WRONG ON RACE

WRONG ON RACE

The Democratic Party's Buried Past

Bruce Bartlett

palgrave
macmillan

WRONG ON RACE
Copyright © Bruce Bartlett, 2008.

All rights reserved. No part of this book may be used or reproduced in any manner whatsoever without written permission except in the case of brief quotations embodied in critical articles or reviews.

First published in 2008 by
PALGRAVE MACMILLAN™
175 Fifth Avenue, New York, N.Y. 10010 and
Houndmills, Basingstoke, Hampshire, England RG21 6XS
Companies and representatives throughout the world.

PALGRAVE MACMILLAN is the global academic imprint of the Palgrave Macmillan division of St. Martin's Press, LLC and of Palgrave Macmillan Ltd. Macmillan® is a registered trademark in the United States, United Kingdom and other countries. Palgrave is a registered trademark in the European Union and other countries.

ISBN-13: 978-0-230-60062-1
ISBN-10: 0-230-60062-X

Library of Congress Cataloging-in-Publication Data

Bartlett, Bruce R., 1951–
    Wrong on race : the Democratic Party's buried past / by Bruce Bartlett.
        p. cm.
    Includes bibliographical references and index.
    ISBN 0-230-60062-X
        1. Democratic Party (U.S.)—History. 2. United States—Race relations.
    3. Presidents—United States—History. 4. Politicians—United States—
    History. 5. United States—Politics and government. I. Title.

JK2316.B37 2008
323.1196'073—dc22   2007024934

A catalogue record for this book is available from the British Library.

Design by Newgen Imaging Systems (P) Ltd., Chennai, India.

First edition: January 2008

10 9 8 7 6 5 4 3 2 1

Printed in the United States of America.

EXPLANATORY NOTE

This book contains racially insensitive words and language. However, they are not used gratuitously, but only in direct quotations from prominent figures and are essential to the accurate portrayal of important historical persons and events. I apologize in advance to anyone who may be offended. However, I would remind readers that the offense was perpetrated by those who said these words, not by the historian who accurately quoted them.

CONTENTS

SECTION III
DEMOCRATS IN THE WHITE HOUSE:
BLACKS SENT TO THE BACK DOOR

SECTION IV
DEMOCRATIC RACISM
FINALLY REPUDIATED

INTRODUCTION

Like everyone, I learned about slavery in grammar school and about Jim Crow laws in high school and college. I'm old enough to have seen separate counters for black and white customers in restaurants while growing up. Even today, I sometimes go into old federal office buildings that have two sets of restrooms and drinking fountains on each floor. They are a reminder that, in the not-too-distant past, blacks and whites were required to use separate facilities in government buildings.

Still, all of this knowledge was cordoned off in the analytical side of my brain. I didn't start to understand what slavery and institutionalized racism really meant until I began to study nineteenth-century political history intensively. I was taken aback to read speeches by important national leaders—presidential nominees, long-serving senators, chairmen of congressional committees, and so on—hurling racial epithets that were crude and tasteless even by the standards of that era.

But it was the content of those speeches that was most appalling: displaying an utter disregard for the humanity of black people, they included justifications for treating them worse than we treat farm animals today and spirited defenses of the barbaric practice of lynching. When I discovered that some of those holding these views were people like Thomas Jefferson, whom I've always admired as one of the greatest thinkers of all time, I wanted to know more.

So I began studying the political history of race in America. Having worked in Congress and at the White House, I have some familiarity with the nature of politics and how politicians think. I thought I could use this knowledge to illuminate this one aspect of the race problem in America in ways that might help us better deal with its long, sordid history.

What quickly jumped out at me is a fact that seems obvious in retrospect, but which I had never really thought about: virtually every significant racist in American political history was a Democrat. Before the Civil War, the Democratic Party was the party of slavery. It was based largely in the South and almost all of its leaders were slave owners, including Andrew Jackson and Thomas Jefferson, considered by Democrats to be the co-founders of their party.

It was illuminating to discover how many debates in American history about the federal government's taxing power, some of its lesser wars, and its westward expansion were fundamentally about the race issue. For example, I never thought carefully before about the clause of the Constitution that counted slaves as three-fifths of a man for purposes of apportionment. Had they been counted as whole persons, it would have increased the South's power in the House of Representatives and the Electoral College. Thus, rather than being a provision that disparaged black people, it actually was an effort to diminish the power of their oppressors.

Having lived in Texas as a youth and been forced to study Texas history, I thought I knew the story of its admission to the Union pretty well. But I never knew the profound importance of race to that history. In particular, I did not know that Mexico had abolished slavery and that this was a key reason for the war for Texas independence. The Texans were determined to keep their slaves and were willing to fight to the death for that right. And of course, the admission of Texas as a state was critical to the maintenance of slavery in the United States, which was threatened both economically and politically in the 1840s.

Like all Republicans, I knew that my party was founded in opposition to slavery. But I hadn't understood why this was so necessary until I came to realize how deeply entrenched racism was in Congress and just how critical the power of the South was in presidential politics. I came to greatly admire Martin Van Buren, whom I had always thought to be a political hack, for breaking with the Democratic Party, which he virtually created in its modern form, over its unwillingness to reject slavery. I also came to really admire John Quincy Adams. I knew that he had been a member of Congress after being president, but I didn't know what a heroic figure he was in the antislavery fight.

Until I studied Andrew Johnson's presidency more deeply, it had never occurred to me that he was always a Democrat. I just assumed that he belonged to the party of Abraham Lincoln. Like most people, I knew he had been impeached by the House of Representatives and saved from conviction in the Senate by a single vote. But I never really understood what that was all about. It, too, was really about the race issue, with Johnson taking such an extreme Southern position that it made the sacrifices of all those who died to end slavery seem in vain.

Like most college history majors, I read C. Vann Woodward's great book, *The Strange Career of Jim Crow*, but it wasn't until I began reading biographies of some of the Southern Democrats of that era—including Woodward's own book on Georgia's Tom Watson—that I came to appreciate just how vicious and nasty these people were.

This led me to write several chapters on some of the worst Southern Democrats of the late nineteenth and early twentieth centuries—people like James Vardaman and Ben Tillman, who are largely forgotten today but were very important in their time. Some may wonder why I wasted the space on such obscure figures. I did it for the same reason that those on the political left never let us forget Senator Joe McCarthy. It's a rare year when there isn't yet another Hollywood film about him or a new biography because those on the left want to ensure that no one like McCarthy ever gains political power in this country again. Not coincidentally, they also want to remind us that McCarthy was a Republican.

The Democrats, however, have skeletons in their own closet and it's worth remembering them, too. For example, Democrat Woodrow Wilson's Attorney General, A. Mitchell Palmer, who was just as rabid an anti-Communist as McCarthy, did far more to repress free speech and political freedom than McCarthy ever attempted. It wasn't a Republican president who locked up thousands of loyal Americans of Japanese descent in con-centration camps for years; it was Democrat Franklin D. Roosevelt. And it wasn't a Republican who wiretapped and snooped on Dr. Martin Luther King Jr., but Democrats John F. Kennedy and his brother Robert, who signed the order as Attorney General.

In the twentieth century, the Democratic Party has been largely identi-fied with political liberalism or progressivism—conscious efforts to expand government and use its power to better the human condition. The first of the party's great liberal leaders was Woodrow Wilson, who was probably the best qualified man ever elected president in our history, at least on paper. He implemented many progressive reforms, such as the income tax and the Federal Reserve System, that are still with us today. And most of us learned in school about his strenuous yet futile effort to get America into the League of Nations, which cemented for all time our image of Wilson as a modern liberal.

I had this image as well before looking more carefully into Wilson's record. It was disturbing to discover just what an overt racist he was. It will probably come as a revelation to most readers that one of Wilson's very first acts in office was to institute comprehensive racial segregation throughout the federal government, a policy that had not previously existed under Republican presidents. Where Wilson's appointees were unable to put blacks and whites into separate offices and buildings, room dividers were installed to prevent whites from even having to gaze upon their darker-skinned co-workers.

Franklin Roosevelt was not much better. He wouldn't even allow his black and white servants at the White House to eat together. Although he has a reputation for being a progressive on the race issue, it is undeserved. Roosevelt sat on his hands for twelve years, never lifting a finger to redress racial injustice, never offering a word of support for antilynching legisla-tion or any other measure that would materially aid black people in America. The reason was that the center of the Democratic Party still lay in the South and Roosevelt worried more about losing its support than doing what was right for the descendents of slaves.

I started my chapter on Harry Truman thinking that he was a Roosevelt clone in this regard—someone who really did nothing to advance civil rights. Careful study of Truman's record, however, forced me to change my opinion. His accomplishments in terms of improving the condition of blacks are very much underrated. More important, they were taken at great political risk to himself. I can find no other explanation for Truman's actions except that he thought they were the right things to do, and I came to admire him greatly for it.

Truman's politically risky efforts to help blacks led to establishment of the Dixiecrats, a rebellious group of racist Southern Democrats who nominated Strom Thurmond to run against him in 1948. Though they knew they could not win the presidency, they ran to split the vote and thereby bring about Truman's defeat. There was every reason to believe it would work, which makes Truman's victory that year all the more miraculous. I think it is telling that the Democratic Party never punished the Dixiecrats or their supporters in Congress in any way. The South was still viewed as the Democrats' political base. Consequently, its national leaders pretended that the Dixiecrats weren't traitors to the party, just as post–Civil War Democrats pretended that those who fought for the Confederacy weren't traitors to their country.

Although this book is primarily about the Democratic Party, I found that I could not discuss its history without also considering the Republicans. This led me to look more carefully into Dwight Eisenhower's record, which I'd believed was devoid of any real accomplishment on racial issues. I thought Eisenhower had been too preoccupied with foreign policy and other matters throughout his presidency.

I was intrigued to discover how much was done on the race issue during the Eisenhower years. He made key appointments to the Supreme Court, especially Chief Justice Earl Warren, knowing that they held liberal views on race and expecting that they would make rulings like *Brown v. Board of Education* that would fundamentally alter the political landscape. Eisenhower also passed the first civil rights bills since Reconstruction over very intense Southern Democratic opposition. These bills tend to be dismissed by historians as insubstantial, at least compared to those enacted in the mid-1960s. But Eisenhower's efforts were critical in showing that it was possible to get *some* civil rights legislation enacted—no small feat when every civil rights bill after 1875 was systematically torpedoed by Southern Democrats.

While Eisenhower has been underrated in terms of what he did on civil rights, John F. Kennedy has been grossly overrated. Like FDR, he was a master of the symbolic gesture, which disguised the fact that he did absolutely nothing of substance in the area of civil rights. Kennedy's reason for inaction was the same as FDR's—he feared the power of racist Southern Democrats, especially in the Senate, and needed their votes to get elected and reelected, and to enact his program. Only extreme outside pressure from the growing civil rights movement pushed Kennedy into doing anything on civil rights beyond appointing a few token blacks to his administration.

Lyndon Johnson deserves credit for ensuring passage of the Civil Rights Act of 1964 and the Voting Rights Act of 1965. As a Southerner who toed the segregationist line throughout most of his political career, it was not easy for him to break with his closest friends, such as Senator Richard B. Russell of Georgia, or to repudiate his own past. But Johnson was too good a politician not to see that the racial landscape was changing. As a leader, he saw which way the troops were running and ran to get in front of them.

Richard Nixon's reputation continues to suffer for his alleged implementation of the infamous "Southern strategy," which is often said to have turned the South into a bastion of Republicanism by skillfully using code phrases like "law and order" to appeal to racist Southern Democrats. In reality, Nixon had an excellent record on civil rights. He did more to integrate the public schools than any other president in history, and also initiated affirmative action and minority set-asides for government contracts.

As a consequence of the mythology surrounding the alleged Southern strategy, the Republican Party has been unfairly tagged as the party of racism in America today—a view commonly expressed by liberals and black leaders to the point where it has become the conventional wisdom. The simple logic seems to be that since the Republican Party is now based in the South, and since Southerners are presumed to be racists, then the Republican Party must be the party of racism. In the process, the Democratic Party's long and deep history of racism has been largely expunged from the national consciousness. Implicitly, people have come to think that since the Democratic Party has been good on civil rights since the 1960s, it must have always been the party of racial tolerance and equality.

As this book amply proves, nothing could be further from the truth. The Democratic Party was the party of slavery and Jim Crow, and the "Solid South" was solidly Democratic for one hundred years. All of the racism that we associate with that region of the country originated with and was enforced by elected Democrats. It could not have been otherwise—there were virtually no Republicans in power in the South for a century after the end of Reconstruction.

Democrats undoubtedly will charge that this book is unbalanced, that I have spotlighted their party's rotten eggs and understated Democrats' positive accomplishments. Perhaps, but my purpose is to redress a larger historical imbalance in the way people perceive the two major political parties. Democrats have been effectively cleansed of their racist past, their sins implicitly transferred to the Republicans.

I especially hope that Republicans will read this book. They may not be the quasi-racists that they are often made out to be in the mainstream media, but neither have they made any real effort to reach out to African

Americans, politically, for a very long time. This is bad for the Republican Party, bad for black people, and bad for the country. It would be much better for everyone if the black vote was "in play" and both major parties had to compete for it. As virtual captives of the Democrats since 1936, blacks have ended up being taken for granted by them and mostly ignored by Republicans.

I think Republicans should fight for the black vote and blacks should fight for a place in the Republican Party, just as they fought for their civil rights in the last century. It's a necessary thing and each may find more in common with the other than they imagine. Blacks will be in a far stronger position if both parties must compete for their votes. And the Republican Party is going to need black votes to compensate for the loss of Hispanic votes resulting from the strongly anti-immigrant views of its base—views that many blacks are in sympathy with.

The passing of the generation of black leaders who led the struggle for civil rights in the 1960s and the rise of a new generation of black leaders like Barack Obama and others, who have lived their whole lives in a post–civil rights society, may make possible an alliance that was unthinkable just a few years ago.

In closing, I would urge Republicans to do as I have done and study this nation's racial history. They need to know—I mean really *know*— things about slavery and racism that they think they know, but really don't. It will make it easier for them to empathize with African Americans, who have really suffered very badly during most of their history in this country in ways that the nation has barely started to acknowledge, let alone compensate for. For too long, white America has taken the view that it is sufficient simply to stop being racist to make things right for blacks. But the long, long legacy of past racism has never been redressed by either party.

It may be time to think seriously about the notion of reparations to African Americans. I don't know how this could be done, and obviously there are many, many problems that would have to be overcome. But I think having a debate on the subject would be good for the country— forcing it to confront its racist past in a way that it hasn't for at least forty years. And if reparations were able to wipe the slate clean, then maybe we could get rid of things like affirmative action, which was born of good intentions but has come to poison race relations and act as a barrier to full racial equality. I hope some Republican leader will take it upon himself or herself to make this an issue and start the process of thought and analysis that might lead to a proposal worthy of consideration.

Both parties have much to apologize for in the area of race. The fact that this book focuses largely on the Democrats isn't meant to imply that the Republicans are entirely blameless. However, the great Republican sin was simply taking the black vote for granted during the period from 1865 to 1936, when blacks largely voted Republican because the party of Lincoln set them free. Republicans became complacent and didn't try hard enough to outlaw things like lynching, poll taxes, and other common methods of oppressing blacks in states controlled by Democrats. But in the end, I think the Republican sin was one of omission, while the Democratic sin was one of commission. There's a big difference, and people ought to know it. This book is a step in that direction.

BRUCE BARTLETT
Great Falls, Virginia
July 2007

SECTION I

THE RACIST ORIGINS OF THE DEMOCRATIC PARTY

1

THOMAS JEFFERSON, ANDREW JACKSON, AND STEPHEN A. DOUGLAS SOW THE SEEDS OF CIVIL WAR

If you go to the web site of the Democratic National Committee and click on the page with the history of the Democratic Party, you'll read that Thomas Jefferson founded the party in 1792 in opposition to the Federalist Party.[1] Of course, political parties were fairly informal affairs in those days. Most of the Founding Fathers viewed them with deep suspicion, fearing that they would lead to disunity—a view best expressed by Jefferson's protégé James Madison in Federalist No. 51.[2] It wasn't until the administration of Andrew Jackson—whom the DNC considers to be the Democratic Party's co-founder—that parties really evolved into their modern form.[3]

Historians tend to dwell on the Democrats' differences with the Federalists and later the Whigs during the early years of the republic on economic issues such as a national bank. The Federalists and Whigs favored a strong central government that would be actively involved in economic development through public works, trade, and financial policy. They saw the young nation's future lying in manufacturing and commerce. By contrast, the Jeffersonian and Jacksonian Democrats were more agrarian and skeptical of central government power.

A key reason for the Democrats' fear of the central government was that it might threaten the institution of slavery, upon which the agrarian economy of the South was vitally dependent. The Federalists opposed slavery and supported its protection in the U.S. Constitution only because union was impossible without it. If the Southern states had feared that the federal government would ever try to uproot slavery, the thirteen colonies surely would have split into separate countries right from the beginning—one free, one slaveholding. At the Constitutional Convention in Philadelphia in 1787, much debate ostensibly about other issues, such as taxation and the Electoral College, was in fact about slavery.[4]

During the Jacksonian era, when the Democratic Party really became a party in the modern sense of the term, skilled politicians like Martin Van Buren of New York were able to convince Democrats to subordinate their sectional interests in the name of party unity. This worked very well in the 1820s and 1830s, making the Democratic Party the nation's dominant party. But in the 1840s, westward expansion put pressure on Congress to reconsider the Missouri Compromise of 1820, which limited the spread of slavery into the West. The potential for new states threatened the balance of power in the Senate between slave and free states.

In the 1850s, Democratic Senator Stephen A. Douglas of Illinois engineered the final breakdown and repeal of the Missouri Compromise, thus allowing the spread of slavery into Kansas and Nebraska. He also persuaded Congress to enact a new Fugitive Slave Law to prevent the collapse of slavery through escape to free states. These actions had the effect of turning the Democratic Party into a purely sectional party based in the South, just the kind of development the Founding Fathers had feared. In effect, the Democratic Party became the party of slavery, fighting to save and protect that institution right down to the Civil War.

THOMAS JEFFERSON AND
BLACK INFERIORITY

As a prominent Virginian, a slaveholder, and the leading intellectual force in the early republic, Jefferson was a central player in all of this. He was author of the Declaration of Independence, the nation's first secretary of state, its second vice president, and third president. Directly or indirectly, Jefferson shaped much of the United States' present and future identity.

Central to Jefferson's views on slavery were those he held on blacks in general. As a scientist, he observed them closely and tried to understand the ways in which they differed from whites beyond mere skin color. Jefferson recorded his thoughts on the subject mainly in his *Notes on the State of Virginia*, written between 1781 and 1782 and published in 1787. Following are a few of them:

> They [blacks] secrete less by the kidneys, and more by the glands of the skin, which gives them a very strong and disagreeable odor. This greater degree of transpiration renders them more tolerant of heat, and less so of

cold, than the whites. . . . They require less sleep. A black after hard labor through the day, will be induced by the slightest amusements to sit up till midnight, or later, though knowing he must be out with the first dawn of the morning. They are at least as brave, and more adventuresome. But this may perhaps proceed from a want of forethought, which prevents their seeing a danger till it be present. . . . They are more ardent after their female: but love seems with them to be more an eager desire, than a tender delicate mixture of sentiment and sensation. Their griefs are transparent. Those numberless afflictions, which render it doubtful whether heaven has given life to us in mercy or in wrath, are less felt, and sooner forgotten with them. In general, their existence appears to participate more of sensation than reflection. To this must be ascribed their disposition to sleep when abstracted from their diversions, and unemployed in labor. . . . Comparing them by their faculties of memory, reason, and imagination, it appears to me, that in memory they are equal to the whites; in reason much inferior, as I think one could scarcely be found capable of tracing and comprehending the investigations of Euclid; and that in imagination they are dull, tasteless, and anomalous.[5]

Jefferson considered the possibility that blacks' backwardness resulted from the institution of slavery, rather than biology. But he noted that the ancient Romans treated their slaves even worse than Americans did, yet Roman slaves often excelled at art and science, and were frequently employed as tutors for the children of slaveholders. Jefferson reasoned that the critical difference was that Roman slaves were white, while American slaves were black. "It is not their condition then, but nature, which has produced the distinction," he wrote; it is nature that "has been less bountiful to them in the endowments of the head." Jefferson concluded that blacks "are inferior to the whites in the endowments both of body and mind."[6]

This racist conviction really explains the contradiction between Jefferson's views on individual liberty, so well expressed in the Declaration of Independence, and the fact that he not only owned slaves himself, but steadfastly avoided taking any action that would end or even undermine the institution of slavery.[7] Of course, it is easy enough to find comments by Jefferson in private letters that indicate opposition to slavery.[8] But discussions based on this source tend to gloss over Jefferson's lifelong ownership of slaves and the fact that he took no *actions* to end slavery, and very seldom made any *public* statements against it.[9] In the view of CUNY historian Frederick Binder, Jefferson's concern for the economic and political welfare of his state and nation, and the purity of the white race, "took precedence over his desire to see the Negroes freed."[10] Or as University of Alaska historian Kenneth O'Reilly put it, "He disliked slavery only in theory."[11]

The way historian William Cohen sees it, the idea that blacks were inherently inferior to whites is the only way Jefferson could reconcile his often expressed libertarian beliefs with his implicit support for slavery. To Jefferson, black people were, in effect, not altogether human and therefore not endowed by God with the same rights as whites. The only other possible explanation for Jefferson's position is that he had been flatly wrong when he said that "all men are created equal." Since Jefferson's statement about the equality of men was the most famous thing he ever said, he could hardly repudiate it and say that black men were not equal to white men. Therefore, his "scientific" analysis of racial differences was really an exercise in rationalization meant to justify his obviously contradictory position.[12]

Jefferson held similarly contradictory views on many civil liberties whose foremost defender he is often considered to be. For example, he fully supported the prosecution of newspapers for publishing "falsehoods"—really just opinions differing from his own—on political matters.[13] And during wartime, Jefferson was willing to go much further, forcibly suppressing all speech that was injurious to the war effort. He also supported bills of attainder when he felt that circumstances warranted, as in the case of Josiah Philips. Historian Leonard Levy has documented many other conflicts between Jefferson's rhetoric and his actions (or inactions) on questions of civil liberty. As with slavery, there was a sharp contrast between what he professed to believe in principle, and what he did or didn't do when confronted with opportunities to apply his beliefs in the real world.[14]

JEFFERSON AND SLAVERY

One might argue that Jefferson's position on slavery was simply dictated by political necessity. He was from a slave state and could hardly hope for any kind of future in politics as an opponent of slavery.[15] When Jefferson was elected president in 1800, it was mainly on the strength of his support from slave states.[16] He knew that union was impossible without the Constitution's explicit support for slavery.[17] And Jefferson also knew that there weren't enough votes in Congress to do anything about it anyway. When the first Census was used to allocate seats in the House of Representatives, thirty out of sixty-five total seats went to states with significant slave populations. The number of congressmen from the slave states would have been even greater had those states not agreed to count slaves as three-fifths of a man for the purposes of representation.[18]

Another possibility is that slaves represented an important part of Jefferson's wealth; he could not free them personally nor support abolition of slavery without suffering a huge financial loss that would have severely crippled his lifestyle. Jefferson inherited slaves from both his parents and acquired many more through marriage. By 1783, he owned more than 200 slaves, making him one of the richest men in Virginia. During his life, Jefferson would often buy and sell slaves. There is no evidence that he treated them either more or less humanely than was common at that time.[19] His slaves often sought escape—thirty of them went over to the

British during the war—and Jefferson had them hunted down and flogged as punishment. As secretary of state, he worked hard to get the British to compensate him and other slave owners for their losses.[20] In that position, Jefferson also supported watering down the slavery prohibition in the Northwest Ordinance by permitting slaveholders entering the Northwest Territory to keep their slaves and forcing the children of slaves to remain in slavery.[21]

President Jefferson was "functionally proslavery," in Stanford University historian Don Fehrenbacher's words. He did nothing to diminish the institution and significantly expanded slavery by permitting it in the new territory acquired by the Louisiana Purchase.[22] As historian David Brion Davis put it, "The extension of what Jefferson called an 'empire for liberty' was also extension of an empire for slavery."[23] Later, Jefferson opposed the Missouri Compromise because it restricted slavery in the Louisiana territory.

The explanation for this position is that he came to believe that diffusing slavery over a broader geographical area would somehow undermine the institution.[24] Dispersion was Jefferson's solution for dealing with the Indians as well.[25] In many ways, his policy toward them anticipated and led inevitably to the removal policy later implemented by Andrew Jackson and Martin Van Buren.[26]

In Haiti, President Jefferson supported French efforts to suppress a slave revolt that American slaveholders feared might spread northward.[27] In 1806, he even pushed a law through Congress that embargoed trade with Haiti in order to deny American arms and provisions to the black revolutionaries.[28] As historian Forrest McDonald put it, "the Jeffersonians sentenced the black revolution in St. Domingo to death by starvation."[29]

Of course, it is easy to criticize those who lived in different times and circumstances for not living up to today's standards. But Jefferson didn't even live up to those of his own time. In this respect, it is worth comparing his actions with those of George Washington, a fellow Virginian and slave owner. As historian Gordon Wood explains, before the Revolution, Washington's views on slavery were probably even more orthodox than Jefferson's. But the war changed Washington in a way that it didn't change Jefferson:

> Washington as commander in chief in Massachusetts for the first time saw blacks as human beings rather than as slaves. He began recruiting free blacks into the Army and even invited the black poet Phillis Wheatley to his headquarters. By the time of the battle of Yorktown, a quarter of Washington's Continental Army was made up of blacks. With peace and the prodding of Lafayette, Washington began gradually and quietly to rethink the issue of slavery. By 1786, he vowed never to purchase another slave and expressed a wish to see slavery in America "abolished by slow, sure and imperceptible degrees." Eventually he found slavery to be

morally repugnant, and he did what no other Southern slaveholding Revolutionary leader was able to do. In his will, which he drew up secretly, he freed upon the death of his wife, Martha, all the slaves under his control and urged that they be educated. He did this in the face of Martha's and his family's bitter opposition.[30]

By contrast, Jefferson freed only one slave during his lifetime; one other bought his own freedom and another ran away, leading Jefferson to free her rather than bothering to chase after her. At his death, he freed only five of his 200-plus slaves.[31] Like Washington, many of Jefferson's contemporaries freed all their slaves in their wills.[32] Contrary to what some historians have asserted, there was no legal obstacle to freeing slaves in Virginia after 1782, except that after 1806 freed slaves had to leave Virginia within twelve months.[33]

In the end, we can draw no other conclusion except that Jefferson's record on race was dreadful. By today's standards, he unquestionably was a racist. In the words of University of Mississippi historian Winthrop Jordan, "His derogation of the Negro revealed the latent possibilities inherent in an accumulated popular tradition of Negro inferiority; it constituted, for all its qualifications, the most intense, extensive, and extreme formulation of anti-Negro 'thought' offered by any American in the thirty years after the Revolution."[34]

But we have never honored Jefferson so much for his actions as for his ideas, which stand on their own merit regardless of how flawed and hypocritical their author was. The same is true for other slaveholders among the Founding Fathers.[35] Nevertheless, it is important for our understanding of American political history to know that one of the men credited by the Democrats as a founder of their party was someone who undoubtedly would be the subject of harsh criticism by them if he had instead been a founder of the Republican Party.

ANDREW JACKSON AND THE INDIANS

As noted earlier, political parties were rather casual operations in the early days, more like loose alliances than the formal organizations we know today. It was Andrew Jackson who was really responsible for building the Democrats into the first modern political party. The glue that held them together was slavery and the exploitation of Indians. Indeed, one of Jackson's greatest accomplishments in office was the removal to the west of most Indians east of the Mississippi, often utilizing methods so harsh that they constituted virtual genocide.

Jackson was born in South Carolina in 1767 but moved to Tennessee in 1787, becoming the state's first congressman in 1794. He was elected to the Senate two years later, but served only two years. Jackson served again in the Senate from 1822 to 1826. Before becoming president in 1828, he achieved his greatest fame as a soldier. Jackson joined the Continental Army at the age of 13 and was taken a prisoner of war by the British. He became a colonel in the Tennessee Militia in 1801 and thereafter engaged in a number of battles with local Indian tribes.

Jackson had great military success during the Creek War of 1813–14, which is sometimes considered a theater of the War of 1812. The treaty he imposed upon the Indians was extremely harsh, especially since it punished those who had allied themselves with him as well as those he had fought. Jackson demanded 23 million acres of land in Alabama and Georgia as reparations. The Indians had little choice but to accede to his demands because Jackson's scorched earth policy had destroyed their farms and villages, leaving them to face starvation without federal aid.[36]

Jackson's harshness toward the defeated Indians was motivated not so much by cruelty as by a sincere belief that they simply could not survive where they were in their traditional ways. There were too few of them spread out over a large territory coveted by land-hungry whites. The federal government was essentially powerless to prevent white encroachment on Indian land or protect the Indians from attacks by whites. Conflict was inevitable. Moreover, the young nation needed those lands to be settled and populated quickly to protect against Spanish and British invasions. Therefore, in Jackson's view, it was absolutely essential to get the Indians off their lands by any means necessary, including annihilation if it came to that. Moving them to the West, where he thought they would be able to live in peace, was the humane policy in Jackson's eyes. The option of allowing them to stay and live where they were just wasn't viable.[37]

The immediate problem facing Jackson after he became president had to do with state sovereignty versus tribal sovereignty. In 1827, the Cherokee Nation adopted a formal constitution and asserted sovereignty over its territory, much of which was in Georgia, which refused to recognize the Cherokee claims.[38] Subsequently, Georgia moved to impose its laws upon the Cherokee and seize their lands.[39] The Cherokee believed that this was a violation of the Indian Trade and Intercourse Act of 1802, which gave the federal government sole jurisdiction in relations with the Indians.[40] But Jackson refused to intervene. He had long believed that the Indians had no sovereignty whatsoever and were simply subjects of the United States, despite the many treaties that the government had signed with them. In Jackson's view, the treaties were mere sops to Indian vanity and carried no force of law.[41]

In 1830, the Cherokee petitioned the Supreme Court for an injunction against the state of Georgia. The court denied the petition the following year in *Cherokee Nation v. Georgia* on the grounds that the Cherokee were neither a state nor a foreign country with standing to petition the court. Said Chief Justice John Marshall, "If it be true that the Cherokee Nation have rights, this is not the tribunal in which those rights are to be asserted."[42] In 1832, however, the Court held in *Worcester v. Georgia* that the state of

Georgia did indeed lack the authority to impose its laws on the Cherokee.[43] Unfortunately for the Indians, the Court failed to provide a mechanism whereby they could obtain redress.[44] Consequently, both the federal government and the state of Georgia were essentially free to ignore the decision, and neither did anything substantive to aid the Indian cause.[45]

In the meantime, at Jackson's behest, Congress passed the Indian Removal Act of 1830. The law sought to resolve the Indian problem by authorizing the federal government to trade land west of the Mississippi for Indian land in the east. It was hoped that the Indians could be induced to relocate from areas in which white encroachment was creating increasingly uncontainable tensions to uninhabited areas where they could live in peace and safety. Jackson repeatedly emphasized that relocation was to be voluntary; those Indians who wanted to stay in the east could if they desired and would be given good title to allotments of land. In his State of the Union message of December 8, 1829, he said:

> This emigration should be voluntary, for it would be as cruel as unjust to compel the aborigines to abandon the graves of their fathers and seek a home in a distant land. But they should be distinctly informed that if they remain within the limits of the states they must be subject to their laws. In return for their obedience as individuals they will without doubt be protected in the enjoyment of those possessions which they have improved by their industry.

The promise that Indian removal would be voluntary was crucial to the legislation's passage. Although the South, where most Indians were located, had no objection to evicting them forcefully, many Northerners were sympathetic to the plight of the Indians and uncomfortable with the removal policy.[46] Even with Jackson's solemn promise that removal would be voluntary, the Indian Removal Act passed the House of Representatives by just five votes (102 to 97), with Northern congressmen voting heavily against it.[47]

INDIAN REMOVAL

University of Toledo historian Alfred Cave believes that Jackson was being fundamentally dishonest about the voluntary character of removal. Although he would use voluntary methods where possible, Jackson had every intention of using force if necessary, even though the legislation specifically proscribed it.[48] He looked the other way at state harassment of Indians, threatened them with the loss of self-government, and did nothing to protect them from fraud perpetrated by corrupt officials. In Cave's words:

> Indian removal as carried out by Jackson and his successor Martin Van Buren was anything but a voluntary relocation program. Numerous

contemporary witnesses provide damning testimony regarding fraud, coercion, corruption, and malfeasance both in the negotiation of removal treaties and in their execution. In their zeal to secure removal treaties, agents of the Jackson administration resorted to extensive bribery of compliant and corrupt tribal officials and frequently threatened independent Indian leaders opposed to relocation. In a series of blatant violations of the specific guarantees that Andrew Jackson and his supporters had offered to Congress in 1830, federal officials, by a variety of ruses, in effect denied antiremoval majorities within Indian tribes the right to vote on the ratification of removal treaties. Furthermore, the administration systematically removed Indian agents who either opposed the removal policy or were less than zealous in coercing compliance. Moreover, Indians endeavoring to make good on Jackson's promise that they could remain within the states as individuals were subjected to all manner of harassment from state officials, speculators, and Indian-hating mobs as the federal government looked the other way.[49]

Historian Mary Young has detailed many of the ways in which the Indians were defrauded of their property. One technique was to send into Indian territory agents who sold Indians goods and liquor on credit, receiving the deed to their property as collateral. When they could not come up with cash to repay the loan, speculators got title to the property. Speculators also used Negro slaves to harass and intimidate Indians into selling their property. In the event that fraud was later claimed, the slaves were understandably unwilling to testify against their masters. Lastly, the states did everything in their power to evict Indians by failing to protect them from white intruders on their land and by requiring the Indians to pay taxes, muster with the militia, and work on public roads. In the end, most of the Indians who wanted to stay were forced off their land and emigrated west.[50]

Alexis de Tocqueville was appalled by the perversion of law to exterminate the Indians, but he was also impressed by its ability to accomplish relatively peacefully what war had not. As he wrote in *Democracy in America*:

> The Spaniards, by unparalleled atrocities which brand them with indelible shame, did not succeed in exterminating the Indian race and could not even prevent them from sharing their rights; the United States Americans have attained both these results with wonderful ease, quietly, legally, and philanthropically, without spilling blood and without violating a single one of the great principles of morality in the eyes of the world. It is impossible to destroy men with more respect to the laws of humanity.[51]

Jackson turned a blind eye to the mistreatment of Indians and the theft of their land under the cover of law because he fundamentally believed that they needed to move west and not remain in the east among white people. The Indians were too backward and their racial and tribal ties were too strong, he thought, making them obstacles to national unity and a hindrance to economic growth. As Jackson put it in his fifth State of the Union message on December 3, 1833:

> That those tribes cannot exist surrounded by our settlements and in continual contact with our citizens is certain. They have neither the intelligence, the industry, the moral habits, nor the desire of improvement which are essential to any favorable change in their condition. Established in the midst of another and a superior race, and without appreciating the causes of their inferiority or seeking to control them, they must necessarily yield to the force of circumstances and ere long disappear.

Another problem with the Indians was that they exacerbated growing problems with slavery. Tribal areas, which were mostly located in the midst of the slave states, were an easy place for runaway slaves to escape. There was also the possibility of a black–Indian alliance that could threaten internal security. In an 1817 letter to the local Army commander, the governor of Georgia warned that an Indian leader named Woodbine was stirring both blacks and Indians into "acts of hostility against this country."[52] In 1835, a group of blacks and Indians annihilated an army unit of one hundred men in Florida, spreading fear throughout the Southeast.[53]

The issue of slavery was both political and personal for Jackson. He was a longtime slave owner who had as many as 150 slaves. Throughout his life, Jackson never expressed the slightest moral qualms about slavery. Says University of Tulsa historian Andrew Burstein, "He was insistent in the belief that liberty-loving white Americans had every right to own slaves, and to prosper from their unpaid exertions." Burstein notes that Jackson once advertised for a runaway slave promising $10 extra ($220 today) for every 100 lashes the person recovering the slave gave the runaway, up to 300 lashes.[54]

To Jackson, slavery was mainly a political issue to be dealt with in whatever way was necessary to maintain unity and protect national security.[55] As historian Frederick Binder explains:

> In his attitude toward the Negro problem, Andrew Jackson reflected both the glory of his era and the tragedy that was to come. Accepting slavery's existence as necessary to his economic way of life, he viewed any attempt to enter the Negro into the mainstream of politics as an act of selfish political intent with consequences destructive to the Union he revered. . . . He seems to have been unable to comprehend that some looked upon the Negro slave as the necessary foundation of a great civilization, and still others looked upon him as a human being denied the basic rights.[56]

This made Jackson ideal as the first presidential candidate of the modern Democratic Party, which came into being largely in opposition to growing antislavery sentiment in the North.[57] As historian David Brion Davis explains, this opposition was reflected in the party's agenda throughout the Jacksonian era:

> From its very start, the Democratic Party of Martin Van Buren and Andrew Jackson sought to suppress criticism of slavery by blocking the delivery of abolitionist mail in the South, by enforcing the gag rule that tabled anti-slavery petitions in Congress, by challenging the judiciary when President Van Buren did everything he could to prevent a publicized trial of the *Amistad* captives, and by favoring the annexation of Texas as a slave state or a cluster of slave states.[58]

In the words of historian Edward Pessen, "It was no accident that the national leader of the party was Andrew Jackson, slave owner and friend to slavery, rather than John Quincy Adams, its enemy." In 1824 and 1828, "proslavery voters knew Adams was not their man." Wherever blacks were free to vote, they all voted against Jackson and the Democrats.[59]

It was left to Van Buren, Jackson's vice president who succeeded him in 1836, to finish the job of Indian removal. Through a combination of incompetence, bad luck, and duplicity, the process led to massive depravation and the loss of thousands of Indian lives. When the last of the Cherokee were removed to Oklahoma in 1838 in the infamous "trail of tears," the government's tactics anticipated those of the Nazis against the Jews one hundred years later. Anthropologist Anthony Wallace describes what happened:

> Detachments of soldiers arrived at every Cherokee house, often without any warning, and drove the inhabitants out at bayonet point, with only the clothes on their backs. . . . The captives were marched to hastily improvised stockades—in language of the twentieth century, concentration camps—and were kept there under guard until arrangements could be made for their transportation by rail and water to the Indian territory west of the Mississippi. . . . Conditions in the stockades were poor and the imprisoned Indians suffered from malnutrition and contracted dysentery and other infectious diseases. The horror of the situation appalled the regular army officers charged with executing the removal plan. . . . The total cost in Cherokee lives was very great. Perhaps as many as a thousand of the emigrants died en route, and it is estimated that about three thousand had died earlier during the roundup and in the stockades. In all, between 20 percent and 25 percent of the Eastern Cherokees died on the "trail of tears."[60]

In 1841, former president John Quincy Adams called Jackson's Indian policy an "abomination." Said the former president in his diary, "It is among the heinous sins of this nation, for which I believe God will one day bring to them judgment."[61]

SLAVERY AND THE WEST

Jackson was able to avoid dealing directly with the slavery problem during his administration, but Van Buren was not so lucky. Growing American settlements in Texas, and the desire of both Texans and many in the United States to admit it to the Union, brought to a head unresolved questions about the future of slavery west of the Mississippi.

A key factor in the dispute between the Texans and Mexicans was slavery. Mexico outlawed slavery in 1829, but the Texas climate and soil had proven themselves very hospitable to the growing of cotton, which meant that slaves were necessary. When war broke out in 1836, the Texas revolutionaries were fighting as much to keep their slaves as they were for any of the other issues behind their desire for independence.[62]

Because most of the Texas territory was below the 36°36' latitude set by the Missouri Compromise, it could be admitted as a slave state under existing law. In 1838, the Van Buren administration felt out Congress on the possibility of Texas annexation. But John Quincy Adams, now a Whig congressman from Massachusetts, strenuously attacked the effort to bring another slave state into the Union. So strong was the public reaction from abolitionists that Van Buren and the Texans mutually agreed to put the issue of annexation aside for the time being.[63]

Democrat Van Buren was defeated for reelection in 1840 by Whig William Henry Harrison, mainly because of poor economic conditions following the Panic of 1837.[64] Harrison died shortly after his inauguration and was succeeded by Vice President John Tyler, who quickly started to feud with his fellow Whigs. This effectively made him a man without a party and largely powerless during his administration, which left unresolved the issues of Texas and slavery.

In 1844, Van Buren hoped to make a comeback and again sought the Democratic nomination. But since leaving the White House, he and his political supporters in the North had come to oppose slavery and therefore the annexation of Texas.[65] However, annexation was extremely popular throughout the South, and the issue was seized upon by former House Speaker and Tennessee Governor James K. Polk, whose strong support for bringing Texas into the Union propelled him to the Democratic nomination and the presidency.[66] Proslavery and a slave owner with some fifty slaves, he even replaced the White House service staff with slaves and turned its basement into slave quarters. Polk clearly had no problem with bringing Texas into the Union as a slave state and was successful in doing so in 1845.[67]

An important factor that animated the Texas issue was a fear that Britain had designs on it and the California territory as well.[68] Since Britain had abolished slavery throughout its empire in 1833, this raised the possibility that British control would prevent the expansion of slavery into much of the land west of the Mississippi, where it would be permissible if under American control.[69] With continued settlement of the Oregon territory in the Northwest, where slavery was prohibited and probably not viable anyway, the South rightly saw the end of slavery not too far down the road unless new slave states like Texas were admitted to bolster its ranks in Congress.[70]

The admission of Texas as a state solved a big part of the Southern problem, but there was still the California territory to the west that was also viewed as a prime area for the expansion of slavery. And with Britain resisting settlement of the U.S. boundary with Canada, its possible designs on California could not be dismissed.[71] Consequently, Polk did everything he could to provoke a fight with Mexico that would give him an excuse to seize the rest of its northern territory outside of Texas, which Mexico continued to claim. Although the British tried to restrain Mexico from reacting to American provocations, Mexican troops crossed the Rio Grande in early 1846 to claim the land south of the Nueces River. The United States immediately declared war, winning a swift victory and thereby gaining control of California, Nevada, Utah, and parts of several other Western states.[72]

Polk hoped that the issue of slavery in the new territory could be finessed by simply extending the Missouri Compromise's 36°30' line west to the Pacific. Slavery would be permissible below that line, prohibited above. In fact, Polk's personal view was that Congress had no power to stop any state from permitting slavery if it chose to do so. As he explained in his State of the Union message on December 5, 1848:

> No enactment of Congress could restrain the people of any of the sovereign states of the Union, old or new, North or South, slaveholding or nonslaveholding, from determining the character of their own domestic institutions as they may deem wise and proper. Any and all the states possess this right, and Congress cannot deprive them of it. The people of Georgia might if they chose so alter their constitution as to abolish slavery within its limits, and the people of Vermont might so alter their constitution as to admit slavery within its limits. Both states would possess the right, though, as all know, it is not probable that either would exert it.

Historians are divided on whether Polk was expressing a genuinely held principle or was merely using the Constitution as a gloss to make the expansion of slavery into California more palatable.[73] In any case, there was resistance in Congress. When Polk asked for a $2 million appropriation ($53 million today) to help negotiate the peace settlement with Mexico on August 8, 1846, a junior congressman from Pennsylvania named David Wilmot attached an amendment to the House bill, later rejected by the Senate, prohibiting slavery in any territory acquired from Mexico.[74] Wilmot represented a number of Northern Democrats, led by Van Buren, who suspected that the war with Mexico was less a legitimate response to attack by a foreign power than a Southern power-play to expand slavery. They saw the appropriation as a down payment to buy the Mexican territory acquired during the war and thus avoid further conflicts over its ownership. With strong support for the Wilmot Proviso from Northern Democrats, it became a key factor in the breakdown of the New York–Virginia Democratic alliance that had dominated American politics since the rise of Jackson.[75]

Polk had run in 1844 on a pledge to serve only one term, which left the Democratic nomination open in 1848. The party's nominee, Senator Lewis Cass of Michigan, argued that the Wilmot Proviso was unconstitutional and pledged to veto it if it ever got through Congress. This led to Van Buren's final break with the Democratic Party and creation of the Free Soil Party, which opposed expansion of slavery into the West.[76] Van Buren himself was its first presidential nominee. Despite the fact that the new party was formed just three months before the election, he managed to garner 10 percent of the votes in 1848. The winner was Zachary Taylor of the Whig Party, who won mostly on his record as a hero of the Mexican War. The owner of one hundred slaves, he also proved more acceptable to many southerners than Cass, and he carried Virginia, Georgia, and Louisiana.

The discovery of gold in California in 1849 brought thousands of settlers westward, forcing the issue of statehood—and therefore slavery—onto the front burner. When California applied for statehood on October 13 of that year as a free state, it forced the first serious debate on slavery in Congress since 1820. Congressman Robert Toombs of Georgia spoke for many in the South when he said that admitting California and New Mexico as free states would "fix a national degradation" upon his region. In that event, he warned, ominously, "I am for disunion."[77]

The end result was the Compromise of 1850, which admitted California as a free state, but allowed Utah and New Mexico to choose or reject slavery at their own discretion.[78] As part of the compromise, Congress enacted the Fugitive Slave Law of 1850, which forced state officials to aid in the capture and return of runaway slaves.[79] State laws and court decisions had left the Fugitive Slave Law of 1793 effectively unenforceable, making the North a haven for blacks able to escape bondage.[80] Everyone knew that without an effective means of preventing slaves from escaping to free states, the cost of slavery would soon become prohibitive.[81] In short, a tough fugitive slave law was absolutely essential to the continued viability of slavery. It was enacted only with overwhelming support from the Democratic Party.[82]

Although the 1850 compromise kept the slavery issue bottled up for a little while longer, it also set in motion forces that would finally make it uncontainable. One of them was to strengthen abolitionist sentiment. For many Northerners, it was one thing to permit slavery in the South and quite another to force those in free states to, in effect, subsidize it by paying slavery's enforcement costs. Consequently, the Fugitive Slave Law did much to radicalize the abolitionists and attract new supporters to their cause.

THE FAILURE OF COMPROMISE

The architect of the 1850 compromise was Stephen A. Douglas, Democrat of Illinois, perhaps the most talented politician of his generation.[83] He had been elected to the House of Representatives in 1842, becoming a U.S. Senator in 1847. As chairman of the Senate Committee on Territories, Douglas exerted significant influence on all issues related to the admission of new states, including slavery.

In 1854, there was heavy pressure from settlers and the railroads to admit Kansas and Nebraska as states. When Douglas introduced legislation to this effect, however, he also sought to repeal the restriction on slavery imposed by the Missouri Compromise. Instead, he favored "popular sovereignty," allowing those living in Kansas and Nebraska to decide for themselves whether or not to sanction slavery.[84] This was a clever political strategy because it appealed to moderates on both sides of the issue. Proslavery people could live with it because the institution itself was not threatened by federal law, and many of those opposed to slavery strongly supported the principle of states' rights.

Reading the published debates in the *Congressional Globe* doesn't fully indicate how deeply Douglas' racism underlay his motives. On one occasion, the *New York Times* reported his actual words during debate on the Kansas-Nebraska Act. "His speech as delivered abounded in such delectable terms as 'nigger,' 'base falsehood,' 'abolition confederates,' and 'unadulterated, free soil, abolition niggerism,'" the *Times* reported. These words were all deleted from the published version of Douglas' speech that day at his request, which at least shows that he knew they were offensive.[85] One wonders whether he thought the unexpurgated version would be more effective with his Senate colleagues.

In Congress, Democrats basically used raw political power to ram the Kansas-Nebraska Act through over Whig opposition, and it was signed into law by Democratic President Franklin Pierce.[86] Historian Michael Holt describes the public reaction to the legislation:

> Passage of the Kansas-Nebraska Act ignited an explosion of rage in the North, an outpouring of wrath that was almost universal. Because the law seemed to provide an opportunity for slavery to spread to Kansas, which was directly adjacent to slaveholding regions in Missouri, it reinforced all of the existing reasons for Northern hostility to slavery expansion—moral antipathy to black slavery, fear that the Northern free labor economy would be prevented from growing, racism, and jealousy of the Slave Power. But Northern animosities were much more intense in 1854 because the areas involved were not distant like New Mexico but contiguous to populated states. . . . More important, the area involved had been promised to free soil for thirty-five years. The overthrow of the Missouri Compromise seemed like concrete evidence of a genuine Slave

Power conspiracy to use its domination of the national government to spread slavery against the will of the majority of Americans.[87]

The feebleness of the Whigs in opposing this legislation was the final straw for many of those opposed to slavery, who now realized that a new political organization was needed. Among these was former Whig Congressman Abraham Lincoln of Illinois, who argued that the Compromise of 1850 was no compromise at all because only the antislavery side gave up anything. The Kansas-Nebraska Act was more of the same, he believed. In Lincoln's view, slavery's supporters got elimination of the prohibition above 36°30′, and its opponents got nothing.[88]

Revulsion toward the Kansas-Nebraska Act led to a collapse of the Democratic Party throughout the North, and it lost 74 seats in the 1854 congressional elections. However, the ineffectual Whig Party was not the beneficiary. Instead, the party system basically broke down in the North. Out of the chaos emerged the modern Republican Party on an explicitly antislavery platform.[89] In the South, the Whig Party disappeared, and the Democratic Party solidified its position. As historian Arthur Schlesinger Jr. put it, voters in that region now saw the Democrats as having "more formidable equipment for the protection of slavery."[90]

By 1856, Democrats in Congress, almost all of whom were now from slave states, were becoming extremely agitated by the growing political opposition to slavery. On May 19 of that year, Senator Charles Sumner of Massachusetts, who would shortly join the Republicans, rose to denounce the "crime" against Kansas. He fingered Senators Douglas and Andrew Butler of South Carolina as the key perpetrators. Sumner called Douglas "the squire of slavery" and said that slavery was Butler's mistress.[91]

A few days later, Representative Preston Brooks, Democrat of South Carolina, entered the Senate chamber and approached Sumner, who was sitting at his desk doing paperwork.[92] Without warning, Brooks severely beat Sumner with the metal end of a stout cane, inflicting injuries on him serious enough to require hospitalization and a long convalescence. Brooks said he was defending the honor of Butler, who was a relative of his. For many in the North, Brooks' cowardice in attacking an unarmed man this way symbolized the impossibility of reasoning with Southerners on the issue of slavery. They would simply lash out like wild animals at any threat to their chattel. The incident ended up being a powerful factor in the rise of the Republican Party.[93]

Also in 1856, the Republican Party fielded its first presidential candidate, John C. Frémont, a hero of the Mexican War who was California's first U.S. Senator. The Democrats quickly subjected him to vicious race-baiting, including charges of being a "nigger lover." As historian Michael Holt recounts, Democrats "charged that the Republicans would abolish slavery in the South and thus inundate the North with a horde of freed blacks who would rob white workers of their jobs, ruin their neighborhoods, and even marry their daughters."[94]

Because of the Republican Party's newness and lack of organizational infrastructure, Frémont got only a third of the vote. However, he carried a number of states in New England and the upper Midwest. The winner was Democrat James Buchanan of Pennsylvania, a former congressman, senator, and secretary of state.

Almost immediately after Buchanan took office in 1857, the Supreme Court poured fuel on the smoldering political fire of slavery. In *Dred Scott v. Sanford*, it ruled that all blacks, free or slave, were mere property and therefore could not become citizens. This meant that they could neither vote nor sue in court. Chief Justice Roger Taney, a Democrat who had been appointed by Andrew Jackson, justified his ruling on the grounds that blacks were "a subordinate and inferior class of beings who had been subjugated by the dominant race."[95] President Buchanan hailed the decision:

> The right has been established of every citizen to take his property of any kind, including slaves, into the common territories belonging equally to all the States of the Confederacy, and to have it protected there under the Federal Constitution. Neither Congress nor a territorial legislature nor any human power has any authority to annul or impair this vested right. The supreme judicial tribunal of the country, which is a coordinate branch of the government, has sanctioned and affirmed these principles of constitutional law, so manifestly just in themselves and so well calculated to promote peace and harmony among the states. . . . Had it been decided that either Congress or the territorial legislature possess the power to annul or impair the right to property in slaves, the evil would be intolerable.[96]

In the words of historian Don Fehrenbacher, "Here, straight from a Pennsylvanian in the White House, was proslavery doctrine pure enough to have satisfied John C. Calhoun."[97] South Carolina Democrat Calhoun was, of course, the leading defender of slavery in Congress for a generation.[98]

That same year, there was strenuous debate in Kansas about whether it should enter the Union as a slave state or a free one. Competing constitutions were drawn up, but the one that Democrats in Washington chose to accept was the constitution adopted in September in Lecompton, Kansas, which permitted slavery and protected slaveholders. President Buchanan supported it enthusiastically. His letter of endorsement was hailed as "the greatest state paper for the South that has ever emanated from the executive chair since the days of Washington."[99] Although the admission of Kansas as a slave state under the Lecompton constitution was rejected in the House, Senate Democrats supported it overwhelmingly, including those from the North, two of whom disregarded instructions from their state legislatures to oppose the measure.[100]

ABRAHAM LINCOLN AND
STEPHEN A. DOUGLAS

The *Dred Scott* decision and Lecompton constitution greatly energized the fledgling Republican Party and drove the last remaining antislavery politicians from the Democratic Party. Growing Republican pressure on the Democrats intensified the latter's need for superior political leadership to counter it. Senator Douglas tried to provide that leadership, but ultimately failed to bridge a gap between slavery supporters and abolitionists that had grown too wide for any kind of compromise to cope with.

Although nominally from the North, Douglas' politics and views about black people and slavery were very Southern.[101] He was a slave owner (through his wife) who believed that the black race was clearly inferior and utterly incapable of self-government. Douglas was also strenuously opposed to racial intermarriage, viewing "amalgamation between superior and inferior races" as a disaster that would only drag down the superior (white) race while doing nothing to raise up the inferior (black) race.[102]

The great Civil War historian Allan Nevins believed that Douglas was not so much proslavery as amoral on the issue. Douglas had "no moral repugnance to slavery," Nevins wrote. "His attitude toward slavery was completely and exclusively materialistic. When it paid it was good and when it did not pay it was bad." Consequently, Douglas was simply incapable of comprehending the deep repugnance that increasing numbers of people in the North held for the South's peculiar institution.[103]

In 1858, Douglas was up for reelection to the Senate. In those days, before the Seventeenth Amendment to the Constitution, state legislatures chose their states' senators. Consequently, those seeking a Senate seat might campaign for the election of legislators that would support their appointment. When Douglas began doing so, Abraham Lincoln started following him around, challenging him to impromptu debates in hopes that a Republican majority might be elected that would send him to the Senate instead of Douglas. Lincoln announced his campaign for the Senate with a stirring denunciation of the middle-of-the-road policy on slavery championed by Douglas. In his famous "House Divided" speech on June 16, 1858, he said of the Kansas-Nebraska Act:

> We are now far into the fifth year since a policy was initiated with the avowed object and confident promise of putting an end to slavery agitation. Under the operation of that policy, that agitation has not only not ceased, but has constantly augmented. In my opinion, it will not cease until a crisis shall have been reached and passed. A house divided against itself cannot stand. I believe this government cannot endure permanently half slave and half free. I do not expect the Union to be dissolved. I do not expect the house to fall. But I do expect that it will cease to be divided. It will become all one thing or all the other.

In this instance, Lincoln was not so much attacking Douglas for being proslavery as for being a classic moderate—someone who tries to skirt difficult issues by splitting the difference and refusing to take a firm position.[104] As a political strategy, it was excellent; if Lincoln could just force Douglas to take a side, it would probably lead to his downfall. If Douglas sided forthrightly with slavery, he would lose one group of supporters; if he opposed it, he would lose another. Douglas' only hope of winning was to make enough people on each side think he favored their position by pushing his idea of popular sovereignty.

Lincoln and Douglas eventually agreed to a formal series of seven debates, which are rightly renowned as possibly the most famous debates in history. Although many issues were debated, the issue of slavery was dominant. Douglas frequently restated his view that the fundamental problem was the basic inferiority of black people. Said Douglas in the second debate on August 27, 1858: "Those of you who believe that the nigger is your equal and ought to be on an equality with you socially, politically and legally, have a right to entertain those opinions, and of course will vote for Mr. Lincoln."[105]

In the third debate on September 15, 1858, Douglas said that the generally understood meaning of the Declaration of Independence was wrong, that all men were not created equal, that blacks were not equal to whites, and that the Founding Fathers never meant to say any such thing. As Douglas explained:

> I hold that a Negro is not and never ought to be a citizen of the United States. I hold that this government was made on the white basis; made by the white men, for the benefit of white men and their posterity forever, and should be administered by white men and none others. I do not believe that the Almighty made the Negro capable of self-government. . . . Now I state to you my fellow citizens, in my opinion the signers of the Declaration of Independence had no reference whatever to the Negro when they declared all men to have been created equal. The signers of the Declaration were white men of European birth and European descent and had no reference either to the Negro or to savage Indians or the Fiji or the Malay or any other inferior or degraded race when they spoke of the equality of men. . . . Thus, my friends, I am in favor of preserving the government on the white basis as our fathers made it.[106]

In the end, Douglas' popular sovereignty approach won the day against Lincoln's principled opposition to slavery. Douglas was reelected to the Senate, but quickly discovered that the increasing radicalization of proslavery forces within the Democratic Party had left him outside its mainstream.[107] Whereas Republicans saw Douglas' support for popular sovereignty as a ruse to spread slavery into the West, Southerners saw it as a betrayal because he was conceding that slavery could be restricted by local law. The Southern position was that the *Dred Scott* decision made slave ownership a constitutionally protected right, allowing slave owners to take their property anywhere in the country they pleased without governmental hindrance.

With Southerners firmly in control of the Democratic Party in Congress, Douglas was now viewed as squishy, someone who could not be depended upon to vigorously defend slavery. Senator Jefferson Davis, Mississippi Democrat and later president of the Confederate States of America, denounced Douglas for throwing a "delusive gaze" over the public mind and said his popular sovereignty doctrine was "full of heresy."[108] Consequently, Democrats in the Thirty-Sixth Congress removed Douglas as chairman of the Committee on Territories, a position he had held for eleven years, because he was no longer considered trustworthy on the slavery question.

Douglas and Lincoln met again during the presidential election of 1860, the former as the candidate of the Democratic Party and the latter as the standard-bearer for the Republicans. However, while the Republicans were united around their candidate, the Democrats were not. Southerners skeptical of Douglas' commitment to slavery and suspicious of popular sovereignty demanded a plank in the Democratic platform explicitly protecting their interests. When this was not forthcoming, they nominated their own presidential candidate, Vice President John Breckinridge of Kentucky, who also ran as a Democrat. With two different Democrats running for president and dividing the vote, Lincoln was able to win relatively easily, even though he garnered just 40 percent of the ballots.[109]

The election of Lincoln left no doubt in the minds of Southerners that the tide had turned decisively against them. The result was secession and war—the bloodiest in American history.[110] Historians are divided on whether war was inevitable—baked in the cake by the Constitution itself— or could have been avoided with the right leadership. But once the Democratic Party became almost purely a sectional party based in the South—in effect making it the party of slavery—secession probably became impossible to avoid.

2

ANDREW JOHNSON

The Democrat Who Tried to Wreck Reconstruction and Paved the Way for Jim Crow

When schoolchildren study the presidents of the United States, they learn that Abraham Lincoln was the first Republican. After his assassination in 1865, he was succeeded by his vice president, Andrew Johnson. Most schoolchildren, therefore, naturally assume that Johnson was also a Republican and they probably continue to think so as adults. In fact, he was a Democrat his whole life, including the time he served as president, and never said otherwise. University of California historian Kenneth Stampp called him "the last Jacksonian."[1]

During the Civil War, there were many in the North who opposed it strenuously. Some were pacifists, some genuinely thought the problem of slavery could be solved through compromise without war, and some supported the continuation of slavery even though they may not have been slaveholders themselves. There was one thing that almost all such people had in common: they were Democrats.

After the war, those who opposed the war mostly disagreed with meaningful reconstruction as well. They thought that bygones should be bygones—forgive and forget, let's move on, put the past behind us, etc. Those who murdered, tortured, abused, and enslaved millions of black people should be given a pass, they implicitly said. Let's just pretend that nothing happened; in effect saying that hundreds of thousands of people on both sides died for nothing.[2] Anyone who thought the war was for a larger purpose and ought to accomplish something more than simply the end of fighting was viewed by most Southerners as a dastardly person motivated only by vengeance. They did everything in their power in every state of the former Confederacy to undermine the whole point of the war, to reinstate *de facto* slavery in every way possible, and to claim victimhood in the process.

If one reads the literature on Reconstruction written in the first hundred years after the war, one would think that it, rather than slavery, was the worst thing that ever happened to the South.[3] The "carpetbagger" and the "scalawag" are still deeply reviled figures in the South to this day. One would think that Southerners did absolutely nothing to deserve the privation and punishment they endured in the aftermath of war. In fact, they got off absurdly easy. Many Confederates deserved what the Nazis got at Nuremberg.[4] Yet only one was ever executed for his wartime actions: Henry Wirz, superintendent of Andersonville Prison in Georgia, where some 13,000 Union soldiers died in unspeakable conditions.

Democrats opposed every civil rights measure proposed by the Republican Congress, supported fellow Democrat Andrew Johnson in his efforts to block legislation that would give rights and dignity to former slaves, and cleverly found ways to keep black people in their place. The denial of voting rights for blacks was pervasive throughout the South, as were pettier forms of discrimination such as separate rail cars, rest rooms, and drinking fountains, which persisted well into the 1960s. Much more serious were laws and perverted legal systems that put many black men on chain gains, where they were rented out at hard labor for a pittance, effectively reestablishing, under state supervision, the worst slave conditions. Arguably, the new chain gangs were even worse than slavery because slaves at least belonged to someone who would protect them as they would any valuable piece of property, and occasionally show them some compassion.

Yet those on chain gangs were sometimes the lucky ones. Lynching of blacks for the most trivial of offenses was pervasive throughout the former Confederacy. Indeed, it was virtually a form of entertainment that even children were permitted to watch. But through it all—indeed even to the present day—many Southerners will claim that Reconstruction was so terrible that their actions were somehow justified. Instead of blaming slavery, they blame Lincoln and the Republican Party, which is the main reason why the "Solid South" elected only Democrats for a century after the war.[5]

We have come to call the latter half of the nineteenth century in the South as the era of "Jim Crow," during which the oppression of blacks throughout the region became institutionalized. It is seldom pointed out that *all* of the Jim Crow laws were enacted by Democratic legislatures and signed into law by Democratic governors. It could not have been otherwise, since there were virtually no Republicans in positions of authority in state governments in the South after the end of Reconstruction in 1877.

Throughout much of this period, Andrew Johnson was the central figure. As president during perhaps the most critical period in all of American history, he established the foundation for race relations in this country that continues to affect every American to this day.

JOHNSON'S RISE

Andrew Johnson was born in Raleigh, North Carolina, in 1808, but moved to Tennessee as a young man. Poor and self-educated, he became a tailor in the town of Greenville. Through hard work, Johnson soon achieved financial success. Like many others in the western part of this rapidly growing nation, he was drawn to Andrew Jackson's ideas about equality and democracy. Johnson found that he was good at espousing them and became known as a powerful and articulate speaker. This skill naturally pushed him into politics, and he became the mayor of Greenville in 1834. Among his early political accomplishments was helping to pass a new state constitution that disenfranchised free blacks.[6]

As time went by, Johnson sought higher office and he rose through the ranks of the Democratic Party in the Tennessee legislature. He was elected to the U.S. House of Representatives in 1842, where he became closely allied on racial issues with members from the South. For example, in an 1844 speech, Johnson defended the gag rule that automatically tabled anti-slavery petitions. Slavery was justified, he said, because blacks "were inferior to the white man in point of intellect." Moreover, the black race was "many degrees lower in the scale of gradation that expresses the relative relation between God and all that he has created than the white man; hence the conclusion against the black man and in favor of the white man."

Going on, Congressman Johnson denounced the idea of allowing free blacks to vote. That would, he said, "place every splay-footed, bandy-shanked, hump-backed, thick-lipped, flat-nosed, woolly-headed, ebon-colored Negro in the country upon an equality with the poor white man."[7]

In debate on the race question, Johnson could be vicious. In 1848, Congressman John Palfrey, a Massachusetts Whig, made some comments on the House floor about a fine young black man whom he knew to be charming and highly intelligent. Palfrey said he would be very disappointed if his son failed to treat such a man with proper respect regardless of his race. Johnson immediately jumped up to ask whether Palfrey therefore viewed this black man to be the equal of his son? And if that were the case, would he permit him to marry his daughter?[8]

This was an old racist trick—equating opposition to slavery with advocacy of interracial marriage. Since virtually all whites opposed social equality with blacks and were horrified by the thought of race-mixing, this was a clever debating tactic, which Abraham Lincoln often encountered. His response was always to carefully separate the issue of slavery from the question of equality. As Lincoln succinctly put it in his fourth debate with Stephen A. Douglas on September 18, 1858, "I do not understand that because I do not want a Negro woman for a slave, I must necessarily want her for a wife."[9]

Although voting with the proslavery bloc against the Wilmot Proviso and in favor of Texas annexation, Johnson occasionally exhibited independence as well. He opposed the idea of secession and strongly supported the Union. His pet legislation was a Homestead Act to give 160 acres of government land to those who would settle and work it, a measure opposed in the South because it was thought to hinder the spread of slavery in the West.[10]

In 1852, Johnson gave up his House seat to run for governor of Tennessee and was elected in 1853. The following year, he signed into law legislation requiring freed slaves to be deported to Africa. Johnson's own son Robert accompanied several free blacks to the port of Norfolk in 1856, where they were put onboard a ship bound for Liberia. "This unsavory business did not faze the governor," historian Hans Trefousse writes. "He was interested in the welfare of whites, not freed blacks."[11]

Johnson ran for reelection as governor in 1855. When his opponent questioned his credentials as a defender of slavery, Johnson responded that he had "never cast a single vote upon any Southern question not up to the extremist standard of Southern rights."[12] He chose not to seek a third two-year term in 1857. Instead, Johnson worked hard to elect a majority of Democrats to the state legislature in hopes that it would name him to the U.S. Senate. During the campaign, he often defended his record on slavery, denouncing blacks as inferior and declaring his opposition to abolitionism.[13]

SENATOR JOHNSON

A big Democratic victory in the statehouse elections gave Johnson his wish: he was named to the Senate on October 8, 1857. In one of his first speeches as senator, he put forward a vigorous defense of slavery, often citing his own ownership of several slaves. Said Johnson, "Servitude or slavery grows out of the organic structure of man." Therefore, in his view, it was foolish to debate the question of whether or not slavery was justified; the only question was what form it should take.

Siding with the most radical Southerners, Johnson went on to denounce the compromises of the 1850s. "I think it is time for the North and the South to abandon the idea of compromise," he said; the reason being that slavery was well grounded in the Constitution. Therefore, Johnson concluded, any further compromise on slavery must necessarily amount to an undermining of the Constitution itself. It was equivalent, he argued, to truth compromising with falsehood or virtue compromising with vice. Nothing good could come of it.[14]

During Senate debate in 1860, Johnson perceptively recognized that racism, rather than slavery, was the root of the problem. He emphasized that even if slavery were abolished, racism would remain, uniting poor and wealthy Southerners in opposition to black equality. As Johnson explained:

> I say that if the day ever does come when the effort is made to emancipate the slaves, to abolish slavery, and turn them loose on the country, the non-slaveholder of the South will be the first man to unite with the slaveholder to reduce them to subjugation again; and if one would be more ready to do so than the other, it would be the non-slaveholder. I have said that; and that if their resistance to subjugation were obstinate and stubborn, the non-slaveholder would unite with the slaveholder, and all this abolition philanthropy, all this abolition sympathy, when pressed to its ultimatum, would result in the extirpation of the Negro race. . . . Press this question to its ultimatum, and the non-slaveholder will unite, heart and hand, in subjugating the Africans, and if resistance be made, in extirpating the Negro race; and that is where this question will end. . . . I repeat now, that the idea of there being any difference between the feelings of the slave-holder and non-slaveholders of the South on this question, is a mistaken one, a false one. . . . When there was agitation in Tennessee in 1856, I saw that the non-slaveholder was the readiest man to rise up and reduce the Negro to subjugation; and he would join the master in extirpating, if necessary, this race from existence, rather than see them liberated and turned loose upon the country.[15]

Here is one of the clearest explanations one will ever read about why war was ultimately necessary to free the slaves. Even though only a small minority of Southerners owned slaves, and though there was class conflict between the few wealthy slave owners and the much larger number of non-slaveholding whites, Southerners were as one in their fear of millions of black slaves being given freedom.[16] This is why so many uneducated, dirt-poor whites, who never owned a slave and never would, fought to the death to defend the institution of slavery. They believed they were fighting for the very survival of their race.

Remember, in 1860 blacks outnumbered whites by a substantial margin in Mississippi and South Carolina. In Louisiana, Virginia, Alabama, and Florida, blacks made up almost half the population. In no state of the Confederacy did blacks represent less than 25 percent of the population.[17] Since the cities were largely white, this meant that in the bulk of the South's geographical area, blacks were a majority of the population—often overwhelmingly so.[18] The only way the minority whites could keep control and avoid being overwhelmed by the black majority was by brutalizing them, keeping them down, and denying them the tiniest bit of human dignity.[19] Not surprisingly, there is much similarity in the way whites treated blacks in the old South and in twentieth-century South Africa before the end of apartheid.[20]

The idea that the South was fighting against Northern tariffs, as some analysts still maintain, is simply nonsense.[21] People won't risk their lives in war to fight against a tariff; no war in history can be traced to that origin. But they will fight to the death to save their race or nationality. A great many wars can be traced to this cause. It is true that Southerners complained about the tariff and some even cited it as the cause of the war. But this was just for political effect, to make it seem as if the South had a more noble justification for secession than the maintenance of slavery.

Summing up Johnson's prewar career, historian David Bowen describes him as an "ardent if sometimes unorthodox defender of slavery . . . often found in the company of the strongest pro-slavery extremists."[22]

CIVIL WAR

With the shelling of Fort Sumter on April 12, 1861, war became inevitable. Democrats in the North were forced to choose sides. Some took positions like Johnson's, siding with Lincoln, supporting the Union, and defending the war even though they opposed abolition. Others were steadfast in their opposition, coming to be called "Copperheads" because of their allegedly traitorous, snake-like qualities.[23] Historians today tend to downplay the more lurid charges that Peace Democrats, as they preferred to be called, engaged in active conspiracies to undermine the Union.[24] On the other hand, there is no doubt that most Northern Democrats remained sympathetic to the South, highly tolerant of slavery, and doubtful that war was necessary.[25] University of Connecticut historian Richard Curry describes the wartime Democratic Party in the North in these words:

> Stated in its simplest form, the Democratic Party was the party of tradition—the defender of the *status quo*, the bitter opponent of political and social change. The ideology of the Democratic Party *before, during* and *after* the Civil War was remarkably consistent. The wartime Democratic motto, "The Union As It Was, The Constitution As It Is, And The Negroes Where They Are" accurately reflects the determination of Civil War Democrats to maintain Jacksonian ideals of limited government and racial subjugation.[26]

Perhaps the outstanding example of a Copperhead was Congressman Clement Vallandigham, Democrat of Ohio, who strenuously opposed the war and defended slavery to the bitter end, despite representing a free state. After being defeated for reelection in 1862, he gave a farewell speech to the House of Representatives summarizing his view that there really wasn't anything wrong with slavery; certainly nothing worth fighting a war over. Said Vallandigham:

> Domestic slavery in the South is a question, not of morals, or religion, or humanity, but a form of labor, perfectly compatible with the dignity of free

white labor in the same community, and with national vigor, power, and prosperity, and especially with military strength. . . . The condition of subordination, as established in the South, is far better every way for the Negro than the hard servitude of poverty, degradation, and crime to which he is subjected in the free states.[27]

When Tennessee went for secession, Johnson sided with the Union, returning to Washington where he continued to represent his state in the Senate. However, to protect his position at home, Johnson insisted that the Senate pass a resolution stating explicitly that the war was not about abolition or anything other than preservation of the Union, which it did.[28]

In 1862, Lincoln appointed Johnson to be military governor of the Union-occupied portion of Tennessee. In hopes of winning slaveholders over to the Union side, Johnson ordered the Army to return runaway slaves to their owners. However, in July Congress passed the Confiscation Act, which freed all slaves belonging to those engaged in rebellion against the United States. Furthermore, any slaves captured within the Confederate states were deemed to be captives of war and automatically set free.[29] A few weeks later, on September 22, Lincoln read a preliminary draft of the Emancipation Proclamation to his cabinet, putting the South on notice that unless fighting ceased, he would set free all slaves in the rebellious states on January 1, 1863.[30] The idea was to give time for slaveholders in Confederate border states to pressure their states to reenter the Union so that they could keep their valuable property.[31] It was also to head off efforts in Britain to recognize the Confederacy as an independent nation.[32]

Throughout the North, Democrats universally opposed the Proclamation, saying that the war was *only* about reestablishing the Union and *nothing else.* "In one voice, Democrats protested," writes Marquette University historian Frank Klement. "The proclamation of September 22 stirred the Democrats to political activity. They stirred anew the coals of Negrophobia."[33] Princeton University historian James McPherson describes the strategy Democrats took in the November 1862 congressional elections:

> As they had done in every election since the birth of the Republican Party, northern Democrats exploited the race issue for all they thought it was worth in 1862. The Black Republican "party of fanaticism" intended to free "two or three million semi-savages" to "overrun the North and enter into competition with the white labor masses" and mix with "their sons and daughters." "Shall the Working Classes be Equalized with Negroes?" screamed Democratic newspaper headlines.[34]

As University of Kansas historian Jennifer Weber notes, rather than base their opposition to the Proclamation on constitutional principles, which they could easily have done, Democrats instead wrapped their complaints "in racist rhetoric designed to appeal to people's basest fears." Nor did they ever offer any alternative to Lincoln's strategy, never once putting a plan on the table other than the Crittenden Compromise of 1860, which would have amended the Constitution to permit slavery forever.[35]

Johnson was not at all happy with the prospect of emancipation. He feared that it would encourage slaveholders in Tennessee, which was not entirely under Union control at the end of 1862, to continue fighting. However, Johnson was able to intercede with Lincoln to exempt his state from the final Emancipation Proclamation, thus preserving slavery in Tennessee. But in 1863, Johnson finally conceded the necessity of emancipation, if only for political reasons, and pushed for an amendment to the state constitution prohibiting slavery. Yet he was still no friend to blacks; Johnson wanted a strict black code to keep them in their place, and resisted pleas to assist runaway slaves, whom he usually referred to as "contraband." Only severe pressure from Washington forced Johnson to offer them modest aid.[36]

By the middle of 1863, Union victories at Vicksburg and Gettysburg turned the tide of the war, bolstering the political position of Lincoln and the Republicans. But Lincoln still felt vulnerable to Democratic attacks, which had gained strength from resistance to conscription, inflation, and high taxes. This led him to conclude that he needed to replace Vice President Hannibal Hamlin, a solid Republican from Maine, with a Democrat, so that he could run for reelection in 1864 on a national unity ticket. Lincoln first sounded out Massachusetts Democrat Benjamin F. Butler, who rejected the offer.[37] Lincoln appears to have then allowed the Republican Convention, which was held in Baltimore in June, to choose Johnson, who had gained renown for his strenuous defense of the Union as a War Democrat.[38]

PRESIDENT JOHNSON

In 1864, the Democratic Party nominated for president General George B. McClellan, whom Lincoln had sacked as head of the Union Army and relieved of command in 1862 for excessive caution in pursuing the enemy. Consequently, there was no love lost between the two opposing presidential candidates. In private, McClellan had been known to call Lincoln "a well meaning baboon" and "the original gorilla." Nor did McClellan have any use for black people. In 1861, he wrote to a friend, "Help me to dodge the nigger—we want nothing to do with him."[39]

During the campaign, McClellan's surrogates hammered the race issue relentlessly. One was Jeremiah Black, attorney general and secretary of state under James Buchanan, who charged that Republicans were robbing the white man of his property just to bestow it on blacks. "You can degrade the white man to the level of the Negro," he said, "but you cannot lift the Negro up to the white man's place."[40]

A key Democratic tactic during the 1864 election was to accuse Republicans of advocating race-mixing or amalgamation, as it was often called. Indeed, some Democratic operatives coined a new term, "miscegenation," during the campaign, producing a widely-read anonymous pamphlet, seemingly from an abolitionist, arguing that those of mixed race were superior to those of pure race. Democrats like Congressman Samuel "Sunset" Cox of Ohio eagerly bandied the new term around, saying that the Republican Party was "moving steadily forward to perfect social equality of black and white, and can only end in this detestable doctrine of—miscegenation!"[41] Sarcastically, the *New York Times* suggested that very soon there would hardly be a Republican family left in the city without a black son-in-law and those without one would be read out of the party.[42]

The success of General William Tecumseh Sherman's march to the sea and Admiral David Farragut's naval victory at the Battle of Mobile Bay in the late summer of 1864 essentially clinched Lincoln's reelection, and he won with 55 percent of the vote in November. With the outcome of the war no longer in doubt, Lincoln turned his attention to reconstruction.

In his State of the Union message on December 6, 1864, Lincoln asked for swift enactment of the Thirteenth Amendment to the Constitution to permanently abolish slavery. It had passed the Senate in April, but failed in the House of Representatives in June, as Democrats voted overwhelmingly against it.[43] At Lincoln's request, the House tried again in January. During debate, some Democrats still insisted that there was absolutely nothing wrong with enslaving black people. One was Congressman Fernando Wood, Democrat of New York. On January 10, 1865, he told the House:

> The Almighty has fixed the distinction of the races; the Almighty has made the black man inferior, and, sir, by no legislation, by no military power, can you wipe out this distinction. . . . The condition of domestic servitude as existing in the southern states is the highest condition of which the African race is capable, and when compared with their original condition on the continent from which they came is superior in all the elements of civilization, philanthropy, and humanity. . . . Admitting all the sins with which slavery is charged, it cannot be denied that it has been an instrument in the hands of God by which to confer a benefit upon that unfortunate race.[44]

Despite the fact that Republican gains in the 1864 elections ensured that the amendment would pass easily in the next Congress, making it essentially a free vote, only fourteen Democrats in the House supported passage of the Thirteenth Amendment the second time around, with fifty-one voting "nay."[45] Every Republican supported passage.[46]

Historians have spent considerable time trying to determine what, exactly, Lincoln's postwar policy would have been. Many believe that he would have adopted a policy of reconciliation and treated the South with great leniency—"with malice toward none; with charity for all," as Lincoln put it in his second inaugural address. What little he did and said on the subject, however, was colored by the fact that the war was still in progress. This is especially the case with the most complete statement of Lincoln's reconstruction plans, his Proclamation of Amnesty and Reconstruction, issued on December 8, 1863.[47] Interpreting the president's power to pardon as broadly as possible, Lincoln said that all rebellious states could be readmitted to the Union on the basis of full equality, with no penalty, if just 10 percent of the state's qualified voters in the 1860 presidential election took an oath of loyalty and established new state governments.

Issued as it was in the midst of a war that would continue for another seventeen months, Lincoln was obviously trying to encourage an early end to hostilities by offering seceding states the best possible peace terms. Since these terms were not accepted, we cannot necessarily assume that Lincoln would have offered the same ones in 1865. Indeed, in his last State of the Union message, Lincoln warned that unless his terms were accepted quickly, "more rigorous" measures would almost certainly be imposed. It's worth remembering that in 1862 Lincoln had signed the Confiscation Act, which provided for the total forfeiture of all property belonging to those engaged in the rebellion. Historian Kenneth Stampp points out that if Lincoln had chosen to enforce its provisions, "it would have resulted in the economic liquidation of the old planter aristocracy."[48]

In short, Lincoln's comments suggesting leniency may have been as much war propaganda as true indications of what he would actually do after the war.[49] Moreover, we cannot know how Lincoln would have dealt with Congress, which may have rejected his approach and enacted its own. In 1864, Congress passed the Wade-Davis bill, which would have imposed harsh terms for the readmission of rebellious states.[50] Although Lincoln vetoed it, he left open the door to supporting it at a later time. Said Lincoln, he was not "inflexibly committed" to one particular plan and the Wade-Davis bill was "one very proper plan" for restoration.[51] Nor do we know how Lincoln would have reacted to the South's continued brutalizing of black people, which might have radicalized him.

In the end, as a matter of history, we have no choice but to look at what was and not overly concern ourselves with what might have been. What we know with certainty is that Lincoln was assassinated on April 14, 1865, a few days after General Robert E. Lee's surrender at Appomattox Courthouse effectively ended the war, making Andrew Johnson president of the United States during one of the most critical periods in American history. Hence, Lincoln was never able to implement his agenda, whatever it would have been, and instead it was Johnson who implemented his.

RADICALIZED REPUBLICANS

One belief Johnson and Lincoln clearly shared was that reconstruction was almost solely an executive responsibility; Congress had no real role to play as far as they were concerned. With Congress in adjournment since before Lincoln's assassination and not scheduled to reconvene until December 1865, Johnson simply undertook to carry out reconstruction by himself. He offered blanket pardons to all but the top economic, military, and political leaders of the Confederacy and moved swiftly to set up new state governments and recognize them as legitimate.[52] By the time Congress returned to Washington, Johnson thought that reconstruction was essentially finished.

Even if Congress had agreed entirely with the substance of Johnson's actions, it certainly would have been highly annoyed at being left entirely out of the process by an accidental president and a Democrat at a time when Republicans controlled both houses of Congress by large majorities. Combined with glaring problems in Johnson's approach and honest disagreements about how to proceed, the result, predictably, was a monumental political confrontation.[53]

The biggest problem was that in his haste to bring the South back into the Union, Johnson had blithely assumed that new leaders would emerge, and that those who had brought so much pain and misery upon the South would be rejected out of hand. In reality, the average Southerner still looked up to and respected the class of people who had brought about secession and immediately put them back in charge of the former Confederate states. Even more galling to congressional Republicans was the fact that most of those in control didn't qualify for pardons even under Johnson's liberal criteria. Yet rather than fix the problem by refusing to recognize the new governments and insisting upon leadership untainted by association with the rebellion, Johnson simply handed out additional pardons to almost all of those he had originally excluded.

This left many Republicans feeling as if the war had been fought for nothing, especially when they saw the Southern states swiftly enact severe black codes, which kept the former slaves in virtual bondage despite passage of the Thirteenth Amendment to the Constitution, which became effective on December 18, 1865, and refuse to give them basic rights such as voting.[54] Under these codes, blacks were commonly required to have available for inspection at all times either written labor contracts for at least a year or government licenses permitting them to practice a trade. In the absence of such documentation, they were deemed to be vagrants and subject to arrest. Black workers were not allowed to leave their employers and were liable for arrest if they did. Those convicted of vagrancy were fined heavily and could be hired out by the state for a pittance until the fine was paid. Blacks were prohibited from possessing knives, firearms, or liquor.[55]

The great black leader Frederick Douglass tried to explain all this at a White House meeting on February 7, 1866. "The masters have the making of the laws and we cannot get away from the plantation," he told Johnson, who appeared incapable of grasping the point.[56] Afterwards, however, the president was overheard saying, "Those damned sons of bitches thought they had me in a trap. I know that damned Douglass. He's just like any nigger and he would sooner cut a white man's throat than not."[57]

When Congress reconvened on December 4, 1865, Johnson quickly dismissed its concerns about the way black people were being treated in the South. In a message to the Senate on December 18, he said, "systems are gradually developing themselves under which the freedman will receive the protection to which he is justly entitled, and, by means of his labor, make himself a useful and independent member in the community in which he has a home."[58]

Of course, nothing could have been further from the truth. Numerous reports from the South made clear to Congress, if not to the White House, that great suffering was occurring among the former slaves. After all, they previously had someone responsible for their care and feeding, if only to make them fit for arduous labor. Now they were almost entirely on their own, owning nothing except their own labor, but still under the *de facto* control of their former masters, who wanted nothing more than to reestablish their previous relationship to the greatest extent possible.[59]

During the war, a Freedmen's Bureau had been established in the War Department to provide food, clothing, and fuel to displaced former slaves who had sought out or been captured by the Union Army.[60] Johnson wanted the Bureau to wind up its work and close down, feeling that its job was essentially finished by the end of 1865. But Republicans in Congress recognized that there was still a pressing need for a federal agency to continue providing aid and protection to black people, since virtually none was forthcoming from the Southern state governments. In early 1866, Congress sent Johnson legislation renewing the Freedmen's Bureau and expanding its authority. Among other things, it would have set aside three million acres of public land in the South to be given to former slaves in forty-acre plots.[61] Johnson wasted little time vetoing it and the Senate upheld his veto, with every Democrat voting to sustain.[62]

Republicans next passed the Civil Rights Act of 1866, which addressed the systematic denial of basic legal protections to black people in Southern states. It would have guaranteed them the same rights to make contracts, own property, and have that property protected by law. The Act also would have ensured that the criminal laws applied equally to white and black people. Mechanisms were provided for the federal courts to enforce these guarantees. Democrats strenuously attacked the bill as both unconstitutional and unnecessary. Among the most vigorous opponents was Senator Willard Saulsbury, Democrat of Delaware. Said Saulsbury during floor debate on January 29, 1866:

> I think the time for shedding tears over the poor slave has well nigh
> passed in this country. The tears which the honest white people of this

country have been made to shed from the oppressive acts of this government in its various departments during the last four years call more loudly
for my sympathies than those tears which have been shedding and dropping and dropping for the last twenty years in reference to the poor,
oppressed slave—dropping from the eyes of strong-minded women and
weak-minded men, until, becoming a mighty flood, they have swept
away, in their resistless force, every trace of constitutional liberty in this
country.[63]

President Johnson sided with the critics and vetoed the Civil Rights Act
on March 27, 1866. Among his reasons for opposing the legislation was
that it would have applied to Chinese, Gypsies, and Indians. Johnson also
objected to the exclusion of foreigners from its provisions. "The bill, in
effect, proposes a discrimination against the large number of intelligent,
worthy, and patriotic foreigners, and in favor of the Negro," he complained. Among Johnson's other concerns was that the measure might prohibit states from outlawing interracial marriage and leave them powerless
to exclude blacks from voting and holding office. Finally, he argued, new
laws were unneeded because blacks were getting along just fine without
them. Indeed, Johnson warned that giving the same rights to blacks as
enjoyed by whites would somehow create reverse discrimination and ultimately hurt blacks by interfering with the free market.[64] Racists applauded
his veto and reasoning.[65]

The Senate overrode Johnson's veto on April 6, 1866, even though
every Democrat in that body voted to uphold it.[66] The House followed suit
on April 9, with forty Democrats and one Unionist voting to sustain.[67] The
Civil Rights Act thus became law despite the best efforts of Johnson and
the Democratic Party to kill it.

THE ROAD TO IMPEACHMENT

Johnson's veto of the Civil Rights Act and persistence in trying to restore
full political rights to the former Confederate states produced a deep breach
between him and the Republican majority in Congress.[68] Taking advantage
of the fact that proposed constitutional amendments cannot be vetoed by
the president and go directly to the states for ratification after congressional
passage, Republicans drafted the Fourteenth Amendment to the Constitution
in early 1866. Its purpose was to resolve once and for all the questions of
whether Americans of all races enjoy the full protection of the Constitution
and whether the federal government has the right to enforce such protection in cases where the states abrogate that responsibility.

Although he could not veto the Fourteenth Amendment, Johnson
made clear his displeasure with it in an extraordinary message to Congress
afterwards. He argued that as long as the Southern states remained unrep-
resented in Congress, such an amendment was *per se* unconstitutional.[69]

The fact that he never made a similar case with regard to the Thirteenth Amendment, however, shows the disingenuousness of his argument. The truth is that Johnson simply objected to the substance of the amendment because he was a racist who didn't believe that blacks were entitled to equal rights.

Rather foolishly, Johnson believed that the country was behind him in trying to block equal rights for black people. In fact, his position was politically weak, and he would have been much better off negotiating with Congress on things like the Civil Rights Act and the Fourteenth Amendment, rather than taking a totally confrontational stance. And by making the congressional elections in 1866 a virtual referendum on his approach, Johnson was playing a very risky game, with much more to lose than to gain. Consequently, when the Republicans won big, they had every reason to believe that voters were repudiating Johnson's conciliatory policies toward the South.[70]

Nevertheless, on January 5, 1867, Johnson continued his obstructionism by vetoing a bill to give black people in the District of Columbia the right to vote. His main concern was that because of the large number of blacks in Washington, they would gain "supreme control over the white race, and to govern them by their own officers, and by the exercise of all municipal authority."[71] Two days later, the Senate, which did not yet have the new members elected in 1866, overrode the veto by a vote of 29 to 10. The next day, the House did the same on a vote of 112 to 38.

Soon, Congress was on a roll. In early February, it admitted Nebraska as a state over Johnson's veto. On March 2, it overrode his veto of a bill limiting the president's ability to remove from office officials in Senate-confirmed positions. That same day, Congress also overrode Johnson's veto of the first Reconstruction Act, which put the Southern states under direct military supervision pending the establishment of new state constitutions and civilian governments. But the thing that really irritated Johnson was the requirement that blacks be allowed to vote in new elections. "The Negroes have not asked for the privilege of voting—the vast majority of them have no idea what it means," he argued. The result, Johnson went on, would be the "Africanizing" of the Southern states.[72]

A second Reconstruction Act was vetoed by Johnson on March 23. Again, his main concern was allowing blacks to vote. He called black enfranchisement a "fearful and untried experiment" that would have dire consequences.[73] The veto was overridden by Congress the same day. In July, Johnson's vetoes of two more Reconstruction Acts were also immediately overridden.

In his State of the Union message on December 3, 1867, Johnson threw down the gauntlet to Congress and challenged its actions in exceptionally strong language. As always, the undesirability of allowing black people to vote—he called it "madness" and "peculiarly unpropitious"—was his paramount concern. Said Johnson:

> It must be acknowledged that in the progress of nations Negroes have shown less capacity for government than any other race of people. No independent government of any form has ever been successful in their hands. On the contrary, wherever they have been left to their own devices they have shown a constant tendency to relapse into barbarism. . . . Of all the dangers which our nation has yet encountered, none are equal to those which must result from the success of the effort now making to Africanize the half of our country.

By early 1868, Republicans felt that they had had enough from Johnson and instituted impeachment proceedings. Over the years, this event has been the subject of much interest; until recently, it was the only case of presidential impeachment. The textbooks still portray Johnson as the injured party and the Republican Congress as the bully—using extra-constitutional methods to usurp presidential power. In fact, the Congress had ample grounds for impeachment.[74] Its mistake was in believing that it had to find Johnson guilty of violating the law to justify removing him from office, rather than simply saying that Johnson was not doing his job properly and removing him for that reason.[75] But Johnson really hadn't broken the law, and the specific grounds upon which the House based impeachment were extremely weak. The Senate was right not to convict on them.[76] The most important effect of the impeachment debacle was to make Johnson into a martyr, causing historians to long downplay his dreadful performance in office.

THE RISE OF JIM CROW

In 1868, the Democrats nominated former New York Governor Horatio Seymour for president and former Congressman Francis P. Blair for vice president. Blair's job, as is often the case for those in his position, was to throw red meat to the party's base, which he did with abandon. He promised that, if elected, Seymour would immediately declare the civil rights acts to be "null and void" and cease their enforcement. At the Democratic Convention, Blair said the election was about saving white people from "an inferior and semi-barbarous race."[77] This was virtually a pledge to start a second civil war.[78] Thankfully, Seymour and Blair lost to Republicans Ulysses Grant and Schuyler Colfax, but more than 47 percent of voters still supported the racist Democrats.

In 1869, Republicans decided that the widespread denial of voting rights for black people in the South required yet another amendment to the Constitution. The Fifteenth Amendment would expressly guarantee the right to vote regardless of race. During the course of debate on this amendment, many Democrats made it clear that racism was the principal basis for their opposition. Senator Thomas Hendricks, Democrat of Indiana and later Vice President of the United States under Grover Cleveland, was among the more outspoken. Said Hendricks:

> I do not believe that the Negro race and the white race can mingle in the exercise of political power and bring good results to society. . . . I do not believe that the two races can mingle successfully in the management of government. I believe that it will bring strife and trouble to the country. . . . While the tendency of the white race is upward, the tendency of the colored race is downward; and I have always supposed it is because in that race the physical predominates over the moral and intellectual qualities. . . . I am speaking of a race whose history for two thousand years has shown that it cannot elevate itself. I am speaking of a race which in its own country is now enshrouded by the darkness of heathenism, the darkest heathenism that covers any land on earth. While the white man for two thousand years past has been going upward and onward, the Negro race wherever found dependent upon himself has been going downward or standing still.[79]

The reaction in the South to the Fifteenth Amendment was the formation of the Ku Klux Klan to suppress the black vote by force. University of North Carolina historian Allen Trelease describes this nefarious organization as the "terrorist arm of the Democratic Party."[80] Columbia University historian Eric Foner concurs, calling the KKK "a military force serving the interests of the Democratic Party."[81]

Republicans immediately recognized the grave threat posed by the Klan and similar groups and swiftly responded. In 1870 and 1871, they passed three laws making it a federal crime to interfere with voting. The first empowered federal marshals to protect that right. The second put state elections, in both the North and South, under federal supervision. And the third was directed specifically at the Klan, making its activities federal crimes and, if necessary, suspending the right of *habeas corpus*—effectively imposing martial law—in areas where it was particularly active. Democrats opposed all three measures, voting *en bloc* against them.[82] The strongest opponents of the anti-Klan bills were those Democrats, like the previously quoted Congressman Cox, who could always be depended upon to blame blacks for their own troubles.[83]

Empowered by the new laws, federal officials worked quickly to arrest, indict, and convict Klan members. The Klan's power in South Carolina was so great that President Grant was forced to call out the Army to suppress its violence. Democrats almost universally condemned Grant's actions and those of the Justice Department officials who sought to enforce the law. However, as Professor Trelease notes, "the degree of Democratic outrage over federal arrests and prosecutions was the measure of their effectiveness."[84] By 1873, the federal prosecutions had largely done their job. Klan violence fell significantly and its power was sharply diminished for the balance of the nineteenth century.[85]

In 1874, Senator Charles Sumner, Republican of Massachusetts and one of the last prewar abolitionists still serving in Congress, died of a heart attack. In his last years, his energy was mainly directed at passing legislation that would prohibit racial discrimination by railroads, hotels, restaurants, schools, and other service providers. With support from President Grant, the Civil Rights Act of 1875 was enacted into law by a Republican Congress as a tribute to Sumner.[86]

This proved to be the last major act of Reconstruction. In the presidential election of 1876, Republican Rutherford B. Hayes got about 250,000 fewer votes nationwide than Democrat Samuel Tilden, but Hayes had a one-vote majority in the all-important Electoral College. There followed a fierce dispute over who really won the election, resolved only when Hayes cut a deal with some Southern Democrats to support him over Tilden, who was from New York, in return for pulling federal troops out of the South, allowing the last Republican state governments in the South to fall, and formally ending Reconstruction.[87]

Republicans may have felt, not unreasonably, that by 1877 there really wasn't anything left to do legislatively with regard to civil rights.[88] All that was necessary was to enforce the laws on the books. Consequently, Republicans thought that keeping control of the White House and Justice Department was what was really paramount to the further advancement of black rights.[89] Since there was overwhelming public pressure to demobilize the Army in the South anyway, Republicans may have felt that the deal cut by Hayes was the best they could do under the circumstances.[90]

What Republicans had not reckoned with was the Supreme Court, which basically dismantled their entire Reconstruction program. In the *Slaughter-House* cases in 1873, the Court severely limited the scope of the Fourteenth Amendment.[91] In *U.S. v. Cruikshank* in 1875, it essentially took away the right to own guns from blacks in the South, ruling that it was permissible for the Ku Klux Klan to forcibly disarm two black men in Louisiana, thus leaving them defenseless since racist state and local governments would do nothing to protect them.[92] And in the *Civil Rights* cases in 1883, the Court basically struck down all of the postwar civil rights laws.[93] The final nail in the civil rights coffin was *Plessy v. Ferguson* in 1896, which upheld the "separate but equal" doctrine that effectively sanctioned racial segregation in all areas of government policy.[94]

Just in case the Supreme Court had neglected to overturn some parts of the civil rights acts, Democrats quickly moved to repeal them when they got control of the House, Senate, and White House for the first time since the war in the 1892 elections.[95] President Grover Cleveland signed the repeal into law on February 8, 1894.[96]

This freed Southern racists to reassert control over the black population by systematically taking away their right to vote; reestablishing *de facto* slavery by putting large numbers of black men in jail on trumped-up charges, and then renting them out to white plantation owners on chain gangs; and using lynching to terrorize blacks into submission so that they would accept laws and practices enforcing comprehensive racial segregation.[97] We now call this the era of "Jim Crow," when blacks were substantively put back in the same place they were before the Civil War.[98] As W. E. B. DuBois famously lamented, "The slave went free; stood a brief moment in the sun; then moved back again toward slavery."[99]

Once blacks lost the right to vote, the Republican Party in the South withered away to virtual nonexistence, and the Democratic Party completely dominated the region for the next one hundred years.[100] Therefore, it was Democratic governors, Democratic state legislatures, Democratic judges, and other government officials who were responsible for all the laws and practices that we associate with Jim Crow. And with the system rigged to make political competition in the South impossible except within the Democratic Party, where party rules kept blacks from voting in primaries—the only elections that mattered—Republicans were powerless to help. Although the Republican Party still had significant strength at the national level—holding the White House for all but 16 years between 1860 and 1932—the Supreme Court's decisions left little executive power with which to redress the racist policies.[101] It was not until the Court's philosophy changed with *Brown v. Board of Education* in 1954 that there was once again an opportunity to pass new civil rights legislation.

SECTION II

SOUTHERN DEMOCRATS: RACIST TO THE CORE

3

BEN TILLMAN, COLE BLEASE, AND JAMES F. BYRNES

Democrats of South Carolina

Among the more colorful Democrats ever to serve in the United States Senate was Benjamin Ryan Tillman of South Carolina, who served from 1894 until his death in 1918, after two terms as governor. Known as "Pitchfork" Ben Tillman, because he had once threatened to stick a pitchfork into President Grover Cleveland, he was undoubtedly the most outspoken racist of his era.

Tillman's protégé and his equal as a racist, if not an orator, was Coleman Livingston Blease. Like Tillman, Blease was a Democrat and a governor of South Carolina. He served in the U.S. Senate from 1925 to 1931, where Blease was known mainly for being an even cruder racist than Tillman.

Another Tillman protégé was James Francis Byrnes, who was first elected to the House of Representatives in 1910. Subsequently, Byrnes was to have an extraordinary career as, in turn, U.S. Senator, Associate Justice of the U.S. Supreme Court, U.S. Secretary of State, and Governor of South Carolina. This last position, a bit of a step down from his lofty positions in Washington, was taken explicitly to block integration of the state's schools.

TILLMAN'S START

Tillman got his start in politics as the member of a rifle club in his home town of Edgefield, South Carolina, after the Civil War. Such "clubs" were in reality racist paramilitary organizations not unlike the Ku Klux Klan, except that they were more political and operated openly, with no effort to disguise the identity of their members. Often called "Red Shirts," because many members wore such shirts as *de facto* uniforms, their main purpose was suppression of the Republican vote, which they accomplished by continual harassment. As University of Wisconsin historian Stephen Kantrowitz explains:

> Masses of armed Red-shirts arrived at Republican rallies and demanded that their opponents "divide time"; then they "howled down" the Republicans and provoked physical conflicts, breaking up the rallies. In effect, Democrats denied their opponents the right to meet independently, much as slaveholders had formally prohibited slaves from assembling without a white man present. They also transformed peaceful political meetings . . . into riots.[1]

In 1876, the Red Shirts ratcheted up their violence. On July 4, there was an incident in the town of Hamburg, where a couple of obnoxious white farmers intentionally provoked a confrontation with the black militia that was parading in an Independence Day celebration. The farmers insisted on driving their carriage right through the soldiers, claiming that they owned the street, despite having plenty of room to go around.[2]

Tillman was among those who had been looking for an excuse to put down those blacks still clinging to power as Reconstruction came to an end. They planned "to seize the first opportunity that the Negroes might offer them to provoke a riot and teach the Negroes a lesson . . . by killing as many of them as was justifiable," he later explained.[3]

On July 8, the Red Shirts invaded Hamburg and attacked the black militiamen for allegedly insulting the white farmers. After a shootout, about thirty of the blacks surrendered. Five were taken aside and immediately executed in cold blood. The rest were told to run and were fired upon as they did.

Although Tillman was not personally involved in the Hamburg Massacre, he did join another Red Shirt assault on a black militia in September. Near the town of Ellenton, thirty blacks were killed before federal troops arrived. Tillman's unit murdered a black Republican state senator named Simon Coker who had come to investigate the reports of violence. They shot him as he knelt in prayer.[4]

"Black Republicans bore the brunt of the terror," Kantrowitz tells us. Not long after the Coker killing, twenty of Tillman's Democratic friends broke down the door of Silas Goodwin, a Republican activist in Edgefield, and murdered him, too. "God damn you," one of the gang exclaimed. "You was bragging about how you was going to vote, but now vote if you can!"[5]

Since Tillman had been too young to fight in the war—he was born in 1847—his involvement in the guerilla war against blacks and Republicans in 1876 demonstrated his willingness to fight to defend white South Carolina. It was important in establishing him as a leader and someone who would do whatever was necessary to defend the white race and the Democratic Party. He later told a reporter, "I was the captain of a company of rangers at that time, and was in several race riots. I never killed a Negro myself. I shot at one, but missed him."[6]

After retaking the governorship in 1877, which they would hold continuously for almost a century, Democrats quickly moved to suppress the Republican vote, which was mostly black, and turn South Carolina into a one-party state. In 1878, voting precincts were eliminated in strong Republican areas, and separate ballot boxes were created for federal and state offices in order to confuse illiterate blacks, often leading to the invalidation of their votes. In 1882, this strategy was extended so that there were eight different boxes for various offices. Unless the right ballot was inserted in the right box, it didn't count. Election officials would move the boxes around before blacks came into vote so they couldn't memorize their order. White Democrats were instructed on the proper place to deposit ballots. Republicans were helpless to do anything about this blatant vote-rigging because they weren't allowed on any of the local election boards.[7]

In spite of these obstacles, blacks continued to vote and Republicans still got elected. In the mid-1880s, Tillman began speaking out on the need to further restrict the black vote. The Greenback Party was attracting white farmers suffering from low crop prices, threatening to split the white vote and give blacks the balance of power. Although sympathetic to some of the Greenback Party's program, Tillman thought it was essential to keep white farmers in the Democratic Party and he believed that the party's leadership was not doing enough toward that end.

Playing the race card helped Tillman organize the white farmers, who viewed blacks as economic competitors.[8] By 1890, he and his farmers' movement were strong enough to get him elected governor of South Carolina. His principal accomplishment in office was to rewrite the state constitution to completely disenfranchise black voters. Initially, Tillman lacked the votes in the legislature, which was dominated by conservative Democrats more inclined to co-opt the black vote than suppress it. Many of these conservatives had been slave owners and they felt that they could control the blacks effectively, so there was no need to risk Northern retaliation through overt disenfranchisement. They were also concerned that Washington might curtail South Carolina's congressional representation, which Section 2 of the Fourteenth Amendment permitted where states abridged the right of black people to vote.

By 1892, however, Tillman's forces in the legislature were strong enough to ram through the authorization for a constitutional convention, which took place in 1895. The Republican Party of South Carolina immediately recognized that the main purpose of writing a new constitution was to get them and blacks out of politics for good. Said the Republicans, "We are simply asking that Republicans and Negroes be spared the right to exist as citizens. . . . The cries of 'white supremacy' and Negro rule are simply exhausted bugaboos which will frighten no man who thinks and are used only by shallow politicians for purposes of deceit."[9] The strongly Democratic *Charleston News and Courier* newspaper replied, "We can trust white men to do right by the inferior race, but we cannot trust the inferior race with power over the white man."[10]

In the end, the convention required all voters to live in the state for two years, in the county for one, and in their election district for four months. A poll tax of one dollar had to be paid six months before the election, and voters had to demonstrate an ability to read and write any section of the state constitution or show that they owned or paid taxes on at least $300 worth of property (more than $7,000 today).[11] Before 1898, however, all those who could demonstrate an understanding of the constitution would also be allowed to vote. Historian William Mabry explains why these provisions effectively disenfranchised blacks:

> Relatively long residence requirements tended to work against the Negro in politics because of his migratory character. . . . The permanent literacy and property clause would, of course, have eliminated the illiterate and impecunious of both races, provided the law was impartially administered and provided further that there had been no loophole to let in the illiterate whites. But there was such a loophole. Negroes who were poor and illiterate—and there were a great many of them—were not expected to be able to "understand or explain" a clause in the Constitution, while the registration officials saw to it that the whites did.[12]

At the close of the constitutional convention, Tillman's brother George, who had served as a Democratic congressman from South Carolina, lamented that black disenfranchisement was even necessary. Instead of having Negro suffrage, he said, South Carolina should still have Negro slavery. Instead of the United States Government, there should be a Confederate States Government, George Tillman said.[13]

The new constitutional provisions were very effective in achieving their goal of total Democratic supremacy in South Carolina. This can be shown by the drastic decline in Republican presidential votes in the state. In 1876, the last year when federal troops were there to ensure fair elections, Republican Rutherford B. Hayes carried South Carolina with 91,786 votes—just over 50 percent. By 1904, Republican Theodore Roosevelt, who was elected nationally in a landslide, got just 2,554 votes—less than five percent, compared with a nationwide figure of better than 56 percent.

SENATOR TILLMAN

Having accomplished what he set out to do in South Carolina state politics, Tillman moved on to the U.S. Senate in 1895. When he got to Washington, he was already well known as a wild man. His 1892 statement as governor that he would "lead a party to lynch any Negro that would criminally assault a white woman" was well known in the capital.[14]

What was not yet known about Tillman was his skill as an orator. When he gave his first major speech in the Senate, the *Washington Post* was highly impressed. Said the paper's account the next day, "For two hours there poured forth from the lips of Senator Tillman of South Carolina, a torrent of invective, a Niagara of abuse, such as never before was listened to upon the floor of the Senate. It abounded in the most vehement tirades . . . uttered with a directness of statement and a dramatic manner of delivery which seemed absolutely to awe both the senators upon the floor and the auditors in the galleries."[15]

On that occasion, his target, as would often be the case, was one of his own: fellow Democrat Grover Cleveland, then in the last year of his second presidential term. "In the entire history of this country the high office of President has never been so prostituted," Tillman charged. Cleveland's crime, it seems, was a commitment to hard money and a refusal to debase it, which silver advocates such as Tillman wanted. As Tillman argued, this was because Cleveland was in league with the Jews:

> [Baron Edmund de] Rothschild and his American agents graciously con- descend to come to the help of the United States Treasury in maintaining the gold standard which has wrought the ruin and only charges a small commission of ten millions or so. Great God! That this proud government, the richest and strongest on the face of the globe, should have been brought to so low a pass that a London Jew should have been appointed its receiver, to have charge of the Treasury, with an option on any addi- tional issue of bonds, and who presumes to patronize us and promises to take care of our country! Is there a man here who can think of it without blushing?

Tillman then turned to the Republican majority and asked, "Why have you not impeached him?"[16] A *Washington Post* editorial concluded that Tillman must be a complete fool. "It is impossible to suppose that any man with the faintest conception of refinement, or the merest gleam of intelli- gence, or the most cursory knowledge of decent behavior, would or could have made such an exhibition of himself as Mr. Tillman did," the newspa- per said. "He is clearly a fool, and a fool of that melancholy and hopeless kind—the fool who is not aware of his infirmity."[17]

During the Spanish-American War in 1898, Tillman began to make a name for himself as an opponent of empire. Like other anti-imperialists of that era, Tillman was less concerned about the morality of imperialism than the negative consequences for the United States of having colonies.[18] Where he differed with his fellow anti-imperialists, however, was in believing that these problems were almost entirely racial in nature.[19] Tillman was terribly worried about all the nonwhites that would, in effect, be absorbed into the United States by the annexation of Hawaii and the Philippines. As he explained during Senate debate:

> With 8,000,000 Negroes already among us, the adding of more colored peoples presents to a student of sociological and political questions a grave problem, a solemn responsibility. Can we afford to enter upon a scheme of colonial expansion by conquest, with the inevitable result that we will incorporate another million and a half of Negroes, 10,000,000 Malays, Negritos, Japanese, and Chinese, to say nothing of the hundreds of thousands of mongrels of Spanish blood, imbued with Spanish thought and action?[20]

Tillman went on to explain that he had great insight into the problems that would inevitably arise from the annexation of nonwhite territories because of his experience with blacks in the South. Either the United States would be forced to assimilate these nonwhite subjects—amalgamation, he called it—or be forced to deal with them the same way Southerners had dealt with blacks—by denying them political rights to prevent them from overwhelming the white minority. Tillman was amazingly blunt about what he had done in South Carolina and why:

> In my State of South Carolina we have by constitutional amendment, as far as the fourteenth and fifteenth amendments of the national Constitution would permit us, disfranchised this ignorant mass and rid ourselves for the time being of danger. . . . Our knowledge of the Negro teaches us that he is inferior, and he stands there creeping forward as he may increase in intelligence, or rather as he may gain the necessary educational qualifications, to act as the balance of power, the arbiter between contending white factions, each bidding for his debased vote, which they can buy as you would buy a bullock in the market.[21]

Back in South Carolina, Democrat violence against Republicans continued unabated. In November 1898, Robert Tolbert, a white Republican from a prominent family in Phoenix, South Carolina, was running for Congress. Black supporters of Tolbert were lynched and shot by white Democrats, who also attacked members of the Tolbert family, wounding several. This incident led hundreds of blacks to depart the state permanently, which caused economic devastation in the area for many years thereafter.[22] Commenting on the incident later, Tillman urged his followers to avoid killing "poor, innocent black wretches" and instead "kill the snake, go kill the Tolberts."[23] For Tillman the one thing worse than being black was being a Republican, which was apparently a capital offense punishable by death as far as he was concerned.[24]

TILLMAN DEFENDS RACISM

In 1900, Tillman became more aggressive in attacking his fellow senators for hypocrisy on the race issue. In his view, Northerners hated blacks just as much as Southerners, but lacked the guts to admit it. "You do not love them any better than we do," he told the Senate. The only difference was that Southerners never made any pretense of believing that blacks were fit to vote, while Northerners manipulated black voters to seize power and loot the South during Reconstruction. "When that happened," Tillman explained, "we took the government away. We stuffed ballot boxes. We shot them. We are not ashamed of it."[25]

In another debate, Tillman argued that the North was really responsible for violence against blacks in the South. When they were slaves, he explained, they were fine people that Confederate soldiers entrusted to care for their wives and children during the war. But once freed, blacks lost all self-control and became a menace. "It cannot be denied," Tillman opined, "that the slaves of the South were a superior set of men and women to freedmen of today, and that the poison in their minds—the race hatred of the whites—is the result of the teachings of Northern fanatics." Freedom, Tillman went on to say, had aroused in black men "lust on our wives and daughters" that necessitated lynching.[26]

In an October 1900 article in the *North American Review*, then one of the most influential magazines in the United States, Tillman returned again to the issue of imperialism and why Southerners opposed it. Said Tillman:

> We of the South have never acknowledged that the Negroes were our equals, or that they were fitted for or entitled to participate in government; therefore, we are not inconsistent or hypocritical when we protest against the subjugation of the Filipinos, and the establishment of a military government over them by force. Conscious of the wrongs which exist in the South, and seeking anxiously for a just and fair solution of the Race Question, we strenuously oppose incorporating any more colored men into the body politic.[27]

Despite the outrageousness of Tillman's views—or perhaps because of them—he became highly popular on the national lecture circuit, earning him the equivalent of hundreds of thousands of dollars per year in today's money.[28] "I do love to go up there and tell those Yankees the truth about the Negro . . . and then tell them what damnable hypocrites they are," he once told a reporter, "and the best part of it all is I make 'em pay me 50 or 75 cents apiece to hear me do it. It's the sweetest money God Almighty ever let me make."[29]

More amazingly, he actually started to get serious national support for his idea of repealing the Fifteenth Amendment to the Constitution.[30] It was even endorsed by the *New York Times* in a May 1900 editorial:

> The Republican Party committed a great public crime when it gave the right of suffrage to the blacks. . . . So long as the Fifteenth Amendment stands, the menace of the rule of the blacks will impend, and the safeguards against it must be maintained. The South cannot hope to command the support of three-fourths of all the States for an amendment to the Constitution revoking the privilege so improvidently given to the Negroes thirty years ago. That would beyond all question be the just remedy, a proper reparation for a great wrong, and it ought to be evident to all the people that such an amendment would be an act of national wisdom.[31]

In a 1902 speech to the Senate, Tillman presented a revisionist history of the Civil War. It was caused, he said, by the New Englanders who brought slaves to the South in the first place. Tillman also said there would have been no peace in 1865 had Southerners even remotely suspected that blacks would be given political rights. "If it had ever entered into the minds of the Southern soldiers that it was not only to restore the Union and destroy slavery and then put the ex-slaves in charge of the state governments and make them control our affairs, I tell you here there would have been guerilla warfare inaugurated throughout . . . the South that would have made it impossible that you should have won in the long run," he ruminated. Tillman called upon the North to help the South solve the race problem by sending the blacks back to Africa. "Let us colonize them," he pleaded. "Let us do anything you please that will get them away and out from among us. They threaten our civilization!"[32]

Of course, Tillman was being completely disingenuous. He knew perfectly well that Southern agriculture could not survive without cheap black labor. His own farm depended upon it. Indeed, as governor Tillman put through a law in 1891 that imposed a prohibitive license fee of $500 (about $10,000 in today's dollars) on emigrant agents who recruited black laborers for jobs in the North and West. As historian George Tindall explains, Tillman "wanted to see the influence of the Negro destroyed while his sinews were retained."[33]

It wasn't only blacks that were the objects of Tillman's ire. As noted earlier, he got his nickname by attacking a president of his own party. In 1902, Tillman turned his wrath on Senator John L. McLaurin, his fellow Democrat from South Carolina. Tillman believed that McLaurin had become too friendly with the Republicans and charged him with treachery while McLaurin was absent from the Senate chamber and unable to reply.[34] When McLaurin heard about Tillman's speech, he ran to the Senate floor and physically attacked Tillman.[35] So disgusted was McLaurin with his fellow South Carolinian that he did not seek reelection and moved to New York.

The altercation with McLaurin also led Tillman to begin a long-running feud with Theodore Roosevelt, who disinvited him from a White House dinner on February 24, 1902 as a consequence.[36] The following year, Tillman excoriated Roosevelt for closing a Post Office in Indianola, Mississippi, because local whites had forced the resignation of a black woman who had been appointed postmaster.[37] And to Roosevelt's last day in office, Tillman fought his appointment of a black man, William Crum, as customs collector in Charleston.[38] Speaking of Crum, Tillman said, "We still have guns and ropes in the South and if the policy of appointing the Negro to office is insisted upon, we know how to use them."[39]

AMALGAMATION CONDEMNED

A consistent theme of Tillman's was that black men had some sort of compulsion to mate with white women. "It was Tillman's belief that by the act of rape upon a white woman the Negro was expressing, in the boldest and more horrible form at his command, his desire to break down the lines of caste and thereby effect racial amalgamation," historian Francis Simkins explains.[40]

Blacks were aided and abetted in this urge, Tillman charged, by white men who seemed equally compelled to mate with black women. "Amalgamation," he said, "is the hope and ultimate purpose of the Negroes. White men are rendering them great aid in this by intimacy with Negro women. The line must be drawn as sternly as possible between white men and Negro women as between black men and white women."

Tillman went on to say that one solution to the race problem might be to require all blacks to carry internal passports, with a concomitant increase in law enforcement officials to make sure that blacks did not venture far from their homes. The *Washington Post* described Tillman's proposal in these words:

> He [Tillman] declared if all [blacks] were shot like wild beasts the country would be better off, but that was unlawful. Therefore, when they were unable to produce passports, they should be placed on chain gangs until they reformed or left the country.[41]

In a 1906 speech, Tillman emphasized the political nature of his crusade. "Republicanism means Negro equality, while the Democratic Party means that the white man is supreme. That is why we Southerners are all Democrats." He went on to complain that Republicans' support for blacks was insincere and that anything they did for them was designed solely to acquire their votes. Said Tillman:

> History has no record of Negro rule. The situation is grave, and calls for wisdom and all manner of statesmanship. If we had our say the Negro

could never vote. I believe that God made the white man out of better clay than that which the Negro was made from, and . . . we don't need another race to help us at this time. In some of the states the Negro holds the vote of control. . . . In Chicago the Republicans needed the Negro vote to elect their whole ticket, so a nigger was nominated for judge and elected.[42]

Two days later, Tillman gave another speech and apparently was offended by the presence of a black man in the audience. "Look down that aisle—there's a nigger as black as the ace of spades," the South Carolina Democrat exclaimed. According to a news report, the man was well dressed and only smiled at Tillman's outburst—showing more class in that moment than Tillman had shown in his entire life.[43]

In 1908, Tillman suffered a stroke and was thereafter unable to speak with his customary gusto. Although he remained in the Senate until his death in 1918, he seldom spoke on the floor and concentrated primarily on constituent service. Tillman became increasingly alarmed, however, by efforts to raise the educational levels of blacks in South Carolina, which he feared would undermine the constitutional provisions he had written to prevent black voting primarily by a literacy test. This increased his resolve to get rid of the Fifteenth Amendment to the Constitution, so that the states could simply ban blacks from voting without having to use indirect methods that were not entirely satisfactory.[44]

In 1913, Tillman was overjoyed to at last have another Southern Democrat in the White House with the inauguration of Woodrow Wilson. As chairman of the Senate Naval Affairs Committee, Tillman was in a good position to support Wilson and Navy Secretary Josephus Daniels in their efforts to institute racial segregation throughout the federal government. When South Carolina Governor Coleman Blease attacked Wilson for not doing even more to get blacks out of government, Tillman cautioned that Wilson was doing everything he could. If he tried to do more, Tillman said, it would "arouse all the old abolition sentiment throughout the North and all to no purpose."[45]

Despite being probably the most vocal racist in U.S. Senate history, Tillman remains a revered figure in South Carolina. His statue stands on the grounds of the statehouse. At its unveiling in 1940, Senator James F. Byrnes lauded Tillman as the state's "first New Dealer."[46] Tillman Hall at Clemson University is named for him. Ironically, it was the site of the admission of Clemson's first black student, Harvey Gantt, in 1963.

COLEMAN BLEASE

Cole Blease was Tillman's protégé. Tillman essentially created him to forestall the emergence of a genuine white reformer.[47] But whereas Tillman's principal following was among South Carolina's poor white farmers, Blease built his political base among the growing number of poor white textile workers. Between 1880 and 1900, the number of textile mills in the state had risen almost tenfold, from a dozen to 115, and by 1914 one out of every seven Democrats in South Carolina lived in a mill village.[48] Tillman had little use for such people, calling them the "damned factory class."[49] This eventually led to tensions between Tillman and Blease. But on the race issue, they were as one. Historian Francis Simkins describes Blease's first race for governor in 1908:

> He [Blease] called his inoffensive opponent, [Democratic] Governor [Martin] Ansel, a "nigger lover" because he had made "an infernal nigger" into a notary. He opposed the state's support of higher education for Negroes, advocated the vigorous application of vagrancy laws against blacks, and let his passion for "cussing niggers" lead him to call them "baboons and apes." He . . . opposed Tillman's plan of importing labor under contract on the grounds that foreigners were "worse than Negroes."[50]

Blease was unsuccessful in 1908, but was elected governor in 1910. When he ran again in 1912, however, a rift developed between him and his old mentor Tillman, who disapproved of Blease's personal behavior, labeling him a drunk, a gambler, and a womanizer.[51] But because both were running in 1912, Tillman was forced to be circumspect in his criticism, lest it threaten his own reelection.

Tillman also disapproved of Blease for having publicly raised the issue of white men having relations with black women. At one point during the Democratic primary campaign in 1912, Blease attacked his opponent, Ira Jones, chief justice of the state supreme court, saying, "You people who want social equality vote for Jones. You men who have nigger children vote for Jones. You who have a nigger wife in your back yard vote for Jones." To Tillman, such behavior was appalling. In the South, one never discussed the sexual liaisons between white men and black women—at least in public.[52]

During the 1912 campaign, Blease was attacked for having pardoned a black man. He defended himself by noting that the man had murdered another black man, "and South Carolina was the gainer in the case," Blease said. He railed against spending state money to educate blacks. As one newspaper explained, he "did not believe in white people's money going to educate baboons and free niggers." Such statements even went beyond Tillman's, earning Blease the reputation of being the foremost racist in the state.[53]

Blease defended the lynching of black men and was even known to do a little "death dance" after they took place. The fear of blacks committing indiscriminate rapes against whites became so absurd in 1912 that two black men were even lynched for raping a white *man* named Joe Childers in the town of Blacksburg, South Carolina. The local newspaper editor blamed the incident on "Bleaseism."[54]

By 1914, Tillman was not on the ballot and he used his influence to defeat Blease in the Democratic primary, the only election that mattered in South Carolina after the disenfranchisement of blacks in 1895. Indeed, so intent was Tillman on defeating his former protégé that he threatened to have the literacy tests designed for blacks used against Blease's poor white followers as well.[55]

Among the more ridiculous tactics Blease used in the 1914 campaign to save his position was an attack on doctors, whom he charged with abusing young women by examining their private parts during physical examinations. He threatened to kill any doctor who examined his daughter against her will and to pardon anyone who did the same. Fearful that other people were not as outraged as he was about doctors simply doing their jobs, Blease implied that doctors were allowing "Negro janitors" to observe their examinations.[56]

Of course, Blease did not avoid attacking blacks directly in his efforts to gin up the votes of ignorant white textile workers. "The Negro race has absolutely no standard of morality," he declared. "They are, in that respect, a class by themselves as marital infidelity seems to be their more favorite pastime." Blease said that giving education to a black man would only "ruin a good field hand and make a bad convict." He warned that "the black ape and baboon" was a constant threat to rape white women whenever the opportunity presented itself.[57]

Partly because of Tillman's efforts, Blease was defeated in the 1914 Democratic primary and again in 1916. In 1918, Blease retaliated by running against Tillman for the Senate himself. However, Blease misread the mood of the people regarding World War I and ran a strongly pacifist campaign, attacking Woodrow Wilson and opposing American intervention in the war. After voters reacted very negatively to this approach, he tried to switch course, but it was too late and he was defeated.[58]

Six years later, Blease ran again for the Senate; this time winning election. As a U.S. Senator, Blease was best known for continuing the Tillman tradition of making racially inflammatory speeches on the Senate floor. For example, in a 1928 speech, Democrat Blease blasted Republican Commerce Secretary Herbert Hoover:

> Republicans are now talking about nominating that man for President of the United States . . . a man who is in favor of making young white girls use the same water-closets as Negro men, making young white girls sit by them day by day. If there was nothing else, Mr. President, a Negro would be offensive because of his natural human smell. You can take a Negro and take a tub of the hottest water you can get him into, and use all the soap you can use, then take him out and cover him with cologne, and in five minutes he will smell just as offensive as he did before you washed him, because it is human nature, and he could not get rid of the odor. Then this man [Hoover], who wants to be President of the United States

of America, this Englishman, wants to make white girls associate on equal terms with Negroes. . . . Mr. President, it is a shame, it is a disgrace.[59]

The only disgrace, of course, was that the Democratic voters of South Carolina—the only ones whose votes counted—sent such an obnoxious racist to Washington to represent them. But by 1930, they came to their senses and replaced Blease with James F. Byrnes, a much more genteel racist.[60] Twice more, in 1934 and 1938, Blease attempted to make a comeback as governor, but was rejected by voters both times. He died in 1942.

JAMES F. BYRNES

Byrnes was born in 1879 and first elected to the House of Representatives as a Democrat from South Carolina in 1910, serving until 1924. There, he became a protégé of the state's senior senator, fellow Democrat Ben Tillman.[61] Although a progressive on many issues, Byrnes always drew the line on anything that touched the race question.[62] For example, he pressured Woodrow Wilson to fire black federal workers in South Carolina even though they had Civil Service protection.[63] In 1917, he opposed conscription for World War I because he did not like the idea of a boy from South Carolina having to serve along side "a Negro from Indiana." Said Byrnes, "If they did this, they would not have to go to Europe for war."[64]

In 1919, Byrnes became unhinged over growing black radicalism, viewing it as proof of Communist infiltration of the black community. This had to be the case, he reasoned, because the black man was pleased and appreciative with all that the white man was doing for him. "He is protected in his life and property," Byrnes told the House. "He is happy and contented." Lynchings were not a matter of concern, Byrnes went on, because they almost never affected any black man who was not in fact guilty of rape against a white woman.[65] (How he knew this with such certainty was left unexplained.)

"This is a white man's country, and will always remain a white man's country," Byrnes pontificated. "As to social equality, God Almighty never intended that a white race and a black race should live on terms of social equality, and that which the Creator did not intend man cannot make possible." Nor did blacks have any interest in political equality, he said. "The Negroes of my district do not seek to participate in politics," Congressman Byrnes went on to say. "I know that they do not seek social equality."[66]

Therefore, Byrnes assumed that the only possible reason for blacks' discontent had to be that Soviet Communists were stirring them up with alien ideas. With prosecutorial skill, he quoted extensively from black newspapers and magazines to prove his point and demanded that the federal government investigate and jail their publishers under wartime sedition laws.[67] Woodrow Wilson's Justice Department confirmed that there was indeed Soviet influence at work and promised an investigation.[68]

Any black person that was not happy to live in America, Byrnes concluded, "can depart for any other country he wishes, and his departure will be facilitated by the white people of this country."[69]

Historian David Robertson says Byrnes' 1919 speech "marks a low point for civil rights in a year that is itself remembered as marking the nadir for civil liberties." Together with Byrnes' opposition to antilynching legislation, it "fixed his reputation for the next three decades as a racist politician." Robertson concluded there is "no doubt" that "Byrnes was an uncompromising segregationist."[70]

In 1921, Republicans again brought up an antilynching bill. Said President Warren G. Harding, "Congress ought to wipe the stain of barbaric lynching from the banners of a free and orderly representative democracy."[71] Congressman Byrnes was in the forefront of those Democrats who fought it tooth and nail.[72] "It may please a few misguided Negro leaders," he said, but it will defeat its purpose and lead to even more lynching. This was a problem that was quickly going away as Southern law enforcement officials stamped it out and public opinion turned against it, Byrnes explained. Therefore, there was no need for federal legislation that would intrude on states' rights.[73]

The evidence of a decline in lynching at the time Byrnes spoke, however, is nonexistent. The best data we have show that there were fifty-nine lynchings of blacks in 1921 and fifty-one in 1922, about the same as had been the case annually since 1905.[74]

In his last year in the House, Byrnes made a strenuous effort to cut off federal aid for Howard University, the nation's leading black university.[75] He also strongly supported the Immigration Act of 1924, which set rigid quotas on immigrants for the first time, especially those viewed as inferior to whites of Northern European stock.[76] During debate on an earlier immigration bill, Byrnes had expressed concern that immigrants from Southern Europe, Greece, and Turkey might be more inclined to "mingle" with blacks, thus aggravating the race problem.[77]

After deciding to leave the House, a Senate seat opened up in 1924 and Byrnes decided to run for it against Cole Blease, who ran primarily on the race issue. For a while, Byrnes tried to keep up with him. At one point he attacked another candidate, Nathanial Dial, for favoring the importation of Italian immigrants to replace the blacks that were leaving South Carolina in droves because of the state's uncompromising racism. Said Byrnes, "I'd rather have one big black nigger working on my cotton farm than half a dozen Italians."[78] But after realizing that he could never out-bait Blease as a racial demagogue, Byrnes took a more moderate tone in the campaign, which probably contributed to his close loss to Blease in the Democratic primary.[79] Citadel historian Winfred Moore summarizes Byrnes' position on race during this period:

> Because Byrnes was both a political representative of, and a philosophical heir to, a predominantly white, racist constituency, he evidently found it

to be both politically and philosophically logical to remain, like most white Southerners of his time, an ardent white supremacist. In the early 1920s, then, Byrnes was a man unable to rise above the long-held, racial prejudices of his section of the country. . . . Both in his House career and his campaign statements, he made it clear that he did not believe in racial equality and would not hesitate to fight any development which he felt might jeopardize white supremacy.[80]

BYRNES WEARS MANY HATS

After a few years in private legal practice, Byrnes reentered the political area and was elected to the U.S. Senate in 1930. In 1932, he became an enthusiastic supporter of Franklin D. Roosevelt for the White House and was instrumental in helping him secure Southern support for the Democratic nomination. This early commitment served him well when Roosevelt was elected that year. Subsequently, Roosevelt relied heavily on Byrnes for political advice and leadership in the Senate, especially among Southern Democrats who were not always inclined to support the New Deal.[81]

In 1935, liberals and Republicans made yet another effort to enact an antilynching bill and Byrnes again stood firmly with its opponents. As Moore explains, "his Senate position on lynching proved that the racial problem remained as one issue on which neither he nor his Southern constituents could tolerate compromise."[82] The following year, Byrnes personally blocked a Senate investigation of lynching.[83]

Byrnes opposed Roosevelt's plan for a national minimum wage in 1937 because he was afraid that it would raise the wages of black as well as white workers. "This wage would have to be paid to every Negro working in any store as well as to white employees," he complained.[84] That same year, Byrnes fought efforts by the Department of Agriculture to appoint blacks to state committees established by the Farm Security Administration, which helped tenant farmers buy land. Blacks had no interest in such representation, he argued. Unfortunately, because of Byrnes' power on the Senate Appropriations Committee, Secretary of Agriculture Henry Wallace caved in and blocked the appointments.[85]

In early 1938, the antilynching bill came up again. Although President Roosevelt refused to endorse it, the measure had strong national support and could only be defeated by a filibuster, which Byrnes helped lead. He spoke forcefully and at length against the measure, personally attacking Walter White of the NAACP for pushing it, as well as the growing influence of blacks in the Democratic Party. "The Negro has not only come into the Democratic Party, but the Negro has come into control of the Democratic Party," Byrnes charged.[86] After weeks of debate, all efforts to end the filibuster by Southern Democrats failed and the antilynching bill died once again.

In 1940, Roosevelt asked Byrnes to replace John Nance Garner as vice president. Byrnes declined the offer because he believed that the 1940 race for the White House was going to be close and that his presence on the ticket would cost Roosevelt too many black votes in the North.[87] Considering how easily Roosevelt won the election that year, however, he would probably have done just as well with Byrnes as his running mate as he did with Henry Wallace of Iowa. Since Byrnes undoubtedly would have stayed on the ticket in 1944, he, rather than Harry Truman, would have become president in 1945 when Roosevelt died.

In 1941, Justice James McReynolds, one of the Supreme Court's most conservative members, announced his retirement. After having appointed three justices in a row from the North, Roosevelt looked to the South for McReynolds' replacement and chose Byrnes. Byrnes was strongly opposed by the NAACP because of his poor record on race; in a telegram to the White House, it said, "If Senator Byrnes at any time in his long public career failed to take a position inimical to the human and citizenship rights of 13 million American Negro citizens, close scrutiny of his record fails to reveal it." Nevertheless, Byrnes was nominated by Roosevelt and confirmed to the Supreme Court the same day, June 12, 1941, eight minutes after the nomination was officially received by the Senate.[88]

Quickly bored with the Court after a lifetime in the rough-and-tumble world of electoral politics, Byrnes left after a little more than a year to become head of war mobilization, a very powerful position during World War II that earned him the informal title of "assistant president."[89] When his old Senate colleague Harry Truman assumed the presidency in 1945, Byrnes was eager to join him in some capacity and was offered the job of secretary of state, which he assumed on July 3. But as with the Supreme Court, Byrnes stayed only a short time in this position, resigning in December 1946. It is not clear why he left so soon, but there are indications that he was unhappy with Truman's policies toward blacks, which were the most inclusive of any Democratic president until that time.[90]

Despite a moderate record on race during his brief time on the Supreme Court, it is apparent that Byrnes was at heart always a white supremacist.[91] The proof of this is that he reentered politics in 1950 to run for governor of South Carolina expressly for the purpose of thwarting integration of the schools, something every Southerner knew that the Supreme Court was going to order shortly. After an easy election, Byrnes promised that he would do whatever it took to maintain segregation. As he said in his 1951 inaugural address as governor:

> Whatever is necessary to continue the separation of the races in the schools of South Carolina is going to be done by the white people of the state. That is my ticket as a private citizen. It will be my ticket as Governor.[92]

Byrnes promised that if the federal government forced the states to integrate their public schools, he would ask the South Carolina legislature to abolish public education altogether.[93] He was convinced that allowing black and white children to go to school together would inevitably cause them to socialize together, leading to a crumbling of the wall between the races and resulting in social chaos.[94]

On May 17, 1954, the Supreme Court handed down its long expected decision in *Brown v. Board of Education*—which was actually a consolidation of several separate cases, including one from South Carolina—and Byrnes' worst fears were realized. But he left office the following year without making good on his threat to abolish public education. However, Byrnes was highly critical of the decision for years afterward, and his criticisms carried considerable weight because of his status as a former Supreme Court justice.[95] In his last years, the race issue caused him to become deeply alienated from the Democratic Party to which he had devoted so much of his life. He died in 1972.

4

TOM WATSON, HOKE SMITH, EUGENE TALMADGE, AND RICHARD B. RUSSELL

Democrats of Georgia

During the first half of the twentieth century in Georgia, three demagogues dominated the Democratic Party: Tom Watson, Hoke Smith, and
Eugene Talmadge. Richard B. Russell was no demagogue, but he carried the
same message of white supremacy well into the 1960s.

Watson started out as a populist in the late nineteenth century and
organized the poor white farmers of the state into a powerful electoral
force. Although economic and agricultural issues were important, Watson
knew that the race issue would always dominate all others for these people, who were ever so slightly better off than Georgia's blacks. Rather than
recognize that their economic interests were virtually identical to those of
the blacks, poor whites clung to the belief that they were socially better
and would vote to maintain that distinction whatever the cost.

Smith was a city lawyer who had little in common with Watson, but he
understood the political power of Watson's followers and their devotion to
racial superiority. This power derived from the peculiar nature of Georgia's
electoral system, which greatly magnified the influence of thinly populated
rural counties at the expense of urban counties.[1] By appealing to racism,
Smith was elected both governor and U.S. senator from Georgia.

When Watson and Smith departed the political scene in the 1920s, Talmadge stepped into the vacuum and became leader of the poor white farmers—"wool hat boys," as he affectionately called them. Between 1926 and 1946, he was a candidate for statewide office in virtually every election. Talmadge was elected governor four times and would have been elected to the U.S. Senate as well, except for an utter lack of self-control that unnecessarily antagonized many of his friends and allies.

For almost forty years, Russell was one of the most powerful men in the U.S. Senate. So great was his influence, he was able to install Lyndon Johnson, whom he adopted as his protégé, as the Democratic leader of the Senate just four years after Johnson's election. Russell always preferred to work behind the scenes, and the Senate named one of its office buildings after him as a sign of respect when he died. But on the race issue, he was a diehard segregationist who used every bit of his power every day he was in office to maintain white supremacy.

TOM WATSON: REACTIONARY POPULIST

Thomas Edward Watson is among the more enigmatic figures in American history. A populist by nature and for many years by political affiliation as well, he was a strong supporter of economic reform in the late nineteenth century, with a national audience that went far beyond his native Georgia. During those years, he was strongly opposed to the Democratic Party, which often used violence and intimidation to suppress Populist Party votes just as it did those of Republicans. But in 1906, Watson reconciled with the Democrats, after deciding that suppression of the black vote was critical to his reform agenda. He was rewarded with election to the U.S. Senate as a Democrat.

In the 1880s, Watson became a spokesman for populism, which he felt better represented the needs of rural farmers than the Democratic Party. Under Grover Cleveland, he believed the Democrats had sold out to Eastern industrial and commercial interests. In the populist view, the chief source of the farmers' distress was falling prices, which neither the Democrats nor the Republicans would address because both were committed to the gold standard.[2] Nor could farmers turn to socialism because Karl Marx also believed in hard money.[3] Between 1874 and 1886, the general price of commodities fell by a third and did not really recover until World War I.[4] Low prices and high interest rates forced tenant farmers, both black and white, into debt peonage from which they were virtually helpless to extricate themselves.[5]

Watson became involved with the Farmers Alliance, which was open to both black and white farmers. Interestingly, membership was denied to bank and railroad officials, real estate agents, cotton brokers, and lawyers, thus excluding Watson himself from joining.[6] Nevertheless, he strongly supported the group's efforts, which rapidly grew into a nationwide movement demanding an abolition of national banks, free coinage of silver, government ownership of railroads, and other staples of populism in that era.[7]

In 1890, Watson was elected to Congress as a Populist. This created great fear among racists in the Democratic Party. Their perennial nightmare was a third party that would split the white vote and give blacks the balance of power.[8] Consequently, Democrats used all the tools of violence, intimidation, bribery, and fraud that had so effectively destroyed the Republican Party against the Populists as well. In the election of 1892, Watson was defeated by such methods, after serving only a single term in the House of Representatives. In one town in his district, more than twice as many votes were cast for his Democratic opponent than there were registered voters.[9]

Watson ran again in 1894, and Democrats used the same methods to defeat him again. Nevertheless, he remained committed to the Populist cause and in 1896 became William Jennings Bryan's running mate on the national Populist Party ticket. However, Bryan also had the Democratic Party nomination as well, for which he chose a different running mate, Arthur Sewall, a hard-money Democrat like Cleveland. In so doing, Bryan basically stabbed Watson and the Populists in the back, leading to subsequent disintegration of the Populist Party.[10]

For eight years, Watson was largely disengaged from politics. He wrote books and tended to his newspaper and magazine businesses. During this time, Watson concluded that blacks had been the major cause of his political frustration in the 1890s. As long as they were involved in politics, he reasoned, there was no hope for a third party in the South. Such a party would always be viewed as a vehicle through which blacks would become politically empowered. Therefore, the only hope of a populist party was to totally disenfranchise blacks, eliminating them from the political process altogether. In short, Watson came to view blacks as the principal stumbling block to populist political power.[11]

After concluding that populism as a distinct political party was unviable, Watson made his peace with the Democrats in 1906. Henceforth, the populist cause would be waged inside the Democratic Party as a faction, rather than outside as a third party. Because Watson retained the strong allegiance of about 20,000 populist voters, whose votes would go to the candidate of his personal choice, he ended up holding the balance of power within the Georgia Democratic Party, which was always split between different factions (based on geography, support for particular individuals based on personalities, or the historical city/rural or agricultural/industrial divisions). For the next fourteen years, Watson more or less decided who would be governor of the state of Georgia.[12]

ANTI-CATHOLIC, ANTI-SEMITIC,
AND RACIST

Watson's bitterness toward black people as the barrier to the success of the Populist Party turned him into a virulent racist. Whereas he had once preached racial inclusiveness and the common class interests of blacks and poor whites, he now preached racial hatred. For example, in 1905 Watson wrote an editorial attacking Booker T. Washington, undoubtedly the most respected black man in America. "What does civilization owe to the Negro?" Watson asked. His response: "Nothing! Nothing!! NOTHING!!!"[13]

To Watson, blacks had no capacity for virtue, honesty, truth, gratitude, or principle. He defended lynching as a sign that justice lived among the people. Lynching, in Watson's view, was no more a sin than shooting a mad dog. According to historian C. Vann Woodward, "No Southern leader of post-bellum times ever equaled Tom Watson in his scathing ridicule of 'Negro domination' as the 'stock-in-trade' of the Southern demagogue."[14]

But blacks were not the only objects of Watson's hate. He also became the leading voice of anti-Catholic and anti-Semitic thought in America during the early part of the twentieth century. Beginning in 1910, Watson launched a long-running attack on the Catholic Church that Woodward calls "pathological." His series on Catholic Cardinal Gibbons was "matchless in its insulting offensiveness," in Woodward's estimation. Priests were routinely called "chemise-wearing bachelors," "shad-bellies," and "foot-kissers." To Watson, the Catholic faith was "jackassical."[15]

In 1914, Watson became positively unhinged over the Leo Frank case. Frank was a Jewish factory manager who was accused of the vicious murder of a young Gentile girl named Mary Phagan. That the accused was a Jew was really all Watson needed to know in order to convict him in his magazine. He fanned the flames of anti-Semitism and mob psychology throughout the trial. Sadly, the atmosphere of intimidation that Watson created made it almost impossible for the jury to return anything except a guilty verdict; any juror voting for acquittal undoubtedly would have had good reason to fear for his own life. Indeed, after commuting Frank's sentence from death to life in prison, the governor himself was forced to flee the state to escape mob violence. When a gang of vigilantes broke into the prison where Frank was being held and dragged him off to be lynched in 1915, Watson congratulated them:

> In putting the sodomite murderer to death, the Vigilance Committee has done what the Sheriff would have done, if [Governor John] Slaton had not been of the same mould as Benedict Arnold. Let Jew libertines take notice. Georgia is not for sale to rich criminals.[16]

"Tom Watson is the murderer of Leo Frank," Frank's lawyer Louis Marshall asserted.[17] The *Atlanta Journal* agreed that although Watson had not been an actual member of the lynch mob, he was as much to blame as anyone for the awful miscarriage of justice against Frank, who was later found to be completely innocent. "God may be able to forgive him," the paper said of Watson, "but Georgia will never be able to forget him and his hellish work."[18]

Despite widespread national disgust with the people of Georgia over the Frank case, Watson's stand was very popular within the state, making him even more powerful than he was before. In 1916, Watson virtually took control of the state government, with his candidates winning across the board. He was even able to induce the legislature to pass a law requiring strict state inspection of Catholic convents. Watson had long held that these were not places of worship at all, but rather dens of iniquity where priests and nuns engaged in lurid sexual debauchery.[19]

Watson encouraged reconstitution of the Ku Klux Klan in Georgia, which he used as a kind of private army against his political enemies. One of them was the American Legion, which took issue with Watson's opposition to American entry into World War I.[20] Although the war was popular in Georgia, Watson's position did nothing to diminish his power and he was elected to the U.S. Senate as a Democrat in 1920. *The Nation* magazine called it a victory for "sinister forces of intolerance, superstition, prejudice, religious jingoism, and mobbism."[21]

Watson spent most of his brief time as a senator giving long-winded speeches on forgettable topics and starting fights with his colleagues. Among his targets: motorcycles and failure of the Capitol police to stop squirrels from eating the birds.[22] Few of Watson's fellow senators mourned his death on September 26, 1922. The largest floral bouquet at his funeral was from the Ku Klux Klan.[23]

HOKE SMITH: ESTABLISHMENT RACIST

Hoke Smith was a prosperous trial lawyer and newspaper publisher whose political power in Georgia rivaled Watson's in the early part of the twentieth century. Although they shared many views, Smith was always a Democratic Party loyalist and never flirted with third parties as Watson did. Smith later went on to become governor of Georgia and U.S. senator. Like Watson, he was a political Jekyll-and-Hyde, supporting tolerance and reform early in his career but becoming a virulent racist later.

Born in North Carolina, where his father was a college professor, Smith studied law in Atlanta and took up practice there in 1873. He became one of the wealthiest lawyers in Georgia by specializing in personal injury cases against the railroads, often taking 50 percent of the settlements.[24] In 1887, he purchased the *Atlanta Journal*, the city's principal afternoon newspaper, which Smith often used to assist his legal practice by attacking those against whom he had suits pending.[25]

Smith was sympathetic to the plight of the farmer and he strongly endorsed free silver, tariff reform, and trust-busting. But he always remained a loyal Democrat even when the party went in a different direction, as when former President Cleveland, a supporter of the gold standard, was renominated in 1892. Despite his difference with Cleveland on this issue, Smith supported him wholeheartedly and was rewarded by being appointed secretary of the interior in 1893.

Among those with doubts about Smith's appointment was Woodrow Wilson, then a college professor, who questioned his qualifications.[26] Indeed, Smith didn't know very much about Interior, the newest of the eight cabinet departments then in existence. Among its functions were many that later were parceled out to other departments, including pensions, patents, the census, education, railroads, and others. One of Smith's appointments at Interior was Josephus Daniels, the North Carolina racist who later served as secretary of the navy under Wilson.

Smith's tenure at Interior was fairly successful and he left office in 1896 to generally positive reviews. He returned to Atlanta, where he resumed the practice of law and other business pursuits. But in 1905, Smith was lured back into politics when he was recruited to run for governor. He immediately reached out to Tom Watson, whose support was essential if he hoped to win the whites-only Democratic primary, the only election that mattered. Although Smith and Watson differed on some issues, there was one of overriding importance on which they both agreed: black disenfranchisement. Convinced of Smith's support for this goal, Watson agreed to endorse him. The *Atlanta Journal* immediately reversed its long-held position in favor of voting rights for blacks and also endorsed disenfranchisement.[27]

The *Macon Telegraph* characterized Smith's campaign for governor as "anti-nigger and anti-railroad."[28] After being attacked by the *Atlanta Constitution*, the principal morning paper, for having appointed some blacks to minor positions at the Interior Department while he was secretary, Smith became more and more outspoken in his support for disenfranchisement.[29] Although he had previously been considered a moderate on the race issue—favoring black education, supporting Booker T. Washington, opposing lynching and disenfranchisement—Smith soon became one of the leading race-baiters in Georgia.[30]

Smith's conversion to racial demagogue pleased Watson, but Watson's support for Smith was controversial owing to his long involvement in the Populist Party. Finally, in order to quell such concerns, Watson formally rejoined the Democratic Party to aid Smith's campaign.[31] This assured his victory in the primary on August 22, 1906, effectively making Smith Georgia's next governor.

ATLANTA RACE RIOT

The extreme racism of Smith's campaign stirred up racial tensions throughout Georgia and helped ignite a race riot in Atlanta on the night of

September 22, 1906. As historian Charles Crowe explains, "The tide of white aggressiveness produced by Hoke Smith's vituperative Negro baiting campaign for the governorship . . . left in its wake inflamed emotions and unsatiated desires for more repression."[32] Triggered by an alleged assault by a black man on a white woman, a white mob quickly arose to roam the central city beating, torturing, and killing any black man it could find. This went on for hours while the police stood by doing nothing to stem the violence. Finally, in the early morning hours, after the mob had largely exhausted itself, the militia was called out to restore order. Twenty-five black men lay dead.[33] Although repeatedly asked to speak out on the situation to help calm tensions, Governor-elect Smith chose to remain silent.[34]

In his inaugural address on June 29, 1907, Smith showed no signs of letting up on the race-baiting that had characterized his campaign. Slavery, he said, had been good for blacks, improving their condition. This improvement ceased once they became free, Smith continued. The reason was that blacks were incapable of anything except manual labor; those that received education spurned such labor, Smith went on, making them useless. "The Negro school, to be useful, needs less books and more work," he concluded.[35]

Smith's first action in office was to press black disenfranchisement into the state constitution, as he had promised during the campaign. "I favor," he had said, "and if elected will urge with all my power, the elimination of the Negro from politics."[36] Six tests were devised and a citizen needed to meet at least one of them in order to vote: service in any war, descent from someone who fought in an American war, standing as a person of good character, ability to read and write any provision of the U.S. or Georgia constitutions, ownership of forty acres of land, or ownership of $500 worth of taxable property (about $11,000 today). It was assumed that local registrars would ensure that no black people met any of these conditions.

The only debate on the provision was whether it might lead to the disenfranchisement of some poor white voters as well. Its supporters responded that for every white voter disenfranchised, 490 blacks would also lose the right to vote. On balance, the white community would gain, they said. With this assurance, the Democrat-controlled legislature enacted the constitutional change overwhelmingly in 1908, and it was later ratified in a statewide referendum.[37]

Smith was less successful in another of his plans to deal with the race problem: inducing white settlers to come to Georgia and blacks to move away. As he explained:

> Experience shows that Negroes improve most rapidly where there are fewest Negroes in proportion to the number of whites. The best friend of the Negro should seek his distribution to all sections. This can be accomplished by more white settlers coming south, and more Negroes going North, East, and West.[38]

After falling out with Watson over his failure to grant clemency to a Watson pal convicted of murder, Smith was defeated for reelection in 1909 and returned to his law practice. The following year he ran again for governor and was reelected, despite lurid charges during the campaign by his former ally Watson. However, Smith's term as governor proved to be brief because he was almost immediately elected to the U.S. Senate by the state legislature.

Smith quickly made a name for himself in Washington as a defender of white supremacy. In July 1912, a white boy from Macon, Georgia was visiting the District of Columbia and saw his first black policeman. He made some derogatory remarks toward the policeman, who proceeded to arrest him. Senator Smith instantly came to the boy's defense, saying he would take the word of a white boy over that of one hundred black policemen. Smith went on to denounce the whole idea of having black policemen in the nation's capital:

> I am opposed to the practice of having colored policemen in the District. It is a source of danger by constantly engendering racial friction, and is offensive to thousands of Southern white people who make their homes here. These places ought to be filled by good white men.[39]

After the election of Democrat Woodrow Wilson, Smith worked hard to make sure that no blacks received any federal appointments.[40] This earned Smith a reputation for being one of the leading racists in Congress.[41] In 1919, he even rejected the League of Nations because he was "opposed to Oriental immigration." What this had to do with the League was left unexplained.[42]

In 1920, Smith was opposed for reelection by his old mentor Watson, who wanted the seat for himself. Although Smith tried to play the race card by denouncing "ignorant and purchasable" black voters, there was no way he was going to win the racist vote against Watson, who was a racist's racist. Smith rightly attacked Watson as a liar and hater. "He preaches no doctrine but bitterness and strife," Smith said.[43] But it was to no avail. Watson won easily and Smith retired from politics. He died in 1931.

EUGENE TALMADGE: OUTSIDER AS INSIDER

Eugene Talmadge was a natural outsider who never fit into the machine politics that characterized Georgia's political system. Because of the unit vote system, local county political machines were especially important. They were also cliquish and hostile to newcomers and outsiders like Talmadge. Thus, early in his political career he rejected the traditional path to power through the county machines and resolved to run outside the system.

Although from a well-to-do family and trained as a lawyer, Talmadge had an instinctive feel for the soil and the men who tilled it. He worked the land himself and could always identify with and speak the language of the poor white farmers, whose influence in Georgia's elections was overwhelming in the early part of the twentieth century. This skill enabled Talmadge to win his first statewide office in 1926 as agricultural commissioner against a powerful machine candidate.

Early on, Talmadge recognized that there was a hunger in Georgia for another Tom Watson and he aimed to satiate it.[44] Although the two had the same views on race, Talmadge came of age during an era when blacks had been completely eliminated from Georgia politics and were no longer an issue. Moreover, Talmadge's racist views were shared by virtually all whites in the state, including those deemed "liberals" in the North.[45] Consequently, it was unnecessary for him to play the race card until late in his political career, when increasing urbanization diluted his rural political base and Supreme Court decisions forced integration on the South.

Today, Talmadge is probably best known for being one of the most anti-Roosevelt Democrats of the 1930s. Often compared to Louisiana Senator Huey Long, Talmadge was really his polar opposite ideologically. While Long was virtually a socialist, Talmadge was an extreme conservative who opposed debt, taxes, unions, and the federal government with a passion.[46] One of his first acts in office was to use the National Guard to break a textile strike by putting strikers into what was essentially a concentration camp.[47] Said Talmadge, "When anyone quits a job, he does not have the right to hang around the place of business and interfere with anyone else who wants to work on the job."[48] On another occasion, he told a federal agent that the best unemployment relief program would be to emulate Italy's Mussolini and use the Army to force people to work.[49]

Talmadge's feuds with the Roosevelt Administration were legendary.[50] He called the National Industrial Recovery Act "a form of Nazism, fascism, bolshevism."[51] The National Recovery Administration, the Agricultural Adjustment Administration, and the Tennessee Valley Authority were "all in the Russian primer," Talmadge said, and Roosevelt had read it twelve times.[52] On numerous occasions he even made fun of President Roosevelt's inability to walk.[53]

By 1936, Talmadge's hostility to Roosevelt was so great that he flirted with a third-party run against him. At the "convention" of a proposed Grass Roots Party in January 1936, attendees were greeted by a giant Confederate flag and heard from luminaries like *Clansman* author Thomas Dixon, who spoke in defense of lynching, saying there wasn't enough of it. Scattered throughout the meeting hall were copies of a magazine with a prominent picture of Eleanor Roosevelt walking with a black woman on the cover. The rest of it was filled with articles attacking President Roosevelt for being too cozy with blacks.[54] But in the end, the effort went nowhere.

When his presidential bid died, Talmadge turned his attention to Senator Richard B. Russell, who preceded him as governor and was running for reelection. Deciding that Russell was vulnerable on the race issue, Talmadge ran against him in the Democratic primary. Russell was for the New Deal, he said, and the New Deal was for racial equality.[55] "This is a white man's country," Talmadge thundered, "and Georgia don't want any dictation from any federal bureaus and boards of a mixed race, and by the eternal God we won't have it!"[56]

Although just as much in favor of white supremacy as Talmadge, Russell was initially thrown off by this attack. But he quickly regained his footing and went on the offense. Said Russell, "When a politician runs out of arguments, when he hasn't any more soap and knows that in the minds of the people he is convicted of pure cussedness in keeping the old people of Georgia from getting their pensions, then he comes hollering, 'nigger, nigger, nigger.'"[57]

In the end, Talmadge's strategy didn't work and Russell was reelected.[58] Georgians were content to let Talmadge rail against the New Deal as long as he was governor and couldn't do anything about it. But they weren't going to put him in a position were he might actually be able to cut off the flow of federal dollars into the state. This reality also doomed Talmadge's run against Senator Walter F. George in 1938, despite Roosevelt's effort to purge George and other conservative Democrats that year.[59]

UNIVERSITY WITCH HUNT

In 1940, Talmadge was returned again to the governorship. Almost immediately, he became embroiled in a major fight with the state university system. Talmadge charged that Walter Cocking, dean of the school of education at the University of Georgia, was promoting racial equality by suggesting that blacks be allowed to use some white educational facilities.[60] "We don't need no niggers and white people taught together," Talmadge said and moved to have Cocking fired. Talmadge explained:

> Dr. Cocking favored the teaching of whites and Negro children in the same classrooms. I am opposed to social equality and so long as I am governor of Georgia, no such teaching will be permitted in our school system. Dr. Cocking, as you know, was reared in Iowa where white and colored are taught in the same classrooms. His conduct since being in Georgia is proof of the fact that he retains the views and ideas gained by him in the State of Iowa. I am not in favor of such foreign ideas . . . being taught in our university system.[61]

When the Board of Regents refused to fire Cocking, Talmadge had several of them removed and replaced by those that would rubber stamp everything he asked for. The new board fired Cocking and several other professors and university administrators on trumped-up charges.[62] There was a national outcry against this blatant attack on academic freedom, which soon led to a loss of accreditation for the entire university system on the grounds of grossly inappropriate political interference.[63]

While running for reelection in 1942, Talmadge sought to bolster his credentials as a race baiter by admitting to having once personally flogged a black man for eating apples out of the same sack as a white woman. It seems that the woman was from the North and the black man was her driver. They were just passing through Georgia and had stopped briefly for some car repairs. Nevertheless, Talmadge was determined to teach them both a lesson about how things are done in the South. As he later recounted the incident:

> I jus' picked up mah buggy whip an' I walked down to that niggah an' that red-headed woman an' I stopped 'em. I cut that big niggah with that whip, an' y'know th' impudent sonuvabitch wanted to fight *me*. Jus' shows how Yankees mistreat niggahs. So I jus' [drew] mah gun on him an' let 'im have that whip till he hollered Sweet Jesus. It was the funniest thing y'ever saw. . . . They still tell down there how fast that big niggah an' that red-headed woman got that old white automobile out'a Jawjuh.[64]

Talmadge was opposed in the Democratic primary that year by Attorney General Ellis Arnall, who thought Talmadge's actions in the Cocking affair were both wrong-headed and illegal. Arnall struck a chord with Georgia voters who knew that education was the best way to a better life and were appalled by Talmadge's denigration of the university system and its loss of accreditation. Talmadge responded by hitting the race issue even harder. In July, after an internationally-known black singer named Roland Hayes was beaten by police in Rome, Georgia, Talmadge's response was that any black person who didn't like the state's segregation laws should "stay out of Georgia."[65]

Although Arnall appeared more moderate on the race issue, in private his views on the subject were the same as Talmadge's. On race mixing in the schools, Arnall was overheard to say, "Any nigger who tried to enter the university would not be in existence [the] next day. We don't need a governor [or] a sheriff to take care of that situation."[66] But Arnall benefited from being more understated in his racism in a rapidly urbanizing state, and for supporting the universities against Talmadge's heavy-handed political interference. Arnall won the 1942 gubernatorial election easily. *Time Magazine* wrote Talmadge's political obituary: "Thus ended the reign of the most high-handed, low browed local dictator that U.S. politics has known since the days of the late Huey Long."[67]

But the obituary was premature. After sitting out the 1944 election, Talmadge decided to run for governor one last time in 1946. His opponents were ex-governor Ed Rivers, who replaced Talmadge in 1936 and then proceeded to bankrupt the state with liberal spending programs modeled after the national New Deal, and political newcomer James Carmichael, running as a moderate. Despite their differences, however, all three candidates favored white supremacy. According to columnist Drew Pearson, Rivers had been a member of the Ku Klux Klan.[68] And during the campaign, Carmichael promised that he would never permit the mixing of races in Georgia.[69]

If it had been a normal political year, Talmadge's old-fashioned, over-the-top style of racism might have put him at a disadvantage. But the race issue was unusually hot in Georgia that year because of two federal court cases. The first ordered Georgia's Democratic primary to be opened to blacks. The second said that blacks could sit where they wanted on interstate buses, rather than being confined to the rear. Talmadge promised that if elected he would ban interstate bus travel through Georgia. Buses would have to stop 50 feet from the border and passengers would walk across the state line and board intrastate buses, in which blacks would remain segregated, for the balance of their trip through Georgia.[70]

In the June 17 primary, Talmadge lost the popular vote to Carmichael. But because he carried more of the rural counties, Talmadge won a majority of the unit votes and thus the election.[71] Columnist Pearson compared his victory to Hitler's in 1933.[72] Talmadge obliged him by appointing a long list of Ku Klux Klan members to key positions in the Georgia Democratic Party.[73] But he didn't live to reenter the governor's mansion for a fourth time. Talmadge died on December 21, 1946.

RICHARD B. RUSSELL

Richard Brevard Russell Jr. was from a prominent Georgia family—his father served for many years as chief justice of the state Supreme Court—and he was on the political fast track his whole life. Born in 1897 in Winder, Georgia, Russell became a member of the state House of Representatives in 1921 and was elected Speaker of the House just six years later. He became governor of Georgia in 1931 and was elected to the U.S. Senate in 1932, where he served continuously until his death in 1971.[74]

From the minute he got there in 1933, Russell loved the Senate, which fit him like a glove. But he knew he needed to tend to his state, especially in his first term, if he hoped to be reelected. This meant toeing the line on racial matters. In his first year in office, Russell heard that some blacks had received positions with the Georgia Relief Commission and he protested. The chairman of the commission promised that only whites would be hired in the future. Two years later, Russell complained to the Federal Emergency Relief Administration that white girls had to serve under black executives. The Roosevelt Administration assured him that no such thing would be allowed to happen.[75]

In 1935, Eugene Talmadge wrote Russell a letter suggesting that he had not been sufficiently diligent in defending white supremacy. Russell replied, "As one who was born and reared in the atmosphere of the Old South, with six generations of my forebears now resting beneath Southern soil, I am willing to go as far and make as great a sacrifice to preserve and insure white supremacy in the social, economic, and political life of our state as any man who lives within her borders."[76]

Russell received a routine constituent request in 1936, asking for a recommendation for a position with the Tennessee Valley Authority. He was happy to comply and the young Georgia man got the job. But when Russell discovered that he was black, he not only withdrew his recommendation, but insisted that the letter of recommendation be returned.[77]

Facing a tough reelection in 1938, Russell bolstered his segregationist credentials by leading the fight against a federal antilynching bill. Speaking against the legislation at extraordinary length, he called it a Communist plot designed to destroy the United States itself. Said Russell:

> It has been pointed out on this floor time and time again that this bill is but the first step of this program to which I referred, a program which, if it were adopted in its entirety, would destroy the white civilization of the South if it did not undermine and destroy the entire civilization of the United States. . . . The pending bill is the first step in the Communist program and has the hearty support of the Communist Party and every organization affiliated with the Communist Party. . . . Those who are supporting this proposed legislation, whether unwittingly or not, are contributing to a horrible and sickening situation and are encouraging this nefarious movement of the Communist Party in the South.[78]

As was the case in every previous effort to enact an antilynching bill, this one died from a Southern Democratic filibuster in the Senate. Similarly, efforts to abolish poll taxes were also routinely filibustered by Democrats from the South, whose states used such taxes to restrict voting by poor blacks.[79] When an effort was made in 1942 to pass a bill abolishing poll taxes, Russell joined the filibuster against it. Again, he saw the hand of the Communist Party behind the legislation: "Mr. President, I do not appreciate the fact that Mr. Earl Browder, the head of the Communist Party in the United States, is identified as one of the leaders in connection with the proposed legislation."[80]

In 1944, Russell turned his fire on the Fair Employment Practices Committee, which had been created by President Roosevelt to guarantee that blacks had equal access to jobs in businesses receiving government defense contracts. Russell charged that the FEPC's true goal was to "enforce social equality" and promote "the intermingling of the races throughout the nation." Consequently, it was "the most ruthless agency of the entire government. . . . The most dangerous force in existence in the

United States today. . . . A greater threat to victory than 50 fresh divisions enrolled beneath Hitler's swastika."[81]

In 1945, President Truman asked that the FEPC be made a permanent government agency. When a bill to implement this request came up in the Senate in early 1946, Russell led yet another filibuster by Southern Democrats. They recognized that the world was changing and that added resolve was needed to block any civil rights legislation, no matter how modest, lest it open the floodgates and put an end to white supremacy in the South for good. "We will resist to the bitter end, whatever the consequences," Russell told the Senate, "any measure or any movement which would have a tendency to bring about social equality and intermingling and amalgamation of the races in our states."[82]

Russell was too smart a man not to see the handwriting on the wall indicating the eventual end of white supremacy in the South. He got the idea that one way of minimizing the pain would be to encourage the migration of blacks out of the South by offering them financial incentives to move elsewhere.[83] Russell thought that if the ratio of blacks to whites was reduced in the South, then this would dilute the impact of dismantling the laws and policies ensuring segregation in the South. He also thought that if Northerners had more direct contact with blacks, they would better understand the need for segregation and stop pressuring the South to end it.[84]

What Russell apparently didn't know is that his goal was already being realized. Because of the decline of small farm agriculture in the South and growing opportunities for blacks in Northern factories, there had already been a huge migration of black people out of the South. In 1900, the states of the South were 32.3 percent black; by 1950, the black percentage had fallen to 21.7 percent. In Russell's own state of Georgia, the percentage of blacks in the population fell from 46.7 percent in 1900 to 30.9 percent in 1950.[85]

In the 1950s, Russell realized that the Senate filibuster, which had protected the South against federal integration efforts for so many years, was becoming less and less effective; too many Southern senators were unwilling to undertake the arduous task of mounting an effective filibuster.[86] This forced Russell to work harder at couching his opposition to civil rights legislation in broader philosophical language in order to attract support from the growing number of libertarians like Senator Barry Goldwater being elected from the West. They had no brief for Southern racism, but were ideologically opposed to any federal intrusion into state and private affairs. One of Russell's efforts in this regard was the so-called Southern Manifesto that he drafted to explain Southern opposition to the Supreme Court's *Brown* decision in purely constitutional terms. It was signed by every senator from the Confederacy except Lyndon Johnson, who was not asked because of his position as majority leader, and Tennessee's two senators, Estes Kefauver and Albert Gore Sr.[87]

In the 1960s, Russell was still defending the discredited separate-but-equal doctrine against growing pressure for integration from demonstrations, marches, court cases, and public opinion. Absurdly, he rationalized segregation by saying that he had seldom heard any whites complain about having to use whites-only facilities. Said Russell:

> If there is any inferiority involved in this system . . . it is in the minds of the Negroes who object to associating with members of their own race. I have never seen very many white people who felt they were being imposed upon or being subjected to any second-class citizenship if they were directed to a waiting room or to any other public facility to wait or to eat with other white people. Only the Negroes, of all the races which are in this land, publicly proclaim they are being mistreated, imposed upon, and declared second-class citizens because they must go to public facilities with members of their own race.[88]

Russell's greatest triumph was in some ways his greatest disappointment: Lyndon Johnson. When Johnson was elected to the Senate from the old confederate state of Texas in 1948, he had an impeccable record of supporting the Southern position on race. Johnson was also supremely ambitious and immediately latched on to Russell as someone who could further his ambitions. At the same time, Russell saw in Johnson the South's best hope of maintaining white supremacy, so Russell promoted Johnson into his election as majority whip in 1951, minority leader in 1953, and majority leader in 1955—an extraordinarily rapid ascent up the Senate leadership ladder, which no one except Russell could have engineered. Russell eschewed a formal leadership position for himself because he feared that it would force him to compromise his racial beliefs and support legislation he opposed.

Despite their closeness, Russell and Johnson did not see eye-to-eye on civil rights after Johnson became president, and their relationship was deeply strained in Russell's last years.[89] Although Russell remained committed to white supremacy until his death in 1971, he was nevertheless a revered figure in the Senate for his long service, parliamentary skill, and deep commitment to the Senate as an institution. In 1972, he was honored by having what was simply known as the old Senate Office Building renamed the Russell Senate Office Building.[90]

JAMES VARDAMAN AND THEODORE BILBO

Democrats of Mississippi

A great admirer of South Carolina's Ben Tillman, Democrat James Kimble Vardaman, who served as both governor and senator from Mississippi, sought to emulate him by organizing poor white farmers around the principle of total black disenfranchisement.[1] He was best known for claiming that the Fifteenth Amendment to the Constitution was the root of all evil and for his strenuous attacks on Republican President Theodore Roosevelt for every effort he made to help black people.

Democrat Theodore Gilmore Bilbo was Vardaman's protégé and also served as governor and senator. While Vardaman was a large, imposing man, Bilbo was small and wiry. What he lacked in physical stature, however, Bilbo more than made up for in toughness. As a racist, he even outdid his mentor—going so far as to make his major legislative effort in the Senate a bill that would send all blacks back to Africa.

VARDAMAN'S START

Born in 1861, Vardaman came of age politically after blacks had effectively been removed from Mississippi politics in 1890. This resulted from adoption of a provision in the state constitution requiring voters to demonstrate an ability to read or understand any provision of it. Said the new Section 244:

> On and after the first day of January, A.D., 1892, every elector shall, in addition to the foregoing qualifications, be able to read any section of the constitution of this State; or he shall be able to understand the same when

read to him, or give a reasonable interpretation thereof. A new registration shall be made before the next ensuing election after the first, A.D., 1892.

Despite the fact that violence and intimidation had made the black vote in Mississippi politically inconsequential since the end of Reconstruction in 1877, Democrats in the state were worried that the federal government might step in to force free elections. In 1890, Congressman Henry Cabot Lodge, Republican of Massachusetts, had gotten through the House of Representatives legislation that would have greatly expanded federal monitoring of elections in Southern states. Often referred to as the Force Bill of 1890, it struck terror in the hearts of Southern Democrats, who managed to defeat it in the Senate by a single vote.[2]

Fear of another force bill led Southern states to find more subtle means of depriving blacks of the right to vote—ones that were seemingly even-handed, but easily rigged to allow whites to vote while disenfranchising virtually all blacks. This led to literacy tests, poll taxes, and primaries limited to whites throughout the South. Henceforth the elections in the Democratic conventions or primaries to choose candidates for various offices were the only ones that mattered. Since the Republican Party was nonexistent, winning the Democratic nomination for any office was tantamount to victory in the general election.

Although Vardaman strongly supported the disenfranchisement of blacks, he chaffed at the convention system because it put most of the political power in the hands of a small group of conservatives, often called Bourbons, based in the cities and supported by business and commercial interests. Being more of a populist, Vardaman wanted to empower the white farmers, whom he saw as the economic backbone of the state.

Vardaman expressed his views in several newspapers that he owned and edited in Mississippi. In them, he called blacks "a blight, a caterpillar that destroys everything in sight and leaves nothing behind." Vardaman also said, "Sambo is the only man that will suit the Delta farmer."[3] During the 1890s, he became the most outspoken advocate of white supremacy in Mississippi—no mean accomplishment in a state where lynchings were a form of entertainment.[4]

Having missed the Civil War, Vardaman saw the Spanish-American War as his ticket to political advancement. He volunteered for it despite a bad arm, dating back to a childhood injury, and was able to serve in Cuba as a lawyer in the judge advocate's office. The main impact of his experience seems to have been to convince him that Cubans were even more inferior than American blacks. As he wrote in his newspaper:

> The Almighty when He made Cuba, did a pretty good job, but He turned it over to a class of people that would cause hell itself to deteriorate. I think of all the weak, weary and altogether worthless people that I have ever had the misfortune to come into contact with the Cuban is . . . the

most trifling. The American nigger is a gentleman and scholar compared with him. Indeed, I am disposed to apologize to the nigger for making the comparison.[5]

Vardaman was also appalled by the Catholic Church's tolerance of social equality—even intermarriage—between the races in Cuba. This made him extremely wary of imperialism. Vardaman was deeply fearful of the consequences of bringing nonwhites, especially from Catholic nations, into the American orbit. He began editorializing strongly against colonialism in his newspaper, which was "opposed to injecting any more niggers, chinamen and other mongrel races into the body politic of this country, with all the accompanying evils—bubonic plague, leprosy, ignorance and superstition."[6]

Although Vardaman approved of lynching in cases of a black man raping a white woman, he was opposed to making a spectacle of such things. In 1902, he editorialized against those who burned alive a suspected black rapist. Said Vardaman:

> Much has been said and written about the people of Corinth burning the brute who killed Mrs. Carey Whitfield. I am sorry they burned him. It would have been better to have buried him alive, or shot him, or hanged him in the jail. I think they did right to kill the brute, but it would have been better had the crowd been denied admission. It does not help a man morally to look upon a thing of that kind. It is rather hardening. But I sometimes think that one could look upon a scene of that kind and suffer no more moral deterioration than he would by looking upon the burning of an Orangutan that had stolen a baby or a viper that had stung an unsuspecting child to death. He ceases to be regarded as a human being, and is only looked upon as a two-legged monster. But then, it is not elevating to even look upon the burning of a big monkey. However, when one of these devils commits such deeds as this nigger did, someone must kill him and I am in favor of doing it promptly. In this case I only regret the brute did not have ten thousand lives to pay for his atrocious deed.[7]

That same year, the Mississippi legislature changed the law to require primary elections instead of conventions for choosing candidates for office. This was extremely important to Vardaman's ambitions, because he had little hope of achieving high office if it were only up to the snotty Bourbons who controlled the conventions and looked down on populists like him. But if the people were empowered to make the decision, Vardaman knew he had a chance.[8]

BECOMES GOVERNOR

With the new primary law, Vardaman immediately began running for governor in 1903. His strategy was to mobilize the poor white farmers mainly by appealing to their racism.[9] Vardaman attacked Governor Andrew Longino for trying to put a stop to lynchings and for breaking-up white gangs known as Whitecaps that were similar to the Ku Klux Klan.[10]

Vardaman also spent considerable time attacking Theodore Roosevelt, who had become president in 1901 after the assassination of William McKinley. One of his first acts as president was to have dinner at the White House with the great black leader Booker T. Washington. Roosevelt had earlier planned to visit Washington's Tuskegee Institute in Alabama, but was forced to cancel because of McKinley's death.[11] The dinner took place on October 16, 1901.

Although a low-key affair, the Roosevelt-Washington dinner caused a storm of controversy throughout the South when it was disclosed.[12] Vardaman was incredulous. He could not believe that Roosevelt had taken "this nigger bastard into his home" and entertained him on terms of social equality.[13] To Southerners, social equality was one small step away from race-mixing. Vardaman later said of the Washington dinner that the White House had become "so saturated with the odor of the nigger that the rats have taken refuge in the stable."[14] Even non-Southern Democrats criticized Roosevelt. William Jennings Bryan said the dinner was "unfortunate, to say the least."[15]

Among the matters that Roosevelt and Washington undoubtedly discussed was the appointment of blacks to positions in the federal government. Roosevelt felt strongly, for both political and moral reasons, that highly qualified black people ought to have an opportunity to advance within the federal government. In consultation with Washington, he began giving patronage jobs to blacks in the South, where even low-level appointments deeply offended racist whites like Vardaman.[16] When Southerners protested, Roosevelt responded in a November 1902 letter:

> It has been my consistent policy in every state where their numbers warranted it to recognize colored men of good repute and standing in making appointments to office. . . . I cannot consent to take the position that the door of hope—the door of opportunity—is to be shut upon any man . . . purely upon the grounds of race or color. Such an attitude would, according to my convictions, be fundamentally wrong. . . . It seems to me that it is a good thing from every standpoint to let the colored man know that if he shows in marked degree the qualities of good citizenship the qualities which in a white man we feel are entitled to reward—then he will not be cut off from all hope of similar reward.[17]

Shortly thereafter, Roosevelt announced his intention to appoint Dr. William Crum, a black physician, as collector of the customs in Charleston, South Carolina. This set off racists throughout the South. Crum's actions as a delegate to the Republican National Convention in 1892 caused some to raise questions about his political trustworthiness, however, which forced

Roosevelt to hold off on the appointment. In the meantime, Roosevelt further enraged Southern racists with another action in defense of black political appointees—this time in Vardaman's own backyard.

Mrs. Minnie Cox, a black woman, had been in charge of the post office in Indianola, Mississippi, since Republican President Benjamin Harrison's administration, doing her job without complaint from anyone. In late 1902, Vardaman suddenly took notice of this inoffensive black woman. He chided the people of Indianola for "tolerating a Negro wench as postmaster." This led to a confrontation between Cox and some local whites.[18] Without offering any evidence of misfeasance, malfeasance, or failure to discharge her duties properly, they demanded that she step down, threatening violence unless she did so forthwith. Cox immediately resigned and sent a telegram to Washington to that effect.[19]

Roosevelt was outraged by the action of the Indianola racists and refused to accept Cox's resignation. Instead, he ordered the post office in Indianola closed, with Mrs. Cox remaining on the government payroll. The White House issued the following statement on January 2, 1903:

> The resignation [of Cox] was forced by a brutal and lawless element, purely upon the ground of her color, and was obtained under terror of threats of physical violence. . . . By direction of the President the following telegram was sent by the Postmaster General to the bondsmen: "The Postmaster's resignation has been received but not accepted. In view of the fact that the office at Indianola is closed all mail addressed to that office will be forwarded to Greenville."[20]

Vardaman was apoplectic at Roosevelt's action. He called it "contemptible," "craven," and "malignant." Roosevelt, Vardaman said, was "a human coyote who would destroy civilization. . . . He would break down the barriers which keep back and hold in restraint the black waves of ignorance, superstition and immorality with which the South is perpetually threatened." Writing in his newspaper on January 10, Vardaman went on to attack Roosevelt's mother for giving birth to such a reprobate. "Probably old lady Roosevelt during the period of gestation was frightened by a dog and that fact may account for the qualities of the male pup which are so prominent in Teddy," Vardaman speculated. "I would not do her an injustice but I am disposed to apologize to the dog for mentioning it."[21]

Shortly thereafter, Roosevelt decided that the charges against Crum were baseless and he sent his name to the Senate for confirmation. When it was rejected, Crum was given a recess appointment on March 30, 1903. This gave Vardaman another powerful election issue. As he told his readers:

> My election will mean and will be taken by the aspiring, trouble-breeding, ambitious Negroes as a condemnation by the white people of Mississippi of Roosevelt's criminal policy of social and political equality. It will have a

most salutary restraining influence upon them. My defeat will, on the other hand, encourage these same Negroes to aspire to the unattainable and trouble, discord and demoralizing will follow.[22]

Vardaman's victory in the August 26, 1903, Democratic primary ensured his election as governor and he took office on January 19, 1904. In his inaugural address, he asked for new laws to rigidly divide the races in all public places, including separate cars for blacks and whites on railroads. Vardaman called for repeal of the Fifteenth Amendment to the U.S. Constitution and curtailment of education for blacks in Mississippi.

Although Vardaman's campaign against the Fifteenth Amendment was hopelessly quixotic, it received a surprising amount of serious national attention. In 1905, *Harper's Weekly* published a positive discussion of the topic, and in 1907 the *Saturday Evening Post*, a hugely popular national magazine at that time, ran a highly favorable article as well, both quoting Vardaman at length.[23]

On black education, even most racists believed that it was a good thing. But not Vardaman. He thought it only instilled aspirations that could not be met, leading to frustration and violence. The only sort of education Vardaman favored for blacks was technical, in order to make them better workers. Toward this end, he closed the Holly Springs State Normal School, which trained black teachers, and slashed the salaries of "literary" teachers at Alcorn Agricultural and Mechanical College, a black school, while raising those of vocational teachers.[24]

Surprisingly, however, as governor Vardaman was strongly opposed to lynching. He felt that it was the government's job to enforce the law and he personally intervened in several cases to prevent lynchings. In one instance, the fellow about to be lynched actually ended up being acquitted in a jury trial. Vardaman also permanently broke up the Whitecaps, using undercover agents and a determination that was admirable.[25] One can only speculate that the demands of governing imposed a degree of responsibility on him that was absent when he was an outsider.

THE SENATE

In 1907, a U.S. Senate seat opened up when Hernando DeSoto Money announced that he would not seek reelection in 1910. Governor Vardaman sought the seat against his bitter rival, Congressman John Sharp Williams, then serving as minority leader of the House of Representatives in Washington. Although the legislature still chose senators, Mississippi law provided that the appointment would be determined by the winner of a state primary on August 1, 1907.

Williams was Vardaman's equal as a racist; on one occasion he even called for the extermination of black people. But he was also less of a populist than Vardaman and therefore more acceptable to Mississippi's

Bourbons and business interests. In a very tight election, Williams defeated Vardaman and on January 12, 1908 the Mississippi state legislature named Williams a senator beginning on March 4, 1911.[26]

Vardaman retired from the governorship at the end of 1908 with a fairly progressive record of accomplishment.[27] He returned to the newspaper business, where he further developed his idea that the Fifteenth Amendment needed to be repealed in order to solve the race problem in America.

In 1909, another U.S. Senate seat opened up when Senator Anselm McLaurin died suddenly. Vardaman immediately announced for the position. But he had made many enemies in the legislature, which in this case would decide without a primary who would fill the balance of McLaurin's term. The major event of the deliberations was State Senator Bilbo's charge that anti-Vardaman forces tried to bribe him.[28] In the end, Vardaman lost, but immediately made plans to challenge the winner, Le Roy Percy, in the 1911 Democratic primary.

Running together with his protégé Bilbo, who was seeking the lieutenant governorship in the same election, both Vardaman and Bilbo won easily. Vardaman made plans to be in Washington when the new president was inaugurated on March 4, 1913. He was overjoyed when it turned out to be Woodrow Wilson, a Southern Democrat like himself. Vardaman strongly supported Wilson's policy of segregating blacks throughout the federal government.[29] He urged Wilson not to appoint blacks to any patronage positions whatsoever, no matter how qualified they might be.[30]

True to his philosophy, Vardaman made repeal of the Fifteenth Amendment to the Constitution his top priority in the Senate. He even argued that it was, in fact, unconstitutional because the former Confederate states had been coerced into endorsing it as a condition for being readmitted to the Union.[31] Vardaman spoke out in favor of lynching and the Ku Klux Klan.[32] In a February 6, 1914, Senate speech, he went on at length about the inferiority of black people. Said Vardaman:

> The Negro as a race, in all the ages of the world, has never shown sustained power of self-development. He is not endowed with the creative faculty. . . . He has never created for himself any civilization . . . He has never had any civilization except that which has been inculcated by a superior race. And it is a lamentable fact that his civilization lasts only so long as he is in the hands of the white man who inculcates it. When left to himself he has universally gone back to the barbarism of the jungle.[33]

Yet in this same speech, Vardaman declared himself to be the black man's "real friend." The love of his life, he said, was his "old black mammy, the recollections of whose tender ministrations to me are among the sweetest assets of my life." Such cognitive dissonance—hatred of blacks in general combined with genuine love for some individual blacks—was common among Southern racists. Journalist Ray Stannard Baker explained this phenomenon in a 1908 book:

> [The South] loves the ignorant, submissive old Negroes, the "mammies" and "uncles;" it wants Negroes who, as one Southerner put it to me, "will do the dirty work and not fuss about it." It wants Negroes who are really inferior and *feel* inferior. The Negro that the South fears and dislikes is the educated, property-owning Negro who is beginning to demand rights, to take his place among men as a citizen.[34]

This helps explain Vardaman's strenuous objection to black education. It was opening a Pandora's box that racists like himself knew would inevitably lead to political equality. And for Vardaman and those like him political equality led inexorably to social equality, which was one step away from race-mixing and the end of the white race.[35] Also, it was embarrassing to whites that blacks often made better use of their educational opportunities than they did.[36]

Although he had been a strong supporter of Wilson, Vardaman turned against him on World War I. Vardaman's opposition to imperialism had made him an across-the-board isolationist and he strongly opposed American intervention in the war. He feared that it would lead to the conscription of blacks, who would return from combat with military training and new demands for equal rights. War would also strengthen the federal government—power that might later be turned against the states to enforce voting rights for blacks.[37]

Despite the racist rationale for his opposition to the war, Vardaman's position proved highly unpopular back in Mississippi. Sensing his political weakness, Vardaman's protégé Bilbo broke from him and sought his seat in 1918. By splitting the populist rural vote, Bilbo and Vardaman both went down in defeat, leading to the election of Pat Harrison, a Bourbon allied with Senator Williams. This marked the end of Vardaman's career in politics. He died in 1930.

THE RISE OF BILBO

Bilbo was elected governor of Mississippi in 1915. Having failed to replace Vardaman in the Senate, he left office in 1920 because of term limits. Like his former mentor, Bilbo started a newspaper, the *Mississippi Free Lance*, which he used to promote himself for the next available political office. Although a Senate seat opened up when John Sharp Williams announced plans to step down in 1923, Bilbo decided instead to run for governor again in 1927. He won and took office for a second time in 1928.

During his first term as governor, Bilbo, like Vardaman, turned out to be a fairly competent and progressive executive. But the Great Depression hit the second time around, devastating state finances. Bilbo staggered from one financial crisis to another and left office in 1932 with little to show for it, either personally or politically.

Desperate to find some way of making a living, Bilbo prevailed upon Senator Harrison to compel the Roosevelt Administration to give him a patronage appointment. Although no fan of Bilbo's, Harrison agreed to help him in order to get a potential rival out of the state. Bilbo got a job clipping newspapers at the Agricultural Adjustment Administration for $6,000 per year—an excellent salary during the Depression, equal to about $94,000 today.

Bilbo stayed in Washington just a short time, however, returning to Mississippi to run against Senator Hubert Stephens in the 1934 Democratic primary. Vowing to emulate Louisiana's Huey Long and raise hell in Washington, Bilbo was elected that year to the Senate, where he became a diehard supporter of Franklin Roosevelt. In V. O. Key's words, Bilbo "went down the line for the New Deal."[38]

In 1938, Bilbo's Democratic Party loyalty was sorely tested by efforts to pass a federal antilynching bill. Although the legislation not supported by Roosevelt, Bilbo threatened to leave the party if it was enacted, saying it was "monstrous" and "insulting." It was supported only by "a few negrophilists or Negro lovers" and a "great host of mulattoes, octoroons, quadroons, and time-serving politicians." Passage would "open the floodgates of hell in the South," Bilbo warned.[39]

Bilbo went on to offer two plans for permanent resolution of the race problem in America. First was repatriation of all blacks back to Africa. "Millions of acres of rich and fertile lands have already been set apart and dedicated by the Republic of Liberia for the colonization of the American Negro," Bilbo said, "where he could live under a government of his own people; where there would be no discriminations; where he would have equal opportunities in all things."[40]

The payoff, Bilbo went on to say, is that with the departure of twelve million blacks to "their fatherland" there would now be ample jobs for all white Americans and the government would no longer have to spend vast sums caring for the unemployed. And with the black problem solved, America could then turn its attention to the "Asiatic colored problem, the yellow peril . . . the mixed breeds of Latin America and . . . the hybrid and mongrel races" from elsewhere.[41]

The second plan was creation of a new forty-ninth state somewhere in the West, "where none but the Negro would be permitted to live, where they could have a government all their own, with a Negro Governor, Negro Senators, Negro Representatives, Negro schools, Negro society, Negro everything." Getting blacks to go there was no problem, Bilbo explained, because America's treatment of the Indians established a precedent for forcibly moving large numbers of people from one section of the country to another in the national interest. "We moved the Indians," he said, so "why can we not move the Negro in the same way?"[42]

A few months later, Bilbo offered his plan for black repatriation to Africa as an amendment to some pending legislation. It would have established a Repatriation Commission empowered to pay for the transport of any black person living in America to Liberia or any other suitable territory established by the Commission, and to offer settlement assistance for those taking advantage of this opportunity. The Commission would be empowered to enter into negotiations with Britain, France, and other colonial powers for the purchase of African lands within their control to further assist in the resettlement of American blacks in Africa. Bilbo claimed that seven million blacks supported his plan and that two million had already signed a petition to that effect. He discussed his amendment's benefits for several hours before withdrawing it from consideration.[43]

The following year, Bilbo returned again to his idea of repatriating black people to Africa. This time he had some new arguments. First, it would establish an outlet for the export of American goods to Africa. Second, France and Britain could discharge their war debts to the United States by ceding some of their African territory for the repatriation effort. And third, this would also be in their interest because Germany and Italy had designs on Africa. Bilbo likened his plan to Napoleon's sale of Louisiana to the United States in order to thwart British ambitions in the Americas.[44] Bilbo went on to say that he had become convinced this was all part of God's master plan:

> I am one of those who believe that, in accordance with His plan, God Almighty sent the children of Israel down into the land of Egypt in slavery in order that they there might absorb and take on the cultural trades and arts and training and literature of the Egyptians, who at that time had the greatest civilization in the world, and that later, through Moses and Aaron, they were led out into the promised land; and it is not far-fetched to say that, in the wisdom of God Almighty himself, the Negro was brought from the wilds of the jungles of Africa in his heathen condition and planted on the American shore as a slave in order that he might learn the arts and trades and culture and music and education and religion of the American people; and having been thus prepared, it is a further plan of the Almighty that the Negroes may be transferred back to the land of their forefathers, a land where there still remain a few of their brethren who are without Christianity, without education and training, to teach them the American way of life and to reclaim and save their less fortunate kith and kin.[45]

Historian Thurston Doler notes that Bilbo had expressed support for repatriating black Americans to Africa as early as 1923. However, it really had very little political support in Mississippi even among the rabid racists, who may have been concerned about the loss of cheap black labor. Doler concludes that Bilbo supported the legislation mainly because he really believed in it.[46]

Although it appears absurd today, Bilbo's proposal actually had a considerable amount of genuine support in the black community. Black militants like Marcus Garvey supported the idea of repatriation and some even worked directly with Bilbo on his legislation. The onset of war, however, drained what little support there was for the plan, which was strenuously opposed by mainstream black organizations such as the NAACP. Some historians now suggest that the repatriation campaign was tragic because it sidetracked growing black militancy, distracting it into a hopeless cause that may have delayed the achievement of civil rights by splitting the black community at a crucial time during the war when the government was heavily dependent on black workers.[47] If so, then perhaps Bilbo's efforts were not entirely wasted from his point of view.

BILBO'S DOWNFALL

Having won reelection in 1940, Bilbo returned to Washington with enhanced seniority. In 1944, he became chairman of the Senate Committee on the District of Columbia, giving up a more prestigious chairmanship so that he could use the heavily black city of Washington as a laboratory for his racial schemes, such as outlawing intermarriage between blacks and whites and preventing residents of the city from voting.[48] As Bilbo once explained:

> Some niggers came to see me one time in Washington to try to get the right to vote there. The leader was a smart nigger. Of course he was half white. I told him that the nigger would never vote in Washington. Hell, if we give 'em the right to vote up there, half the niggers in the South will move into Washington and we'll have a black government. No Southerner could sit in Congress under those conditions.[49]

Much of Bilbo's second term was taken up with filibusters. He fought national legislation to repeal the poll tax, but not because he feared that it would lead to an increase in black voting. "The poll tax won't keep 'em from voting," he said. "What keeps 'em from voting is Section 244 of the Constitution of 1890, [which] damn few white men and no niggers can explain."[50] Indeed, Bilbo actually favored repeal of the poll tax in Mississippi because he thought it would lead to the enfranchisement of many poor whites likely to support him. His fear of a federal law was that it would set a precedent for federal intervention in state affairs on the race issue.[51] On one occasion, Bilbo said the idea of a federal law banning poll taxes came from Russia as a way of destroying the Constitution.[52]

On March 22, 1944, Bilbo was invited to address a joint session of the Democrat-controlled Mississippi Legislature. He used the opportunity to summarize his philosophy on the inherent inferiority of blacks, the necessity of maintaining segregation to prevent intermarriage and race-mixing, and the benefits of repatriating blacks to Africa. In one widely quoted comment, Bilbo said that should the North try to force Mississippi colleges to admit black students, "We will tell our Negro-loving Yankee friends to go straight to hell!"[53] Bilbo urged even more strenuous efforts to keep the races separated:

> Reduced to its simplest form and laid bare for all the world to judge, we declare that the South is justified in the absolute denial of social equality to the Negro regardless of what his abilities or accomplishments may be. This the South must do, in behalf of her blood, her essence, and the stock of her Caucasian race. . . . We people of the South must draw the color line tighter and tighter, and any white man or woman who dares to cross the color line should be promptly and forever ostracized. No compromise on this great question should be tolerated, no matter who the guilty parties are, whether in the church, in public office, or in the private walks of life. Ostracize them if they cross the color line and treat them as a Negro or as his equal should be treated.[54]

Commenting on this speech, the *Washington Post* said, "Dr. Goebbels himself could not have hewed more faithfully to Nazi racial doctrine."[55]

In 1945, much of Bilbo's time was occupied by killing legislation to create a permanent Fair Employment Practices Committee. A temporary FEPC had been created by Roosevelt's executive order barring discrimination in defense industries, but the authority for this organization would end with the expiration of the president's wartime powers. Legislation was offered to make the FEPC permanent, but Bilbo successfully filibustered it to death. At one point, he complained that the staff of the FEPC had too many minorities. It consisted, he said, of "66 Negroes, 12 Jews, a few gentiles, and two Japs, just to be 'lollypops' for this country, 'sugar boys' going around pacifying."[56]

Bilbo was strenuously attacked in the North for killing the FEPC and he often received hate-mail, which he was delighted to answer. He addressed a letter to one New York City critic, apparently of Italian descent, as "My Dear Dago." When Bilbo was attacked for anti-Semitism, he blamed "kikes that are fraternizing and socializing with Negroes for selfish and political reasons." Those opposed to him, Bilbo said, consisted of "Communists, nigger-lovers and Yankee crackpots."[57]

By 1946, Bilbo had become so notorious for his racism that a new term was coined: Bilboism. The *New York Times* defined it as "a combination of racial hatred, Ku Klux Klannery, intimidation at the polls and a narrow parochialism to which all national interests are subordinated." The *Times* excoriated the Senate's Democratic majority for keeping such a reprehensible member in their midst, saying that his right to a Senate seat did not necessarily entitle him to membership in the Democratic caucus.[58]

Bilboism, it should be noted, is different from a practice known as Bilboing. This is when a congressman or senator uses every available opportunity to sing the praises of his state or the accomplishments of its citizens with remarks in the *Congressional Record.*[59] Sadly, this is a Bilbo legacy that lives on to this very day. There are a goodly number of members of Congress who almost never rise to speak on the House or Senate floors except to congratulate Jimmy Jones for becoming an Eagle Scout or Jane Smith for her prize-winning rhubarb pie at the county fair.

Bilbo's attacks on the FEPC proved very popular down in Mississippi. He explained that it was "nothing but a plot to put niggers at work next to your daughters." Bilbo went on to say, "I don't mind having the nigger for my brother in Christ, but I'm damned if I want him for a son-in-law." He said that attacks on him in the Northern press came from "Communists and nigger-lovers."[60]

During a radio interview in 1946, Bilbo confessed to being a member of the Ku Klux Klan. He said that the Klan lodge in his home town of Poplarville, Mississippi, was named for him: Bilbo Klan No. 40. However, Bilbo said that he had only attended one meeting.[61] No doubt, he felt that his attendance at Klan meetings would be superfluous, since he was already spending every waking hour pursuing its agenda.

Bilbo was reelected easily to a third term in 1946. But his victory was short-lived because Republicans won control of the Senate that year for the first time since 1932. Among the first things they planned to do was look into charges of corruption that had swirled around Bilbo for years, which Democrats had systematically turned a blind eye toward. For example, early in his first term, Bilbo had talked openly about using the Civilian Conservation Corps to lay out a golf course on his farm. "Mighty convenient, I can tell you," he bragged.[62]

With the knowledge that the Republicans would make an issue of Bilbo when they took control on January 3, 1947, Democrats suddenly moved furiously to cleanse themselves of Bilbo first. In December 1946, during the final days of Democratic control, a special Senate committee was empanelled to look into charges that Bilbo had enriched himself with war contracts and kickbacks. Testimony indicated that he had, among other things, received a new Cadillac, a swimming pool, excavation for a lake on his property, and furnishings for two houses he owned. The estimated value of these "gifts" came to between $57,000 and $87,000 in 1942 alone. This is equivalent to between $700,000 and $1.1 million in today's dollars.[63]

Given the strength of the evidence against him, as well as charges that he had suppressed black votes during the election—something else that Senate Democrats had ignored for many years, but now suddenly found appalling—there was little Bilbo could do except lash out at his attackers and play the race card. He accused one critic, Congresswoman Clare Boothe Luce, Republican of Connecticut, of being "the greatest nigger-lover in the North" except for Eleanor Roosevelt. Mrs. Roosevelt, Bilbo claimed, had "forced our Southern girls to use the stools and toilets of damn syphilitic nigger women."[64]

When the new Congress convened, an effort was made to prevent Bilbo from taking his seat until the investigations into corruption and voter fraud had concluded. In retaliation, Southern Democrats filibustered the election of new leaders in the Senate. This impasse was broken only when Bilbo decided to return to Mississippi for medical attention. The question of whether he should be seated was put aside and Bilbo remained on the Senate payroll. Although his departure was politically convenient, it turned out that he really was sick with cancer, which would take his life later in the year.[65]

Bilbo's last act was seeing into print a book that brought together all the research on black inferiority that he had compiled over the years. Published in 1947, it was entitled *Take Your Choice: Separation or Mongrelization.*[66] The book appears to consist mainly of excerpts from speeches he had given in the Senate over the years with a few footnotes thrown in. In many ways, it summarized Bilbo's life better than any autobiography would have.

EPILOGUE

Although Vardaman and Bilbo have been the focus of this chapter on Mississippi Democrats, they were merely the best-known of that state's race-baiters. Every other major elected Democrat in Mississippi shared the same opinions to one degree or another. For example, Senator Williams was just as much of a racist as Vardaman and Bilbo, and he even lectured at Columbia University on the subject. In one lecture he defended Thomas Jefferson's refusal to free his slaves:

> It was harder to be a good master then, than it was to emancipate a lot of ignorant, and for the most part foolish creatures—welcome nowhere—unable to take care of themselves and with nobody under obligations to take care of them. With an emancipation universal—as it was when it finally came—these difficulties were for the most part obviated, but to turn a whole race free, under conditions that their labor *must* be sought and paid for, is a different thing from turning a few free to be unwelcome everywhere as men and impossible as laborers—to be objects of suspicion as "free niggers" and possibly victims of kidnapping by rough men and sale into slavery a half a thousand miles or more away.[67]

Williams agreed with Vardaman that the Fifteenth Amendment to the Constitution should be repealed. He called it "one of the greatest blunders, and therefore one of the greatest crimes in political history." And Williams was just as virulent as Vardaman in attacking Theodore Roosevelt for the Indianola affair. He compared Roosevelt's actions to those of King George in terms of high-handedness and tyranny.[68]

During Senate debate in 1918, Williams confessed that he belonged to the "slave-holding class," but never to the "nigger-hating and nigger-baiting class." He took care of his "darkies," Williams said, and treated them like members of his family. "Nobody can make a nigger baiter out of me," he told the Senate. "I not only have no hate for them," Williams went on, "I have a positive gratitude to them."[69] Not surprisingly, Williams was among Woodrow Wilson's closest friends in the Senate.[70]

Congressman John Elliot Rankin, a Democrat who represented Mississippi in the House of Representatives from 1921 to 1953, was another class act. In one of his first speeches in Congress, he showed that he was a match for Vardaman and Bilbo when it came to racism. As Rankin told the House in 1922:

> What has the Negro done for himself or for civilization to entitle him to equality with the white race? The only civilization he has ever imbibed was that imposed upon him by the white people of the South through the unfortunate institution of slavery—unfortunate for the white man; fortunate for the Negro.

Slavery, Rankin went on to say, was "the greatest blessing the Negro has ever known." One reason, he explained, was that it stopped blacks from eating each other. But freed from slavery, they now went about raping white women indiscriminately. Rankin suggested that "extermination" might be necessary if black agitation for equal rights continued.[71]

In 1944, Rankin attacked radio commentator Walter Winchell as a "little kike." He also took umbrage at those who accused him of disloyalty to the Democratic Party; he was a true Democrat, Rankin said:

> I voted the Democratic ticket in 1904 when President Roosevelt voted the Republican ticket. I voted the Democratic ticket when [Secretary of the Navy Frank] Knox was running on the Republican ticket. I voted the Democratic ticket when the Taft Administration was going down to defeat with Secretary [of War Henry] Stimson as a Republican in the Cabinet. I voted the Democratic ticket when [Interior Secretary Harold] Ickes was a Bull Mooser. I voted the Democratic ticket when [Secretary of Commerce] Harry Hopkins was a Socialist. I do not want any fly-by-night or fair-weather Democrats trying to tell me how to vote.[72]

In 1946, Rankin went ballistic over union efforts to register voters in the South. "They'll be trying to give the nigger a vote," he said, but "no nigger will ever run against me."[73] That same year, Rankin killed an investigation of the Ku Klux Klan by the Democrat-controlled House Committee on Un-American Activities. "After all," he said, "the Klan is a completely American institution, and its members are Americans."[74]

With the death of Bilbo in 1947, Rankin picked up his mantle as principal congressional foe of a permanent FEPC. For this, he said, "nigger Communists" were out to defeat him in his effort to replace Bilbo in the Senate. "They know I'll take the floor and tear to shreds the arguments for the Communistic FEPC—one of the most dangerous pieces of legislation ever introduced."[75]

Rankin was defeated for the Senate and redistricted out of his House seat in 1952. Upon his departure from Congress, the *Washington Post* said his "prime claim to notoriety as a legislator was as the personification of bigotry."[76] Rankin died in 1960.

This review does not exhaust the long list of racist Democrats sent to Washington or put in the governor's mansion by Mississippi voters. During the long one hundred years from the total disenfranchisement of blacks in the 1880s to the 1980s, when Republicans finally cracked the Democratic monopoly, virtually every major officeholder in Mississippi shared the view that segregation was good or at least required, and that black participation in politics should be prevented by any means necessary.[77] They were just more circumspect than Vardaman, Bilbo, Williams, and Rankin about expressing themselves so forcefully or publicly on the subject. In short, these men were not exceptions, but the rule in Mississippi's Democratic Party for most of its history.

SECTION III

DEMOCRATS IN THE WHITE HOUSE: BLACKS SENT TO THE BACK DOOR

WOODROW WILSON

Reactionary Progressive

The typical textbook portrays Woodrow Wilson, who served from 1913 to 1921, as one of our great liberal presidents. They point to his institution of the federal income tax, creation of the Federal Reserve System, implementation of tariff and antitrust reform, development of the first child-labor law, and passage of women's suffrage among his progressive accomplishments, as well as to his efforts to get the United States into the League of Nations.[1] Consequently, he has long ranked among our greatest presidents according to polls of academic historians. One, conducted by Arthur Schlesinger in 1962, put Wilson in the top five, along with George Washington, Thomas Jefferson, Abraham Lincoln, and Franklin D. Roosevelt.[2] In a more recent survey by his son, Arthur Schlesinger Jr., Wilson fell a bit, but still ranked number seven overall and was judged "near great."[3]

A different picture emerges, however, when one studies Wilson's writings and record more deeply. His record on race relations, in particular, is appalling; he set black progress in the United States back fifty years by instituting racial segregation throughout the federal government and greatly empowering the most racist Southern faction within the Democratic Party. Furthermore, he was responsible for repressive measures against political radicals vastly greater than anything Senator Joe McCarthy ever contemplated, let alone did. The actions of Wilson's Attorney General, A. Mitchell Palmer, should send a chill down the spine of anyone whose politics puts them outside the mainstream.[4]

In all of this, Wilson was aided and abetted by the Democratic Party, which saw him as a savior after fifty-two years of almost continuous Republican control of the White House, broken only by Grover Cleveland's two non-consecutive terms. This was especially true of Southern Democrats, who had been isolated within the Democratic Party since the war. They saw Wilson as one of them—someone who would restore their power and influence in both the Democratic Party and national politics. They were right.

AS THE TWIG IS BENT

To the extent that people know anything about Wilson's life before entering the White House, they may remember that he was governor of New Jersey or president of Princeton University. Thus, they probably assume that he was a Northerner by birth. In fact, he was a man of the South, born in Staunton, Virginia, in 1856. Much of his childhood was spent in Augusta, Georgia; Wilmington, North Carolina; and Columbia, South Carolina.

Wilson's father, Joseph Wilson, was a Presbyterian minister who defended slavery on biblical grounds. One of his sermons on this topic in 1861 was so popular that it was published. Joseph Wilson also wrote many columns for the church newspaper in which he expressed typical Southern conservative views, such as opposing voting rights for blacks and ridiculing the idea of women preachers.[5] During the war, his church was used as a hospital by the Confederate Army and young Woodrow witnessed General William Tecumseh Sherman's devastating march to the sea. The Civil War and its aftermath left a deep impression on Wilson for the rest of his life.[6]

Wilson went to Princeton University, got a law degree at the University of Virginia, and a Ph.D. in political science from Johns Hopkins. He took up a career in academia, teaching at Bryn Mawr and Wesleyan before settling back at Princeton in 1890. But he was never really an academic at heart, his principal interest always being politics.[7]

In his academic writings, Wilson expressed clear sympathy for the South, the land of his birth, even to the point of defending slavery. For example, in his book, *Division and Reunion: 1829–1889*, first published in 1893, Wilson had this to say about the condition of slaves:

> Domestic slaves were almost uniformly dealt with indulgently and even affectionately by their masters. . . . "Field hands" on the ordinary plantation came constantly under their master's eye, were comfortably quartered, and were kept from overwork both by their own laziness and by the slack discipline to which they were subjected.

Wilson denied that slaves were generally mistreated and argued that conditions such as those depicted in *Uncle Tom's Cabin* were "exceptional." Slaves, he said, were "often commanded in brutal language, but they were not often compelled to obey by brutal treatment." Wilson claimed that Southerners were as intolerant of cruelty toward slaves as were those in the North.[8]

In his *History of the American People*, Wilson strongly empathized with Southern suffering after the war and made light of the activities of the Ku Klux Klan. Here is how he described the origin of that notorious group:

> In May, 1866, a little group of young men in the Tennessee village of Pulaski, finding time hang heavily on their hands after the excitements of the field, so lately abandoned, formed a secret club for the mere pleasure of association, for private amusement—for anything that might promise to break the monotony of the too quiet place, as their wits might work upon the matter, and one of their number suggested that they call themselves the *Kuklos*, the Circle.

Wilson said that the main activities of the group consisted of "pranks," "mischief," and "frolicking." Although he admitted that the Klan often preyed upon helpless blacks, he described the latter's fear as "comic." Eventually, the Klan did do some bad things, Wilson conceded, but only because "malicious fellows of the baser sort who did not feel the compulsions of honor" took control of the organization from the "sober men" who founded it.[9]

In an article in the *Atlantic Monthly* in 1901, Wilson defended the black codes, which were enacted by Southern states after the war to keep blacks under control, on the grounds that the former slaves were "unpracticed in liberty, unschooled in self-control; never sobered by the discipline of self-support, never established in any habit of prudence; excited by a freedom they did not understand, exalted by false hopes; bewildered and without leaders, and yet insolent and aggressive; sick of work, covetous of pleasure—a host of dusky children untimely put out of school."

Reconstruction, Wilson lamented, had disenfranchised the "better whites." Of course, the only ones who lost their voting rights were those who had served in the Confederacy or refused to swear an oath of allegiance to the United States of America. He also complained that the federal government had gone too far in saying that the Fifteenth Amendment to the Constitution not only guaranteed blacks the right to vote, but to hold public office and to have a public education as well.[10]

For what it is worth, Wilson did once admit, "I am not only not a scholar, but I don't want to be one."[11] On another occasion he said, "I am not an historian; I am only a writer of history."[12] His principal biographer was even forced to concede, "His intellect was not especially profound."[13] But soon enough, Wilson was able to stop pretending to be a scholar, intellectual, or historian after becoming the thirteenth president of Princeton University in 1902.

When Wilson took over the presidency of Princeton, it had never admitted a single black student, despite the fact that most other top universities had already graduated a number of them. Yale granted its first degree to a black student in 1857. Harvard graduated its first black in 1870, and

W. E. B. DuBois earned a Ph.D. there in 1895. Rutgers, just down the road from Princeton, graduated a black student in 1892. But as long as Wilson was president of Princeton, the policy of excluding blacks continued.[14]

Eventually, Wilson's first love, politics, beckoned him, and he was elected governor of New Jersey in 1910. Although he solicited the votes of black people during the campaign, once in office he turned his back on them. Two years later, the *New York Age,* the nation's most prominent black newspaper, took him to task for indifference to blacks during his time in Trenton:

> Everyone knows that without the vote of the Negro people in the State of New Jersey Mr. Wilson could have never been elected governor. In spite of the fact that his election as governor was due to the Negro vote, he has not by a turn of the finger recognized a single Negro in New Jersey since he has been governor. He has treated the race in New Jersey as if they were foreigners and outcasts.
>
> It is reported on seemingly good authority that when a delegation of colored people called to see him soon after he was inducted into the office of Governor to request him to retain a colored man who had been messenger in the Governor's office for a number of years, Mr. Wilson told the committee of colored people that he would retain the colored man not because of their political influence but because the man was a "good darky."[15]

This pattern was followed during Wilson's race for the White House in 1912 as well. He solicited black support privately, but was never willing to make any concrete promises. And whenever there was any threat to his support in the racist South, Wilson quickly distanced himself from blacks. For example, when Tom Watson, the notorious Georgia racist, accused Wilson of having once sent a letter of condolence to Booker T. Washington, the great black leader, Wilson's campaign vehemently denied that he had ever done any such thing.[16]

Throughout the 1912 campaign, Wilson emphasized his ties to the South and desire to lift the political fortunes of his native region. After all, he would be the first Southern president since Andrew Johnson left office in 1869. Indeed, it is clear that one of Wilson's primary motivations for becoming president was precisely to restore the political influence of the South in the Democratic Party. He thought that ending the South's isolation and bringing it back into the mainstream of national politics would undermine the racial fanatics and empower moderate conservatives like himself to retake control of the party. Wilson explained this strategy in a 1906 letter:

> Unquestionably the conservative elements at the South have for a long time been latent and in the background. The radical element has been allowed to

play fast and loose with Southern politics, because the conservative men, as I take it, were disinclined to go into affairs which were complicated by the necessity of handling the Negro vote. What a great many of us hope is that this latent conservatism, stronger in the South than anywhere else in the country, will in the new and happier circumstances of the time, assert itself, particularly in the reclamation of the Democratic Party.[17]

Toward this end, Wilson walked a fine line throughout the 1912 campaign, seeking black support, but never at the expense of losing white votes in the South. This philosophy defined his presidency as well. Although he played the part of the modern progressive in public, he made sure to mollify his Southern base by appointing prominent Southerners to high-level positions, and by looking the other way when they used blatantly racist tactics to appeal for Southern votes or implemented racist policies.

JOSEPHUS DANIELS

A prime example of Wilson's effort to implement a Southern strategy was his appointment of Josephus Daniels as his campaign manager in 1912. Daniels was owner and editor of the *Raleigh News & Observer* newspaper in North Carolina and Wilson's closest ally in the South.

Daniels had been aware of Wilson's presidential possibilities as early as 1886, when they were brought to his attention by fellow North Carolinian Walter Hines Page.[18] After Wilson gave a laudatory speech about Robert E. Lee at the University of North Carolina in 1909, Daniels was totally smitten with the man.[19] He helped him secure the Democratic presidential nomination and used his newspaper for all it was worth to help Wilson carry North Carolina and the rest of the South. Daniels did this by making sure that his readers were perfectly clear about where Wilson stood on the race question. He made this point most directly in an editorial in the *News & Observer* a few weeks before the election.

Daniels started by condemning the Republican Party, especially former President Theodore Roosevelt, who was running again in 1912 on the Progressive Party ticket. Roosevelt, Daniels said, had offended the South by making a Negro the customs collector in Charleston, South Carolina, and by closing a post office in Indianola, Mississippi, after local whites objected to his having made a Negro the postmaster there.[20]

But Roosevelt's greatest sin, Daniels wrote, his affront to the "sensibilities of every white man in the South," was daring to have lunch at the White House with Booker T. Washington.[21] Roosevelt also sinned by allowing two black politicians to pat him on the back three months earlier "with a comradery quite surpassing that of the commonest white Republican office-seeker in the South." Daniels went on to explain at length that no politician would be deserving of support in the South unless he understood the realities of the race issue:

> The South is serious with regard to its attitude to the Negro in politics. The South understands this subject, and its policy is unalterable and uncompromising. We desire no concessions. We seek no sops. We grasp no shadows on this subject. We take no risks. We abhor a Northern policy of catering to the Negro in politics just as we abhor a Northern policy of social equality. . . .

> Out of bitter experience, the South has evolved certain convictions on the race question; and she takes her place in the Nation with those convictions. They are paramount convictions. It is not conceivable that any man or any party that is not clear upon those convictions will ever receive her support: She is seeking not merely a sectional but a national policy on this subject; for she knows that short of a national policy on the race question, she will never be secure. . . .

> The subjection of the Negro, politically, and the separation of the Negro, socially, are paramount to all other considerations in the South short of the preservation itself of the Republic.

There was but one man in America deserving of Southern support, Daniels said: "The Anglo-Saxon South hails Woodrow Wilson as the Restorer of the Republic from the Privileged Classes of [William Howard] Taft and the Deliverer of the Republic from the Dictatorship of [Theodore] Roosevelt."[22]

Daniels had long been the leading spokesman for North Carolina's most racist element. In 1898, he even supported the only confirmed *coup d'etat* in American history, when Democrats forced the lawfully elected Republican leaders of Wilmington, North Carolina, out of office at gunpoint.[23]

The genesis of this event goes back to the early 1890s, when Republicans managed to crack the Democratic Party's stranglehold on North Carolina by working with the Populist Party, which had developed a strong following among poor white farmers. With the white vote split, Republicans were able to take control of the state legislature in 1894 and the governorship in 1896.

Once in office, Republicans moved quickly to expand voting rights for blacks, who had been largely disenfranchised by literacy tests, poll taxes, and other measures enacted by Democrats following the end of Reconstruction. After taking control of the *News & Observer* in 1895, Daniels used it any way he could to end Republican control and restore Democrats to office, primarily by playing the race card shamelessly.[24]

A recent report by the state of North Carolina on the Wilmington race riot of 1898 documents the Democratic Party's responsibility for that event and Daniels' deep involvement.[25] In his memoirs, Daniels freely admitted his role in the "white supremacy campaign."[26] Among other things, he published the names of every black officeholder in the state, accused the Republican Party of slandering white women, and published front-page stories of all cases in which a black justice of the peace or sheriff had the temerity to force a white man to obey the law in the run-up to the 1898 election.

In Daniels' own words, the *News & Observer* was "the militant voice of White Supremacy, and it did not fail in what was expected, sometimes going to extremes in its partisanship."[27] He even defended the Red Shirts, a racist group similar to the Ku Klux Klan that had been active in South Carolina and spread across the border into North Carolina in 1898.[28] The Wilmington Race Riot Commission called the Red Shirts "effectively a terrorist arm of the Democratic Party."[29] Without them and their threats of violence, which kept Republicans and Populists home on Election Day, Democrats would have lost several counties, Daniels acknowledged.[30]

The result was an across-the-board victory for Democrats in 1898. Daniels was among those who urged an immediate change to the state constitution that would forever keep most blacks from voting. Modeled after a provision adopted in Louisiana, it required all voters to demonstrate detailed knowledge of the state constitution before being allowed to vote. However, whites were effectively excused from this requirement by an exemption for those descended from any man who had been a registered voter prior to January 1, 1876; i.e., before the Fifteenth Amendment to the U.S. Constitution took effect. This is where the term "grandfather clause" comes from.[31]

Daniels was very pleased with this constitutional change, which was ratified in 1900 and became effective in 1902. It would remove the "nigger question" from politics and put an end to the Republican Party in North Carolina, he said.[32] "After 1902, when the bulk of the Negro vote is eliminated, the Republican Party will virtually disappear," Daniels bragged.[33]

Not content to rest on his laurels, Daniels continued his efforts to maintain white supremacy in every corner of North Carolina. In 1903, for example, he was incensed when a respected professor at Trinity College (now Duke University), John Spencer Bassett, dared to write an article in a scholarly journal in which he said that Booker T. Washington was the greatest man born in the South in the previous one hundred years except for Robert E. Lee.[34]

The *News & Observer* carried multiple stories on page one saying that the South had been slandered. In an editorial, the paper demanded that the professor be fired from the university. Childishly, it even spelled the professor's name as "bASSett." Although the university refused to accept Bassett's resignation, he soon left the state for a more hospitable position at Smith College in Massachusetts.

In his memoirs, Daniels expressed no regret over his actions in the Bassett affair, which remains a famous case of the suppression of academic freedom.[35] Even his admiring biographer, who bent over backward to excuse Daniels' racism, had to admit that "he was not in his best form" regarding Bassett.[36]

Today, the *News and Observer*, which was owned by Daniels' family until 1995, views its former owner and editor as a stain on its record. His racist activities "are an embarrassing blot" on its past that brings "shame" to the paper, it editorialized in 2005. A *News & Observer* columnist called Daniels' transgressions "inescapably execrable."[37]

RESEGREGATION

After winning the election of 1912, Wilson's first order of business was choosing a cabinet. He made certain that the South was well represented, designating Albert Burleson of Texas as postmaster general and fellow North Carolinians David F. Houston as secretary of agriculture and Josephus Daniels as secretary of the Navy. Although Secretary of the Treasury William Gibbs McAdoo was living in New York at the time of his appointment, he was born in Georgia and spent much of his life in Tennessee. In the words of one historian, "The President surrounded himself with men whose racial views were Southern in the narrowest sense."[38]

Burleson was a seven-term member of the House of Representatives whose father had been a Confederate officer during the war. His principal qualification for the cabinet seems to have been an extreme degree of loyalty to the Democratic Party and Wilson, who often relied upon Burleson for political advice.[39] At one of the first cabinet meetings of the new administration on April 11, 1913, Burleson urged the institution of racial segregation throughout the federal government. In his diary, Daniels offers these details:

> The Postmaster General brought up a matter that is always the hardest matter to deal with—to wit: policies that are affected by race relations. In the railway mail service there are a great many Negroes who are employed and it often happens that there are four railway mail clerks in one and when this happens, the white men might often have to do all the work. It is very unpleasant for them to work in a car with Negroes where it is almost impossible to have different drinking vessels and different towels, or places to wash and he was anxious to segregate white and Negro employees in all Departments of the Government, and he had talked with Bishop Walters and other prominent Negroes and most of them thought it would be a great thing to do. Mr. Burleson thought the segregation would be a great thing as he had the highest regard for the Negro and wished to help him in every way possible, but that he believed segregation was best for the Negro and best for the Service.[40]

The idea that Bishop Alexander Walters, one of the principal black leaders in the United States, would approve the idea of instituting racial segregation throughout the federal government is ludicrous. Indeed, at that very moment he was doing everything in his power to get as many blacks appointed to positions in the Wilson Administration as possible.[41] Yet no one at the meeting disputed Burleson on this point, including Wilson, who knew Walters well because he had been a major supporter of his during the campaign.[42] Only Treasury Secretary McAdoo argued against the proposal and then only on grounds of practicality.

Burleson, Daniels, and McAdoo interpreted Wilson's silence as constituting permission for them to impose segregation within their departments at their own discretion.[43] No announcement was made of the new policy, but it quickly became clear that the Wilson Administration was instituting a major departure from the way black workers throughout the federal government had been treated under Republican presidents. Historian Kathleen Wolgemuth describes the changes:

> By the end of 1913, segregation had been realized in the Bureau of Engraving and Printing, the Post Office Department, the Office of the Auditor for the Post Office, and had even begun in the City Post Office in Washington, D.C. This involved not only separated or screened-off working positions, but segregated lavatories and lunchrooms. . . . In the office of the Auditor of the Navy . . . screens set off Negroes from whites, and a separate lavatory in the cellar was provided for the colored clerks.[44]

In 1914, the Civil Service began demanding photographs to accompany employment applications for the first time. It was widely understood that the only purpose of this requirement was to weed out black applicants.[45]

According to Wilson biographer Arthur Link, "Burleson and McAdoo made a clean sweep of Negro political appointees in the South and allowed local postmasters and collectors of internal revenue either to downgrade or dismiss Negro workers with civil service status."[46] The postmaster in Atlanta fired thirty-five blacks, and the chief federal tax collector in Georgia said publicly, "A Negro's place is in the cornfield."[47]

Sensing an opportunity for whites to replace blacks throughout the federal government, white civil service workers and those seeking government jobs organized a group called the National Democratic Fair Play Association to pressure Congress and the White House to remove blacks wherever possible. A major concern was that Southerners were underrepresented in federal jobs because they would not work for or alongside blacks. The association also considered it reprehensible that white women were sometimes supervised by black managers.[48] As one of the group's leaders complained, absurdly:

> I would not have believed that such conditions could exist in the government service had I not seen it myself. In one of the rooms I visited I saw a Negro employee leaning over the desk of a white woman, evidently

giving her instructions relative to her work. This state of affairs cannot exist, and I for one cannot understand how it has gone on for so many years with no apparent attention being paid to it.[49]

On other occasions, the Fair Play Association expressed outrage that whites and blacks used the same tables at the Census Bureau and often shared the same wash rooms, and that white stenographers were forced to take dictation from blacks.[50] Even Ellen Wilson thought it was wrong for blacks and whites to work together. The *Washington Post* reported this incident in September 1913:

> An interesting occurrence followed a recent visit of Mrs. Wilson, wife of the President, to the bureau of engraving and printing. There she saw white and Negro women working side by side. Mrs. Wilson came from Georgia and seemed very much surprised. Shortly afterward Assistant Secretary of the Treasury John Skelton issued an order segregating the races in the bureau.[51]

Not surprisingly, politicians soon added their voices to the demands for segregation. Congressman Joseph Thompson, Democrat of Oklahoma, introduced legislation to require segregation.[52] Senator James Vardaman, Democrat of Mississippi, warned Wilson that if he kept his promise to reappoint blacks to the high-level positions that they historically had held, it "will create in every Negro in the country a hope that he may some day stand on social and political equality with the white man."[53]

OUT OF THE CLOSET

Wilson's liberal supporters hoped that the stories about segregation in the government were lies spread by his political enemies. But by the middle of 1913, Wilson himself acknowledged that this was indeed the new policy. In a letter to Oswald Garrison Villard, Wilson defended his action:

> It is true that the segregation of the colored employees in the several departments was begun upon the initiative and at the suggestion of several of the heads of the departments, but as much in the interest of the Negroes as for any other reason, with the approval of some of the most influential Negroes I know, and with the idea that the friction, or rather the discontent and uneasiness, which had prevailed in many of the departments would thereby be removed. It is as far as possible from being a movement *against* the Negroes. I sincerely believe it to be in their interest. . . . My own feeling is, by putting certain bureaus and sections of the service in the charge of Negroes we are rendering them more safe in their possession of office and less likely to be discriminated against.[54]

A few racists, such as *Clansman* author Thomas Dixon, encouraged Wilson to be even more segregationist, but Wilson told them he was doing as much as he could. "We are handling the force of colored people who are now in the departments in just the way they ought to be handled," Wilson told Dixon. "We are trying—and by degrees succeeding—a plan of concentration which will put them all together and will not in any one bureau mix the two races."[55]

In a letter to Howard Bridgman, Wilson confirmed his support for the segregation policy. "I do approve of the segregation that is being attempted in several of the departments," he wrote. "I think if you were here on the ground you would see, as I seem to see, that it is distinctly to the advantage of the colored people themselves that they should be organized, so far as possible and convenient, in distinct bureaus where they will center their work."[56]

The Nation magazine blasted Wilson for creating a caste system in the federal government for the first time. The Negro sections of the departments, it said, would soon become "nigger sections" that would become neglected and despised. "So far from helping the Negro to retain office, it will soon make it impossible for self-respecting Negroes to enter a service which begins by classifying them as people who must be set off lest mere contact with them should result in some kind of moral contamination," it argued.[57]

Republicans in Congress, such as Congressman John Rogers of Massachusetts, tried to call attention to the issue, but with the House and Senate both under Democratic control, their efforts fell on deaf ears.[58] Black leaders worried that as white racists learned about Wilson's policy, they would be emboldened to enact even more discriminatory policies in the states.[59]

Despite Wilson's private admissions, the government's official position was that nothing had changed. After a public attack on the Wilson Administration's segregation policy by Villard on October 27, 1913, Secretary McAdoo called the charge "an unjust and mischievous exaggeration."[60] Congressman James Aswell, Democrat of Louisiana, came to Wilson's defense:

> Mr. Villard seems to be shedding crocodile tears because someone in Atlanta said the Negro's place is in the cornfield. He thinks that to segregate the races in the government service is a stupid political policy. Every informed and right-thinking white man, while sympathizing with and anxious to help the Negro in his place, recognizes the necessity of preserving the integrity and the supremacy of the white race.[61]

On March 6, 1914, the House Committee on Reform in the Civil Service held a hearing on the Wilson Administration's policy of segregating blacks and whites in the civil service. But it was mainly a forum for complaints that the policy didn't go far enough. The first witness was Aswell, who proceeded to deliver this racist rant:

> The Almighty by the stamp of color decreed that the Caucasian race should occupy positions of authority and control the destinies of this country. Fear of losing the Negro vote in the doubtful States and personal desire for office through his vote, which are the real causes of the existing conditions, are usually covered by the pretense of justice. If we would be just to each race, we would recognize the eternal fitness of things in this Government as did Lincoln and Jefferson. We would know that this is a white man's country whose future is to be controlled by the Caucasian race. It is unjust to a member of this inferior race to put him in positions of authority even over his own race. Every informed and right thinking white man, while sympathizing with and anxious to help the Negro in his place, recognizes the necessity of preserving the integrity and supremacy of the white race. No nation ever destroyed itself except by amalgamating with an inferior race. Are we blindly drifting that way?[62]

He was followed by Congressman Charles Edwards, Democrat of Georgia, who told the committee, "I do not think the Government ought to place white men and women in a position where they have to bend the racial pride and the racial dignity of the great Caucasian races in this manner."[63] Both congressmen urged the committee to report legislation that would make segregation mandatory throughout the entire federal government.

Finally, at the very end of the hearing, Archibald Grimké of the NAACP was allowed to offer some comments on Wilson's policy. When he suggested that blacks should one day become part of the nation's ruling class, committee chairman Martin Dies, Democrat of Texas, exclaimed, "I do not want to live to see the Negro race a part of the ruling class!" Since Dies had just proclaimed his great love for the black race a few minutes earlier, Congressman Martin Madden, Republican of Illinois, offered this retort: "It comes with bad grace to have a man put his arm around your neck and tell you how much he loves you and then stick a knife under your fifth rib."[64]

BLACK DISAPPOINTMENT

Although blacks had traditionally voted Republican, Wilson actively solicited their support in 1912.[65] In a letter to Bishop Walters that was widely circulated in the black community, Wilson assured it that, should he become president, "they may count on me for absolute fair dealing and for everything by which I could assist in advancing the interests of their race in the United States."[66] It wasn't much, but it was enough to persuade some prominent black leaders to throw their support to Wilson in the campaign. Chief among these was W. E. B. DuBois, who editorialized in

Wilson's favor in the NAACP's magazine, *The Crisis:*

> We sincerely believe that even in the face of promises disconcertingly
> vague, and in the face of the solid caste-ridden South, it is better to elect
> Woodrow Wilson President of the United States and prove once and for all
> if the Democratic Party dares to be democratic when it comes to black
> men. It has proven that it can be in many Northern states and cities. Can
> it be in the nation? We hope so and we are willing to risk a trial.[67]

DuBois wasn't naïve about Wilson. He knew that election of a
Democrat would also empower the racist Southern segment of that party.
"We have helped call to power not simply a scholar and a gentleman, but
with him and his closest counsels all the Negro-hating, disenfranchising
and lynching South," DuBois wrote just after the election. Nevertheless, he
felt that Wilson was better than the alternatives, Roosevelt and Taft, and
hoped that his personality would keep him from being controlled by party
reactionaries.[68]

Consequently, the revelations about Wilson's segregation policy were a
harsh blow to his black supporters. After a trip to Washington in the summer of 1913, Booker T. Washington said, "I have never seen the colored
people so discouraged and bitter as they are at the present time."[69] On
August 15, 1913, the NAACP officially protested Wilson's actions. In a letter from the board, it said:

> The National Association for the Advancement of Colored People . . .
> respectfully protests the policy of your administration in segregating the
> colored employees in the departments at Washington. It realizes that this
> new and radical departure has been recommended, and is now being
> defended, on the ground that by giving certain bureaus or sections wholly
> to colored employees they are thereby rendered safer in possession of their
> offices and are less likely to be ousted or discriminated against. We believe
> this reasoning to be fallacious. It is based on a failure to appreciate the
> deeper significance of the new policy; to understand how far reaching the
> effects of such a drawing of caste lines by the Federal Government may be,
> and how humiliating it is to the men thus stigmatized.
>
> Never before has the Federal Government discriminated against its civil-
> ian employees on the ground of color. Every such act heretofore has been
> that of an individual state. . . . It has set the colored apart as if mere con-
> tact with them were contamination. . . . Behind screens and closed doors
> they now sit apart as though leprous. Men and women alike have the
> badge of inferiority pressed upon them by government decree. How long
> will it be before the hateful epithets of "nigger" and "Jim-Crow" are
> openly applied to these sections? . . . And wherever there are men who
> rob the Negroes of their votes, who exploit and degrade and lynch those
> whom they call their inferiors, there this mistaken action of the Federal

Government will be cited as the warrant for new racial outrages that cry out to high Heaven for redress.[70]

African Americans were also dismayed by Wilson's policy of replacing black political appointees with whites in positions they had held for many years through Republican and Democratic administrations. For example, the American envoys to Liberia and Haiti, as well as the Register of the Treasury, had traditionally been blacks. Wilson replaced them all with whites, denying blacks even the tiniest bit of political patronage.

Historians have long been critical of Wilson's racial segregation policy. "Negroes not only failed to make progress toward equality in securing patronage . . . during Wilson's administration but actually lost ground in their struggle for equal recognition by the national government," historian George Osborn observed in 1961.[71] "What happened in Washington in 1913 involved more than the growing toleration of petty prejudices," historian Henry Blumenthal wrote two years later. "Worse than that, trust was violated, and hope was lost."[72]

After being put off for a year, a delegation of black leaders was finally able to meet with Wilson to discuss their concerns in November 1914. The meeting did not go well. According to a *New York Times* report, Wilson "resented" the attitude of the group, especially that of its principal spokesman, William Monroe Trotter, whom Wilson said he would never meet with again.[73] Wilson said he had never been addressed in such an insulting fashion since taking office. He insisted that the segregation policy was for the comfort and best interests of both blacks and whites. Afterwards, Trotter had this to say:

> What the president told us was entirely disappointing. His statement that segregation was intended to prevent racial friction is not supported by facts. For fifty years Negro and white employees have worked together in the government departments in Washington. It was not until the present Administration came in that segregation was drastically introduced.[74]

Trotter later noted, bitterly, that during the election he and other black leaders had been greeted by Wilson with open arms. "The Governor had us draw our chairs right up around him, and shook hands with great cordiality. When we left he gave me a long handclasp and used such a pleased tone that I was walking on air," Trotter recalled. "What a change between then and now!"[75]

In 1915, blacks were again insulted when Wilson arranged for a private showing at the White House of the notoriously racist movie, *The Birth of a Nation*, based on his friend Dixon's book. Even by the standards of the time, it was over the top in its glowing portrayal of the Ku Klux Klan, and there were many protests against it in Boston, New York, and elsewhere. But the producers of the film were successfully able to counter them by pointing to the White House showing, which was viewed by Wilson, senior members of Congress, and the Supreme Court.[76] Afterwards, Wilson reportedly said of the movie, "It is like writing history with lightening. And my only regret is that it is all so terribly true."[77]

Also in 1915, blacks were dismayed by Wilson's invasion of Haiti. They felt that he would not have acted in such a high-handed manner if the revolutionary activity that motivated his action had occurred in a white nation.[78]

By 1916, most blacks who had voted for Wilson in 1912 realized they had made a terrible mistake. As historian Herbert Aptheker put it, "after four years of his administration, the return to the Republican Party was fairly complete."[79] It didn't change the result, however, with Wilson winning reelection over Republican Charles Evans Hughes and gaining more total votes than he did in 1912. This meant that whatever political need Wilson had for maintaining good relations with blacks was now completely gone.

WAR AND AFTER

World War I brought no improvement in Wilson's policy toward blacks. They were put in segregated military units, mostly relegated to support positions, and kept out of combat.[80] One reason was a fear of giving them training with guns, which they might use to defend themselves from racist violence once the war was over. "I know of no greater menace to the South than this," said Senator Vardaman, the Mississippi Democrat, in opposing conscription for blacks.[81] "It will mean there will be arrogant strutting representatives of the black soldiery in every community."[82]

Despite numerous reports of racial attacks on black soldiers, Wilson did nothing.[83] Although urged simply to speak out against them by black leaders, he maintained his silence, just as he had done consistently on the issue of lynching. In private, Wilson even made racial jokes. His friend Raymond Fosdick wrote of swapping "Negro stories" with him in December 1918. Wilson himself told one about a "darky" who commented on an Episcopalian church service, saying, "Dey spend too much time readin' de minutes of de las' meetin'."[84]

After the war, Wilson was very concerned about its long-term impact on race relations. He feared that blacks would return from Europe emboldened with foolish notions about equality. Wilson expressed some of these concerns to his physician after reading a newspaper article about how the new German government was recognizing soldiers and workers councils. The doctor recorded this in his diary:

> After reading this article the President said that this looked bad; that if the present government of Germany is recognizing the soldiers and workers councils, it is delivering itself into the hands of the bolshevists. He said the

American Negro returning from abroad would be our greatest medium in conveying bolshevism to America. For example, a friend recently related the experience of a lady friend wanting to employ a Negro laundress offering to pay the usual wage in that community. The negress demands that she be given more money than was offered for the reason that "money is as much mine as it is yours." Furthermore, he called attention to the fact that the French people have placed the Negro soldier in France on an equality with the white man, and it "has gone to their heads."[85]

At the Paris Peace Conference in 1919, Wilson fought measures that might aid black equality. The Japanese delegates to the conference, for example, were very keen on adding a racial equality clause to the peace treaty, which had strong support among Asian Americans. But Wilson was warned by his close adviser Colonel Edward House that acceptance of the clause "would surely raise the race issue throughout the world." Consequently, Wilson told the Japanese that it was a mistake to make too much of a fuss about racial prejudice and he was able to kill the racial equality amendment even though it had majority support at the conference.[86]

University of Alaska historian Kenneth O'Reilly sums up Wilson's racist policies in these words: "At his direction Jim Crow within the federal bureaucracy grew every day of his eight White House years, and at the direction of others Jim Crow had swept the entire capital by the second term's end."[87]

Even without considering Wilson's actions regarding World War I, it is clear that he was neither a great president nor a liberal one.[88] In my view, Wilson is best seen as a reactionary who turned back the clock on race relations and civil liberties. Whether his progressive reforms were enough to offset or compensate for his deplorable treatment of blacks and political dissidents, I will let his defenders argue if they wish. The important thing is to take into account everything Wilson did in office when rendering a judgment on his presidency and not cherry-pick those that may still be praiseworthy, while sweeping his ugly side under the rug. Both sides make up the man, and history's verdict must take both into account.

7

FRANKLIN D.
ROOSEVELT

Insensitive Liberal

By all accounts, Franklin D. Roosevelt was not especially sensitive, racially. As Arthur Schlesinger Jr. diplomatically put it, before 1933 he was "fairly conventional in his racial attitudes."[1] By the standards of the white upper class of the time, this meant that he was a borderline racist. It wasn't that he had any particular dislike of blacks or was ever known to mistreat them. It's just that in his world, they were more likely to be servants than anything else. Roosevelt paid no more attention to them than he would the furniture. He was oblivious to them.[2] Thus Roosevelt could write a letter to his wife Eleanor about a trip to Jamaica in which he mentioned receiving "a drink of cocoanut water, procured by a naked nigger boy." His casual use of the N-word was not uncommon. As Roosevelt biographer Geoffrey Ward tells us:

> As a young man, Franklin used the word "nigger" privately without embarrassment, just as his father had when young. His handwritten caption for one of the snapshots he made at St. Thomas on his 1904 Caribbean cruise reads: "Niggers coaling the P.V.L." and the margin of a 1911 speech contains a crisp penciled reminder to himself: "story of nigger."[3]

At the White House, Roosevelt maintained Woodrow Wilson's policy of segregation among the household staff. There were separate dining rooms for whites and blacks until all the white staff were removed, leaving only black servants to wait on Roosevelt and his family. Even at Hyde Park, the

Roosevelts required the black staff to eat in the kitchen, rather than the staff dining room.[4]

From 1913 to 1920, Roosevelt was assistant secretary of the Navy, where he served under the notorious racist Josephus Daniels, who instituted racial segregation throughout the department immediately upon taking office. Although there is no indication that Roosevelt supported Daniels' policy, neither is there any evidence that he opposed it. In Schlesinger's words, "he served with no visible discomfort under Woodrow Wilson and Josephus Daniels—two liberal southerners who rapidly dropped their liberalism when it came to the race question."[5]

In 1920, Roosevelt was the vice presidential nominee of the Democratic Party and went along with the party's race-baiting tactics to get votes.[6] He made Georgia his second home in the 1920s, a time when the state was still deeply racist.[7] Roosevelt bought the Warms Springs resort there and turned it into a world famous polio treatment facility—for whites only. Not only were blacks excluded from treatment at Warm Springs, the black staff were forced to live in the basement, while the white staff lived in the hotel or surrounding cottages.[8]

According to Schlesinger, as Governor of New York (1928–32), Roosevelt "showed no special concern for Negroes either in appointments or in legislation." And as late as 1929, Roosevelt felt compelled to deny reports that he had entertained blacks at a public function. When running for president in 1932, he courted racist Southerners and appealed to them by appointing a congressman from the old Confederacy as his running mate, John Nance Garner of Texas.[9]

There is no mention of blacks in the Democratic Party's 1932 platform. Much of the black community was, in fact, less than enthusiastic about the Roosevelt-Garner ticket. Said the *New York Amsterdam News*, a prominent black newspaper, "We fear that equal rights in the National Democratic Party means exactly what they meant in 1913 when the Woodrow Wilson administration came into power—equal rights for the white man but hell and damnation for the colored man."[10]

From the black perspective, the best thing Roosevelt had going for him in 1932 simply was that he wasn't Herbert Hoover. Hoover was certainly no racist—he abolished segregation in the Commerce Department while secretary.[11] But he had the tinniest of tin ears when it came to practical politics, especially when it came to blacks. Hoover needlessly alienated them by purging blacks from Republican organizations in the South in order to appeal to whites; nominating a justice to the Supreme Court, John J. Parker, who was widely viewed, rightly or wrongly, as a racist; and allowing the War Department to segregate black Gold Star Mothers during a government-financed trip to European graveyards.[12] Many blacks also believed that Hoover had condoned discriminatory treatment while he was in charge of federal relief after the Great Mississippi Flood of 1927.[13]

Once in the White House, Roosevelt was more sensitive to black concerns. His Interior secretary, Harold Ickes, had long been actively involved in the NAACP, and Eleanor Roosevelt was personally concerned about the problems of black people, especially the awful practice of lynching. Government positions were created for minority affairs for the first time.[14]

On the other hand, Roosevelt never used his political capital to do anything meaningful for blacks. Many of his economic policies actually hurt them and he never publicly supported an antilynching bill in Congress, allowing every effort to fall victim to filibusters by Southern Democrats. Roosevelt never spoke to the NAACP or gave a single speech devoted to black concerns, and even banned black reporters from White House press conferences.[15] His calculation seems to have been to do just enough to win the black vote without doing anything to alienate the Democratic Party's racist Southern base.

Blacks weren't the only minority group to suffer from Roosevelt's insensitivity. Japanese-Americans were singled out for internment during World War II, while whites of German and Italian descent were spared this humiliation. He also turned a blind eye to the horrors faced by European Jews, denying many refugees entrance to the United States. Nor did Roosevelt allow news of the Holocaust to influence conduct of the war, thereby prolonging that tragedy.

BLUE EAGLE OR BLACK HAWK?

When Roosevelt took office in 1933, the Great Depression was well underway. He and his economic advisers believed that deflation—a falling price level—was at the heart of the nation's economic problems. Falling prices reduced profits, forcing employers to lay off workers, which reduced purchasing power throughout the economy. With unemployed workers lacking the income to buy goods and services, sales fell, leading to further layoffs and negative growth.

Roosevelt thought the way to break this downward spiral was to fix prices and wages so that they could not fall further.[16] This was the basic rationale of the National Industrial Recovery Act (NIRA), one of the first key pieces of New Deal legislation, enacted on June 16, 1933. The National Recovery Administration (NRA) was established to enforce industrial codes that created minimum prices and wages throughout the economy in order to staunch deflation. Its symbol was a blue eagle, which complying businesses were encouraged to display.

Unfortunately for black workers, it quickly became clear that minimum wage rates established by the NRA tended to disadvantage them relative to whites. Previously, blacks had often been able to overcome discrimination and get jobs even from racist employers by agreeing to work for lower wages or longer hours. But the NRA effectively eliminated these options. Faced with the necessity of paying blacks and whites the same wages for the same hours, employers generally kept their white workers and laid off their blacks.[17] As historian Philip Foner explains:

> It rapidly became clear that the code mechanism under the NRA was valueless for black workers; it merely legalized for all American industry the pattern of racial discrimination that had long been the practice of Southern employers. Conditions of blacks worsened under the NRA. Thousands were fired and replaced by white workers on jobs where blacks were being paid less than established minimum-wage scales; by August 1933, blacks were calling it the "Negro Removal Act." NRA wage minimums were considered "too much money for Negroes."[18]

As early as August 1933, the *New York Times* warned that the NIRA was inadvertently hurting blacks.[19] A year later, the liberal *New Republic* magazine expressed great bitterness about the Roosevelt Administration's unwillingness to acknowledge the unintentionally racist impact of the legislation or to hire any blacks to help administer the program and mitigate its effect on minorities.[20] John P. Davis wrote in that magazine:

> There is not a section of the country where Negroes have not suffered because of the Blue Eagle. That bird has become for them a black hawk, a predatory bird which makes prices go up but not their wages, which makes them lose their jobs, which weakens their economic position. To them the N.R.A. has but one meaning: "Negroes Ruined Again."[21]

In August 1934, the federal government's highest-ranking black economist, Dr. Robert C. Weaver of the Interior Department, admitted that "Negroes have lost jobs as a result of the NRA." The minimum wage policy, he said, "resulted in wholesale discharges in certain areas."[22] A 1937 study by the NRA itself concluded that the minimum wage provisions of the NIRA put 500,000 blacks out of work in 1934 alone.[23]

The idea of forcing prices up also underlay Roosevelt's agriculture policy. Farmers were paid not to grow crops in order to restrict supply and thereby raise prices for farm commodities. But the Agricultural Adjustment Administration (AAA) only paid those who owned the land, thus excluding sharecroppers and tenant farmers. This policy hurt black farmers because most were not landowners. Although landlords were supposed to share government payments with their tenants, in practice they did not. Indeed, the AAA effectively encouraged landlords to evict tenant farmers in order to maximize their payments.[24] Historian Paul Moreno recently summarized the impact of Roosevelt's policies on black farmers:

> Scholars generally agree that New Deal farm policy had a disastrous effect on blacks, despite the bureaucrats' claims of sensitivity to black hardships. . . . New Deal agricultural policies amounted to an "American

enclosure movement," pushing blacks off the land in a period when the pull of northern industrial employment was slack.[25]

Black farmers were also shortchanged by the Tennessee Valley Authority (TVA), which viewed most of them as too small to be efficient. As part of its mandate, it tried to raise agricultural productivity by consolidating acreage wherever possible to obtain economies of scale. This almost always benefited white farmers. When farmers needed to be relocated to make way for dam construction, blacks were often forced off the land altogether. TVA also refused to hire any blacks. According to historian Melissa Walker, it "maintained a policy of institutionalized segregation and discrimination against blacks."[26]

LICENSE TO DISCRIMINATE?

Section 7a of the NIRA was another Roosevelt initiative that proved injurious to blacks. This provision made it easier for labor unions to organize. Unfortunately, most unions had long excluded blacks.[27] There was also historical antipathy between black workers and white unionists because the former were often used as strikebreakers.[28] Consequently, the spread of unionism resulting from Section 7a, which was later replaced by the Wagner Act, tended to put jobs in unionized industries off limits to blacks.[29] Although the Roosevelt Administration attempted to make union jobs in federal construction projects available to blacks, these efforts were at best marginally successful.[30] To the extent that black workers were able to get public works jobs at all, they were mostly in lower-level job categories than they had previously held before the New Deal.[31]

Adding to the difficulties of black workers in the construction industry was implementation of the Davis-Bacon Act, which was passed in the waning days of the Hoover Administration. This legislation required that "prevailing wages" be paid on federal construction projects. In practice, this meant the union wage, which generally excluded non-union construction companies from bidding on federal public works projects. The effect was to keep blacks from working on them. Indeed, that was one of the law's purposes.[32]

Another problem relating to construction was the development of federal housing programs such as the National Housing Act of 1934, which established the Federal Housing Administration (FHA) to guarantee private mortgages and make them more widely available and on better terms than had been the case previously.[33] The goal was to stimulate home-building to create jobs. Although there was no racist intent in the law's creation, there was a deeply racist result in the way it operated in practice. Because the FHA favored single-family homes in racially homogeneous neighborhoods, it drained the cities of their white middle class. The FHA also instituted a practice known as "redlining," which meant that loans would not be made for housing in inner-city neighborhoods that were viewed as too poor and run-down. This effectively made homeownership impossible for blacks and other minorities by making it prohibitively difficult for them to get insured loans in the places where they lived, thus creating ghettoes in all our major cities, ringed by lily-white suburbs.[34]

In 1935, the Supreme Court declared the NIRA unconstitutional in *Schechter Poultry Corporation v. U.S.*[35] Roosevelt was enraged by this and other Supreme Court cases that invalidated much of his program. But after his big reelection victory in 1936, the Court shifted direction and became more supportive of Roosevelt's efforts. This shift was signaled in *West Coast Hotel Company v. Parrish*, handed down on March 29, 1937.[36] Because Roosevelt had been threatening to pack the Supreme Court by expanding its membership, the Court's new direction obviated this necessity.[37] Hence, the *Parrish* case is often called "a switch in time that saved nine."[38]

Before the Court shifted direction, the Department of Labor had been working on a narrow minimum wage bill that would pass constitutional muster.[39] The shift, however, led Roosevelt to propose a broad minimum wage bill on May 24, 1937, providing for a forty-cent per hour minimum wage and a forty-hour maximum workweek.[40] This was equivalent to $5.74 in 2006 dollars—higher than the $5.15 minimum wage then in existence.

The idea of a national minimum wage was not new. It had been under discussion for decades, although not in the way most people think. Rather than being seen as a means of lifting up the poor, it was instead viewed as a way of intentionally pricing certain groups out of the labor market, especially those viewed as mentally deficient. As Princeton University economist Thomas Leonard explains, "Progressive economists . . . believed that binding minimum wages would cause job losses. However, the progressive economists also believed that the job loss induced by minimum wages was a social benefit, as it performed the eugenic service of ridding the labor force of the 'unemployable.'"[41]

Among the most vocal advocates of this view was economist Frank W. Taussig of Harvard, whose work on international trade is still frequently cited. In his *Principles of Economics*, a commonly-used university textbook in the 1920s, Taussig was unequivocal in his advocacy of a minimum wage for the very purpose of creating unemployment among the feeble-minded to prevent them from reproducing:

> There would unfailingly be a certain number not capable of earning the minimum—the aged, feeble, maimed, the destitute or half dissolute. It would be impossible to compel employers to pay the minimum to those whose services were not worth it. . . . Neither the feeble minded, nor those saturated by alcohol or tainted with hereditary disease, nor the irretrievable criminals and tramps, should be allowed at large, still less should be allowed to breed.[42]

Two other groups were also targets of the Progressive Era minimum wage advocates: immigrants and women. It was thought that immigrants from poor countries would always be able to undercut the wages of the native born because it was thought that they could survive on practically nothing. Thus there was a kind of race to the bottom in which the living standards of American workers were steadily reduced to those of the marginal immigrant. Moreover, it was thought that the availability of a large pool of laborers who would work for very little discouraged businesses from investing in training and productivity-enhancing equipment, thus reducing the overall productivity level in the economy.[43]

As for women, it was felt that they undercut the wages of men because most working women still lived at home in those days and were, in effect, subsidized by their parents. Second, it kept white women from marrying and having children. Since women were assumed to be less productive than men, because they had less physical strength and seldom received higher education, it was thought that a minimum wage would tend to force women out of the labor market—a desirable outcome in the progressive view at the time.[44]

Although there is no evidence that minimum wage advocates in the 1930s intended to price blacks out the labor market, nevertheless this was one of its effects, as was the case with the NIRA. After the law went into effect, the most racist member of Congress, Senator Theodore Bilbo, Democrat of Mississippi, spoke approvingly of its discriminatory impact:

> With the wage and hour law on the statute books . . . the white man will receive a wage which will enable him to accept the job which the poor Negro has been filling in the South, because the wage will now be sufficiently high so that the white man can maintain his standard of living in the South. So that the poor Negro who has been having the labor job heretofore will be out of luck. We will find in the South a great army of millions of Negroes who are going to lose their jobs to white men because the wage scale has been increased.[45]

It is worth noting that the apartheid government of South Africa at this time was intentionally using minimum wage laws for the express purpose of discrimination. A high minimum wage was instituted there in 1925 precisely to put black workers at a disadvantage relative to whites. As the South African Economic and Wage Commission explained, "The method would be to fix a minimum rate for an occupation or craft so high that no Native [black] would be likely to be employed."[46]

There is nothing in the record to indicate that an adverse impact on black workers was anticipated in the United States, despite the experience of the NIRA. But it was well understood that there would be a negative effect on the South, where the vast majority of blacks lived. Because it was the poorest and least productive region of the country, it was feared that a national minimum wage, which might be borne with ease in the Northeast or West, might be debilitating in the South. The *New York Times* explained that the minimum wage would act as a tariff wall in the North against Southern goods. "It might make it so difficult for Southern employers to compete that many of them would be forced to close down," the paper warned.[47]

Consequently, much of the debate over the minimum wage bill in Congress revolved around the question of a differential wage for the South. This idea was categorically rejected by Roosevelt, who believed that national uniformity was essential for fairness and administrability. The *New York Times* repeatedly editorialized that imposition of a single minimum wage throughout the country with no adjustment for local conditions, such as between city and rural businesses, would impose undue hardship.[48] Nevertheless, in the end, a uniform national minimum wage was established, forcing many Southerners in Congress to break with Roosevelt for the first time on a major issue.[49] This incident helped create the notorious Southern Democrat/Republican coalition that soon brought New Deal legislation to a halt.[50]

It is impossible to calculate precisely to what extent New Deal policies raised black unemployment above what otherwise would have been the case. But it is revealing that well after the beginning of the Depression but before the New Deal began, unemployment for black workers was actually lower than for whites. In April 1930, the unemployment rate was 6.3 percent for black males and 6.9 percent for white males. Seven years later, in late 1937, after implementation of most New Deal programs, the unemployment rate for black males was well above that for white males: 19.1 percent for the former versus 13.9 percent for the latter.[51]

POLITICAL REALIGNMENT

Despite all of this, black support for Roosevelt grew sharply between 1932 and 1936. Contrary to popular belief, Hoover actually carried a majority of the black vote in 1932. It was not until 1936 that blacks really deserted the Republican Party in large numbers.[52] A key reason appears to have been the federal government's welfare efforts through the Federal Emergency Relief Administration, which literally put food on the table for a large percentage of black families.[53] According to one estimate, 30 percent of the entire black population was receiving relief in January 1935.[54] As a contemporary analyst explained, blacks were profoundly grateful for this aid, little as it was, and rewarded the political party that delivered the goods:

> Many Negroes in Chicago came in for a large share of relief funds and, consequently, were greatly impressed with the humanitarian aims of the New Deal. This sentiment was played upon and encouraged by both the national and local Democratic organizations. It was soon evident that their security was tied up with direct relief.

This same analyst quoted a Republican precinct captain in Chicago, who explained his party's loss of the black vote this way: "That Abe Lincoln was a Republican is not near so important as their daily bread."[55] It didn't matter that the disbursement of aid was in the hands of local officials who often discriminated severely against blacks. They were grateful that they were getting *something*, even if it was less than whites received.[56] "Let Jesus lead me and welfare feed me," Depression-era blacks would say.[57]

Ironically, on August 14, 1935, Roosevelt signed into law the biggest expansion of social welfare in American history—the Social Security Act—and left most blacks out of it. Although initially proposed as universal legislation that would benefit all workers, the bill Roosevelt ultimately signed excluded most blacks by exempting domestic and agricultural workers from coverage. For this reason, many historians today view the original law as inherently racist. As Robert Lieberman of Columbia University recently wrote:

> The Old-Age Insurance provisions of the Social Security Act were founded on racial exclusion. In order to make a national program of old-age benefits palatable to powerful Southern congressional barons, the Roosevelt administration acceded to a Southern amendment excluding agricultural and domestic employee from OAI coverage. This provision alone eliminated more than half of the African Americans in the labor force and over three-fifths of black Southern workers.[58]

While Roosevelt himself was not responsible for the provision that limited Social Security coverage for blacks, it is also a fact that he didn't fight very hard to prevent his proposal from being watered down this way.[59] Nor can Roosevelt be excused for ignorance. The NAACP even testified against the Social Security Act before the Senate Finance Committee. Said the NAACP representative, Charles H. Houston, the more the organization studied the legislation, "the more holes appeared, until from a Negro's point of view it looks like a sieve with the holes just big enough for the majority of Negroes to fall through."[60]

KLANSMAN TO THE COURT

Much harder to rationalize is Roosevelt's appointment of a member of the Ku Klux Klan to the Supreme Court, particularly since this was his first opportunity to make an appointment to the Court and influence its direction. He had been denied this opportunity throughout his entire first term. Finally, on May 18, 1937, Justice Willis Van Devanter, one of the conservatives who had found many New Deal programs to be unconstitutional, told Roosevelt he planned to leave the Court on June 2.[61] Obviously, Van Devanter's replacement was a matter of great importance to Roosevelt and he thought deeply about who to appoint in his place. On August 12, 1937, he selected Senator Hugo Black, Democrat of Alabama.

Black's primary qualification for the position was a slavish loyalty to the New Deal. Roosevelt was determined to get someone on the Court who could be depended upon to support his program without question. But there were any number of other politicians and legal scholars Roosevelt could have chosen who probably would have been equally supportive.[62] It wasn't necessary for him to appoint someone from the Deep South who was sure to have a questionable record on race simply by virtue of history and geography. Roosevelt clearly did so in order to help solidify the South as part of the Democratic coalition. He shouldn't have been surprised when Black turned out to have been a member of the Ku Klux Klan.

Born in Ashland, Alabama, in 1886, Black graduated from the University of Alabama and became a practicing lawyer in Birmingham in 1907 specializing in personal injury cases, which made him a wealthy man. After serving as a municipal judge and prosecuting attorney, he was elected to the Senate in 1926. In those days, the Klan's endorsement was pretty *de rigueur* for anyone wishing to achieve major political office in the state of Alabama.[63] As *The Nation* magazine explained in a 1927 report:

> Alabama is the most completely Klan-controlled state in the Union. . . .
> The Klan is so well entrenched politically, that so many judges, solicitors,
> sheriffs, jury commissioners are members of the Klan or submissive to it,
> that state and county governments are so thoroughly beholden to the
> Klan, that Alabama is a veritable Eden to the Knights.[64]

Black became a member of the Klan on September 13, 1923. His biographer Roger Newman says, "It was a decision he did not take lightly." Furthermore, "Black could not have had any illusions about the group he joined." He became active in the Klan, too, marching in parades, speaking at Klan meetings throughout Alabama, and wearing the Klan regalia, including hood and mask.[65] Historian J. Mills Thornton says Black's involvement in the Klan was "extensive and ardent."[66]

Black had been introduced to the Klan when he took Crampton Harris as his law partner. Harris was Cyclops of the Birmingham Klavern and he soon persuaded Black to join as well. He knew Black would fit in because he was not shy about using the race card whenever he thought it would help him win a case. For example, while cross-examining a witness, Black once asked, "Was he standing at the door where this nigger woman came in?" And the woman in question was his client.[67] Black later explained that so many members of the jury were members of the Klan that such tactics were necessary to have a chance of winning.[68]

Black knew what he was talking about. On one occasion, the Klan handed him a huge victory in a murder case. In 1921, a Methodist minister named Edward Stephenson became enraged when his daughter Ruth not only converted to Catholicism, but married a Puerto Rican. He decided to take his rage out on Father James Coyle, who had performed the ceremony.

Stephenson shot him a few hours afterward and immediately confessed to the local sheriff.[69]

Although it was an open-and-shut case, Black played the race card for all it was worth. While on the witness stand, he asked Stephenson if he knew his daughter's husband was Puerto Rican. Stephenson replied, "You can call him a Puerto Rican, but to me he's a nigger." That was about all it took for the Klan-dominated jury to acquit him. The victory made Black famous throughout Alabama.[70]

At different times, Black gave different reasons for joining the Klan, but it seems pretty clear that the fundamental one was politics. He had political ambitions and he needed Klan support. As he once explained, "The Klan was, in effect, the underground Democratic Party in Alabama."[71] And the Democratic Party controlled Alabama.

Black's involvement with the Klan was no secret. When he ran for the Senate, his campaign manager was James Esdale, Grand Dragon of the Alabama Klan. The *New York Times* reported at the time that Black was first elected to the Senate that it was with the support of the Klan, which he had solicited by, among other things, attacking New York Governor Al Smith.[72] Smith was seeking the Democratic Party's presidential nomination in 1928 and was opposed by the Klan because he was a Catholic.[73] In 1930, the *Washington Post* reported that Black had been drafted by the Klan for the Senate in order to give it some respectability.[74]

KLAN MEMBERSHIP SHOCK

Therefore, it is surprising that Black's Klan connection should have taken so many people by surprise after his confirmation to the Supreme Court. Apparently, his membership was well known among Washington insiders.[75] Indeed, when Black's nomination was announced, one said, "Hugo won't have to buy a robe; he can dye his white one black."[76] But Black's nomination was rammed through the Senate so quickly that there was no time to investigate or publicize the matter. He was confirmed by a vote of 63 to 16 on August 17, 1937, just five days after Roosevelt nominated him, and sworn-in two days later.[77]

The same day Black joined the Supreme Court, a reporter for the *Pittsburgh Post-Gazette* named Ray Sprigle arrived in Birmingham to look into Black's membership in the Klan, which had never been confirmed. He had no trouble finding people who would talk about it because they saw nothing wrong with it.[78] One in particular was Esdale, who offered documentary evidence that Black had joined the Ku Klux Klan in 1923.[79]

Sprigle's story broke on September 13, 1937, and was nothing short of sensational. It ran in a six-part series that was reprinted throughout the country.[80] One startling revelation was that Black had accepted a life membership in the Klan following his election to the Senate. After winning the Democratic primary in 1926, tantamount to winning the general election as well, Black was feted by his fellow Klan members, who presented him with a gold passport signifying life membership. In accepting it on September 2, 1926, he was most appreciative:

> This passport which you have given me is a symbol to me of the passport which you have given me before. I do not feel that it would be out of place to state to you here on this occasion that I know that without the support of the members of this organization I would not have been called, even by my enemies, the "Junior Senator from Alabama."[81]

Although the *Post-Gazette* series left no doubt as to Justice Black's membership in the Klan, the Democratic Party quickly circled the wagons around him. Senator William King, Democrat of Utah, said that he saw no reason why membership in the Klan should disqualify anyone from being a member of the Supreme Court. Senator Marvel Logan, Democrat of Kentucky, denied that Black was ever a Klansman and said the whole thing was just a political smear.[82]

Black himself was on vacation in Europe when the Klan story broke and he refused comment until his return to the States. Roosevelt claimed no knowledge of Black's Klan involvement until the *Post-Gazette* series began. "I know only what I have read in the newspapers," he told reporters.[83] However, in a 1968 memo, Black admitted that Roosevelt knew perfectly well about his Klan membership. Said Black:

> President Roosevelt, when I went up to lunch with him, told me there was no reason for my worrying about my having been a member of the Ku Klux Klan. He said that some of his best friends and supporters he had in the state of Georgia were strong members of that organization. He never in any way, by word or attitude, indicated any doubt about my having been in the Klan nor did he indicate any criticism of me for having been a member of that organization. The rumors and statements to the contrary are wrong.[84]

In a brilliant public relations move, Black declined all interview requests and asked instead for national radio time to address the issue of his membership in the Ku Klux Klan. It was granted and he made an eleven-minute speech to the nation on the evening of Friday, October 1, 1937. It was estimated that an astonishing forty million people—almost a third of the U.S. population—heard the broadcast.

Black admitted his membership in the Klan, but said that he had resigned in 1925.[85] In response to charges that he had been given a life membership in the Klan, he said that he had never accepted it. Since joining the Senate, Black said that he had had no further involvement with it: "I have had nothing whatsoever to do with it since that time. I abandoned it. I completely discontinued any association with the organization."[86]

Press reaction was overwhelmingly negative. Typical was the view of the *New York Times:* "Regardless of the present views he holds, and his affirmation of faith in the principles of religious and racial tolerance, it is a deplorable thing that a man who has ever taken the oath of allegiance in a sinister and destructive organization should now take his place on the highest court of justice in this country."[87]

The public, however, reacted positively for the most part because it was convinced that Black was speaking from the heart. Consequently, the furor quickly blew over. In the words of journalist Max Lerner, he "turned what might have been, in a sense, a lynching bee into something like a triumphal homecoming."[88] The main impact of the Klan controversy was probably to make Black even more liberal in his court philosophy than he otherwise would have been, lest any hint of conservatism—especially in the racial area—be construed as reflecting his racist past. As prominent left-wing lawyer William Kuntsler later put it, "If there was ever any doubt of his disaffiliation with the Klan, it was dispelled by his decisions in *Chambers v. Florida* and *Smith v. Texas.*"[89]

Needless to say, Black's court record stands on its own and his membership in the Klan is little more than a footnote to his life.[90] This episode really tells us much more about Roosevelt than Black. There appears to be little doubt that he knowingly appointed a member of the Ku Klux Klan to the Supreme Court and saw nothing wrong with it since he had many "friends and supporters" who were also members. It is further evidence of Roosevelt's insensitivity when it came to matters of race.

INTERNMENT AND THE HOLOCAUST

The advent of war on December 7, 1941, ended the debate about American intervention and the Great Depression as well, at least in the popular perception. Fortunately for Roosevelt, Hitler declared war on the United States a few days later, sparing him from having to figure out how to join the European conflict when our only attacker was Japan.[91] Absent a German attack, there would have been enormous public and political pressure on him to concentrate all U.S. forces in the Pacific, even if it meant letting Hitler have his way in Europe.

Naturally, the federal government immediately started to round up German, Italian, and Japanese foreign nationals, especially those who were suspected of being spies or potential saboteurs. But there was considerable debate within the Roosevelt Administration about how to deal with American citizens of German, Italian, and Japanese descent. Attorney General Francis Biddle and FBI Director J. Edgar Hoover thought there was no need to isolate such people as a war measure.[92] But Secretary of War Henry Stimson argued that the large Japanese-American population on the West Coast presented a serious security threat. With a Japanese invasion of California being a real possibility in the weeks following Pearl Harbor,

Roosevelt sided with Stimson and on February 19, 1942, signed the infamous Executive Order 9066, which authorized the military to prescribe areas from which "any or all persons may be excluded" at its discretion.

There was no mention of Japanese-Americans or any other national or ethnic group. Indeed, a small number of people of German and Italian descent were initially caught up in the military dragnet. But there was a critical distinction between them and those of Japanese descent: the German-Americans and Italian-Americans were all quickly given the opportunity to plead their cases, prove their loyalty to the United States, and be released from confinement. No such opportunity was offered to any of the American citizens of Japanese descent, most of whom ended up in concentration camps for the duration of the war, long past the point when a Japanese invasion was possible.[93]

Another distinction is that the roundup of German-Americans and Italian-Americans was highly selective, whereas the confinement of Japanese-Americans was universal. Over 100,000 of the latter ended up in camps for years.[94] Moreover, they were rounded up so quickly that they lost almost all of their possessions, not to mention their jobs, thereby suffering a massive economic loss on top of their loss of freedom. A recent history refers to this event as the "most tragic act" of the Roosevelt Administration and a "tragedy of democracy."[95] In the 1980s, the U.S. Congress officially apologized for the internment policy and offered belated reparations. Most of those involved in the internment were later remorseful about it. Typical was the view of Earl Warren, then attorney general of the state of California and later chief justice of the Supreme Court. In his memoirs he wrote:

> I have since deeply regretted the removal order and my own testimony advocating it, because it was not in keeping with our American concept of freedom and the rights of citizens. . . . It was wrong to react so impulsively, without positive evidence of disloyalty, even though we felt we had good motive in the security of our state.[96]

Roosevelt's order may have been influenced by a longstanding animosity toward Japan and all things Japanese. This was due to a family history with China that caused him to view Japan's invasion of China in 1931 very negatively.[97] But Roosevelt also seems to have harbored what can only be described as a racial bias against the Japanese. In the 1920s, he even wrote a newspaper column condemning intermarriage between Japanese and (presumably white) Americans. As Roosevelt wrote:

> Anyone who has traveled to the Far East knows that the mingling of Asiatic blood with European or American blood produces, in nine cases out of ten, the most unfortunate results. . . . The argument works both ways. I know a great many cultivated, highly educated and delightful Japanese. They have all told me that they would feel the same repugnance

and objection to have thousands of Americans settle in Japan and inter-marry with the Japanese as I would feel in having large numbers of Japanese coming over here and intermarry with the American population.

In this question, then, of Japanese exclusion from the United States it is necessary only to advance the true reason—the undesirability of mixing the blood of the two peoples. . . . The Japanese people and the American people are both opposed to intermarriage of the two races—there can be no quarrel there.[98]

Rivaling the Japanese internment in terms of tragedy was Roosevelt's steadfast refusal to aid European Jews or to take any action against the Holocaust. In his book, *The Abandonment of the Jews*, historian David Wyman offers this withering indictment:

- The American State Department and the British Foreign Office had no intention of rescuing large numbers of European Jews. On the contrary, they continually feared that Germany or other Axis nations might release tens of thousands of Jews into Allied hands. Any such exodus would have placed intense pressure on Britain to open Palestine and on the United States to take in more Jewish refugees, a situation the two powers did not want to face. Consequently, their policies aimed at obstructing rescue possibilities and dampening public pressures for government action.

- Authenticated information that the Nazis were systematically exterminating European Jewry was made public in the United States in November 1942. President Roosevelt did nothing about the mass murder for fourteen months, then moved only because he was confronted with political pressures he could not avoid and because his administration stood on the brink of a nasty scandal over its rescue policies.

- The War Refugee Board, which the President then established to save Jews and other victims of the Nazis, received little power, almost no cooperation from Roosevelt or his administration, and grossly inadequate government funding. . . .

- Because of State Department administrative policies, only 21,000 refugees were allowed to enter the United States during the three and one half years the nation was at war with Germany. That amounted to 10 percent of the number who could have been legally admitted under the immigration quotas during that period. . . .

- In 1944 the United States War Department rejected several appeals to bomb the Auschwitz gas chambers and the railroads leading to Auschwitz, claiming that such actions would divert essential air-power from decisive operations elsewhere. Yet in the very months that it was turning down the pleas, numerous massive American bombing raids were taking place within fifty miles of Auschwitz.

Twice during that time large fleets of American heavy bombers struck industrial targets in the Auschwitz complex itself, not five miles from the gas chambers.

Wyman concludes that "Franklin Roosevelt's indifference to so momentous an historical event as the systematic annihilation of European Jewry emerges as the worst failure of his presidency."[99] Probably the best that can be said for Roosevelt in this regard is that his failure to acknowledge the Holocaust or act against it was widely shared by the American media, especially the *New York Times*, which systematically ignored, misunderstood, and downplayed evidence of the event. In 2006, the Newspaper Association of America officially offered regrets for its inaction at the time.[100]

ASSESSMENT

Most blacks were deeply saddened by Roosevelt's death in 1945. They felt that they had not had a better friend in the White House since Abraham Lincoln. Also, with many high-paying jobs with defense contractors having been opened to blacks by Roosevelt's order banning discrimination in the defense industry, they were in the best economic position in their entire history in America.[101] Within a few years, however, blacks began to reassess the Roosevelt legacy. One of the first to offer a revisionist viewpoint was *Negro Digest* editor Allan Morrison. In a 1951 article, he saw the substance of Roosevelt's accomplishments with regard to blacks as being very meager indeed. Said Morrison:

> Mr. Roosevelt did not do as much for the Negro as is believed and was never as liberal as he seemed. His thinking on the Negro was fuzzy and he always had to be pressed for remedial action which seldom came. . . . Tragically, the gnawing problem of the Negro people's marginal existence in the world's strongest democracy did not seem to have a very high priority on his list of things to be done. He regarded the Negro as an integral part of the nation, entitled to but often denied equal citizenship rights. But he did not apparently consider the Negro's cause vital enough to jeopardize the bulk of his legislative program to which he was committed and for which he needed the votes of anti-Negro Southern congressmen and senators. . . . The record shows that throughout his years at the White House FDR leaned over backwards to keep from offending Southern legislators and thus losing votes he believed to be crucially important. His failure to vigorously champion civil rights legislation can only be explained by his desperate resolve to maintain the unholy alliance he had formed with the Southerners in his party.[102]

In 1967, black sociologist Kenneth Clark attributed black support for Roosevelt to "folk wisdom." He conceded that this was "in spite of the fact that FDR never clearly defined civil rights goals." Clark concluded that blacks understood that Roosevelt's paramount concern was getting the economy going again and that they would benefit from this even if their concerns weren't addressed directly.[103]

In 1970, black historian Charles Crowe of the University of Georgia wrote, "Franklin D. Roosevelt gave explicit sanction to the Southern caste system and allowed officials to maladminister Federal and state programs according to the dictates of white supremacy."[104]

In 1982, Roy Wilkins, who edited the NAACP's magazine in the 1930s, said, "I have always felt that F.D.R. was overrated as a champion of the Negro. He was a New York patrician, distant, aloof, with no natural feel for the sensibilities of black people, no compelling inner commitment to their cause."[105]

Historians today are disinclined to believe that blacks could have been expected to benefit proportionately even if Roosevelt's policies were successful in reviving the economy as a whole. Too much of the New Deal simply bypassed them altogether. In a recent review of Roosevelt's policies toward blacks, Trinity College sociologist Steve Valocchi came to this conclusion:

> This survey of the impact of New Deal programs on African Americans suggests that most of the positive evaluations of this period need to be, at the very least, significantly qualified. Most of these evaluations are done with categories that leave invisible the farm laborers, domestic and service workers, sharecroppers, and tenant farmers, a large number of whom were black. These evaluations implicitly assume that once African Americans participated more fully in industrialized society that they too would qualify for and receive New Deal largesse; they do not consider the legal and extra-legal restrictions on blacks' economic and political freedoms that kept many blacks out of or subjugated within the industrializing economy.[106]

Perhaps Roosevelt's greatest failure regarding blacks was his utter cowardice in failing to press for an antilynching bill.[107] Several attempts to pass one in the 1930s were mounted, all falling to filibusters by Southern Democrats. Among the participants: Senator Hugo Black, who somehow viewed an antilynching bill as anti-labor; Senator James F. Byrnes, Democrat of South Carolina, whom Roosevelt also appointed to the Supreme Court; and Senator Claude Pepper, Democrat of Florida, whose left-wing politics on issues other than race gave him the nickname of "Red" Pepper.[108] Roosevelt's excuse was simply that he had bigger fish to fry. As he told Walter White of the NAACP in 1935:

> I did not choose the tools with which I must work. Had I been permitted to choose them I would have selected quite different ones. But I've got to

get legislation passed by Congress to save America. The Southerners, by reason of the seniority rule in Congress, are chairmen or occupy strategic places on most of the Senate and House committees. If I come out for the antilynching bill now, they will block every bill I ask Congress to pass to keep America from collapsing. I just can't take that risk.[109]

I believe Roosevelt was being disingenuous. The idea that Southern Democrats would block legislation widely viewed as essential for economic recovery in the middle of the Great Depression just to protest Roosevelt's support for an antilynching bill is ridiculous. It would have been an act of political suicide.[110] Roosevelt's support for an antilynching bill may or may not have been able to overcome a filibuster, but there is no excuse for him not to have made a public issue of the matter and shame those who insisted upon defending the indefensible. "No government pretending to be civilized can go on condoning such atrocities," journalist H. L. Mencken declared in 1935 congressional testimony. "Either it must make every possible effort to put them down or it must suffer the scorn and contempt of Christendom."[111] Had Roosevelt spoken words such as these in one of his fireside chats, I believe it might have turned the tide in the Senate.[112]

Another important failure was Roosevelt's unwillingness to integrate the armed forces during World War II, maintaining instead the historical policy of segregated units. As he said in a 1940 statement confirming continuation of the practice: "This policy has proven satisfactory over a long period of years and to make changes would produce situations destructive to morale and detrimental to the preparation for national defense."[113] Indeed, the war years presented many golden opportunities to advance civil rights for blacks that Roosevelt consistently ignored.[114]

Even taking all these factors into account, one may still conclude, as most historians do, that Roosevelt was among our greatest presidents. Seeing America through both its worst economic crisis and the bloodiest war in world history is an important achievement—second only to Lincoln's salvation of the Union itself. Any of the many, many books about the New Deal and Roosevelt's life will tell the curious all they could possibly want to know about his praiseworthy accomplishments, because almost all are unabashedly positive.[115] But Roosevelt had his dark side, too, and both sides make the man.

SECTION IV

DEMOCRATIC RACISM FINALLY REPUDIATED

HARRY S. TRUMAN

Unsung Civil Rights Hero

Harry Truman's home state of Missouri entered the Union as a slave
state and long thereafter was in many ways the northernmost Southern
state. Both sets of his grandparents were slave owners, and his mother was
so Southern in her attitudes that she refused to sleep in the Lincoln bed-
room when she visited her son in the White House.[1]

By the time Truman entered politics in the 1920s, the Ku Klux Klan had
achieved a significant revival nationally and was particularly strong in
Missouri, where it had over 100,000 members.[2] Truman was up for reelection in 1924 as a judge in Jackson County, just outside Kansas City, and
may have thought that being a member of the Klan would further his political ambitions.[3] In an interview with the Truman Library in 1962, a
Klansman named Edgar G. Hinde, who served with Truman in World War
I, discussed Truman's involvement with the Klan:

> We had quite a wave of Ku Klux around here at that time [1924] and there
> are so many stories on Harry joining the Ku Klux Klan. I was instrumen-
> tal in that thing. Some of us had joined to see what it was, to see what was
> going on, you know. So they got after me to get Truman to join the
> Klan. . . . So I talked to him and he said, "All right." So I took [his] ten dol-
> lars and went down to this organizer, and he took it and then they wanted
> to have a meeting with him [Truman] over in Kansas City at the Hotel
> Baltimore. There was a fellow by the name of Jones, who was an organ-
> izer. He wanted to talk to Truman and see what his intentions were. . . .
> This fellow Jones wanted him [Truman] to agree that he wouldn't give a
> Catholic a job if he was elected and Harry told him no, he wouldn't do
> that. He said he commanded a battery of artillery that was about 90 percent

Catholic and if any of those boys wanted a job—needed a job—and he could give it to them, he was going to give it to them. Jones said, "Well, we can't be for you." So that was it and they gave me the ten dollars back.[4]

Truman's rejection of the Klan for its anti-Catholicism may have cost him the election of 1924, the only political loss he ever suffered. But he rebounded in 1926 and was elected presiding judge of Jackson County. Among Truman's major undertakings was building a new courthouse. Although racial segregation was standard practice in Kansas City at that time, he ensured that the Jackson County courthouse would not have separate rest rooms for blacks and whites, as was the case in the nearby Clay County courthouse.[5] This suggests that Truman's flirtation with the Klan was more of a misguided political calculation than any indication that he agreed with its philosophy.

It would not have been surprising if Truman had sympathized with the casual racism that was pervasive at that time in rural Missouri. That he didn't is early evidence of an independent streak in his personality that fully emerged once he became president. But long before that happened, Truman spent many years as a functionary in one of the country's biggest, best known, and most corrupt political machines.

THE PENDERGAST CONNECTION

Truman owed his career in politics to Thomas J. Pendergast, perhaps the most corrupt big city boss of his era.[6] From the early 1920s until 1939, when he was convicted of tax evasion, Pendergast ran the city of Kansas City, Missouri, with an iron hand. He routinely made and broke city and state politicians. For many years, Truman was one of his most trusted lieutenants and was rewarded with a U.S. Senate seat in 1934 that Pendergast basically handed to him as a gift.[7] As the *Washington Post* put it at the time, Truman was elected "because Boss Pendergast so willed it."[8] He remained loyal to Pendergast until Pendergast's death in 1945.

Pendergast was heir to a political machine originally built by his older brother Jim. When Jim died in 1911, Tom took over and steadily built it up, forcing out or subordinating all competitors, until by the 1920s his control was complete. He then moved to expand his empire outside the city limits of Kansas City to encompass surrounding Jackson County as well, where the town of Independence was the county seat. In 1922, Pendergast anointed Independence native Truman, whose haberdashery business was going bankrupt, to be judge for the Eastern section of Jackson County. A loyal Democrat eager to get into politics, Truman gratefully accepted Pendergast's offer and was duly elected.

Being a county judge in those days was more of an administrative position than a judicial one and Truman had responsibility for things like road building and repair. By all accounts, he did his job responsibly and well. But Truman was also beholden to his master, Pendergast, whose appetite for graft was insatiable, owing to a severe gambling addiction. Among other things, this meant that Truman was required to use only machine-approved contractors and suppliers, who in turn paid kickbacks to Pendergast.

Although there is no evidence that Truman personally profited from the graft, he had no choice but to look the other way at inflated contracts that ultimately came out of taxpayers' pockets. On one occasion, Truman was forced by Pendergast to allow one of his henchmen to just steal $10,000 of county funds (about $120,000 today) and Truman was very upset about it. "Am I an administrator or not?" Truman asked himself. "Or am I just a crook to compromise in order to get the job done?" He was unable to answer his own questions.[9]

Truman's loyalty to the Pendergast machine was rewarded by his appointment as vice president of the Jackson County Democratic Club. Basically, he ran the Pendergast machine outside the Kansas City limits. With machine support, Truman was easily reelected as presiding judge in 1930.

In 1931, Pendergast was an early supporter of Franklin D. Roosevelt for president, helping him roll up a 64 percent majority in Missouri in 1932.[10] That same year, a Pendergast lackey named Guy Park was elected governor. The State Capitol became known as "Uncle Tom's Cabin."[11] This removed the last obstacle to Pendergast's exercise of total power in Kansas City.

His support for Roosevelt got Pendergast control of federal patronage in Missouri, which gave him command of all the millions of dollars flowing from Washington for jobs, welfare, public works, and other New Deal programs. It also made him more desperate to maintain his power and he began using more and more "ruffians" and common criminals to enforce party discipline. Such discipline was essential to Pendergast in order to protect him from the law and maintain the flow of graft and kickbacks that financed his horse race betting habit.

Roosevelt's victory also got Pendergast some protection against federal investigations. In 1935, Roosevelt fired E. Y. Mitchell as assistant secretary of Commerce because Mitchell, a Missouri native, kept trying to get the administration to do something about the massive corruption in Kansas City by the Pendergast machine. But that machine delivered a lot of votes for Roosevelt and so he threw Mitchell over the side after repeated efforts to shut him up failed.[12]

Gambling, narcotics sales, and prostitution were conducted openly and widely throughout Kansas City, which became the "sin city" of the Midwest. (Las Vegas was still just a railroad junction.) What Pendergast didn't control directly, he received payoffs from. He reportedly made an astonishing $20 million annually from gambling alone and another $12 million from prostitution and narcotics.[13] This would be close to $500 million in today's dollars.

But as fast as the money came in, it flowed back out again. Pendergast spent a significant part of every day placing bets on horse races with Eastern bookies who gave him the codename "Sucker" because he lost so consistently. In one month in 1925, he lost $600,000—equal to $7 million today.[14] Pendergast's heavy demand for cash to cover his gambling losses caused him to get reckless, which ultimately led to his downfall.

In 1935, Pendergast agreed to fix a problem for the insurance industry in Missouri for a payoff of $750,000 ($11 million today). A federal investigation eventually turned two of the participants who then implicated Pendergast. As with Chicago gangster Al Capone, the Feds ultimately got Pendergast for tax evasion and he was convicted in 1939, serving a year in jail. More important, he was banned from all political activity thereafter.

Pendergast's conviction was the culmination of several forces that came together to bring him down. The first was evidence of vote-rigging in Kansas City that became too brazen to ignore. For example, a little over 3,000 votes were cast in the second ward in the 1925 mayoral election. But without any significant increase in population, the number of votes cast in that ward rose to over 8,000 in 1930, almost 16,000 in 1934, and more than 21,000 in 1936. In 1944, after the machine had collapsed, about 4,000 votes were cast in the second ward, suggesting that as many as 17,000 phantom votes were cast in just one Kansas City ward at the height of Pendergast's power.

Federal District Court Judge Albert Reeves took notice of this situation and decided to do something about it. No doubt, he was still nursing a grudge for having lost a race for Congress in 1918 in a fixed election. In one precinct, only thirty people actually cast ballots, but Reeves lost that precinct by a vote of 700 to 1.[15] Reeves convinced U.S. Attorney Maurice Milligan to investigate voter fraud in Kansas City. They empanelled a grand jury made up exclusively of citizens from outside Jackson County to avoid leaks and corruption. In one precinct, it found 113 ballots originally marked for the Republican candidate had been changed to the Democrat. "Some of those damned Republicans marked their ballots so hard it was all I could do to rub them out," the perpetrator complained.[16]

Eventually, some 278 people were indicted for voter fraud and 259 were found guilty, 200 of whom served time. The Pendergast machine covered all their fines and even paid them a salary while they were in jail. However, Pendergast and his top lieutenants managed to escape punishment. Frustrated, Reeves and Milligan looked for some other way of bringing them to justice. This led to an examination of Pendergast's finances in hopes of finding evidence of tax evasion. Investigators found that in 1935, Pendergast spent $568,000 ($8.4 million today) more than he reported on his tax return and $614,000 ($9 million today) more in 1936. Based on this evidence, he was charged with evading $265,000 in federal income taxes (close to $4 million today).[17]

To his discredit, Senator Truman tried to derail Milligan's investigation by opposing his reappointment as U.S. Attorney in 1938. Although renominated by Roosevelt and supported by Missouri's other Democratic senator, Bennett "Champ" Clark, who had recommended Milligan's appointment by Roosevelt in the first place, Truman was vehement in his denunciation of Milligan for incompetence, public immorality, and "Hitler-Stalin tactics."[18] *Time Magazine* later called his speech against Milligan "one of the bitterest . . . ever heard on the Senate floor."[19]

It was obvious to everyone that Truman was simply protecting Pendergast's criminality from the only force capable of bringing him down, the federal government. Truman would have been far better off saying nothing, since Milligan's nomination was going to be approved overwhelmingly anyway. It shows that Truman's commitment to Pendergast went far beyond the loyalty of an elected official to a political ally. Truman was deeply and personally devoted to Pendergast and willing to sacrifice his honor and integrity to defend him, even from the most obvious criminal wrongdoing. It was not Truman's finest hour. Historian Robert Ferrell says he made "an egregious error" in opposing Milligan's confirmation.[20]

Pendergast died a broken man on January 26, 1945. Conspicuous among the mourners at his funeral was Vice President Truman, who said Pendergast "has always been my friend and I was his."[21] Just days after becoming president in April, Truman fired Milligan from his post.[22] Attorney General Francis Biddle protested Truman's action, arguing that Milligan had only been doing his job by prosecuting Pendergast. In response, Truman fired Biddle as well.[23]

PRESIDENT TRUMAN

In 1944, Roosevelt knew that he had to replace Henry Wallace as vice president. Wallace was too soft on Communism and a bit of a flake as well— the word "naïve" is almost always used to describe him. Historian Arthur Schlesinger Jr. notes that Wallace was completely bamboozled by Josef Stalin on a trip to the Soviet Union in 1944 and that Wallace was enamored with a crazy Russian mystic named Nicholas Roerich.[24] But another factor was Wallace's outspoken support for civil rights for blacks, which endangered Roosevelt's support in the South. For example, in a 1943 speech, Wallace harshly criticized racism and the denial of voting rights for blacks:

> We cannot fight to crush Nazi brutality abroad and condone race riots at home. Those who fan the fires of racial clashes for the purpose of making political capital here at home are taking the first step toward Naziism. We cannot plead for equality of opportunity for peoples everywhere and overlook the denial of the right to vote for millions of our own people.[25]

Wallace also implicitly condemned Roosevelt's policy of keeping black soldiers in segregated units. It was "not . . . a happy situation," Wallace said.[26] This is a key reason why liberals lobbied hard to keep him on the ticket.[27] And it is why Roosevelt gave serious consideration to naming South Carolinian James F. Byrnes as his running mate in 1944 in order to placate Southern Democrats.[28] When Southerners realized that no one from their region would be acceptable to the Northern labor unions, they quickly got behind Truman, who had agreed to put Byrnes' name into nomination and was viewed as far more compatible with Southern views on race than Wallace.[29] Alabama Governor Chauncey Sparks spoke for many Southerners at the Democratic convention when it was announced that Roosevelt had chosen Truman as his new vice president:

> The South has won a substantial victory. I find him safe on states' rights and the right of the state to control qualifications of its electors. In the matter of race relations, Senator Truman told me he is the son of an unre-constructed rebel mother.[30]

When Truman became president upon Roosevelt's death on April 12, 1945, there was a huge sigh of relief throughout the South, which antici-pated that Truman would be even more sympathetic to its racial concerns than Roosevelt had been. This hope was confirmed when Truman's earli-est appointments went to prominent Southerners: James F. Byrnes as Secretary of State, Tom Clark of Texas as Attorney General, and James J. Vardaman Jr., son of the notorious racist senator from Mississippi, as his Naval aide in the White House. It should be noted that because Truman had no vice president, Byrnes was next in line to the presidency under the rules then prevailing.[31] The *Chicago Defender*, a prominent black newspa-per, said it was "sickened" that a "Dixie race-baiter" would become presi-dent if Truman died.[32]

In truth, the South's hopes regarding Truman had a weak foundation. In Kansas City, the Pendergast machine treated blacks fairly as long as they delivered their votes to the organization on Election Day.[33] And in the Senate, Truman had a good record on civil rights, supporting a permanent Fair Employment Practices Committee (FEPC) and federal laws against lynching and poll taxes.[34] When asked at his first press conference as pres-ident what his policy toward blacks would be, Truman replied simply, "All you need to do is to read the Senate record of one Harry S. Truman."

Consequently, Southern Democrats shouldn't have been as shocked as they were on June 5, 1945, when Truman asked Congress to continue fund-ing for the FEPC, which Southern Democrats had managed to cut out of the budget for the fiscal year beginning on July 1.[35] Said Truman in a letter to the House Rules Committee chairman:

> Discrimination in the matter of employment against properly qualified persons because of their race, creed, or color is not only un-American in nature, but will lead eventually to industrial strife and unrest. It has a ten-dency to create substandard conditions of living for a large part of our

population. The principle and policy of fair employment practice should be established permanently as a part of our national law.

On September 6, 1945, Truman followed through on his request for funding the FEPC by asking that the organization be made permanent. Since it was created by executive order under wartime powers, the committee did not have a line item in the budget or a continuing authorization. Making the FEPC a permanent government agency was a major goal of civil rights leaders, who had been greatly disappointed by Roosevelt's unwillingness to support it. That Truman was willing to go against the Southerners in his party, who had made abolition of the FEPC their number one legislative priority, was an important sign that he would not take a finger-in-the-wind approach to civil rights as Roosevelt had done.

That same month, Truman began to balance some of his Southern appointments with blacks and whites sympathetic to civil rights. A black judge, Irvin Mollison, was named to the Customs Court, making him the highest-ranking black judicial appointment in U.S. history to that point. Howard University professor Ralph Bunche was named to the Anglo-American Caribbean Commission. And Senator Harold Burton of Ohio was named to the Supreme Court. Not only was Burton active in the NAACP and a supporter of the FEPC, but he was a Republican—the only one appointed between 1933 and 1953. Yet he was the most liberal of Truman's four appointees to the Court.[36]

In a January 3, 1946 radio address, Truman again asked for the FEPC to be made permanent and for the Democratic-controlled House Rules Committee to release the legislation for an up-or-down vote. A few days later, Senate supporters of the FEPC brought the bill up for consideration in that body. This led to a full-scale filibuster by Southern Democrats. Senator James O. Eastland, Democrat of Mississippi, questioned Truman's competence to hold office for making the FEPC a legislative priority. Senator Olin Johnston, Democrat of South Carolina, predicted that there would be riots in major cities if the bill was enacted. Senator Theodore Bilbo, Democrat of Mississippi, threatened to speak against the FEPC continuously for sixty days if necessary. The Senate's most skilled parliamentarian, Richard B. Russell of Georgia, successfully used its rules to prevent supporters of the FEPC from invoking cloture and shutting off debate.[37]

Speaking on the Senate floor, Allen Ellender, Democrat of Louisiana, denounced any federal effort to improve black access to public accommodations. This would just raise their expectations and create friction between the races. Ellender said that all states should follow the example of the South, where blacks were loved and well treated but not coddled. Permitting greater equality, as was done in the North, only led to more black crime. One of the senators who rose to challenge Ellender's racist rant was Republican Robert Taft of Ohio, who dryly noted that when the law prevented black people from earning a living honestly, it was hardly surprising that they were often forced to turn to crime.[38]

TRUMAN'S PROBLEM

In order to fully appreciate Truman's efforts, it is important to keep some context in mind. He was an accidental president who had replaced one of the most beloved presidents in American history, and was widely viewed as less than well qualified for the job. Moreover, the early postwar years were among the most tumultuous the nation has ever seen, both domestically and internationally. Inflation was a very serious problem, but people worried that the Great Depression might start right up again where it left off in 1940 without wartime spending to keep it in check. Meanwhile, there were tremendous challenges in the foreign policy arena from Soviet expansionism; the creation of the United Nations, World Bank, and International Monetary Fund; the partition of Germany; occupation of Japan; and Communist insurgency in China, among other things.

In short, Truman could easily have been forgiven if he had chosen to put civil rights on the back burner. His hands were so full of more pressing matters that no one would have faulted him for devoting his time and political capital to them. Undoubtedly, that is what Roosevelt would have done.

Furthermore, it is clear that Truman's civil rights efforts were hurting him politically. He was alienating the Democratic Party's political base in the South at the same time the Republicans were on an upswing. The Democratic majority in the Senate had fallen from 76/16 in 1938 to 57/38 when Truman became president. In the House of Representatives, the Democratic margin had fallen from 334/88 in 1938 to 242/199 in 1946. And everyone knew that the Republicans were going to do well in the 1946 elections, as voter fatigue weighed heavily on the Democrats, who had controlled the House, Senate, and White House continuously since 1933. Indeed, Republicans did so well in 1946 that they took control of both the House and Senate, gaining a 51 to 45 majority in the Senate and a 246 to 188 majority in the House.

Another consequence of the 1946 election was that Southerners in Congress, who completely escaped the Republican rout, emerged even stronger within the Democratic Party. The twenty-two senators from the Confederacy increased their share of all Democratic seats in the Senate from 40 percent to almost 50 percent—twenty-two out of fifty-six before the election to twenty-two out of forty-five afterward. Thus Southerners came to dominate Senate committees through seniority—a domination that lasted well into the 1970s. Moreover, the power of the Southerners was greatest on the Senate's most powerful committees, such as Finance and Appropriations, which had chairmen from Southern states throughout most of the postwar era.[39] Consequently, Southerners could often use their power over things like taxes and spending to block and frustrate congressional and administration initiatives on civil rights.

Truman's unpopularity was a key reason for the breadth of the Democratic defeat in 1946. Even in the South, where the Democratic Party easily maintained its lock on congressional seats, some Democrats were so fearful of being dragged down by Truman in 1948 that they urged him to step aside. Senator J. William Fulbright, Democrat of Arkansas, suggested that Truman appoint a Republican to be secretary of state and then resign, thus making the Republican president.[40] Although the proposal went nowhere, it shows the depth of Democratic frustration with Truman in part due to his dogged pursuit of civil rights for blacks.

TRUMAN PRESSES ON

Despite huge Democratic losses in the congressional elections and the unpopularity of Truman's civil rights agenda among many Democrats, Truman pressed ahead. On December 5, 1946, he issued an executive order establishing a presidential committee on civil rights, which was to study the problem and issue a report. Truman was moved to act in part because of some appalling racist incidents that made a deep impression on him.

In one horrendous case, a black soldier named Isaac Woodward was returning home to New York City on a bus after having been released from the Army in Augusta, Georgia. Only hours after his discharge on February 12, 1946, he was badly beaten by local police in Batesburg, South Carolina, for allegedly causing a disturbance. The beating was so severe that Woodward was permanently blinded and Truman personally asked the Department of Justice to look into it. Although federal charges were brought, the police chief was cleared by an all-white South Carolina jury after a few minutes of deliberation.[41]

In another widely publicized case, two black men and their wives were dragged from their car and murdered by a white mob in Walton County, Georgia, on July 25, 1946. Again, Truman ordered a Justice Department investigation to forestall the likelihood that local authorities would simply look the other way, as was typically done in lynching cases. Unfortunately, despite a major commitment of federal resources to the investigation, the perpetrators were never identified.[42]

Presidential commissions are oftentimes ways of avoiding or putting off tough issues that the president does not want to deal with, but Truman's commission on civil rights was not one of these. On the contrary, he intended the commission, which was heavily stacked with members known to be supportive of civil rights for blacks, to be a meaningful contribution to the problem of race relations and the first step in a legislative program.[43] As Truman told the committee on January 15, 1947:

> I want our Bill of Rights implemented in fact. We have been trying to do this for 150 years. We are making progress, but we are not making progress fast enough. This country could very easily be faced with a situation similar to

the one with which it was faced in 1922. That date was impressed on my mind because in 1922 I was running for my first elective office—county judge of Jackson County—and there was an organization in that county that met on hills and burned crosses and worked behind sheets. There is a tendency in this country for that situation to develop again, unless we do something tangible to prevent it.

While waiting for the civil rights committee to report, Truman spoke to the annual meeting of the NAACP on June 29, 1947—the first president ever to do so. He used the occasion, which took place at the Lincoln Memorial, to make a stirring attack on mob violence, prejudice, and intolerance. "We cannot wait another decade or another generation to remedy these evils," Truman told a crowd of 5,000 and a national radio audience. "We must work, as never before, to cure them now."[44]

On October 29, 1947, Truman received the civil rights committee report. It was the most thorough analysis of the costs of racial discrimination ever produced by the federal government. It made clear that those costs were paid not only by blacks and other minorities, but the nation as a whole. Segregation and poor educational opportunities for them meant that a large portion of the nation's labor force was severely underutilized. Discrimination in housing and at retail businesses reduced sales and profits throughout the economy. The result was slower economic growth.[45]

Furthermore, the mistreatment of America's black citizens hampered the nation's efforts to contain Communism. Race riots and lynchings were heavily publicized by Communist propaganda throughout the world, making it more difficult for American diplomats to explain why people of color in Africa, Asia, and Latin America should resist Communist entreaties. How could America claim to represent the side of freedom, the committee asked, when it was denied to so many of its own citizens?[46]

In short, civil rights was not just a moral issue, but a practical one with important implications for blacks and whites, the economy, and American foreign policy.[47] This was a very powerful message, backed up with a number of specific recommendations that really spelled out a complete civil rights agenda for the first time. In 1972, former Supreme Court Justice Tom Clark, Truman's first Attorney General, called the report "a blueprint of most everything that's been done in the area of civil rights since that time."[48] Among the committee's recommendations were:

- Creation of a Civil Rights Division in the Department of Justice and a special unit within the Federal Bureau of Investigation to pursue racial crimes.
- Establishment of a permanent Civil Rights Commission.
- Enactment of a federal antilynching law and abolition of poll taxes.
- Legislation to ensure fair employment practices and voting rights, and to prohibit discrimination in education, housing, transportation, and health services.

On February 2, 1948, Truman sent a special message to Congress asking for legislation to implement the civil rights committee report. But he didn't limit himself only to actions that the federal government could take; he made clear that all levels of government needed to act. This was a direct challenge to the states of the South and their Democratic-controlled governments. Said Truman:

> The protection of civil rights is the duty of every government which derives its powers from the consent of the people. This is equally true of local, state, and national governments. There is much that the states can and should do at this time to extend their protection of civil rights. Wherever the law enforcement measures of state and local governments are inadequate to discharge this primary function of government, these measures should be strengthened and improved.

> The federal government has a clear duty to see that constitutional guarantees of individual liberties and of equal protection under the laws are not denied or abridged anywhere in our Union. That duty is shared by all three branches of the government, but it can be fulfilled only if the Congress enacts modern, comprehensive civil rights laws, adequate to the needs of the day, and demonstrating our continuing faith in the free way of life.

Not surprisingly, the reaction to Truman's program throughout the South was almost universally negative.[49] Senator Ellender of Louisiana promised a filibuster if it came up for a vote, and retiring Senator Lee "Pappy" O'Daniel, Democrat of Texas, called it "un-American."[50] Texas Congressman Lyndon Baines Johnson, who was running for O'Daniel's seat in 1948, called Truman's civil rights program "a farce and a sham—an effort to set up a police state in the guise of liberty."[51]

Truman may have been calculating that Southern opposition was a matter of no political importance. On November 19, 1947, he had received a memorandum from his close adviser Clark Clifford, which argued that the South was so totally in the Democratic camp that Truman could safely look the other way at its concerns. Said Clifford:

> It is inconceivable that any policies initiated by the Truman Administration no matter how "liberal" could so alienate the South in the next year that it would revolt. As always, the South can be considered safely Democratic. And in formulating national policy, it can be safely ignored.

The only reason to worry about Southern Democrats, Clifford said, was because of their power in Congress. But with Republicans now in control, that factor was less relevant. Clifford also argued that the black vote was in play and that the putative Republican presidential nominee in 1948, New York Governor Thomas E. Dewey, had shown strength in the black community and was working hard to get its votes.[52] Finally, Clifford saw the greatest political threat to Truman coming from the political left; he expected former Vice President Henry A. Wallace to run a third party campaign in 1948 with strong support from many elements of the civil rights coalition. Indeed, Wallace announced his campaign on December 29, 1947, just as Clifford predicted, and attracted endorsements from several prominent black leaders, including Paul Robeson and W. E. B. DuBois.

Clifford also argued that it was politically beneficial for Truman to support a civil rights program. Clifford theorized that blacks now held the balance of power in several pivotal states: New York, Illinois, Pennsylvania, Ohio, and Michigan. Therefore, it would be "sound strategy" to go as far as possible in pressing measures to protect minority rights. "This course of action would obviously cause difficulty with our Southern friends, but that is the lesser of two evils," Clifford concluded.[53]

But if Truman was pushing his civil rights program purely for political reasons, there was no evidence that the strategy was working. An April 1948 poll showed only 6 percent of Americans supported it. Another poll showed 57 percent of white Southerners disapproving of Truman's performance in office. There was so little support for the civil rights program in Congress that the White House was unable to get the Senate's Democratic leader, Alben Barkley of Kentucky, to even introduce a bill incorporating Truman's recommendations—something normally done as a routine matter.[54]

DIXIECRATS

As soon as Truman's civil rights message was delivered there was immediate talk throughout the South about a third party or even—horror of horrors—voting Republican, at least for president. Said Congressman Mendel Rivers, Democrat of South Carolina, "One of these days the so-called leaders are going to find that the so-called Solid South is not as solid as some of the heads of our so-called leaders."[55] Senator Eastland of Mississippi, later chairman of the Senate Judiciary Committee, suggested that Southern states could withhold their Electoral College votes for Truman, thereby throwing the election into the House of Representatives, where anything could happen.[56] Southern Democrats were further agitated when Republican leaders quickly moved legislation to implement Truman's civil rights proposals, thus assuring a legislative showdown in the Senate.[57]

The first legislative action on civil rights was related to the draft. On March 17, Truman asked Congress to reinstate conscription, which had expired the previous year. With the prospect of many new black servicemen entering the armed forces, the question of segregation in the military came to a head.[58] Senator Russell offered an amendment to the legislation that would maintain the historical segregation of black servicemen in separate units.[59] But it was defeated and the final bill said nothing on the subject of race. This left the matter of segregation in the armed forces entirely in Truman's hands.

In the meantime, Truman had to deal with the Democratic Party's 1948 platform, which was being drafted in Philadelphia, and contend with a "Dump-Truman" movement planned for the convention. He had hoped to finesse the race issue in the platform by supporting the same language that had been in the Democratic Party's 1944 platform. That language, endorsed by Roosevelt and acceptable to the South, said, "We believe that racial and religious minorities have the right to live, develop and vote equally with all citizens and share the rights that are guaranteed by our Constitution."

But liberal delegates to the Democratic convention in July insisted on a stronger statement. Led by Minneapolis Mayor Hubert Humphrey, they noted that the Republicans had already adopted a more forceful plank at their convention in June, which said, "This right of equal opportunity to work and to advance in life should never be limited in any individual because of race, religion, color, or country or origin. We favor the enactment and just enforcement of such Federal legislation as may be necessary to maintain this right at all times in every part of this Republic."

After a bruising fight, the Democratic convention committed the party to "eradicate all racial, religious and economic discrimination." Furthermore, all minorities "must have the right to live, the right to work, the right to vote, [and] the full and equal protection of the laws, on a basis of equality with all citizens." The platform called upon Congress to support equal employment opportunity for all blacks and equal treatment for those serving in defense of the nation.[60]

Although it had not been the approach Truman favored, this was not because he disagreed with its sentiment. Rather, his support for a weaker plank was just a last-ditch effort to avoid a split with the Southern Democrats. But when it became clear that such a split was unavoidable, Truman embraced the civil rights plank wholeheartedly, turning it against the Republicans, who had failed to act in Congress. As he told the convention in his acceptance speech on July 15:

> Everybody knows that I recommended to the Congress the civil rights program. I did that because I believed it to be my duty under the Constitution. Some of the members of my own party disagree violently on this matter. But they stand up and do it openly! People can tell where they stand. But the Republicans all professed to be for these measures. But Congress failed to act.

In protest, many Southern Democrats walked out and regrouped at a rump convention in Birmingham, Alabama, a few days later. They nominated Democratic Governors Strom Thurmond of South Carolina and Fielding Wright of Mississippi as candidates for president and vice president, respectively, on the newly formed States' Rights Democratic Party ticket. Its platform, adopted a month later in Oklahoma City, stood in sharp contrast to both the Republican and Democratic platforms on race.[61]

Unambiguously, it said:

> We stand for the segregation of the races and the racial integrity of each race. . . . We oppose the elimination of segregation, the repeal of misce-genation statutes, the control of private employment by federal bureau-crats called for by the misnamed civil rights program. . . . We oppose and condemn the action of the Democratic convention in sponsoring a civil rights program calling for the elimination of segregation, social equality by federal fiat, regulations of private employment practices, voting, and local law enforcement.

With prospects for being on fifteen Southern state ballots, the Dixiecrats appeared to have a very real chance of denying Truman's reelection, espe-cially with Wallace running to his left at the same time.[62] Truman knew that every vote for Thurmond or Wallace came out of his total and effec-tively became a vote for Dewey. And given Truman's weak poll numbers—he had an approval/disapproval ratio of 39 percent to 46 percent in June 1948—and a strong Republican challenger, there was every reason to think that Truman would be a dead duck in November. Truman himself had no illusions about what he had done. As he wrote in his memoirs:

> I did not discount the handicap which the loss of the "Solid South" pre-sented as far as my chances of winning the election were concerned. I knew that it might mean the difference between victory and defeat in November. I knew, too, that if I deserted the civil-liberties plank of the Democratic Party platform I could heal the breach, but I have never traded principles for votes, and I did not intend to start the practice in 1948 regardless of how it might affect the election.[63]

Just three days after the Dixiecrat convention, Truman made a show of publicly presenting an award to General Benjamin O. Davis, the first black soldier to achieve the rank of general in the U.S. Army. Davis, Truman said, represented "all the best in a soldier of the highest type." Then, on July 26, 1948, Truman issued Executive Order 9981, establishing a presidential committee on equality of treatment and opportunity in the armed services, which set in motion the process of full integration of the Army, Navy, and newly created Air Force.[64] Said the order:

> Whereas it is essential that there be maintained in the armed services of the United States the highest standards of democracy, with equality of treatment and opportunity for all those who serve in our country's defense. . . . It is hereby declared to be the policy of the President that there shall be equality of treatment and opportunity for all persons in the armed services without regard to race, color, religion or national origin. This policy shall be put into effect as rapidly as possible, having due

regard to the time required to effectuate any necessary changes without impairing efficiency or morale.

Simultaneously, Truman signed Executive Order 9980, establishing a fair employment practices board within the Civil Service Commission to guarantee the rights of African Americans to jobs and equal treatment in the federal government.[65] In effect, Truman was finally reversing the policies put in place by Woodrow Wilson and forcing the federal government to undo all the trappings of segregation, including separate restrooms and drinking fountains, which were pervasive throughout the bureaucracy. Historian Michael Gardner explains that this order was no mere window-dressing, but a profoundly important change in policy:

> For African Americans seeking to gain employment in the volatile U.S. marketplace in 1948, President Truman's issuance of Executive Order 9980 represented tangible progress, not mere political rhetoric, for black Americans seeking federal employment. Executive Order 9980 not only mandated the immediate elimination of race-based discrimination in the federal bureaucracy but also established the specific procedures for blacks to follow to gain fair access to jobs long denied them.[66]

The following day, July 27, Truman went before a joint session of Congress to demand action on his legislative program, including civil rights. In the atmosphere of the time, having just come out of a difficult fight on civil rights at the Democratic convention, with the Dixiecrats doing everything they could to keep him from being reelected, Truman's actions were like throwing gasoline on a fire that was already blazing. It was a bold and gutsy response to the white supremacist challenge.

REELECTION

In fairness to the Republicans, they really didn't have the votes to pass Truman's civil rights program over a Southern Democratic filibuster, which Truman knew perfectly well. This fact was demonstrated almost immediately when the Senate took up an anti-poll tax bill that had previously passed the Republican House by a vote of 290 to 112. Republican leaders tried to invoke cloture against the inevitable filibuster on August 2, but were unable to do so because of parliamentary tactics by the leading Democratic opponent of the legislation, Senator Russell of Georgia, whose knowledge of the Senate's rules was legendary. Reluctantly, they had no choice but to pull the bill from the floor.[67] This allowed Truman to berate the "do-nothing" Congress and make it the theme of his reelection campaign.

Foolishly, Dewey ignored the black vote, even though he had a good record on civil rights, and instead campaigned heavily in the South.[68] This allowed Truman to turn his civil rights program, which was clearly a political liability when it was proposed, into a political asset. He calculated that the black vote might mean the margin of victory in some key states and strove to connect with black voters in the last days of the campaign by giving a speech in Harlem, becoming the first president ever to do so. On October 29, Truman reminded a crowd of 65,000 that he had taken the first tangible steps toward black equality since Reconstruction by issuing executive orders effectively integrating the military and the civil service. As historian Robert Garson explains, Truman's Harlem speech marked an important turning point in American political history:

> The Harlem speech was perhaps the most outstanding symbol of the profound change in the geographic and social balance within the Democratic Party. For the first time, a Democratic candidate for the presidency had gone into the black ghettos to solicit votes.[69]

Subsequently, political analysts concluded that the black vote put Truman over the top in California, Illinois, and Ohio. He carried these three states by less than 60,000 total votes. Had they gone for Dewey, the election results would have been reversed. In each state, Truman's strong showing in black precincts provided the margin of victory.[70] He lost four states in the South to Strom Thurmond: Alabama, Louisiana, Mississippi, and South Carolina.[71] But had Dewey gotten all of Thurmond's votes, it would not have changed the outcome of the election.

The election results dramatically altered the politics within the Democratic Party forever. As Appendix I indicates, between 1930 and 1950, there was a massive increase in the percentage of blacks in the population in states like California, Illinois, Michigan, and New York, and an even greater decline in the black population of every Southern state. Whether Truman knew this or simply felt it in his gut, his calculation proved to be exactly correct and Dewey's exactly wrong. In the end, the 1948 election was a profound step forward for the black electorate and a step backward for the white supremacists. Democrats now knew that they could win without the South and that the black vote in the North was potent enough to carry states where Republicans had previously won.

While it is easy enough to see the critical importance of the black vote with the benefit of hindsight, it was not at all apparent beforehand. The safe course for Truman would have been to do just enough on civil rights to keep blacks from open revolt, but not so much that it would offend the Southern base of the Democratic Party. That is what Franklin Roosevelt did so successfully in four consecutive elections, and Truman's advisors knew it. As Clark Clifford wrote in his memoirs, Roosevelt never used his prestige and power to redress racial inequality beyond establishing a *temporary* FEPC, he sidestepped the problem of segregation in the federal government and armed forces, and he never pressed Congress for an antilynching bill.

But, said Clifford, FDR was a master of symbolism and together with his wife Eleanor, he "created an impression of action and commitment, while avoiding an open break with the Southerners in Congress." That is why he won every Southern state in every election.[72]

It would have been very easy for Truman to follow in Roosevelt's footsteps. That he chose a different path was extremely risky, something that tends to be forgotten because he ended up winning. But at the time, almost every political analyst thought Truman had chosen the wrong path, politically.[73] When the Southerners bolted in July, Senator Claude Pepper, Democrat of Florida, saw a replay of 1860, in which John Breckinridge's third-party effort threw the election to Abraham Lincoln, who was elected with less than 40 percent of the popular vote.[74]

Truman was not unaware of the extreme risk in his political strategy. But a key factor motivating him was the simple belief that giving equal rights to America's black citizens was the right thing to do, regardless of the political consequences. Truman explained his philosophy most clearly in an August 18, 1948, private letter to an old friend from the war named Ernie Roberts:

> I am not asking for social equality, because no such thing exists, but I am asking for equality of opportunity for all human beings and, as long as I stay here, I am going to continue that fight. When the mob gangs can take four people out and shoot them in the back, and everybody in the country is acquainted with who did the shooting and nothing is done about it, that country is in a pretty bad fix from a law enforcement standpoint. When a mayor and a city marshal can take a Negro sergeant off a bus in South Carolina, beat him up and put out one of his eyes, and nothing is done about it by state authorities, something is radically wrong with the system.[75]

After the election, Truman was pleased to see Democrats back in control of both the House and Senate. In the former, they now had a majority of 263 to 171, and enjoyed a margin of 54 to 42 in the latter. Had the lack of progress on his civil rights program only been a matter of Republican control of Congress, Truman should have had clear sailing after 1948. But in fact, determined resistance from Southern Democrats killed every item on his agenda for the balance of his presidency.[76] Even changes in Senate rules that weakened the filibuster in 1949 did little good.[77] Civil rights leaders had to be content with general economic measures, such as an increase in the minimum wage, and Truman's appointment of William H. Hastie as the first black judge on a federal appeals court.

Although his legislative agenda stalled in Congress, Truman continued to move aggressively in areas where he could use his executive authority to advance civil rights. For example, in December 1948, the Civil Aeronautics Administration banned discrimination at Washington's National Airport, where blacks had been excluded from the terrace dining room and forced to use a basement cafeteria.[78] In 1949, the Federal Housing Administration and the Veterans Administration announced that they would no longer guarantee mortgages for properties with racially restrictive covenants, despite strong objections from the real estate industry.[79]

Truman's Justice Department was very active in filing court cases and friend-of-the-court briefs on civil rights issues, something it had never done before. It is now forgotten how cautious the department historically had been in this area and how important its views were to the Supreme Court. The Justice Department's actions were a critical signal to the Court that it could move swiftly and boldly on civil rights, which made it easier for it to plow new legal ground in cases such as *Brown v. Board of Education*. Without strong support for such cases throughout the appeals process by the Justice Department, which told the Court that it would have the full support of the administration should it rule in its favor, the Court may have been much more reluctant to make broad, decisive rulings in civil rights cases, and might have settled for more narrowly focused rulings that would not have rocked the boat.[80]

ASSESSMENT

Nevertheless, Truman's record on civil rights tends to be derided by historians.[81] A typical view is that of Stanford University's Barton Bernstein. "Truman was never as bold as Negro leaders or staunch proponents of civil rights desired," he writes. "A decade had passed in the assault upon discrimination, but the Democratic administration remained a cautious friend of civil rights."[82]

A similar view is expressed by William C. Berman of the University of Toronto. Truman, he says, "raised the art of civil rights advocacy to new heights while shying away from anything that resembled a substantive program."[83] University of New Hampshire historian Harvard Sitkoff calls Truman a "reluctant champion" of civil rights who had to be pressured into supporting the issue.[84]

I think this view is unfair. Those who criticize Truman's civil rights record are underestimating the political difficulties of doing more at that point in time. Television was in its infancy and there were no images of Bull Connor beating peaceful civil rights demonstrators on the nightly news to stir people to action. The Supreme Court had not yet overturned *Plessy v. Ferguson*, and separate-but-equal was still the law of the land—the landmark *Brown* case wouldn't be decided until 1954. And it was not until 1955 that the Montgomery bus boycott began, marking the formal start of the modern civil rights movement.

Critics seem to think that Truman could have done the kinds of things Lyndon Johnson did in the 1960s. But the political and societal circumstances were vastly different by then. In the 1940s, the nation was not yet ready for even the limited actions Truman took.[85] He had to lead in this area against determined political resistance. That is why Franklin Roosevelt did almost nothing in the area of civil rights despite being in a far stronger political position than Truman ever was.

Moreover, looking carefully at the timing of Truman's civil rights statements and actions, it is clear that they were detrimental to his political fortunes. Truman knew he was goading Southern Democrats into a third-party run that very likely would doom him in the presidential election, yet he pressed ahead anyway. Although the black vote ultimately provided him with his margin of victory, it cannot be overemphasized that this was not expected at the time Truman decided to make civil rights a major issue. Indeed, there was every reason to think he was destroying his reelection chances by acting as he did. It's hard to find any other explanation for Truman's behavior except that he thought it was the right thing to do and needed to be done. There is certainly nothing in his background or history that would have compelled him to act as he did.

Harry Truman is an unsung hero of the civil rights movement. While the actual results of his actions were modest, the political climate was highly unfavorable to *any* action on civil rights, owing to the still potent power of Southern Democrats in Congress. I agree with the historian who said, "President Truman helped immensely in establishing integration as a moral principle. He thus reversed the long accepted process of passively accepting segregation and discrimination."[86]

Truman took a vastly greater political risk in doing what he did than subsequent presidents, who benefited from Supreme Court cases and the emergence of a broad multiracial civil rights movement with articulate leaders such as Dr. Martin Luther King Jr. at its head. These factors plowed the ground for future civil rights initiatives and made it far easier to be more proactive.[87] But Truman basically did what he did on his own, with little support or encouragement. Consequently, I believe his actions were far more courageous and significant than many historians appreciate.

9

DEMOCRATS JUMP ON
THE CIVIL RIGHTS
BANDWAGON

In the 1950s, the United States finally began to fundamentally change its attitude toward black people and confront the Jim Crow culture of the South. By the 1960s, it was clear, at least at the national level, that overt racial discrimination would no longer be tolerated. Every postwar administration worked to fulfill the promise of Reconstruction, which had fallen victim to assault from Southern Democrats and a Supreme Court that, until 1954, would permit only token federal efforts to enforce equal rights for all Americans.

Most histories, however, give credit only to Democratic administrations for the advancement of civil rights. Dwight Eisenhower is conventionally portrayed as having done nothing for blacks during his eight years, figuratively sitting on his hands and kowtowing to the South. In fact, he did a lot; passing the first civil rights bill since Reconstruction in 1957 and another in 1960, despite determined opposition from Southern Democrats. Eisenhower committed federal troops to enforce school desegregation in Little Rock and made key pro-civil rights appointments to the Supreme Court. In many ways, his actions laid the essential foundation for the more aggressive civil rights actions that came later.

Just as Eisenhower receives insufficient credit for his civil rights efforts, John F. Kennedy receives far more than he deserves. As a U.S. senator, he was never a strong supporter of civil rights and often deferred to the Southern caucus, whose support he hoped to have in a race for the White House. As president, Kennedy did nothing substantive on civil rights, not even fulfilling his own campaign promise to issue executive orders prohibiting discrimination in housing and jobs immediately upon taking office. What little he did in the area of civil rights was either totally symbolic or done under extreme political pressure.

Lyndon Johnson deserves credit for finally repudiating both his own segregationist past and the Democratic Party's. But his actions were less courageous than they appear. Johnson clearly saw the political dynamics moving toward civil rights and had every reason to believe that he would be rewarded at the polls in 1964, which he was. In short, what Johnson did in the area of civil rights was motivated as much by what was right for him politically as what was right for the country.

DWIGHT D. EISENHOWER AND CIVIL RIGHTS

The important work that Harry Truman did was crucial in advancing a federal civil rights program for the first time since 1875. But when he left office in 1953, there was an enormous amount of work left undone. Although Truman had taken some important administrative actions and proven the political importance of the black vote, he got no civil rights legislation enacted to replace that which had been nullified by the Supreme Court and repealed by Democrats in the late nineteenth century.

Eisenhower had to deal with both the rising expectations and increasing impatience of blacks, which at the same time hardened the opposition of white supremacists in the South. And since he was a Republican, the first in the White House in twenty years, Southern Democrats had much more freedom to oppose presidential civil rights initiatives. No longer subject to the pressure of party loyalty to keep them somewhat in line, they could now fight presidential civil rights initiatives more freely and aggressively.

Eisenhower immediately came in for a two-pronged attack on civil rights. On the one hand, he was faulted for not immediately doing all of the things that Franklin Roosevelt and Truman had put off or failed to act upon. At the same time, white supremacists ratcheted up their opposition to the policies put in place by those administrations that Eisenhower inherited. Preoccupied with ending the Korean War and with pressing domestic problems, such as inflation and a large budget deficit, Eisenhower had little choice except to be cautious on civil rights. He also suffered from a preference for working behind the scenes and letting his actions speak for themselves.

This has given Eisenhower a reputation among historians and journalists of basically doing nothing for blacks during his entire presidency. *Washington Post* columnist Richard Cohen probably expressed the conventional wisdom when he said, "The plain fact is that Eisenhower was an indifferent, lethargic president when it came to civil rights."[1] In reality, Eisenhower's accomplishments on civil rights made it much easier for his successors to take more celebrated actions.

Eisenhower signaled throughout the 1952 campaign that he would not turn back the clock on civil rights if elected. The Republican platform that year said, "We condemn bigots who inject class, racial and religious prejudice into public and political matters." It endorsed legislation to outlaw lynching, poll taxes, and segregation in the District of Columbia. Just days after becoming president, Eisenhower told Congress:

> Our civil and social rights form a central part of the heritage we are striving to defend on all fronts and with all our strength. I believe with all my heart that our vigilant guarding of these rights is a sacred obligation binding upon every citizen. To be true to one's own freedom is, in essence, to honor and respect the freedom of all others. A cardinal ideal in this heritage we cherish is the equality of rights of all citizens of every race and color and creed. We know that discrimination against minorities persists despite our allegiance to this ideal. Such discrimination—confined to no one section of the Nation—is but the outward testimony to the persistence of distrust and of fear in the hearts of men.[2]

Eisenhower pledged to use all the power of the White House to end segregation in Washington and throughout the federal government, which had been in place since Woodrow Wilson imposed it in 1913. Among Eisenhower's first actions was an order ending discrimination in schools run by the federal government on military posts. Democratic Governor Herman Talmadge of Georgia, son of Governor Eugene Talmadge, reacted sharply to this action. "Nonsegregation won't work in the South," he said. "The white people don't want it and the Negroes don't either."[3]

In February 1953, Eisenhower set up a group that would advise him on administrative actions he could take to bring about desegregation. The following month, his Justice Department filed a friend of the court brief in a pending lawsuit that would end segregation in Washington, D.C., restaurants. In May, Eisenhower set up a Committee on Government Contracts, chaired by Vice President Richard Nixon, to fight discrimination in federal contracting.[4] Eisenhower also appointed several blacks to senior administration positions, including E. Frederic Morrow, the first black person to serve on the executive staff of the White House. He would have appointed more except that J. Edgar Hoover's FBI repeatedly blocked them on security grounds.[5]

IKE APPOINTS PROGRESSIVES TO THE SUPREME COURT

The most important thing Eisenhower did on civil rights in his first year, however, was appoint California Governor Earl Warren as Chief Justice of the Supreme Court. Warren had provided him with crucial support for the Republican presidential nomination in 1952. In return, Warren demanded to fill the first available Supreme Court vacancy, which opened up on September 8, 1953, when Chief Justice Fred Vinson died.[6] But Eisenhower wouldn't have been the first president to abrogate such a deal, and Warren wouldn't have been able to do much about it. Ultimately, it was Eisenhower's decision and he made it knowing full well that Warren had liberal views on civil rights.[7] In the words of legal scholar Michael Kahn:

> There can be no question whatsoever that when Eisenhower and [Attorney General Herbert] Brownell decided to make Earl Warren Chief Justice of the United States, they fully recognized the fact that they were placing the Court in the hands of a person whose record on civil rights was clearly liberal and whose stewardship on the Court would undoubtedly be progressive.[8]

As proof of this proposition, Kahn notes that none of Eisenhower's Supreme Court appointees was from the South and all were known to have progressive views on race. John Harlan was from New York, William Brennan from New Jersey, Charles Whittaker from Missouri, and Potter Stewart from Ohio. Brennan was a liberal Democrat, and Harlan's grandfather, who was also a Supreme Court justice, had authored the lone dissent in *Plessy v. Ferguson*, which *Brown v. Board of Education* overturned in 1954.[9]

Warren's appointment was important because the *Brown* case was looming—indeed, Eisenhower gave him a recess appointment to the Court on October 5, 1953, to ensure that he would be available to hear new arguments scheduled for the case in December.[10] *Brown* had been working its way through the appeals process for years and the Truman Justice Department had argued the case just before Eisenhower took office. Knowing what a big case it was, the Supreme Court also requested that the Eisenhower Justice Department submit its opinion as well. It is possible that the Court would not have ruled so broadly or decisively if it didn't think the administration would back it up. In that event, the Court might have made a more narrow, technical ruling and avoided a sweeping reversal of *Plessy*, which the Court had reaffirmed 27 years earlier in *Gong Lum v. Rice.*[11]

Eisenhower's Justice Department was unequivocal in urging the Court to declare unconstitutional school segregation based on race. Said Assistant Attorney General J. Lee Rankin in oral arguments before the justices, "It is the position of the Department of Justice that the Fourteenth Amendment does not permit any discrimination based on race or color." When Justice William O. Douglas asked whether he thought the Court had any latitude in this area, Rankin replied, "No. The Court can find only one answer. . . . When they [the defendants] stand before this court and say that the only reason for segregation is color, the court must say that the Fourteenth Amendment does not permit this to happen."[12]

Although Warren joined the Court late in the process of deciding *Brown*, his role was important in making the decision unanimous.[13] This was vital in leaving no doubt about the Court's view. A divided opinion—even 8 to 1—would not have had the same impact, and opponents may have dragged their feet in implementing school desegregation even more than they did in hopes of rearguing the case before a different set of justices.

By the end of 1954, Eisenhower was being praised by the NAACP for "strong and constructive" civil rights leadership.[14] In his 1955 State of the Union Address, Eisenhower denounced "demeaning practices based on race or color." The following year, he asked Congress to establish a Civil Rights Commission, create a Civil Rights Division within the Justice Department, increase the federal government's ability to use civil actions as well as criminal procedures to pursue civil rights cases, and give it broader statutory authority to protect voting rights. Said Eisenhower in his 1956 State of the Union Address on January 5, "It is disturbing that in some localities allegations persist that Negro citizens are being deprived of their right to vote and are likewise being subjected to unwarranted economic pressure."

Southern Democrats universally denounced Eisenhower's initiatives.[15] In Congress, a group of them issued a manifesto on March 12, 1956, demanding a reversal of the *Brown* decision and pledging "all lawful means" to "prevent the use of force in its implementation."[16] At a press conference two days later, Eisenhower responded that school desegregation was now the law of the land and he was sworn to uphold the Constitution. "I can never abandon or refuse to carry out my own duty," he said. The Republican Party's platform that year declared, "The Republican Party accepts the decision of the U.S. Supreme Court that racial discrimination in publicly supported schools must be progressively eliminated." By contrast, the Democratic platform made a special point of saying that the party rejected all proposals for the use of force to implement desegregation decisions by the courts.

Sensing that the black vote was "in play" for the first time in many years, both Eisenhower and Vice President Richard Nixon campaigned hard for it. Nixon went to Harlem and gave a strong pro-civil rights speech, saying, "America can't afford the cost of discrimination."[17] The Republican ticket was even endorsed by Democratic Congressman Adam Clayton Powell of New York, the most prominent black politician in the country, who said that he believed Eisenhower would do more for blacks than Democrat Adlai Stevenson.[18] In November, Eisenhower was easily reelected in large part because he raised his share of the black vote from 24 percent in 1952 to 39 percent in 1956.

EISENHOWER GETS FIRST CIVIL RIGHTS LAW SINCE RECONSTRUCTION

In his January 10, 1957, State of the Union Address, Eisenhower renewed his request for civil rights legislation, which had passed the House but died in the Senate in the previous Congress due to Southern Democratic delaying tactics. He strongly urged Republicans in Congress to do all they could to move the legislation quickly so that Southern Democrats couldn't run out the clock again.[19]

Eisenhower was right to be concerned. Congressman Howard Smith, Democrat of Virginia, immediately bottled up the civil rights bill in the House Rules Committee, which he chaired.[20] In the House, bills normally can't be brought up for a vote unless they have a "rule," which spells out the terms of debate, what amendments will be allowed, and so on.[21] If the Rules Committee fails to act, the only way of getting a bill onto the floor for a vote is if a majority of House members sign a discharge petition. It was only the likelihood that such a petition would be successful that got Smith to finally release the civil rights bill for a vote in June—but only after several days of hearings from opponents of the legislation.[22] Even afterward, he and a group of one hundred Southern Democrats used every parliamentary trick in the book to gut the bill, unsuccessfully.[23] Eventually, the civil rights bill came to a final vote and passed easily by a 286 to 126 margin. Virtually all of the "nay" votes were cast by Democrats.[24]

Everyone knew that the critical fight on the civil rights bill would be in the Senate, long the graveyard for all such initiatives, owing to the filibuster and parliamentary procedures that greatly strengthen the hand of the minority and weaken the majority. In that body, the key figure was Majority Leader Lyndon Johnson, who represented the Confederate state of Texas and had been installed in his position by Southern Democrats precisely in order to block civil rights legislation. Until the late 1950s, Johnson's record of opposition to all civil rights initiatives was spotless.[25] But he was ambitious and wanted to be president, so his political calculation in 1957 was based not just on what was good for his state or even his position in the Senate, but on his view of what would give him the best path to the White House.

After dragging his feet on the civil rights bill throughout much of 1957, Johnson finally came to the conclusion that the tide had turned in favor of civil rights and he needed to be on the right side of the issue if he hoped to become president. As he told a friend at that time, "You can either get out in front and try to give some guidance, or you can continue to fight upstream, and be overwhelmed or be miserable."[26] Historian Robert Dallek explains Johnson's change of heart:

> It was clear to Lyndon that pressure from Southern blacks made change in the region inevitable. Renewed pressure for legislation that would implement the *Brown* decision on school desegregation and enforce black voting rights made these matters ripe for action in Congress. With the House likely to pass a bill, as it did in 1956, the Senate would be the focus of attention. If he could lead a major civil rights bill through the Senate, it would be the first federal legislative advance in this field in eighty-two

years. Such an achievement would have multiple benefits; not the least of which would be a boon to his presidential ambitions. A civil rights bill credited to Johnson would help transform him from a Southern or regional leader into a national spokesman.[27]

At the same time, the Senate's master tactician and principal opponent of the civil rights bill, Democrat Richard B. Russell of Georgia, saw the same handwriting on the wall but came to a different conclusion. He realized that the support was no longer there for an old-fashioned Southern Democrat filibuster, such as the one that killed the antilynching bill in 1938. There just weren't enough senators left who could be depended upon to make it work.[28] So Russell adopted a different strategy this time of trying to amend the civil rights bill so as to minimize its impact.[29] Behind the scenes, Johnson went along with Russell's strategy of not killing the civil rights bill, but trying to neuter it as much as possible. As Johnson explained:

> These Negroes, they're getting pretty uppity these days and that's a problem for us since they've got something now they never had before, the political pull to back up their uppityness. Now we've got to do something about this, we've got to give them a little something, just enough to quiet them down, not enough to make a difference. For if we don't move at all, then their allies will line up against us and there'll be no way of stopping them, we'll lose the filibuster and there'll be no way of putting a brake on all sorts of wild legislation. It'll be Reconstruction all over again.[30]

Southern Democrats directed their fire primarily at section three of the Eisenhower civil rights bill, which would have allowed the Justice Department to seek court injunctions against civil rights violations. Although a seemingly minor provision, the Southerners fought it tooth and nail as the reestablishment of Reconstruction-era force measures. By concentrating their efforts on one section, rather than the whole bill, they were successful in having it deleted.

The Southern Democrats were then keen on adding an amendment to the legislation guaranteeing that those accused of violating its provisions would receive a jury trial. They felt that this would effectively gut the bill since no Southern jury would ever return a guilty verdict for violating a federal civil rights law. When the Southern Democrats were successful in both efforts, they allowed the bill to pass, feeling that it could do little real harm to white supremacy. In the words of legal scholar Bernard Schwartz, "From the Southern point of view, the measure finally passed was so innocuous that . . . it could be considered more of a Southern victory than anything else."[31]

Eisenhower was disappointed at not being able to produce a better piece of legislation. "I wanted a much stronger civil rights bill in '57 than

I could get," he later lamented. "But the Democrats . . . wouldn't let me have it."[32]

Liberals criticized Eisenhower for getting such a modest bill at the end of the day.[33] But Johnson argued that it was historically important because it was the first civil rights bill to pass Congress since 1875. "Once you break virginity," he said, "it'll be easier next time."[34] Moreover, once there was a civil rights law on the books, it would be much simpler to pass strengthening amendments in the future than a whole new bill. In short, the Civil Rights Act of 1957 was a huge political victory for civil rights that went far beyond its specific provisions.[35] As the *New York Times* concluded:

> In the context of history—in the context of the simple fact that nothing substantial whatever had been done before in this field in the eight decades and more since Reconstruction—this was a very long step indeed. And, most important of all and perhaps most useful of all, it has demonstrated that the Senate can act on this subject; that the impenetrable Southern barrier of the past is broken for good, and that a decent accommodation of Southern and Northern views is not only possible but has in fact actually arrived.
>
> This, at least, is the beginning of a curative process in an old national wound; *it is incomparably the most significant domestic action of any Congress in this century*, whether or not this action went so far as ideally it should have gone.[36]

LITTLE ROCK AND IKE'S SECOND CIVIL RIGHTS BILL

Almost immediately after Congress concluded action on the civil rights bill, Eisenhower was faced with a racial crisis in Little Rock, Arkansas. Local white supremacists had decided to protest the integration of Central High School on September 3, 1957, when the school's first black students were set to attend. Democratic Governor Orval Faubus used the threat of violence as an excuse to cancel the integration and called out the National Guard to occupy the school grounds. A federal judge immediately ordered the admission of nine black students, but Faubus refused to act. The crisis escalated until September 24, when Eisenhower federalized the National Guard and ordered them away from the school. The next day, federal troops from the 101st Airborne Division entered the city, and the nine black students finally began taking classes.[37]

Both contemporary observers and historians have been critical of Eisenhower's handling of the Little Rock crisis. He should have acted sooner and more decisively, they assert. The *New Republic* said that the incident revealed the bankruptcy of the presidency and suggested that Eisenhower had become the reincarnation of Democratic President James

Buchanan, considered by many historians to be the worst president in history because his feckless leadership made the Civil War unavoidable.[38] However, such critics don't appreciate how difficult it is for a president to even contemplate the use of military force against a lawfully elected state government.[39] Doing so makes a mockery of federalism and democracy, and bears more than a little resemblance to fascism. Eisenhower knew that Southern racists would exploit this fact, which they did. Senator Russell immediately sent Eisenhower a telegram charging him with using tactics copied from "Hitler's storm troopers."[40]

When confronted with a very similar situation at the University of Mississippi in 1962, John F. Kennedy was just as reluctant as Eisenhower to use federal troops against a legitimate state government. When Kennedy was forced by events to take the same action that Eisenhower had taken, Kennedy viewed it as a failure of his own leadership to resolve the situation without resorting to military force.[41] Yet Kennedy is viewed today as having acted decisively, while Eisenhower's actions in Little Rock are viewed as weak. It is worth asking, however, whether Kennedy would have moved as decisively without Eisenhower's actions at Little Rock as a precedent.

The Little Rock mess encouraged Eisenhower to develop another civil rights bill during 1958. He announced his proposal in a special message to Congress on February 5, 1959. Said Eisenhower, "Two principles basic to our system of government are that the rule of law is supreme, and that every individual regardless of his race, religion or national origin is entitled to the equal protection of the laws." He denounced "mob violence" and asked Congress for stronger laws to deal with force or the threat of force to block school desegregation.

Eisenhower also expressed concern over recent bombings of schools and churches by white supremacists and asked Congress to increase the power of the Federal Bureau of Investigation to pursue those accused of such crimes. He requested that the Justice Department be given the power to inspect federal election records for evidence of racial discrimination. And he asked that a federal agency be established to monitor nondiscrimination in federal contracts, in effect reestablishing the Fair Employment Practices Committee that Southern Democrats had zeroed out of the budget after the Second World War.

This was meaningful civil rights legislation, and Southern Democrats knew it. They managed to block action throughout 1959, but in 1960 the Republican and Democratic leaders in the House and Senate joined forces to ram a bill through. Seeing that this was a more significant piece of legislation than the 1957 bill, the Southern Democrats were forced to launch an old-time filibuster to defeat it.

To get the bill passed, it was eventually watered down. In the end, many liberals considered the legislation to be meaningless.[42] In truth, what they were really upset about had less to do with the provisions of the bill than the fact that Southern Democrats had once again snookered the

Senate majority. Liberals felt that now was the time to finally defang the filibuster dragon and were deeply disappointed when Senate Majority Leader Johnson failed to invoke cloture and instead compromised away the substance of the bill so that he could once again get *something* passed. Consequently, the failure was not Eisenhower's—he proposed a tough bill—but Johnson's. His presidential ambitions dictated that he not overly offend either the Democratic Party's Southern base or the growing civil rights movement, so he split the difference, leaving everyone dissatisfied.[43]

A balanced review of Dwight Eisenhower's record on civil rights reveals that he did much more than he gets credit for. His major accomplishment was the passage of the first civil rights bills since Reconstruction. Compared to the more significant bills enacted in 1964 and 1965, the Eisenhower bills seem puny. But the very fact that they were enacted at all was extremely important in laying the groundwork for what came later. Moreover, his action in Little Rock established an important precedent for the use of federal military force to ensure compliance with court-ordered desegregation. And lastly, it is underappreciated that Eisenhower's appointees to the Supreme Court provided the votes for its actions on civil rights for decades thereafter—Potter Stewart served until 1981 and William Brennan until 1990. In short, while Eisenhower was not by any means a revolutionary in the advancement of civil rights, he was a crucial figure in the transition from Roosevelt's do-nothing administration and Truman's purely administrative efforts to the more legislatively significant Johnson years to follow.

In the tense period following the *Brown* decision, the nation needed time to absorb the necessity of the major changes that were to come. It is highly doubtful that any other president serving during Eisenhower's time could have accomplished more in the area of civil rights than he did, given the power that Southern Democrats still wielded in the Senate.[44] Although historians point to private comments Eisenhower made that were critical of the *Brown* decision, they fail to note that all of them related to the Court's order that school desegregation proceed "with all deliberate speed," which he thought was impractical and unnecessarily provocative. Eisenhower feared that many Southern states might simply abolish public education in response—a cure worse than the disease.[45] But he never questioned the Court's ruling that school segregation was illegal under the Fourteenth Amendment.[46]

JOHN F. KENNEDY TRIES TO HAVE IT BOTH WAYS

In many ways, John F. Kennedy's administration is proof that Eisenhower could not have done much more than he did. Indeed, as a senator in the 1950s, Kennedy's position on civil rights was actually more conservative than Eisenhower's. Kennedy denied that Congress had any role to play in implementing the *Brown* decision, voted against bringing the 1957 civil rights bill up for a vote in the Senate, and supported amendments that weakened its effectiveness.[47] If Eisenhower couldn't get the support of Northeastern liberals like Kennedy for his modest civil rights measures, how could he expect to get moderates from border states?

Throughout his Senate career, Kennedy carefully avoided alienating Southern Democrats, whom he knew would be important to him if he ran for president.[48] In his 1956 book, *Profiles in Courage*, he hewed faithfully to the Southern mythology of Reconstruction as "a black nightmare the South could never forget."[49] When Kennedy made a run at the vice presidential nomination in 1956, the bulk of his support came from Southerners. Thereafter, he continued to court them, including some of the most racist Democrats in the country, such as Alabama Governor John Patterson, who got behind Kennedy's presidential bid as early as 1957.[50]

The liberal *New Republic* magazine expressed concern. "We find ourselves a little uncomfortable over presidential aspirant John Kennedy's flirtation with Southern politicians," it said in 1957.[51] He only backed off when it became clear that Lyndon Johnson was also running for president in 1960 and unquestionably would be the candidate of the South.[52]

Going into the 1960 campaign, Kennedy continued to be dogged by his past equivocation on civil rights. Black leaders mostly preferred Senator Hubert Humphrey of Minnesota. Some even attacked Kennedy openly. In a May 29 speech, Roy Wilkins of the NAACP blasted him for meeting privately with Patterson in 1959, saying, "Anything with an Alabama odor does not arouse enthusiasm among Negro citizens." And on June 3, black baseball star Jackie Robinson said, "Senator Kennedy is not fit to be President of the United States."[53]

Realizing that he had a problem with blacks, in late May 1960 Kennedy impulsively went to see popular black singer Harry Belafonte at his apartment in New York City without even having an appointment. Kennedy complained about Robinson's attack on him and asked Belafonte what he could do about it. Belafonte replied that Robinson was a Republican and not to worry about him. The support he needed, above all others, was that of Dr. Martin Luther King Jr. Kennedy barely knew who he was and asked, "Why do you see him as so important? What can he do?"[54]

Although Kennedy tried to shore up his support among blacks by later meeting with King and other black leaders, he continued to flirt with the South.[55] As historian Nick Bryant notes, "Each modification of his stance on civil rights . . . coincided precisely with a twist in the fight for the nomination."[56] Historian Mark Stern concurs: "There is scant evidence that during his pursuit of the presidency Kennedy treated civil rights as anything other than a problem of vote-optimization."[57] This only exacerbated Kennedy's reputation as an equivocator on civil rights.

After winning the Democratic presidential nomination, Kennedy selected Lyndon Johnson as his running mate, making it clear that he was not writing off the South. At the same time, the Republicans ratcheted up their support for civil rights initiatives. Their 1960 platform made a number of specific promises to enforce voting rights, speed school desegregation, and pressure the Senate to change its filibuster rule to allow passage of new civil rights legislation.[58] The *New York Times* even praised the Republican platform for being stronger on civil rights in many respects than the Democratic platform that year.[59] During his second debate with Kennedy on October 7, Republican presidential nominee Richard Nixon made a strong statement on civil rights and chided Kennedy for selecting as his vice president someone who had long opposed them.[60]

As election day approached, a key variable for both campaigns was how Dr. King might go. He was uncommitted, but known to like and respect Nixon.[61] Both sides hoped for his endorsement. However, when Dr. King was arrested at a demonstration in Atlanta on October 19, Nixon did nothing, despite pleas from his campaign aides to at least make a public statement.[62] By contrast, Kennedy personally called King's pregnant wife Coretta to offer support and worked behind the scenes with Georgia's Democratic governor to secure his release.[63] When word of this got out into the black community, it provided a big boost to Kennedy's campaign.[64] Nixon's missteps cost him dearly in the black community, which reduced its support for the Republican ticket in 1960 by seven percentage points from 1956, probably costing him the election.[65] Had he done as well among blacks as Eisenhower did in 1956, Nixon would have carried New Jersey, Michigan, Illinois, and Texas and won the election easily.[66]

PRESIDENT KENNEDY'S CIVIL RIGHTS LETHARGY

Eisenhower and the Republicans had been excoriated by Kennedy during the campaign for not doing more on civil rights, and Kennedy pledged a comprehensive civil rights bill as soon as Congress reconvened. He also promised executive orders ending discrimination in housing and hiring as soon as he took office.[67] "Many things can be done by a stroke of the presidential pen," Kennedy said.[68] But once in the White House, he basically did nothing on civil rights—no executive orders, no legislation, no nothing.[69] He even had to be pressured into appointing a liaison to the civil rights community—and then named a white man, Harris Wofford.[70] In what Kennedy must have viewed as a low blow, the *New York Times* observed no difference between his policies on civil rights and Eisenhower's.[71]

Kennedy seemed to think that all he had to do was appoint a few token blacks to administration positions and that would be enough to keep civil rights supporters happy. This was the way the Democratic Party in Massachusetts had always gotten the black vote and Kennedy saw no reason to do anything different.[72] But by 1961, it was not nearly enough; the civil rights movement was too far advanced for that.

Moreover, the time was ripe for another legislative effort. In early 1961, House Speaker Sam Rayburn, Democrat of Texas, went to considerable trouble to reform the House Rules Committee just to accommodate Kennedy's anticipated civil rights legislation.[73] Plans were also made to limit an expected Senate filibuster, and Vice President Richard Nixon, as president of the Senate, was prepared to make a critical ruling on the matter before leaving office on January 20.[74] But Kennedy refused to lend his support to the effort for fear of alienating Southerners like Richard Russell, and it died.[75]

When black leaders pressed Kennedy for a civil rights bill, he brushed them off and proposed none.[76] Nor was the Justice Department much interested in using its new powers under the 1957 and 1960 civil rights bills. "I did not lie awake at night worrying about the problems of Negroes," Attorney General Robert F. Kennedy, the president's brother, confessed.[77]

President Kennedy remained sensitive to Southern concerns, appointing conservative judges unlikely to push too hard on desegregation, and resisting pressure to appoint a black to the Supreme Court when Justice Charles Whittaker retired in 1962. A black judge, William Hastie, who had been named to the federal appeals court by Harry Truman, was considered by Kennedy but rejected as unqualified.[78] Among Kennedy's circuit court appointees was William Harold Cox, who had been Mississippi Senator James O. Eastland's college roommate and shared his political philosophy. The Eisenhower Administration had previously rejected Eastland's recommendation of his friend for a judicial appointment on the grounds that Cox was a racist.[79]

When Kennedy finally got around to issuing an executive order against housing discrimination, it was not until after the 1962 elections, when Southern congressmen and senators would be protected from the fallout. The order was also severely watered down from what he promised during the campaign, with so many escape hatches that its impact was mostly symbolic.[80] By the end of the year, liberal historian Howard Zinn was complaining that the Kennedy Administration had an "undeserved reputation" for supporting civil rights.[81]

Meanwhile, the Kennedy Administration was irritated by the Civil Rights Commission—Bobby Kennedy likened it to the House Committee on Un-American Activities and prohibited it from having access to Justice Department files on voting rights abuses.[82] Although the department pressed forward with voting rights cases, it did so slowly and without enthusiasm. Nor did the administration take any action to hasten school desegregation. In fact, Kennedy empathized with white parents, saying it was "really tough" for them to put their children into classes with blacks.[83] University of Alaska historian Kenneth O'Reilly summarizes both Kennedys' approach to civil rights during 1961 and 1962:

> John Kennedy designed the something-for-everyone approach to placate both the Democratic Party's northern liberal wing and southern states'

rights wing. He offered voting rights litigation and affirmative action initiatives to one wing, the appointment of segregationist judges and a rejection of the Civil Rights Commission's legislative agenda to the other wing. . . . The Kennedys saw no political gain in pushing too hard for voting rights for Southern blacks. They also had no moral commitment to the cause. By their own account they pursued voting rights as the least objectionable and least intrusive course of action. If it had not been for the pressure brought by the civil rights movement, in all probability the Kennedys would not have moved at all.[84]

BIRMINGHAM FORCES KENNEDY TO ACT

The Kennedy Administration's half-hearted approach to civil rights—Dr. King branded it "tokenism" in early 1963—led to a radicalization of the movement.[85] Civil rights demonstrations increased in number and intensity, leading to ever more violent responses by local law enforcement officials in the South. The escalation peaked in early 1963, when Dr. King began his Birmingham, Alabama, campaign. Police Commissioner Eugene "Bull" Connor, who was also the state's National Democratic Committeeman, was easily baited into attacking the civil rights demonstrators with police dogs, fire hoses, and nightsticks.[86] Although horrific, *New York Times* reporter Anthony Lewis saw how these attacks on peaceful demonstrators greatly increased support for the civil rights movement among whites in the North, and moved Kennedy to finally propose a civil rights bill:

> Most Northerners had gone through life without thinking about how it would feel to have a black skin. Then came those scenes outside the schools in Little Rock and New Orleans—the women screaming "niggers," the mob clawing at a Catholic priest. Those in the North who saw those events on television, or read about them, were not likely to miss the unreasoning hatred and inhumanity. . . . The pictures of dogs assaulting Negro demonstrators in Birmingham in 1963 were instrumental in President Kennedy's decision to propose . . . civil rights legislation.[87]

Kennedy proposed his civil rights bill in June 1963—two and a half years after entering the White House—to blunt the political impact of the ongoing civil rights demonstrations, which were dragging down his popularity.[88] In May 1963, his approval percentage was down fifteen points from a year earlier and his disapproval rating had doubled from 12 percent to 25 percent.[89] Kennedy's legislation would have provided equal access to hotels and restaurants, broadened the authority of the Justice Department to bring school desegregation law suits, banned discrimination in federal hiring and by businesses holding federal contracts, and created a Community Relations Service to mediate racial disputes.

Many liberals were concerned that the legislation was far more limited than it appeared to be because businesses would have had to have a "substantial" connection with interstate commerce before the equal access provisions applied. They thought the White House erred in basing constitutional authority for the legislation solely on the interstate commerce clause, rather than relying on the broader authority contained in the Fourteenth Amendment.[90] Liberals also believed that Kennedy had the power under existing law to do many of the things authorized by the new law. They were concerned that if the law was defeated, it might foreclose this option. The courts might feel that the president wouldn't have asked for the power if he thought he already had it, and might also take note of Congress's rejection of the legislation to prohibit executive action on civil rights.[91]

In August, black leaders organized a massive march on Washington in support of the civil rights bill. Some had to be restrained, however, from using the occasion to bash the legislation as "too little, too late," as John Lewis, president of the Student Nonviolent Coordinating Committee, planned to do before being talked out of it. Others, like Malcolm X, refused to participate in the march at all, labeling it the "Farce on Washington," because the whole thing was being manipulated by the White House solely for its own political benefit.[92] Indeed, two Kennedy aides stood by the public address system at the Lincoln Memorial, prepared to literally pull the plug in the event that any of the speeches got out of hand.[93]

Some in the administration were alarmed by the march. Among these was J. Edgar Hoover, whom Kennedy reappointed to head the FBI as one of his first actions in office.[94] Hoover was convinced that the entire civil rights movement was basically a Communist front and requested wiretaps on Dr. King and other civil rights leaders. Attorney General Robert Kennedy approved them, which could be done in those days without a court order.[95] Although Hoover may have really believed that Dr. King was a Communist dupe, Kennedy's interest was purely political. Because Dr. King was the central figure in the large and growing civil rights movement, he was plugged into everyone, making him an invaluable source of political intelligence. The Communist connection was just an excuse to get that intelligence as far as Kennedy was concerned.[96]

By late 1963, civil rights leaders were openly disparaging President Kennedy's civil rights record. In the words of University of Nebraska historian Thomas Borstelmann, "the Kennedy Administration was beginning to seem almost as much the enemy as the Ku Klux Klan and local law enforcement officers."[97]

Liberals pointed to a report by the U.S. Civil Rights Commission that was highly critical of federal activities under White House control. For example, the Department of Health, Education and Welfare continued to make construction grants to hospitals reserved for whites only. The Department of Labor was cited for operating training programs in 142 all-white schools and just 14 black schools. The Commission noted that although Kennedy's order banning housing discrimination had been in effect for almost a year, nothing had been done to implement it. In terms of voting rights, the Commission reported that only 8.3 percent of blacks in one hundred Southern counties were registered to vote, a trivial increase over the 5 percent that were registered in 1956.[98]

Nevertheless, when Kennedy was assassinated the following month, he was deeply mourned in the black community despite the paucity of his accomplishments on civil rights. Like Franklin Roosevelt, Kennedy had succeeded in making the most of largely symbolic efforts on behalf of blacks, while consistently shying away from more substantive actions. Historian Garry Wills says that whatever he accomplished in the area of civil rights was "largely inadvertent."[99]

Some historians now believe that if Kennedy had been willing to take on the Southerners in Congress early in his presidency, the country would have been with him. By deferring to them, he unwittingly emboldened the diehard segregationists, making the campaign for civil rights more confrontational and violent than it would have been had Kennedy acted earlier and more decisively.[100]

JOHNSON SEES THE FUTURE

A far better legislator than Kennedy, Johnson knew how weak the Southern caucus was. Its already depleted ranks continued to shrink as senators like Ralph Yarborough of Texas abandoned it, seeing better political prospects among the rising number of black voters than the declining number of white supremacists. Seeing an opportunity where Kennedy had not, Johnson made passage of a civil rights bill his first order of business after succeeding to the presidency. As he told a joint session of Congress just five days after Kennedy's death:

> No memorial oration or eulogy could more eloquently honor President Kennedy's memory than the earliest possible passage of the civil rights bill for which he fought so long. We have talked long enough in this country about equal rights. We have talked for one hundred years or more. It is time now to write the next chapter, and to write it in the books of law.

> I urge you again, as I did in 1957 and again in 1960, to enact a civil rights law so that we can move forward to eliminate from this nation every trace of discrimination and oppression that is based upon race or color. There could be no greater source of strength to this nation both at home and abroad.

The fight to pass the Civil Rights Act of 1964 is typically portrayed as a titanic struggle, with victory achieved only due to Johnson's tenacity and legislative skill. While, to his credit, he did fight hard for the bill, the truth is that the outcome was never really in doubt. Ten years after the *Brown* decision, there was no longer insurmountable resistance in Congress to enactment of legislation that would outlaw the most blatant forms of racial discrimination. A majority of both Republicans and Democrats were agreed on this goal in 1964, and all that the dying remnant of Southern Democrats could do was delay and obstruct unsuccessfully.[101]

The passage of the civil rights bills of 1957 and 1960 had proven that there was majority support for civil rights legislation in both the House and Senate. The Southern Democrats held off more substantive antidiscrimination laws only by the skin of their teeth. But they saw the handwriting on the wall and knew it was only a matter of time before they were defeated. By 1964, the Southern hand was very weak indeed. The moral authority of Dr. King, so brilliantly expressed in his great "I Have a Dream" speech, had captured the nation—both black and white. The absurdly violent tactics of Bull Connor and other racists operating under the cover of state and local governments created massive sympathy for the demonstrators, and television brought the plight of those whose rights they were fighting for into every American home in an unprecedented way.[102]

The enormous desire to memorialize the senseless murder of John F. Kennedy, plus Johnson's determination to demonstrate his power and purge his own racist past by getting a substantive civil rights bill through the Senate, proved a formidable combination. The long filibuster of 1964 was only delaying the inevitable. That all the participants knew this only goes to show how deep their racism was. It's one thing to engage in a filibuster if there is even a glimmer of hope that something might be salvaged as a result. But serious commitment is required to take such action when one knows that ultimate failure is the only conceivable outcome. This fact should be kept in mind when thinking about people like Senator Robert C. Byrd, Democrat of West Virginia, whose individual filibuster of the 1964 civil rights bill is the second longest in history, taking up eighty-six pages of fine print in the *Congressional Record*. Only a true believer would ever undertake such a futile effort.[103]

Even so, one final element was essential to passage of the civil rights bill—the strong support of Republicans. Although Democrats had a historically large majority in the House of Representatives with 259 members to 176 Republicans, almost as many Republicans voted for the civil rights bill as Democrats. The final vote was 290 for the bill and 130 against. Of the "yea" votes, 152 were Democrats and 138 were Republicans. Of the "nay" votes, three-fourths were Democrats. In short, the bill could not have passed without Republican support. As *Time Magazine* observed, "In one of the most lopsidedly Democratic Houses since the days of F.D.R., Republicans were vital to the passage of a bill for which the Democratic administration means to take full political credit this year."[104]

A similar story is told in the Senate. On the critical vote to end the filibuster by Southern Democrats, 71 senators voted to invoke cloture. With 67 votes needed, 44 Democrats and 27 Republicans joined together to bring the bill to a final vote. Of those voting "nay," 80 percent were Democrats, including Robert C. Byrd and former Vice President Al Gore's father, who was then a senator from Tennessee. Again, it is clear that the civil rights bill would have failed without Republican votes. Close observers of the Senate deliberations recognized that the Republican leader, Senator Everett McKinley Dirksen of Illinois, had done yeoman work in responding to the objections of individual Republicans and holding almost all of them together in support of the bill.[105] "More than any other single individual," the *New York Times* acknowledged, "he was responsible for getting the civil rights bill through the Senate."[106]

"I know the risks are great and it might cost us the South," Johnson told Kennedy aide Theodore Sorensen at the beginning of the civil rights legislative fight in 1963, "but those sorts of states may be lost anyway."[107] On Election Day, 1964, Johnson did indeed lose much of the South, but still won one of the greatest victories in American political history, beating Republican Barry Goldwater, a senator from Arizona who had opposed the civil rights bill on constitutional grounds, 61 percent to 39 percent.[108] The impressive size of Johnson's victory owed much to the fact that he got 94 percent of the black vote—26 percent more than Kennedy had gotten in 1960.

Thus Johnson's strategy of abandoning the South—as well as his own past—by embracing civil rights was the right thing to do, both for his own political fortunes as well as for the country. As political scientist Pearl Robinson explains, the effect of Johnson's effort "was to add to the newly enfranchised Southern voters the potential for more solid Democratic support from poor blacks in the North as well as the middle class."[109]

In the end, Johnson's efforts were less heroic than they appeared at the time and more a function of his political self-interest. By 1964, public opinion had shifted decisively in favor of the key civil rights goals of school integration and fair employment.[110] In pushing for strong civil rights legislation, Johnson wasn't so much leading public opinion as following it.

10

SINCE THE CIVIL RIGHTS ACT

A Racial Double Standard?

By the end of the 1960s, the political landscape regarding civil rights had changed dramatically. Although there were still many battles left to fight, the war was essentially won. The fight to maintain government-enforced segregation was lost and everybody knew it. Journalist Theodore White described the new racial dynamic:

> Across the country, every major university scoured the ghetto high schools for promising Negro adolescents who could be lured to their ivied halls, while great corporations combed the universities for promising black talent. A Negro sat on the Supreme Court of the United States; two major cities (Cleveland [Ohio] and Gary [Indiana]) had elected Negro mayors; and over 200 Negro legislators sat in state assemblies and city councils; six Negro congressmen and one Negro Senator sat in Washington. Integration had fostered a Negro leadership which seemed to moving steadily toward its rightful privileges and responsibilities in American life.[1]

White and black people reacted differently to the transformation in race relations. The former wanted time to adjust to all of the changes that had occurred in a remarkably short period of time, while the latter wanted to finish the job and press forward on achieving full racial integration throughout society and the economy. At the same time, the long consensus on using nonviolent methods to achieve this goal broke down as new groups like the Black Panthers emerged advocating "black power."[2]

Tensions were heightened by rioting in many major cities in the summer of 1967 and controversy over the Vietnam War, as prominent civil rights leaders like Dr. Martin Luther King Jr. joined the war protests.

Hubert Humphrey, the 1968 Democratic presidential nominee, had been deeply involved in the struggle for racial equality since 1948, when he led the fight to insert a strong civil rights plank in the Democratic platform. But for younger, more radical black leaders like Stokely Carmichael and H. Rap Brown, this counted for little. Their attitude was, "What have you done for me lately?" And their talk of using violence left white liberals like Humphrey flustered and unsure of their position, creating a split between the traditional civil rights community and the new black power advocates. The assassination of Dr. King in April 1968 turned it into a chasm.

Governor George Wallace, Democrat of Alabama, sought to exploit the rising racial tensions.[3] Along with Governor Lester Maddox, the Georgia Democrat, Wallace hoped to lead a white backlash against integration that would at least slow its advance.[4] In 1964, Wallace had run unsuccessfully for the Democratic presidential nomination, leading him to conclude that the deck was too heavily stacked against him to win that way. So he made plans to run for president in 1968 as a third-party candidate opposed to the pro-civil rights policies of both the Republicans and Democrats. Wallace often said there wasn't a dime's worth of difference between the two major parties.[5]

Richard Nixon was well aware of Wallace's intentions when he made his own plans to run for president in 1968 and, consequently, conceded the Deep South to Wallace right off the bat.[6] According to Theodore White, "Nixon conspicuously, conscientiously, calculatedly denied himself all racist votes, yielding them to Wallace."[7] Indeed, Wallace often attacked Nixon during the campaign for supporting civil rights. Said Wallace, "It started under a Republican administration in 1954 when they appointed Chief Justice Earl Warren and the [Senate] confirmation was presided over by [Vice President] Nixon."[8]

Therefore, contrary to popular belief, Nixon had no "Southern strategy" designed to carry racist votes through coded messages about crime and welfare, as is often alleged.[9] It would have made no sense politically with Wallace in the race. Perhaps if Wallace had not been a candidate, it might have paid for Nixon to court conservative Southerners. But with Wallace running, it was clear that the Alabaman was going to get most of the votes of Southern whites concerned about issues such as black crime and welfare. "Wallace split the conservative electorate," Nixon political adviser Kevin Phillips explained, and "siphoned off a flow of ballots that otherwise would have gone heavily for Nixon, and garnered many of his backers—Northern or Southern, blue-collar or white-collar—from the ranks of 1964 GOP presidential nominee Barry Goldwater."[10] This meant that Nixon had no choice but to find his votes in the more racially tolerant North and West. As historian Glen Moore explains:

> The biggest fallacy in the Southern strategy viewpoint is that it ignores the fact that Nixon had to win in other regions in order to get the 270 electoral votes necessary for winning the presidency. If Nixon emphasized winning southern votes, then he risked losing support in the major industrial states, which would be committing political suicide.[11]

This reality forced Nixon to run in 1968 as a classic centrist—splitting the difference between the ultra-liberal Humphrey and the ultra-conservative Wallace.[12] Thus Nixon actually emphasized his support for the Civil Rights Act of 1964 and began his presidential campaign with a strenuous attack on racism.[13] As he explained in a 1966 newspaper column: "Southern Republicans must not climb aboard the sinking ship of racial injustice. Any Republican victory that would come from courting racists, black or white, would be a defeat for our future in the South and our party in the nation."[14]

In an interview with the *New York Times* in 1967, Nixon went so far as to argue for what today would be called "reparations" to African Americans to compensate for the effects of slavery and racism. Said Nixon, "You've got to realize that these people in the ghettos have got to have more than an equal chance. They should be given a dividend." He went on to say, "On this score, I would be considered almost radical."[15]

It's also worth remembering that when Nixon picked Spiro Agnew as his vice president in 1968, it was largely because Agnew had a reputation for being strong on civil rights. Two years earlier, Agnew had been elected governor of Maryland over Democrat George P. Mahoney, who was strongly opposed to open housing laws. Mahoney's campaign slogan was, "Your Home Is Your Castle—Protect It!" Agnew supported fair housing and was actually the liberal in that race.[16] In a glowing profile of Agnew published in the *New York Times* after Nixon picked him as his running mate, Agnew was described as "a bipartisan liberal hero" in Maryland for pushing through a public accommodations law in Baltimore, a state open housing law, and sharply increasing state taxes and spending.[17]

In the end, even liberal *New York Times* columnist Tom Wicker had to concede that in the 1968 campaign, "it would be hard to charge that Richard Nixon had opposed, or was opposed to, civil rights."[18]

SOUTHERN STRATEGY MYTH

The myth of Nixon's Southern strategy has been maintained for so many years because casual observation sees a shift in Southern voting patterns in the 1960s in which the historical dominance of the Democratic Party in that region began to break down. By the 1980s, the South was solidly Republican in presidential races, with Republicans becoming very competitive in statewide races. By the 1990s, Republicans had become dominant across the board.

Since it is assumed that race is the overriding factor in Southern elections, it therefore follows that Republicans must have displaced the Democrats by exploiting that issue, as Democrats had successfully done since the Civil War.[19] In University of Virginia political scientist Gerard Alexander's words, the linkage goes something like this: "The Republican Party assembled a national majority by winning over Southern white voters; Southern white voters are racist; therefore, the GOP is racist."[20]

In truth, economic changes in the South were the driving force behind the Republican advance. During the period of Democratic hegemony, the South was far and away the poorest region of the United States. It had a per capita income three-fifths that in the nation as a whole. Per capita income in the Northeast and West was twice what it was in the South. However, during World War II, the South's income began to converge toward that of the rest of the country. This resulted from the decline of agriculture, the growth of manufacturing attracted by the region's low taxes and anti-union attitude, and federal income transfer programs like Social Security.[21] By 1980, per capita income in the South was only about 10 percent below the rest of the country and the spread between it and the nation's wealthier regions had fallen by 80 percent.[22]

The rising wealth of the South made the region highly receptive to the Republican Party's message of low taxes and small government, while the Democratic Party's embrace of big government, epitomized by Lyndon Johnson's "Great Society," alienated conservative Democrats from the national party. It was this factor, not the race issue, that was primarily responsible for the shift of Southern Democrats out of the party of their ancestors and into the Republican Party—a fact confirmed by the latest academic research.[23] "This administration has no Southern strategy," Nixon aide Harry Dent explained in a 1969 memo, "but rather a national strategy which, for the first time in modern times, *includes* the South, rather than *excludes* the South from full and equal participation in national affairs."[24]

This is not to say that race played no role in Republican success in the South, but the linkage is quite different from what is usually thought. The same civil rights laws that made it possible for blacks to vote in the South also enabled the Republican Party to compete there—precisely because the race issue had finally been resolved. American University political scientist David Lublin explains:

> The Civil Rights Movement shattered the institutions that were critical to maintaining both white supremacy and Democratic dominance in the South. Once the back of white supremacy had been broken, Democrats

could no longer argue that failure by whites to support the party constituted a racial betrayal that could lead to the end of white supremacy and
black political power. The core institutions of white supremacy had
already been defeated and efforts to maintain it constituted an increasingly rearguard action. Moreover, the national Democratic Party was
aggressively moving to attract black voters. The success of the Civil Rights
Movement actually freed whites to consider other political questions
besides race precisely because the battle for the existing system had been
so conclusively lost. One of the wonderful political results of the 1960s is
that it allowed Southerners to focus on issues besides the racial organization of their society.[25]

Federal civil rights legislation brought an enormous increase in voting
by blacks in the 1960s, and almost all of these new voters became
Democrats. As they brought their political influence to bear in Democratic
primaries, their interests and policy preferences had an impact on the
party's nominees for office. These preferences were well to the left of those
historically held by most Southern Democrats. Black voters tended to favor
expansive government, more spending on welfare and social programs,
and less on national defense.[26] Consequently, politically conservative
Southern Democrats found their position within the party increasingly ten-
uous. Many simply found the Republican Party to be more hospitable on
issues such as economics and national security.

At the same time, liberal Northern Democrats became increasingly
hostile to their conservative Southern brethren. After 1968, Democrats
changed their rules for presidential nominations in ways designed to
reduce the influence of conservative Southerners.[27] When Democrats
scored a huge victory in the post-Watergate congressional election of 1974,
they began stripping Southerners of their chairmanships and changing
House rules to diminish their influence.[28] At this point, there was no reason left for a conservative Southerner to remain in the Democratic Party.

Nixon's 1968 campaign took place in the midst of this political shift,
but he had almost nothing to do with it because Wallace had such a strong
hold on the dying remnants of the Old South. Ironically, Wallace's 1968
effort probably led to federal policies that were more racially liberal than
they would have been if he hadn't run at all. Because Nixon was elected
that year without the support of Southern racists, he was able to pursue a
far more liberal policy on race during his presidency than might have been
the case if he owed his election to them.

NIXON DESEGREGATES THE SCHOOLS

Within days of the election, conservatives picked up signals that Nixon
planned to move to the left on domestic issues, including civil rights.[29] The
appointment of Harvard professor Daniel Patrick Moynihan, who had

lately served as an assistant secretary of Labor in the Kennedy and Johnson administrations, to a high-level position on the White House staff was an early indication that the signals were true.[30] Another was naming California Lieutenant Governor Robert Finch as Secretary of Health, Education, and Welfare. A close personal friend of Nixon, Finch promised to reach out to the black community even though its votes had gone overwhelmingly to Humphrey.[31] Among Finch's first appointments was outspoken liberal Leon Panetta to head HEW's Office of Civil Rights.[32] In his inaugural address, Nixon himself declared his intention to take a vigorous approach to civil rights:

> No man can be fully free while his neighbor is not. To go forward at all is to go forward together. This means black and white together, as one nation, not two. The laws have caught up with our conscience. What remains is to give life to what is in the law: to insure at last that as all are born equal in dignity before God, all are born equal in dignity before man.

Roy Wilkins of the NAACP praised the speech and said Nixon "revealed an awareness of the seriousness of the racial crisis."[33] A few days later, HEW cut off federal aid to five Southern school districts that refused to integrate.[34] The move was assailed by Southern Democrats on Capitol Hill. But when asked about the cutoff at a February 6, 1969, press conference, Nixon replied, "As far as school desegregation is concerned, I support the law of the land. I believe that funds should be denied to those districts that continue to perpetuate segregation."

This encouraged HEW to press ahead with more aid cutoffs to segregated school districts. Secretary Finch also announced that prominent civil rights leader James L. Farmer Jr., a founder of the Congress of Racial Equality, would be named an assistant secretary at HEW to aid the civil rights effort.[35] Just one month into his presidency, any idea that Nixon was pursuing a Southern strategy had been thoroughly discredited.[36]

The Justice Department was also enlisted to speed school desegregation efforts. As early as February 10, 1969, it filed suit against three Louisiana parishes for operating dual school systems—one for blacks and another for whites.[37] In July, Justice filed additional desegregation suits in Illinois and South Carolina, and HEW initiated further school aid cutoffs.[38] And in August, Attorney General John Mitchell announced that he was suing the state of Georgia for failure to desegregate—the first time an entire state had been so targeted.[39] In October, the Supreme Court handed down a decision in *Alexander v. Holmes County* that compelled the states to end all dual school systems immediately.[40] Mitchell pledged that the Justice Department would vigorously enforce the ruling.[41]

Although he agreed with its goal, Nixon was frustrated by the Court's ruling because it offered no guidance as to how it should be implemented. Nevertheless, he was adamant that his administration would enforce the law regardless of the political consequences. As Nixon told John Ehrlichman, his chief domestic policy adviser, in January 1970, "I don't give a damn about the Southern strategy—I care a great deal about decent education."[42] On March 24, 1970, Nixon issued a comprehensive statement that was unambiguous in stating his support for *Brown* and other court cases mandating an end to school segregation. "Deliberate racial segregation of pupils by official action is unlawful, wherever it exists," he said. Writing in the liberal *New Republic* magazine, Yale law professor Alexander Bickel was impressed by Nixon's reasoning.[43]

The problem was that while most Americans favored desegregation in principle, they also supported neighborhood schools and strongly opposed busing solely for the purpose of integration. Unfortunately, in many cases the distribution of an area's population made it impossible to achieve racial balance except by busing students away from their neighborhood schools. Although Nixon was widely criticized by liberals for being reluctant to push for busing, there is little doubt that if a Democrat had been in the White House, he would have been just as sensitive to the widespread opposition to busing and, like Nixon, would have worked to soften the impact of mandated desegregation to the extent that the law allowed.[44]

Nixon hoped that persuasion could do most of the work, getting the states with dual school systems to do as much as possible on their own so that the federal government would not have to resort to force. No one wanted another Little Rock, but its precedent undoubtedly aided Nixon's efforts to achieve voluntary desegregation. Throughout 1970, Nixon and his staff, led by Labor Secretary George Shultz, worked intensively with the states to get the job done.[45] They used both the carrot and the stick: promises of more federal money for schools that desegregated, together with threats of Justice Department law suits against those that resisted.[46]

Remarkably, by the time schools reopened after the summer recess in 1970, the effort had largely succeeded. In June 1971, HEW reported that the percentage of black students in the South in all-black schools had fallen from 68 percent in the fall of 1968 to just 14.1 percent by the fall of 1970, and the percentage of black students attending predominantly white schools rose from 18.4 percent to 39.1 percent over the same period.[47] Among those who were impressed by Nixon's performance was Tom Wicker, who later said:

> There's no doubt about it—the Nixon administration accomplished more in 1970 to desegregate Southern school systems than had been done in the sixteen previous years. . . . There's no doubt either that it was Richard Nixon personally who conceived, orchestrated and led the administration's desegregation effort. Halting and uncertain before he finally asserted strong control, that effort resulted in probably the outstanding domestic achievement of his administration.[48]

NIXON ESTABLISHES
AFFIRMATIVE ACTION

One of the problems a historian or journalist confronts in trying to accurately assess Nixon is that he often did the right thing, but then justified it on political grounds. Most politicians do it the other way around. A good example is affirmative action. It arose from a serious problem that had been around for more than one hundred years, which was labor unions' systematic discrimination against black workers. As long ago as 1874, Frederick Douglass denounced the "wickedness" and "tyranny" of labor unions for refusing to admit black members.[49] A long line of black leaders from Booker T. Washington on the right to W. E. B. DuBois on the left were equally critical of unions for closing off an important avenue to black economic advancement.[50] The unions, of course, didn't think of themselves as being racist, but as simply looking out for the economic interest of their members by restricting competition for jobs. As Samuel Gompers, founder of the American Federation of Labor (AFL), once put it, "Caucasians are not going to let their standard of living be destroyed by Negroes, Chinamen, Japs, or any other."[51]

The situation improved in the 1930s with establishment of the Congress of Industrial Organizations (CIO). Unlike the AFL, which historically represented skilled workers across industry lines, the CIO sought to represent all workers in a given industry. Consequently, the CIO was much more receptive to black membership, since its power was based on representing as many workers as possible, not restricting the supply of workers as the AFL did.[52] The migration of blacks from the rural South into Northern cities, along with the general advance of manufacturing in the 1940s and 1950s, greatly improved the black worker's position. But in the 1960s, there was still a great deal of residual racism in the unions, especially the building trades.[53]

Having chaired a committee on nondiscrimination in government contracting during the Eisenhower Administration, Nixon was well aware of the difficulty of opening up jobs for minorities in federal building projects.[54] Contractors could be pressured relatively easily, but there wasn't much they could do when the only workers they could hire belonged to labor unions that had virtually no minority members.[55] The Davis-Bacon Act required contractors to pay prevailing wages, thus forcing them to use union labor.[56] Therefore, any effort to increase minority hiring in federal building projects had to address the problem of racism in the unions.

Lyndon Johnson issued Executive Order 11246 on September 24, 1965, mandating nondiscrimination in employment on federal construction projects. But little was done to enforce its provisions. In early 1969, Nixon moved to beef up enforcement by requiring federal contracts to be awarded on the basis of nondiscrimination in employment and not go automatically to the lowest bidder. But before he could act, Senator Robert Byrd, Democrat of West Virginia, tried to block the effort, known as the Philadelphia Plan, by attaching a rider to an appropriations bill that would have prohibited the expenditure of federal funds to implement it. After a difficult fight in the House, however, the amendment was rejected and Nixon was able to move ahead with what became known as "affirmative action."[57]

While Nixon's primary motive was to do the right thing—he really did believe in equal opportunity—there was, of course, a political dimension as well. Since the labor unions and the black community were both loyal members of the Democratic Party's base, the issue of affirmative action pitted them against each other.[58] Republicans couldn't help but gain. Nevertheless, Nixon later viewed affirmative action as a political loser. "With our constituency, we gained little on the play," he explained. Regardless, Nixon never backed away from it and in fact greatly increased the size of the Equal Employment Opportunity Commission and expanded its authority.[59] He also established the Office of Minority Business Enterprise and pushed federal agencies to set aside a portion of their procurement for minority-owned firms.[60] Overall, Nixon increased federal spending for civil rights activities more than any other president in inflation-adjusted percentage terms.[61]

In the end, Nixon's civil rights accomplishments were quite substantial. One can argue about whether affirmative action and minority set-asides were good policy in principle, but as a matter of history they should not be ignored by those determined to prove that Nixon's election and administration were based on some quasi-racist Southern strategy.

Some historians are now revising their early emphasis on the Southern strategy to form a more sympathetic portrait of Nixon on the race issue. Yale University historian David Greenberg recently wrote that his administration made "real gains in extending the Great Society's civil rights revolution."[62] Wayne State University historian Melvin Small says Nixon "could have boasted, had he wanted to, about his progressive civil rights policy."[63] And in Indiana University historian Joan Hoff's words, "There is no denying . . . that Nixon's advances in civil and political rights for women and minorities far outweigh those of his predecessors."[64]

Even Leon Panetta, who left the Nixon Administration in 1970 in a huff, protesting that it was dragging its feet on civil rights, now says that with the benefit of hindsight, Nixon "was pretty good on civil rights."[65]

THE REAGAN ERA

After the defeat of Gerald Ford in 1976, the Republican Party hit its lowest point since the 1930s in terms of numbers and influence. One consequence of this was that the party became more receptive to the idea of reaching out to the black community. The feeling was that as barriers to black economic advancement fell, black voters would become more in tune with the Republican low-tax, pro-business message.[66] Serious efforts were made to reach out to blacks and there were signs of success. For example,

Congressman Bob Livingston, Republican of Louisiana, credited his election in 1977 to his cultivation of black voters.[67]

There were even indications that the NAACP, the nation's oldest and largest civil rights organization, was warming to the Republicans. In 1978, it broke with the Democrats on Jimmy Carter's energy bill. Echoing the traditional Republican view that free markets are the best way to regulate supply and demand, the NAACP blasted the Carter bill for being too heavy-handed in its reliance on government regulation. This set off a turmoil within the organization over what was perceived as a rightward turn. It probably didn't help that the NAACP found itself being praised by the conservative *Wall Street Journal* editorial page.[68]

Another venerable civil rights organization, the National Urban League, was also becoming more receptive to the conservative economic message. In 1980, it released a study suggesting that welfare programs were doing little to improve the condition of black people. The League argued instead for greater emphasis on jobs and establishing black businesses.[69] That same year, Republicans picked the city of Detroit to host their national convention largely because it was a heavily black city—tangible evidence that the party leadership was sincere in reaching out to blacks. In Congress, black Representative Parren Mitchell, a Democrat representing inner-city Baltimore, was so alarmed by the impact of inflation on his constituents that he became converted to free market economist Milton Friedman's monetary theories.[70]

By 1981, people were starting to hear more and more about black conservatives like economists Thomas Sowell and Walter Williams, who opposed the minimum wage and affirmative action as barriers to black economic progress. While there have always been a few conservative blacks who resisted the liberal political orthodoxy shared by most members of their race, the new black conservatives were different.[71] They weren't businessmen or politicians, but academics whose work was rigorous and scholarly. Hence, they could not be dismissed as tokens or sell-outs, but had to be confronted on an intellectual level.[72]

The rise of these new black conservatives led to a sharp backlash by black liberals. The harshest attack was delivered by black columnist Carl Rowan, who had served in high-level political positions in both the Kennedy and Johnson administrations. Said Rowan:

> Sowell has a right to be a conservative and to articulate far-right views. But I must exercise my right to say that Vidkun Quisling, in his collaboration with the Nazis, surely did not do as much damage to the Norwegians as Sowell is doing to the most helpless black Americans. Sowell is giving aid and comfort to America's racists and to those who, in the name of conservatism and frugality, are taking food out of the mouths of black children, consigning hundreds of thousands of black teenagers to joblessness and hopelessness, and making government a party to at least the partial resegregation of America.[73]

Ronald Reagan also came in for brutal attack. In another column, Rowan blasted him for encouraging, subsidizing, and defending racism. His administration, said Rowan, "has been not merely insensitive, but brutally hostile to the non-white people of America."[74] So over-the-top was this criticism that the *Washington Post*, which seldom found anything good to say about Reagan's policies, came to his defense in an editorial.[75]

To be sure, Reagan had a bit of a political tin ear when it came to issues affecting African Americans. But his mistakes were honest ones, not borne of malice, but resulting from genuine philosophical disagreement over what policies would best aid the black community, mixed with a bit of naiveté on Reagan's part. He would have avoided a lot of unnecessary trouble by having a high-level black adviser on his staff who could point out the minefields to him. In one case, when Reagan needed some advice on an issue affecting blacks, he was forced to borrow black aide Thaddeus Garrett Jr. from Vice President Bush's staff.[76]

A key problem for Reagan, ironically, is that he believed deeply in the idea of a colorblind society and refused to think about blacks as being separate and distinct from the rest of the nation. He thought that the biggest problems they had were the same ones affecting every other American: high inflation, taxes, and unemployment; slow economic growth, large budget deficits, and so on. If he could get these problems under control, Reagan thought, then the free market would do a better job than government of leveling economic disparities.[77] As he told the annual meeting of the NAACP on June 29, 1981:

> The well-being of blacks, like the well-being of every other American, is linked directly to the health of the economy. . . . A declining economy is a poisonous gas that claims its first victims in poor neighborhoods, before floating out into the community at large. Therefore, in our national debate over budget and tax proposals, we shall not concede the moral high ground to the proponents of those policies that are responsible in the first place for our economic mess—a mess which has injured all Americans. We will not concede the moral high ground to those who show more concern for federal programs than they do for what really determines the income and financial health of blacks—the nation's economy. . . . I genuinely and deeply believe the economic package we've put forth will move us toward black economic freedom, because it's aimed at lifting an entire country and not just parts of it.

It bothered Reagan a great deal that he was often perceived as being a racist. He was particularly upset when Supreme Court Justice Thurgood Marshall said he was one of the worst presidents in history when it came to race in a television interview in 1987. Reagan immediately asked for a meeting with Marshall to explain why he was wrong. Although Reagan believed he had "made a friend," there is no evidence that Marshall changed his opinion of him.[78]

Historians generally treat Reagan as another devotee of the Southern strategy, but there is little evidence to support this view except for his opposition to liberal economic policies.[79] Every effort to cut back the size and scope of government is often treated primarily as a covert effort to hurt blacks.[80] However, as with Nixon, some historians are starting to look a little deeper at Reagan's position on race and find that the charge of racism cannot be sustained by the record. In a book-length study of Reagan and the race issue, historian Nicholas Laham recently came to this conclusion:

> Reagan's civil rights policy was motivated not by any political desire the president may have had to play the race card, but by his sincere and genuine philosophical commitment to achieving two principal tenets of the conservative agenda: colorblind justice and limited government. Reagan was not a practitioner of the politics of racial division, much less a bigot, but a genuine conservative who opposed racial preferences and quotas, believed in the constitutional principle of equality under the law, and opposed many federal regulations, including some related to civil rights, which conflicted with his philosophical commitment to limited government.[81]

By Reagan's second term there was concrete evidence that blacks were doing much better economically and, consequently, their opinion of Reagan was rising quite sharply, from 10 percent approval in 1982 to 28 percent in 1985.[82] However, this did not translate into greater black support for Republicans at the ballot box. In 1988, George H. W. Bush did no better than Reagan had done among black voters, even though the Democratic presidential nominee, former Massachusetts Governor Michael Dukakis, was not especially well liked in the black community.[83] Political scientists concluded that blacks' ties to the Democratic Party were so deep that they transcended specific candidates.[84]

REPUBLICAN RACISM?

One reason for the virtually monolithic support blacks have given to the Democratic Party is that defectors tend to be harshly punished. Black Republicans—at least those that are "out of the closet"—are often treated as traitors against their race. Prominent black television personality Tony Brown, who announced publicly that he was a Republican in 1991, has described the pressure to maintain Democratic conformity in the black community. Many of its leaders, he said, "perpetuate an intellectual fascism and foster a totalitarian environment in which any independent thinking black who breaks lock-step with their often self-serving Democratic worldview is severely condemned, and even ostracized."[85]

This follows from a belief among many blacks that the Republican Party is literally out to destroy them. For example, writing in the *Amsterdam News*, a major black newspaper in New York, columnist

Kwame Okampa-Ahoofe attacked congressional Republicans in 1996 for "genocide against African Americans and other racial minorities." His target was a Republican bill that would increase spending on prisons to keep career criminals off the streets. Adolf Hitler could not have crafted a more anti-black policy, Mr. Okampa-Ahoofe said. He was equally contemptuous of welfare reform, which "squarely aims to destroy African American families."[86] (Bill Clinton's support for welfare reform was not called into question; indeed, even after he signed it into law, famed black novelist Toni Morrison praised Clinton as "our first black president.")[87]

Mr. Okampa-Ahoofe may be a bit over the top in his views, but even well-known black journalists writing in our most respected newspapers often express opinions about the Republican Party that are only a little less extreme. For example, Bob Herbert of the *New York Times* said this in 2005: "I've come to expect racial effrontery from big shots in the Republican Party. The G.O.P. has happily replaced the Democratic Party as the safe haven for bigotry, racially divisive tactics and strategies and outright anti-black policies."[88]

Cynthia Tucker, editorial page editor of the *Atlanta Journal and Constitution* and winner of the Pulitzer Prize for commentary in 2007, is another black journalist who commonly ascribes racist motives to everything the Republican Party does that she disagrees with. In a 2003 column, Tucker said, "the party has acquired a reputation for using race as a blunt instrument in political warfare."[89] In 2004, she asserted, "The GOP has built a Southern base by accommodating racists."[90]

Of course, Mr. Herbert and Ms. Tucker are perfectly free to hold their opinions and express them as strenuously as they choose. After all, it's their job to express strongly held opinions in order to get people talking and thinking. But when those at the top of their profession, writing in our most prestigious publications, express intemperate views that are uninformed by historical fact, they give license to politicians and activists to be even more unrestrained in their opinions, leading to a coarsening of public debate that poisons race relations.

Thus in 2003, black State Representative Garnet Coleman, Democrat of Texas, viciously attacked U.S. Representative Tom DeLay, Republican of Texas, saying, "If you think he represents the interests of our people, you believe that the Grand Dragon of the Ku Klux Klan represents our efforts."[91] In 2006, highly influential left-wing blogger Markos Moulitsas (dailykos.com) said, "Is it any wonder the GOP is the party of racists? Not every Republican is a racist. But the opposite—every racist is a Republican—is just about right."[92]

The point is not to single out these individuals. It's not uncommon to read similar comments—and worse—throughout the blogosphere. And white Republicans like Tom DeLay and New Gingrich are not the only targets. Black Republicans suffer much worse. Black poet Amiri Baraka once referred to Secretary of State Condoleezza Rice as a "skeeza," which is street slang for "whore."[93] Black columnist Sam Fulwood III called former Secretary of State Colin Powell a "spearchucker" for defending Bush's foreign policy.[94] Black singer Harry Belafonte called both Powell and Rice "house slaves" because they worked in Republican administrations.[95] When White House aide Claude Allen was arrested for shoplifting in 2006, black columnist Erin Aubry Kaplan suggested that he was driven to it by the "cognitive dissonance" of being both black and a conservative.[96]

Black Republicans running for office have probably suffered the worst treatment. Maryland Lieutenant Governor Michael Steele often had Oreo cookies thrown at him on the campaign trail—because they are black on the outside and white on the inside, the term "Oreo" is often used to accuse blacks of "acting white" when they don't rigidly follow the liberal Democratic party line.[97] A black blogger posted a doctored image of Steele on a website showing him as a nineteenth-century minstrel in blackface. And the president of the Maryland State Senate publicly referred to Steele as an "Uncle Tom," after the obsequious character in Harriet Beecher Stowe's novel. Even the liberal *Washington Post* was appalled and condemned Maryland Democratic leaders for not denouncing such racist treatment of Steele.[98]

By contrast, when Senator Trent Lott, Republican of Mississippi, made the mistake of appearing to praise the presidential race of his colleague, Senator Strom Thurmond of South Carolina, he was forced to give up his position as Senate Majority Leader despite profuse apologies for the gaffe. (As noted in chapter 8, while still a member of the Democratic Party, Thurmond ran a racist campaign in 1948 on the Dixiecrat ticket.) Even though it was just an innocent remark at a retirement party for Thurmond, Democrats did everything in their power to make Lott look as bad as possible, using the occasion to paint every Republican as a closet racist.[99]

The Lott treatment is typical for any prominent Republican who inadvertently says something that can be construed as racist. In 2005, former Education Secretary Bill Bennett was accused of advocating abortions for black women to reduce crime, when he clearly meant no such thing—he called such an idea "ridiculous and morally reprehensible" during the same radio broadcast.[100] Even though any reasonable person hearing or reading Bennett's complete remarks could easily see that they were taken totally out of context, it didn't stop liberals like Bob Herbert from using the occasion to once again excoriate the Republican Party for racism. Said Herbert, "Bill Bennett's musings about the extermination of blacks in America . . . is all a piece with a Republican Party philosophy that is endlessly insulting to black people and overwhelmingly hostile to their interests."[101]

RACIST DEMOCRATS GET A PASS

What is so galling about these episodes to Republicans is the double standard: blatant racism in the Democratic Party usually passes without notice or denunciation from Democratic leaders or the civil rights establishment. Previous chapters have noted the racist records of highly respected Democrats such as Senators Richard B. Russell of Georgia and Robert C. Byrd of West Virginia, who rose to the highest levels of power in the Democratic Party despite their well-known and often demonstrated hostility to civil rights. Byrd, for example, was elected Senate Democratic Whip in 1971 and Majority Leader in 1977 even though he was known to have once been a member of the Ku Klux Klan and had personally filibustered the Civil Rights Act of 1964.[102]

Down to the present day, cases of overt racists holding high-level positions in the Democratic leadership are not uncommon—Byrd still serves in the Senate, where he chairs the powerful Committee on Appropriations. And as recently as 2001, he was still making racist remarks, referring to "white niggers" on national television.[103] Following are a few other contemporary cases that people may have forgotten.

Senator Sam Ervin, Democrat of North Carolina (1954–1974)

Anyone who remembers the 1970s remembers Ervin for his prominent role in the Watergate investigation. As chairman of the Select Committee on Presidential Campaign Activities in the Ninety-Third Congress, Ervin was well known for his relentless attacks on Richard Nixon for the Watergate cover-up, which made him a folk hero and darling among liberals. Conveniently, they overlooked his long record of opposition to every civil rights measure that came up while he was in the Senate. In 1956, Ervin even wrote an article for *Look Magazine*, one of the largest circulation magazines in America at that time, titled, "The Case for Segregation." Said Ervin in that article, "I believe in racial segregation as it exists in the South today."[104]

Senator Herman Talmadge, Democrat of Georgia (1956–1980)

The son of infamous racist Eugene Talmadge, whose career is reviewed in chapter 4, Herman was a chip off the old block.[105] Having replaced his father as governor of Georgia in 1946, he publicly attended Ku Klux Klan events in his official capacity.[106] In 1955, Talmadge published an entire book devoted to attacking the civil rights movement and defending segregation. He was especially concerned about the degrading effects of intermarriage. Said Talmadge, "history shows that nations composed of a mongrel race lose their strength and become weak, lazy and indifferent."[107] Nevertheless, he was elected to the U.S. Senate in 1956, where, despite his racist past, he rose to the chairmanship of the Senate Agriculture Committee. In 1975, Talmadge was awarded an honorary degree by Morris

Brown College, a historically black school, even though he never renounced his racist past.[108]

Senator John Stennis, Democrat of Mississippi (1947–1988)

Elected to succeed the notorious Theodore Bilbo, who was discussed in chapter 5, Stennis shared his predecessor's opposition to integration. In a 1955 interview, Stennis asserted that contrary to popular belief, blacks really wanted separate schools. Moreover, he argued that allowing black and white children to attend the same schools would "eventually destroy each race." Stennis said it was better to abolish public education altogether than permit integration.[109] Nevertheless, he was among the most respected members of the Senate until his retirement, chairing the Armed Services and Appropriations Committees for many years. Stennis was honored by his fellow Democrats by being elected President *pro tempore* of the Senate during the One Hundredth Congress.

Senator Ernest F. Hollings, Democrat of South Carolina (1966–2004)

Elected governor of South Carolina in 1958, Hollings was a staunch opponent of integration.[110] Among his actions was signing into law a bill that added the Confederate symbol to the state's flag. After his election to the Senate in 1966, Hollings continued his intolerant ways. In 1981, he referred to fellow Democratic Senator Howard Metzenbaum of Ohio as "the Senator from B'nai B'rith" for his opposition to school prayer.[111] In 1983, Hollings was forced to apologize for calling supporters of fellow Democratic Senator Alan Cranston of California "wetbacks."[112] In 1986, Hollings used the word "darkies" to describe minimum wage workers in South Carolina.[113] And in 1993, he said that it was good for African leaders to attend international conferences because they would get a good meal instead of having to eat each other.[114] Yet despite these and other racially offensive comments, Hollings served without reprimand and chaired the Senate Budget Committee and the Committee on Commerce.

Senator Christopher Dodd, Democrat of Connecticut (1980–)

On April 1, 2004, Senator Robert C. Byrd cast his 17,000th vote in the Senate. Many senators rose to congratulate their colleague, but the most effusive was Dodd. As he said that day, "I do not think it is an exaggeration at all to say to my friend from West Virginia that he would have been a great senator at any moment. . . . He would have been right during the great conflict of civil war in this nation."[115] Considering Byrd's well-known and admitted past membership in the Ku Klux Klan, Dodd's words could have been construed as endorsing that nefarious group and he quickly apologized.[116] This incident would not be worth mentioning except that the words spoken by Trent Lott about Strom Thurmond in 2002 were very similar and spoken in the same context of honoring a longtime colleague. But while there was a firestorm of controversy about Lott's comments and he lost his leadership position, Dodd was not punished in any way and the story instantly vanished.

Senator James Webb, Democrat of Virginia (2006–)

During Webb's campaign to unseat Republican Senator George Allen in 2006, the liberal *New Republic* magazine dogged Allen for his alleged pro-Confederacy views.[117] These charges were picked up in the major media and contributed heavily to Allen's defeat by Webb. However, there is no media record of the fact that Webb himself held views even more sympathetic to the Confederacy than Allen's. On June 3, 1990, Webb spoke at the Confederate Memorial at Arlington Cemetery and talked extensively about the "gallantry" of the Confederate soldiers that is "still misunderstood by most Americans." He even voiced sympathy for the idea of state sovereignty and the right to secede from the Union.[118] Yet although it is far more supportive of the Confederacy than anything Allen ever said and was easily available on Webb's personal web site, no mention of this speech ever appeared in the *New Republic, Washington Post,* or other major media outlet.

The point of this review is to show that down to the present day there is a vast double standard, which holds Republicans strictly accountable for the most innocuous racial transgression, but consistently looks the other way at far more egregious offenses committed by Democrats.

A TIME FOR REASSESSMENT?

Many blacks know that their virtually monolithic support for the Democratic Party has not always served them well. They end up being ignored by both major parties—the Democrats take them for granted, while the Republicans have given up hope of attracting their votes and don't really try any more. There's not much doubt, however, that if the black vote were in play, and both major parties had to compete for it by offering policies and patronage, it would increase black political leverage and improve the condition of African Americans.[1]

But when the idea of strategically relocating to the Republican Party is raised, blacks complain that the party doesn't want them. In response, black Republican Arthur Fletcher, an assistant secretary of Labor in the Nixon Administration, points out that blacks weren't wanted by segregated schools, hotels, and lunch counters, either, but they demanded access and fought for it with demonstrations, law suits, and legislation. He says that blacks should fight just as hard for access to the Republican Party by joining local organizations, running for office, and working to develop black-friendly policies acceptable to Republicans. Asks Fletcher, "Why do we have to wait for an invitation to consider the importance of making our influence felt in both major parties?"[2]

In North Carolina, there has been an effort to do exactly that. Black leaders in that state concluded that the Republican hold on it is now so great that they had no choice except to become involved with that party or have no political influence whatsoever. They started a campaign to get blacks to drop their Democratic Party registration and register instead as independents in order to prove that their votes were in play.[3]

One problem for Republicans in reaching out to black people is that the concept of civil rights within the black community has expanded far beyond the abolition of government-enforced segregation to include a broad range of social and economic issues on which there are honest political and philosophical differences unrelated to race. Consider this comment by Delegate Eleanor Holmes Norton, who represents the District of Columbia in Congress:

> I would argue that unemployment benefits are a form of civil rights. Because of the great work of the 1960s, there are only a few clear-cut issues left, like hate crimes and racial profiling. Now we're following the bread-and-butter issues that we share with a broader array of Americans, because issues like health insurance and unemployment affect us so disproportionately.[4]

One the one hand, Ms. Norton is right that there are few issues today on which there is a distinct racial dimension; the interests of blacks are, for the most part, the same as those of whites, Asians, and other groups. However, as long as blacks persist in viewing issues like unemployment compensation exclusively through a racial prism, it will be very difficult for them to engage meaningfully in dialogue with Republicans. Issues like that are too complex to be viewed in such simplistic racial terms. There are too many dimensions to programs like unemployment compensation: economic, fiscal, structural, geographical, and others. To assert an overriding racial dimension when it is obvious that other factors are dominant is to argue that a single tree constitutes an entire forest.

In the 2000s, there have been signs that a new generation of black leaders is emerging who have grown up in the post-civil rights era and are not so firm in their loyalty to the Democratic Party and 1960s-style liberalism.[5] This new generation may be more pragmatic, more open to working with Republicans and considering conservative proposals for improving the lives of African Americans, such as establishing enterprise zones in the inner cites and providing vouchers for private education.

It is revealing that some black businessmen have come out in support of a Republican plan to abolish the estate tax, angering many liberals.[6] It's also revealing that a number of black Democrats, as well as black celebrities such as boxer Mike Tyson and music mogul Russell Simmons, endorsed black Republican Michael Steele in his U.S. Senate race in 2006.[7]

One factor favoring Republicans is the growing income of black families. The wage gap between black and white workers has narrowed significantly since passage of the Civil Rights Act of 1964.[8] According to the Census Bureau, the income of black households has risen from three-fifths of the national median in 1967 to two-thirds in 2005. Where blacks really lag, economically, is in terms of wealth.[9] One key reason is their excessively conservative approach to investing. Studies have found that blacks are much less willing to invest in the stock market than whites. When compounded over a lifetime, this has a significant impact on relative wealth levels at retirement.[10]

This suggests that one easy way Republicans might help themselves and African Americans would be to work with the financial services industry to create a campaign to encourage blacks to invest more in the stock market. Over the long run, it will increase black wealth and, thereby, make blacks more likely to vote Republican.[11] According to a Zogby poll in 2000, those who invest in stocks are 37 percent more likely to be registered Republicans than Democrats, and those who don't invest at all are 18 percent more likely to be Democrats.[12] A 2005 poll by CBS News and the *New York Times* found that 59 percent of Republicans were invested in stocks, while only 40 percent of Democrats were.[13]

IMMIGRATION OPPORTUNITY

Another Republican opportunity to attract black voters may lie in immigration policy. Wisely or unwisely, it is pretty clear that the anti-immigrant wing of the Republican Party has become dominant, thus further pushing Hispanics into the Democratic Party.[14] Since blacks and Hispanics tend to be political rivals and since the Hispanic population is larger and growing faster, it stands to reason that Democrats will tend to favor Hispanics over blacks in the future when there is a conflict of interests.[15] Moreover, blacks tend to share Republican concerns about immigration, legal and illegal.[16] As a recent article in the *National Journal* explained:

> Polls show that African Americans and low-income people mostly oppose greater immigration. A survey of 6,000 people released in March 2006 by the Pew Research Center for People and the Press reported that 58 percent of "financially struggling" Democratic respondents, and 56 percent of black Democratic respondents, believed that legal and illegal immigrants were "a burden."

> Informal polls show even greater opposition to immigration. Up to 80 percent of blacks in Houston oppose further Hispanic immigration, said Michael Harris, a leading talk-show host on KCOH radio in that city. "Most of my audience opposes it. They see Hispanics as competition for jobs . . . [and] rental property," said Harris, who is African American. Crowding in schools and hospitals, as well as Hispanics' use of affirmative action benefits, also angers blacks, who feel excluded from jobs when they can't speak Spanish, Harris said.[17]

Such concerns in the black community are not new. As long ago as 1881, Frederick Douglass complained that immigrants from Ireland were taking jobs from African Americans. Said Douglass, "Every hour sees us elbowed out of some employment to make room for some newly arrived emigrant from the Emerald Isle, whose hunger and color entitle him to special favor."[18] In his famous Atlanta Exposition Address in 1895, Booker T. Washington begged white employers to reject "those of foreign birth and strange tongue and habits" in favor of native-born blacks, who have toiled "without strikes and labor wars."[19] More recently, black poet Toni Morrison observed that whatever an immigrant's nationality or ethnicity, "his nemesis is understood to be African American."[20]

There is growing black activism against Hispanic immigrants. A group called Choose Black America, for example, organized a big demonstration against immigration reform in Los Angeles on June 23, 2007. A leader of this group, veteran black activist Ted Hayes, left no doubt about the point of the rally. "We . . . will not sit by quietly as illegal aliens fill our jobs, our schools and our hospitals," he said.[21] Mainstream black organizations like the National Urban League also opposed the immigration reform bill.[22]

Black concerns about Hispanic immigrants are shared by labor unions.[23] In early 2007, they established a group called the Coalition for the Future American Worker to arouse black opposition to amnesty for illegal aliens. It ran an advertisement in the *Washington Post* on April 19, 2007, with this headline: "Amnesty for Illegal Workers Is Not Just a Slap in the Face to Black Americans. It's an Economic Disaster."[24] The ad cited a study by Harvard economist George Borjas and others showing that a 10 percent increase in immigrants reduces black wages by 4 percent and lowers employment by black men by 3.5 percent.[25]

Democrats are well aware of the adverse effect of immigration on the economic condition of blacks, but they argue that an increase in the number of Hispanic voters will elect more Democrats who will then enact liberal legislation to offset the impact. As Congressman Barney Frank, Democrat of Massachusetts, put it, "If [a Democratic Congress] were to significantly strengthen unions, then you would offset the negative effect on the income of workers."[26]

Whether immigration becomes the breakthrough issue that will open the door to the black community for Republicans remains to be seen. But there is no question that it is in the interest of both blacks and Republicans to form an alliance on the issue. Republicans are going to need new voters to compensate for the loss of Hispanic votes resulting from the party's growing antipathy to illegal immigration, and blacks are going to need leverage to compensate for the fact that Hispanics will tend to be favored over them in the future within the Democratic coalition.

The immigration issue is not going away—there are too many business interests and Democratic politicians that want and need a large and growing Hispanic population that can live, work, and vote legally in the United States. Defeat of George W. Bush's immigration reform proposal in 2007 only put off the day when overwhelming political and economic forces eventually come together to enact some permanent resolution to the problem of illegal aliens that will almost certainly involve amnesty for almost all of them. Once Bush is gone, Republicans will have plenty of time to cultivate black concerns about Hispanic immigrants as a wedge issue.

REPUBLICANS FOR REPARATIONS?

But the immigration issue alone is not going to turn many black voters into Republicans. It only plows the ground so that they may become more receptive to Republican outreach. For Republicans to have any real hope of attracting black votes, they are going to have to put something meaningful on the table that will show they are serious about competing for black voters. I suggest that reparations for slavery may be that issue.

The idea of paying reparations to black people for the cost of slavery has been around for many years.[27] Most conservatives condemn the idea. They argue that the thousands of deaths suffered by Union soldiers in the Civil War paid the debt owed to slaves. They also make compelling arguments about the impracticality of identifying the descendents of slaves and calculating a reasonable amount and type of reparations. And they note that we have had policies like affirmative action for many years that are *de facto* reparations, not to mention the trillions of dollars in government aid that have been paid out over the years to poor blacks in the form of welfare, housing subsidies, food stamps, and so on.[28]

Nevertheless, there is a conservative argument for reparations based on generally accepted legal principles. Put simply, the slaves had something important stolen from them by the slave traders and owners. They lost not only their labor, but their homes, families, and much else. These things were never returned to them when slavery was abolished. The slaves were set free, but never "made whole" as we attempt to do through the tort law whenever someone suffers an injury at the hands of another person. The fact that this debt occurred more than one hundred years ago doesn't alter the fact that there was an uncompensated liability that was unpaid to those who were injured and is still owed to their descendents.[29] Nor does it matter that slavery was legal in the states where it existed, any more than it matters that the Holocaust was technically legal in Nazi Germany. In short, the principle of paying reparations for slavery is perfectly sound on legal grounds that any conservative or libertarian could accept.[30]

Another conservative argument is that affirmative action is such an imperfect form of reparations that it should simply be scrapped. But it may be politically impossible to do that unless something else is offered in its place. If some explicit form of reparations were paid that would settle the debt owed to slaves and their descendents once and for all, then it might be possible to abolish affirmative action, minority set asides, preferential admissions to universities, and other such policies. These quasi-reparations are widely condemned as inefficient, unfair, and poisonous to race relations, and it would indeed be highly beneficial to be rid of them. Hence, there is the potential for a "grand bargain" of swapping one for the other, which has been championed for some years by conservative columnist Charles Krauthammer:

> It is time for a historic compromise: a monetary reparation to blacks for centuries of oppression in return for the total abolition of all programs of racial preference. A one-time cash payment in return for a new era of irrevocable color blindness. . . . The savings to the country will be substantial: an end to endless litigation, to the inefficiencies of allocation by group (rather than merit), to the distortion of the American principle of individualism, to the resentments aroused by a system of group preferences. The fact is, we already have a system of racial compensation. It is called affirmative action. That system is not only inherently unjust but socially demoralizing and inexcusably clumsy. Far better an honest focused substitute: real, hard, one-time compensation.[31]

There is also a public policy case for reparations based on the idea that the cost of slavery and subsequent racial discrimination has done long and lasting damage not just to the actual descendents of slaves, but to all African Americans. There is no question that there is a heavy cost simply to being black.[32] While there may be no payment or policy that would ever cause this to completely disappear, a properly designed reparations program could go a long way toward leveling the playing field, especially if it took the form of college scholarships or some other means of building human capital.

Finally, there is the political dimension. Although reparations for slavery may seem like a Democratic issue, in fact the Democrats have nothing to gain by promoting them. Why should they when blacks already vote Democratic overwhelmingly? By contrast, Republicans have a great deal to gain in terms of earning the credibility of black voters, most of whom, rightly or wrongly, view the Republican Party with deep suspicion. Furthermore, Democrats would look as if they are just pandering to their own base if they endorsed reparations, while a Republican would appear bold and innovative. Influential black political analyst Cedric Muhammad believes that supporting reparations would not only benefit Republicans in terms of votes, but in also in terms of cultivating black support for other elements of a policy agenda that would empower and uplift black people. In Muhammad's words:

> The black electorate would recognize the maneuver as the boldest form of black outreach yet, and be willing, I believe, to give the Republican politician at least 10 percent to 15 percent support on that issue alone. Along the way, the Republican, if he were . . . pro-economic growth in

orientation could style his agenda of vouchers, tax cuts, and health care as "reparations friendly." All that would be necessary would be for the Republican to link the policy with the current problem's genesis in slavery—something the Democrats and black leaders used to do during the sixties and seventies. *In the final analysis, only Republicans are capable of delivering the reparations-for-affirmative action exchange that the American electorate may require.*[33]

It goes without saying that designing any kind of reparations program would be monumentally hard, and implementing it may encounter insurmountable difficulties. But if Republicans would at least embrace the principle of reparations, they might be able to find a way to do *something* that would be mutually beneficial for them and African Americans. Such an effort, if sincere, would at least open the door to the black community even if it ultimately proved impossible to implement.

RAPPROCHEMENT?

For the first 70 years or so after they obtained their freedom and were allowed to vote, blacks cast their ballots overwhelmingly for the Republican Party, the party of Abraham Lincoln. Unfortunately, this didn't necessarily serve them well because Republicans came to take their votes for granted and did little to improve their condition after 1875.

In the 1930s, blacks switched their party loyalty *en masse* because the Democrats seemed more committed to their concerns and well-being. But once the Democrats realized that they had a virtual lock on blacks' votes, they followed the same pattern for the next 70 years that the Republicans had followed earlier and essentially took them for granted.

With equal years of experience in belonging almost entirely to one party or the other, it ought to be apparent to African Americans that such blind loyalty is not in their best interest. They would be far better off if both parties had to bid for their support in every election, with black votes going to the party that was most willing to offer policies and patronage and benefits for them in return. Insofar as the government and the political system are capable of improving their lot, this will clearly accomplish more than blacks have been able to achieve by being captives of just one party, whether it's the Republicans or the Democrats.

It is not necessary for all blacks or even a majority of them to switch to make them attractive to Republicans, and thus gain greater respect from Democrats. If Republicans could just raise their share of the black vote from 10 percent to 20 percent or 30 percent—a figure Republicans achieved under Dwight Eisenhower—it would be enough to shift some elections and make blacks an important constituency worth courting at election time.

The purpose of this book is to encourage Republicans to compete for the black vote and at the same time show blacks why they should be receptive if Republicans should ask for a hearing. Blacks deserve better than being pawns in the political game. It is very much in their interest to be players. But that won't happen unless they are willing to loosen the ties that bind them almost exclusively to the Democratic Party, the party to which their greatest oppressors belonged.

A NOTE ON SOURCES

The Internet has tremendously changed historical research. Documents and data that previously might have taken days or weeks to locate can now be found in seconds with a few clicks of a mouse. Public and university libraries increasingly are making powerful databases available to students and the general public. This is making possible deeper and faster research than previously imaginable.

For example, my local library in Fairfax County, Virginia, makes a number of databases available to anyone with a computer and a library card. One that I used heavily has every issue of the *Washington Post* from 1877 to the present online. As the newspaper of record for politics in the nation's capital, this was invaluable. Many other newspapers are available through their own web sites for a fee. *Time Magazine* makes all of its archives since 1923 freely available and the *New York Times* now makes all of its archives from 1851 to the present available for its subscribers as well.

I also discovered that anyone with a library card from a public library in Virginia also has remote access to the state library in Richmond, which makes additional databases available. I assume that other states have similar resources available to their citizens. Although such databases tend to be geared toward high school and middle school students, there are also a great many academic journals, law reviews, and other sophisticated research sources available. Presumably, the accessibility of theses kinds of sources will grow with time.

Lastly, I should note that one of the colleges I attended, Georgetown University, allows its alumni to have off-campus access to some of its library databases, including one that makes available every historical issue of *The Nation* and *New Republic* magazines. This was especially helpful to me because, although they tilt further to the left than I do, their political coverage of many key people and events critical to this book is incomparable, as evidenced by my endnotes.

I assume that other universities also have similar arrangements for their alumni. In any case, the resources available at a good research library have grown amazingly since I was a student. One extremely valuable database that all have access to is called JSTOR. It makes available a vast number of academic journals from the nineteenth and early twentieth centuries that were formerly accessible only in the largest university libraries. Now, college students everywhere have the same resources, which greatly levels the playing field for those unable to attend a top university. It also makes life much easier for independent researchers such as me.

My only complaint about JSTOR and some other useful databases is that they are presently geared exclusively toward libraries and have no option for individual subscriptions. Personally, I would have been willing to pay several hundred dollars to be able to access JSTOR from my home and not have to drive all the way into Washington to use it. On occasion, I would have been willing to pay a pretty high one-time use fee just to get one article that I needed right that minute. But, alas, JSTOR left my money lying on the table and provided no means by which I could pay for what I needed. I hope this will change.

In terms of freely available resources, I relied heavily on the Congressional Biographical Directory available online here:

http://bioguide.congress.gov/biosearch/biosearch.asp

It lists the name of every person who ever served in Congress along with basic biographical information, terms of service, party affiliation, etc. It also lists bibliographical information when it exists, as well as the location of personal papers and other archival sources if they are known to the Library of Congress. This was extremely valuable to me. This source also points to a severe imbalance in our knowledge of Congress. Some members have been the subject of much research and multiple biographies, while others of equal or greater importance in their day have been completely ignored by historians and biographers. Doctoral students looking for dissertation topics should rescue some of these forgotten congressmen and senators from underserved obscurity.

In terms of congressional history, I would add that the Library of Congress has a vast amount of documentary material online. The most valuable is every issue of the *Congressional Globe*, forerunner to the *Congressional Record*, from 1833 to 1873. It is online here:

http://memory.loc.gov/ammem/amlaw/lwcg.html

Unfortunately, the *Congressional Record* itself is available only for 1874–75 and for the years since 1989. The Library of Congress really should make it a priority to get the material from the intervening 114 years online as soon as possible.

Parenthetically, I should note that one important reason to get historical materials online is that they are wearing out from use and need to be saved in a form that will reduce their physical degradation. Through overuse, misuse, and irresponsibility, many of the books, magazines, and journals in the Library of Congress and other libraries that I used for this book are in dreadful shape. Fortunately, some are being rescued. Cornell University and the University of Michigan have digitalized a number of nineteenth century magazines and journals and made them available online here:

http://www.memory.loc.gov/ammem/ndlpcoop/moahtml/snctitles.html

Among the most valuable periodicals in this collection are the *Atlantic Monthly* and the *North American Review*. The latter is now forgotten, but was once a very important publication that is essential for studying nineteenth century political history.

In terms of the presidency, an extraordinarily valuable resource is the American Presidency Project at the University of California, Santa Barbara. It is available here:

http://www.presidency.ucsb.edu/index.php

It has all of the public papers of the presidents since Herbert Hoover, as well as inaugural addresses and State of the Union addresses for every president since George Washington. It also has presidential polling data and every party platform, among other things. It is incredibly useful and well organized. For this reason, I have not footnoted presidential statements and speeches that are easily found on this web site. It is sufficient only to know the date to find such things and there is no point in citing page numbers in obscure published volumes.

Lastly, I should note that online booksellers have been incredibly helpful in my research. There were occasions when I was able to buy for a few dollars books that didn't exist even in the Library of Congress. When I recall the days when it took at least six weeks to get a copy of a book that was in print and months or even years to find one that was out of print, I feel no nostalgia. However, I was dismayed to see how many of the used books I purchased were withdrawn from libraries that should have kept them. Perhaps one day Google will make them all available online, but until that day comes, students and researchers are going to need access to the books themselves.

Finally, I would like to call readers' attention to a useful website for converting dollars in the distant past to current dollars, which is often essential for understanding economic magnitudes:

http://measuringworth.com/calculators/uscompare

APPENDIX I

Percentage of Blacks in the Population by Region and State, 1790–1990

Region/State	1790	1810	1830	1850	1870	1890	1910	1930	1950	1970	1990
Northeast	3.4	2.9	2.3	1.7	1.5	1.6	1.9	3.3	5.1	8.9	11.0
CT	2.3	2.6	2.7	2.1	1.8	1.6	1.4	1.8	2.7	6.0	8.3
ME	0.6	0.4	0.3	0.2	0.3	0.2	0.2	0.1	0.1	0.3	0.4
MA	1.4	1.4	1.2	0.9	1.0	1.0	1.1	1.2	1.6	3.1	5.0
NH	0.6	0.5	0.2	0.2	0.2	0.2	0.1	0.2	0.1	0.3	0.6
NJ	7.7	7.6	6.4	4.9	3.4	3.3	3.5	5.2	6.6	10.7	13.4
NY	7.6	4.2	2.3	1.6	1.2	1.2	1.5	3.3	6.2	11.9	15.9
PA	2.4	2.9	2.8	2.3	1.9	2.0	2.5	4.5	6.1	8.6	9.2
RI	6.3	4.8	3.7	2.5	2.3	2.1	1.8	1.4	1.8	2.7	3.9
VT	0.3	0.3	0.3	0.2	0.3	0.3	0.5	0.2	0.1	0.2	0.3
Midwest	n/a	2.4	2.6	2.5	2.1	1.9	1.8	3.3	5.0	8.1	9.6
IL	n/a	6.4	1.5	0.6	1.1	1.5	1.9	4.3	7.4	12.8	14.8
IN	n/a	2.6	1.1	1.1	1.5	2.1	2.2	3.5	4.4	6.9	7.8
IA	n/a	n/a	n/a	0.2	0.5	0.6	0.7	0.7	0.8	1.2	1.7
KS	n/a	n/a	n/a	n/a	4.7	3.5	3.2	3.5	3.8	4.8	5.8
MI	n/a	3.0	0.8	0.6	1.0	0.7	0.6	3.5	6.9	11.2	13.9
MN	n/a	n/a	n/a	0.6	0.2	0.3	0.3	0.4	0.5	0.9	2.2
MO	n/a	17.6	18.3	13.2	6.9	5.6	4.8	6.2	7.5	10.3	10.7
NE	n/a	n/a	n/a	n/a	0.6	0.8	0.6	1.0	1.5	2.7	3.6
ND	n/a	n/a	n/a	n/a	1.0	0.2	0.1	0.1	0.0	0.4	0.6
OH	n/a	0.8	1.0	1.3	2.4	2.4	2.3	4.7	6.5	9.1	10.6
SD	n/a	n/a	n/a	n/a	0.6	0.2	0.1	0.1	0.1	0.2	0.5
WI	n/a	n/a	1.8	0.2	0.2	0.1	0.1	0.4	0.8	2.9	5.0
South	35.2	36.7	37.9	37.3	36.0	33.8	29.8	24.7	21.7	19.1	18.5
AL	n/a	29.0	38.5	44.7	47.7	44.8	42.5	35.7	32.0	26.2	25.3
AR	n/a	13.0	15.5	22.7	25.2	27.4	28.1	25.8	22.3	18.3	15.9
DE	21.6	23.8	24.9	22.2	18.2	16.8	15.4	13.7	13.7	14.3	16.9
FL	n/a	n/a	47.1	46.0	48.8	42.5	41.0	29.4	21.8	15.3	13.6
GA	35.9	42.5	42.6	42.4	46.0	46.7	45.1	36.8	30.9	25.9	27.0
KY	17.0	20.2	24.7	22.5	16.8	14.4	11.4	8.6	6.9	7.2	7.1
LA	n/a	55.2	58.5	50.7	50.1	50.0	43.1	36.9	32.9	29.8	30.8

Continued

Appendix I   Continued

Region/State	1790	1810	1830	1850	1870	1890	1910	1930	1950	1970	1990
MD	34.7	38.2	34.9	28.3	22.5	20.7	17.9	16.9	16.5	17.8	24.9
MS	n/a	47.0	48.4	51.2	53.7	57.6	56.2	50.2	45.3	36.8	35.6
NC	26.8	32.2	35.9	36.4	36.6	34.7	31.6	29.0	25.8	22.2	22.0
OK	n/a	n/a	n/a	n/a	n/a	8.4	8.3	7.2	6.5	6.7	7.4
SC	43.7	48.4	55.6	58.9	58.9	59.8	55.2	45.6	38.8	30.5	29.8
TN	10.6	17.5	21.4	24.5	25.6	24.4	21.7	18.3	16.1	15.8	16.0
TX	n/a	n/a	n/a	27.5	31.0	21.8	17.7	14.7	12.7	12.5	11.9
VA	43.4	47.1	47.9	45.0	41.9	38.4	32.6	26.8	22.1	18.5	18.8
WV	9.5	11.5	11.2	7.8	4.1	4.3	5.3	6.6	5.7	3.9	3.1
West	n/a	n/a	n/a	0.7	0.6	0.9	0.7	1.0	2.9	4.9	5.4
AK	n/a	n/a	n/a	n/a	n/a	n/a	n/a	n/a	n/a	3.0	4.1
AZ	n/a	n/a	n/a	n/a	0.3	1.5	1.0	2.5	3.5	3.0	3.0
CA	n/a	n/a	n/a	1.0	0.8	0.9	0.9	1.4	4.4	7.0	7.4
CO	n/a	n/a	n/a	n/a	1.1	1.5	1.4	1.1	1.5	3.0	4.0
HI	n/a	n/a	n/a	n/a	n/a	n/a	n/a	n/a	n/a	1.0	2.5
ID	n/a	n/a	n/a	n/a	0.4	0.2	0.2	0.2	0.2	0.3	0.3
MT	n/a	n/a	n/a	n/a	0.9	1.0	0.5	0.2	0.2	0.3	0.3
NV	n/a	n/a	n/a	n/a	0.8	0.5	0.6	0.6	2.7	5.7	6.6
NM	n/a	n/a	n/a	0	0.2	1.2	0.5	0.7	1.2	1.9	2.0
OR	n/a	n/a	n/a	0.5	0.4	0.4	0.2	0.2	0.8	1.3	1.6
UT	n/a	n/a	n/a	0.4	0.1	0.3	0.3	0.2	0.4	0.6	0.7
WA	n/a	n/a	n/a	12.7	0.9	0.4	0.5	0.4	1.3	2.1	3.1
WY	n/a	n/a	n/a	n/a	2.0	1.5	1.5	0.6	0.9	0.8	0.8
US	19.3	19.0	18.1	15.7	12.7	11.9	10.7	9.7	10.0	11.1	12.1

Source: Campbell Gibson and Kay Jung, "Historical Census Statistics on Population Totals by Race, 1790 to 1990, and by Hispanic Origin, 1970 to 1990, for the United States, Regions, Divisions, and States," Population Division Working Paper No. 56, U.S. Census Bureau (September 2002).

APPENDIX II

Presidential Vote of Black Americans 1936–2004
(percent)

Year	Democratic	Republican
1936	71	28
1940	67	32
1944	68	32
1948	77	23
1952	76	24
1956	61	39
1960	68	32
1964	94	6
1968	85	15
1972	87	13
1976	85	15
1980	86	12
1984	89	9
1988	88	10
1992	82	11
1996	84	12
2000	90	9
2004	88	11

Source: Joint Center for Political and Economic Studies; CNN.

APPENDIX III

Per Capita Regional Income Relative to U.S. Average
(U.S. = 100)

Year	West	Northeast	Midwest	South
1880	190	144	97	54
1900	153	139	103	54
1920	124	132	101	64
1940	118	131	101	64
1960	113	114	103	79
1980	109	107	100	90

Source: Kris James Mitchener and Ian W. McLean, "U.S. Regional Growth and Convergence, 1880–1980," *Journal of Economic History* (December 1999), p. 1019.

NOTES

CHAPTER 1

1. On Jefferson's role in the origins of the Democratic Party, see Jules Witcover, *Party of the People: A History of the Democrats* (New York: Random House, 2003), pp. 23–48.
2. On the Founding Fathers' distaste for political parties, see Richard Hofstadter, *The Idea of a Party System* (Berkeley: University of California Press, 1969), pp. 40–73; A. James Reichley, *The Life of the Parties: A History of American Political Parties* (New York: Rowman & Littlefield, 1992), pp. 17–28.
3. Reichley, *Life of the Parties*, pp. 69–89.
4. See Paul Finkelman, *Slavery and the Founders*, 2nd ed. (Armonk, NY: M. E. Sharpe, 2001), pp. 3–36. See also Walter Berns, "The Constitution and the Migration of Slaves," *Yale Law Journal* (December 1968), pp. 198–228; Paul Finkelman, "The Proslavery Origins of the Electoral College," *Cardozo Law Review* (No. 4, 2002), pp. 1145–57.
5. Thomas Jefferson, *Writings* (New York: Library of America, 1984), pp. 265–66.
6. Jefferson, *Writings*, 267–70. He never changed these views throughout his life. See Frederick Binder, *The Color Problem in Early National America as Viewed by John Adams, Jefferson and Jackson* (The Hague, Netherlands: Mouton Publishers, 1968), pp. 73–74.
7. For an excellent discussion of Jefferson's extreme passivity in opposition to slavery, see David Brion Davis, *Was Thomas Jefferson an Authentic Enemy of Slavery?* (Oxford, UK: Clarendon Press, 1970).
8. See, for example, Andrew Dickson White, "Jefferson and Slavery," *Atlantic Monthly* (January 1862), pp. 29–40.
9. Jefferson did sign into law legislation prohibiting the importation of slaves into the United States after January 1, 1808. Act of March 2, 1807, ch. 22, 2 *Stat.* 426. However, this was not really a Jefferson initiative, but merely the fulfillment of a deal made at the Constitutional Convention in 1787 stipulating that Congress could not outlaw the slave trade until 1808 (Article I, Sec. 9, Clause 1). It was always implicitly understood by everyone that the slave trade would be prohibited after that date. Don E. Fehrenbacher, *The Slaveholding Republic* (New York: Oxford University Press, 2001), pp. 42–43. Also, Britain banned the slave trade in 1807, which pretty much forced the United States to follow suit. Although Jefferson requested the antislave-trading bill in his State of the Union message on December 2, 1806, he did nothing to get the bill passed in Congress, despite significant opposition to specific provisions of the legislation that put its passage in doubt at several points. See Matthew E. Mason, "Slavery Overshadowed: Congress Debates Prohibiting the Atlantic Slave Trade to the United States, 1806–1807," *Journal of the Early Republic* (Spring 2000), pp. 59–81. It should be noted as well that the legislation banning the slave trade

had no enforcement mechanism and provided no additional resources to the Treasury Department, which had jurisdiction through its control of the Customs. By contrast, the British Royal Navy was ordered to treat slave traders the same way it treated pirates. However, the United States refused to allow the British Navy to search American flag vessels, with the result that slave traders worldwide used American ships. See Hugh Thomas, *The Slave Trade* (New York: Simon & Schuster, 1997), pp. 551–57, 649, 660–1.

10. Binder, *Color Problem*, p. 71.

11. Kenneth O'Reilly, *Nixon's Piano: Presidents and Racial Politics from Washington to Clinton* (New York: Free Press, 1995), p. 23.

12. William Cohen, "Thomas Jefferson and the Problem of Slavery," *Journal of American History* (December 1969), pp. 503–6. See also John P. Diggins, "Slavery, Race, and Equality: Jefferson and the Pathos of the Enlightenment," *American Quarterly* (Summer 1976), pp. 206–28; Winthrop D. Jordan, *White Over Black: American Attitudes Toward the Negro, 1550–1812* (Chapel Hill: University of North Carolina Press, 1968), pp. 435–47; Nicholas E. Magnis, "Thomas Jefferson and Slavery: An Analysis of His Racist Thinking as Revealed by His Writings and Political Behavior," *Journal of Black Studies* (March 1999), pp. 491–509; William D. Richardson, "Thomas Jefferson & Race: The Declaration & *Notes on the State of Virginia*," *Polity* (Spring 1984), pp. 447–66. The idea that blacks were biologically inferior to whites was a key defense of slavery before the Civil War, and Jefferson was often cited as an authority. See William Sumner Jenkins, *Pro-Slavery Thought in the Old South* (Chapel Hill: University of North Carolina Press, 1935), pp. 242–84. Long after the end of slavery, the same argument was used to justify racial segregation. See James W. Vander Zanden, "The Ideology of White Supremacy," *Journal of the History of Ideas* (June–September 1959), pp. 385–402.

13. Jefferson, *Writings*, p. 1177.

14. Levy points out that Jefferson never protested laws against seditious libel and favored a provision in the Virginia constitution that would permit prosecution for the publication of "false facts." But, as Levy notes, "In politics one man's truth is another's falsity." Leonard W. Levy, *Jefferson and Civil Liberties: The Darker Side*, revised ed. (Chicago: Quadrangle, 1973), pp. 46–47. Josiah Philips was a British loyalist who was the object of a bill of attainder authored by Jefferson that passed the Virginia General Assembly making Philips liable for execution without the benefit of trial. See W.P. Trent, "The Case of Josiah Philips," *American Historical Review* (April 1896), pp. 444–54.

15. Robert McColley, *Slavery and Jeffersonian Virginia* (Urbana: University of Illinois Press, 1964), pp. 124–25; John Chester Miller, *The Wolf by the Ears: Thomas Jefferson and Slavery* (New York: Free Press, 1977), pp. 278–79.

16. Forrest McDonald, *The Presidency of Thomas Jefferson* (Lawrence: University Press of Kansas, 1976), p. 22. It is worth noting that at least twelve of Jefferson's electoral votes resulted from the counting of slaves (at three-fifths each) for the purpose of apportionment in the House of Representatives and therefore the Electoral College. Since he won by only eight electoral votes in 1800, Jefferson would have lost had slaves been treated solely as property and not boosted the South's electoral clout. See Garry Wills, *"Negro President": Jefferson and the Slave Power* (New York: Houghton Mifflin, 2003), pp. 2, 234. The Federalists were well aware of this fact and thereafter made a strenuous attack on slave representation that ended only with the Missouri Compromise. See Albert F. Simpson, "The Political Significance of Slave Representation, 1787–1821," *Journal of Southern History* (August 1941), pp. 315–42.

17. Especially Article IV, Sec. 2, Clause 3, which provided that slaves could not free themselves by escaping to a state where slavery was prohibited. See Earl M. Maltz, "Slavery, Federalism, and the Structure of the Constitution," *American Journal of Legal History* (October 1992), pp. 467–71.

18. The reason that slave states agreed to this diminution of their political power is that the three-fifths clause also limited the federal government's ability to tax them. It is no coincidence that the Constitution's three-fifths clause—Article I, Sec. 2, Clause 3—discusses

apportionment both for purposes of representation and taxation. See Robin Einhorn, *American Taxation, American Slavery* (Chicago: University of Chicago Press, 2006), pp. 162–69; E. James Ferguson, "Public Finance and the Origins of Southern Sectionalism," *Journal of Southern History* (November 1962), pp. 450–61; Erik M. Jensen, *The Taxing Power* (New York: Praeger, 2005), pp. 25–27; Merrill Jensen, *The Articles of Confederation* (Madison: University of Wisconsin Press, 1940), pp. 146–48; Calvin Johnson, *Righteous Anger at the Wicked States: The Meaning of the Founders' Constitution* (New York: Cambridge University Press, 2005), pp. 107–8; Edwin R. A. Seligman, *The Income Tax* (New York: Macmillan, 1914), p. 551.

19. See the testimony of Jefferson's slave Isaac recorded in 1847. He talks of receiving "more whippings than he has fingers and toes." James A. Bear, *Jefferson at Monticello* (Charlottesville: University of Virginia Press, 1967), p. 15.

20. Cohen, "Thomas Jefferson," pp. 506–20; Lucia Stanton, "'Those Who Labor for My Happiness': Thomas Jefferson and His Slaves," in Peter S. Onuf, ed., *Jeffersonian Legacies* (Charlottesville: University Press of Virginia, 1993), pp. 147–80.

21. Fehrenbacher, *Slaveholding Republic*, p. 257. Article 6 of the Northwest Ordinance, the basic law on admission of new states to the Union, plainly prohibited slavery in them: "There shall be neither slavery nor involuntary servitude in the said territory, otherwise than in punishment of crimes, whereof the party shall have been duly convicted: Provided always, that any person escaping into the same, from whom labor or service is lawfully claimed in any one of the original States, such fugitive may be lawfully reclaimed, and conveyed to the person claiming his or her labor or service as aforesaid." Act of August 7, 1789, ch. 8, 1 *Stat.* 50.

22. Fehrenbacher, *Slaveholding Republic*, pp. 259–60. See also Roger G. Kennedy, *Mr. Jefferson's Lost Cause: Land, Farmers, Slavery, and the Louisiana Purchase* (New York: Oxford University Press, 2003), pp. 210–16. Jefferson was one of only two Southerners who voted for the antislavery provision of the Northwest Ordinance the first time it came up for a vote in 1784. See Jordan, *White Over Black*, pp. 321–22. It is not altogether clear why the slave states permitted enactment of a law restricting the spread of slavery. For discussion, see David Brion Davis, "The Significance of Excluding Slavery from the Old Northwest in 1787," *Indiana Magazine of History* (March 1988), pp. 75–89; Paul Finkelman, "Slavery and the Northwest Ordinance: A Study in Ambiguity," *Journal of the Early Republic* (Winter 1986), pp. 343–70; Staughton Lynd, "The Compromise of 1787," *Political Science Quarterly* (June 1966), pp. 225–50.

23. David Brion Davis, *Inhuman Bondage: The Rise and Fall of Slavery in the New World* (New York: Oxford University Press, 2006), p. 270.

24. Jefferson, *Writings*, pp. 1433–34, 1448–49. Economist Daniel Raymond commented at the time, "Diffusion is about as effectual a remedy for slavery as it would be for the smallpox or the plague." Quoted in Davis, *Inhuman Bondage*, p. 277.

25. Harold Hellenbrand, "Not to 'Destroy But to Fulfil': Jefferson, Indians, and Republican Dispensation," *Eighteenth-Century Studies* (Autumn 1985), pp. 523–49. Jefferson held Indians in a higher regard than he did blacks, believing that Indians were capable of greater advancement with proper education. Jefferson, *Writings*, pp. 189, 266; Roger Kennedy, "Jefferson and the Indians," *Winterthur Portfolio* (Summer-Autumn 1992), pp. 105–21. Indeed, he even favored "amalgamation" between the white and Indian races as one solution to the Indian problem. See Binder, *Color Problem*, pp. 112–19.

26. Stephen G. Bragaw, "Thomas Jefferson and the American Indian Nations: Native American Sovereignty and the Marshall Court," *Journal of Supreme Court History* (July 2006), pp. 155–80.

27. Laurent Dubois, *Avengers of the New World: The Story of the Haitian Revolution* (Cambridge: Harvard University Press, 2004), p. 225; Tim Matthewson, "Jefferson and Haiti," *Journal of Southern History* (May 1995), pp. 209–48; Tim Matthewson, "Jefferson and the Nonrecognition of Haiti," *Proceedings of the American Philosophical Society* (March 1996), pp. 22–48.

28. Stanley Elkins and Eric McKitrick, *The Age of Federalism* (New York: Oxford University Press, 1993), pp. 660–62.

29. McDonald, *Presidency of Thomas Jefferson*, p. 105.

30. Gordon S. Wood, "Slaves in the Family," *New York Times Book Review* (December 14, 2003), p. 10. See also Kenneth Morgan, "George Washington and the Problem of Slavery," *Journal of American Studies* (August 2000), pp. 279–301; Henry Wiencek, *An Imperfect God: George Washington, His Slaves, and the Creation of America* (New York: Farrar, Straus & Giroux, 2003). In Wiencek's view, it is revealing that Washington freed *all* of his slaves in his will and not just a few of the most favored, as was often the case with manumissions such as Jefferson's.

31. These were all members of the Hemings family—strong evidence that Jefferson may have fathered children by his slave Sally Hemings. Nevertheless, I don't believe that he in fact fathered any children by her, as is commonly alleged. First, it runs contrary to everything we know about Jefferson's character, views about black inferiority, and opposition to race mixing—he once said that amalgamation between the races "produces degradation." Jefferson, *Writings*, p. 1345. Second, I cannot believe that Jefferson would have enslaved his own children, as he did those of Hemings until his death. This point was emphasized by Jefferson's granddaughter in an 1858 letter commenting on the Hemings allegations. See Dumas Malone, "Jefferson's Private Life," *New York Times* (May 18, 1974). Third, the DNA evidence is inconclusive, suggesting only that someone in Jefferson's family—perhaps his brother or one of his nephews who lived nearby—fathered Hemings' children, not necessarily Thomas Jefferson. On serious problems with the DNA evidence, see Lori B. Andrews *et al.*, "Constructing Ethical Guidelines for Biohistory," *Science* (April 9, 2004), p. 216; Eliot Marshall, "Which Jefferson Was the Father?" *Science* (January 8, 1999), pp. 153–55; David Murray, "Paternity Hype Visits Monticello," *Washington Post* (November 15, 1998). For a review of some recent historical literature on this topic, see Alexander O. Boulton, "The Monticello Mystery-Case Continued," *William and Mary Quarterly* (October 2001), pp. 1039–47.

32. For evidence that manumissions were not uncommon in Jefferson's Virginia, see Art Budros, "Social Shocks and Slave Social Mobility: Manumissions in Brunswick County, Virginia, 1782-1862," *American Journal of Sociology* (November 2004), pp. 539–79; Luther P. Jackson, "Manumission in Certain Virginia Cities," *Journal of Negro History* (July 1930), pp. 278–314.

33. Paul Finkelman, "Thomas Jefferson and Antislavery: The Myth Goes On," *Virginia Magazine of History and Biography* (April 1994), pp. 214–22.

34. Jordan, *White Over Black*, p. 481.

35. See Stephen E. Ambrose, "Flawed Founders," *Smithsonian Magazine* (November 2002), pp. 126–33; William W. Freehling, "The Founding Fathers and Slavery," *American Historical Review* (February 1972), pp. 81–93; Douglas L. Wilson, "Thomas Jefferson and the Character Issue," *Atlantic Monthly* (November 1992), pp. 57–74.

36. Even Jackson's friendly biographers acknowledge that the Treaty of Fort Jackson was extremely harsh. See H. W. Brands, *Andrew Jackson: His Life and Times* (New York: Doubleday, 2005), pp. 231–35; Robert Remini, *The Life of Andrew Jackson* (New York: Harper & Row, 1988), pp. 84–85. The treaty can be found in *American State Papers: Indian Affairs*, vol. 1, pp. 826–27. On the suffering of the Indians after Jackson's victory, see Sean M. O'Brien, *In Bitterness and In Tears: Andrew Jackson's Destruction of the Creeks and Seminoles* (Westport, CT: Praeger, 2003).

37. For a sympathetic view of Jackson's philosophy regarding the Indians, see Francis P. Prucha, "Andrew Jackson's Indian Policy: A Reassessment," *Journal of American History* (December 1969), pp. 527–39.

38. A copy of the Cherokee constitution can be found in Theda Perdue and Michael D. Green, *The Cherokee Removal*, 2nd ed. (New York: Bedford/St. Martin's, 2005), pp. 60–70.

39. In its defense, Georgia pointed out that the articles of cession in 1802 obliged the federal government to extinguish all Indian title in the state in return for ceding the state's western lands to the federal government. The articles can be found in *American State Papers: Public Lands*, vol. 1, p. 114. For the Georgia laws extending its jurisdiction over the Cherokee, see Perdue and Green, *Cherokee Removal*, pp. 76–79.

40. Act of March 30, 1802, ch. 13, 2 *Stat.* 139.

41. Francis P. Prucha, *The Great Father: The United States Government and the American Indians* (Lincoln: University of Nebraska Press, 1984), pp. 192–94.

42. 30 U.S. 15 (1831).

43. 31 U.S. 515 (1832).

44. Jackson is reputed to have said, "John Marshall has made his decision. Now let him enforce it." Although this quote accurately reflects Jackson's sentiment, there is no record of him actually saying those words. See Paul F. Boller Jr. and John George, *They Never Said It* (New York: Oxford University Press, 1989), p. 53. In 1833, the *Worcester* decision became a key element in the nullification controversy between Jackson and South Carolina. After Jackson asked Congress for a force bill that would empower him to use the army to compel South Carolina to respect the 1828 and 1832 tariff laws, which the state had sought to nullify unilaterally, he feared that Congress might also give him power to enforce the *Worcester* decision, an impediment to his Indian removal policy. This led to much behind the scenes negotiating to resolve the issues in the *Worcester* case and keep it separated from the nullification debate. See Edwin Miles, "After John Marshall's Decision: *Worcester v. Georgia* and the Nullification Crisis," *Journal of Southern History* (November 1973), pp. 519–44.

45. See Ronald A. Berutti, "The Cherokee Cases: The Fight to Save the Supreme Court and the Cherokee Indians," *American Indian Law Review* (1992), pp. 291–308; Joseph C. Burke, "The Cherokee Cases: A Study in Law, Politics, and Morality," *Stanford Law Review* (February 1969), pp. 500–31; William S. Hoffman, "Andrew Jackson, State Rights: The Case of the Georgia Indians," *Tennessee Historical Quarterly* (December 1952), pp. 329–45; William Swindler, "Politics as Law: The Cherokee Cases," *American Indian Law Review* (1975), pp. 7–20.

46. Ronald N. Satz, *American Indian Policy in the Jacksonian Era* (Lincoln: University of Nebraska Press, 1975), pp. 20–31; Anthony F. C. Wallace, *The Long, Bitter Trail: Andrew Jackson and the Indians* (New York: Hill and Wang, 1993), pp. 66–70.

47. *House Journal* (May 26, 1830), p. 729. See also Leonard A. Carlson and Mark A. Roberts, "Indian Lands, 'Squatterism,' and Slavery: Economic Interests and the Passage of the Indian Removal Act of 1830," *Explorations in Economic History* (July 2006), pp. 486–504.

48. Section 7 of the law stated, "Nothing in this act contained shall be construed as authorizing or directing the violation of any existing treaty between the United States and any of the Indian tribes." Act of May 28, 1830, ch. 148, 4 *Stat.* 411.

49. Alfred A. Cave, "Abuse of Power: Andrew Jackson and the Indian Removal Act of 1830," *The Historian* (Winter 2003), p. 1337.

50. Mary E. Young, "The Creek Frauds: A Study on Conscience and Corruption," *Mississippi Valley Historical Review* (December 1955), pp. 411–37; Mary E. Young, "Indian Removal and Land Allotment: The Civilized Tribes and Jacksonian Justice," *American Historical Review* (October 1958), pp. 31–45. See also Michael Paul Rogin, *Fathers and Children: Andrew Jackson and the Subjugation of the American Indian* (New York: Alfred A. Knopf, 1975), pp. 219–30.

51. Alexis de Tocqueville, *Democracy in America*, trans. George Lawrence, ed. J. P. Mayer (New York: Harper & Row, 1966), p. 339.

52. *American State Papers: Indian Affairs*, vol. 2, p. 155. For complaints about Indians harboring runaway slaves, see pp. 253 and 698.

53. Kenneth W. Porter, "Negroes and the Seminole War, 1835–1842," *Journal of Southern History* (November 1964), pp. 427–50.

54. Andrew Burstein, *The Passions of Andrew Jackson* (New York: Alfred A. Knopf, 2003), p. 24.

55. John M. McFaul, "Expediency vs. Morality: Jacksonian Politics and Slavery," *Journal of American History* (June 1975), pp. 24–39; Sean Wilentz, *Andrew Jackson* (New York: Times Books, 2005), pp. 121–31.

56. Binder, *Color Problem*, p. 135. Some historians claim that Jackson was merely neutral on the slavery question, but University of Massachusetts historian Leonard Richards calls such claims "far-fetched." Leonard L. Richards, *The Slave Power: The Free North and Southern Domination, 1780–1860* (Baton Rouge: Louisiana State University Press, 2000), p. 113.

57. Richard H. Brown, "The Missouri Crisis, Slavery, and the Politics of Jacksonianism," *South Atlantic Quarterly* (Winter 1966), pp. 55–72.

58. Davis, *Inhuman Bondage*, p. 279. The so-called gag rule adopted by the House of Representatives ordered that all antislavery petitions be tabled automatically. *Register of Debates* (May 26, 1836), pp. 4052–53. Democrats overwhelmingly supported this effort to stifle debate on slavery by a vote of 92 to 21. Whigs opposed it by a vote 46 to 19. Albert Castel and Scott L. Gibson, *The Yeas and Nays: Key Congressional Decisions, 1774–1945* (Kalamazoo, MI: New Issues Press, 1975), p. 47. For further evidence that Democratic Party loyalty, rather than sectional interests, was central to enactment of the gag rule, see Gordon M. Weiner, "Pennsylvania Congressmen and the 1836 Gag Rule: A Quantitative Note," *Pennsylvania History* (July 1969), pp. 335–40.

59. Edward Pessen, *Jacksonian America: Society, Personality, and Politics* (Homewood, IL: Dorsey Press, 1969), pp. 156, 215.

60. Wallace, *Bitter Trail*, pp. 93–94. Other tribes suffered similar cruelties. For details, see Grant Foreman, *Indian Removal* (Norman: University of Oklahoma Press, 1932).

61. John Quincy Adams, *Memoirs of John Quincy Adams*, ed. Charles Francis Adams (Philadelphia: J. B. Lippincott, 1876), vol. 10, p. 492. On the evolution of Adams' thinking about the Indians, see Lynn H. Parsons, "'A Perpetual Harrow Upon My Feelings': John Quincy Adams and the American Indian," *New England Quarterly* (September 1973), pp. 339–79.

62. Lester G. Bugbee, "Slavery in Early Texas," *Political Science Quarterly* (December 1898), pp. 648–68. The constitution adopted by the Republic of Texas in 1836 legalized slavery and prohibited free blacks from living there. Section 9 of the general provisions stated: "All persons of color who were slaves for life previous to their emigration to Texas, and who are now held in bondage, shall remain in the like state of servitude, provided the said slave shall be the bona fide property of the person so holding said slave as aforesaid. Congress shall pass no laws to prohibit emigrants from the United States of America from bringing their slaves into the Republic with them, and holding them by the same tenure by which such slaves were held in the United States; nor shall Congress have power to emancipate slaves; nor shall any slave-holder be allowed to emancipate his or her slave or slaves, without the consent of Congress, unless he or she shall send his or her slave or slaves without the limits of the Republic. No free person of African descent, either in whole or in part, shall be permitted to reside permanently in the Republic, without the consent of Congress, and the importation or admission of Africans or Negroes into this Republic, excepting from the United States of America, is forever prohibited, and declared to be piracy." Downloaded at http://tarlton.law.utexas.edu.

63. William L. Miller, *Arguing About Slavery* (New York: Alfred A. Knopf, 1996), pp. 297–98.

64. Peter L. Rousseau, "Jacksonian Monetary Policy, Specie Flows, and the Panic of 1837," *Journal of Economic History* (June 2002), pp. 457–88; Peter Temin, *The Jacksonian Economy* (New York: W.W. Norton, 1969), pp. 113–71.

65. Arthur M. Schlesinger Jr., *The Age of Jackson* (Boston: Little, Brown, 1945), p. 431.

66. Joel H. Silbey, *Storm Over Texas: The Annexation Controversy and the Road to Civil War* (New York: Oxford University Press, 2005), pp. 69–79.

67. William J. Cooper Jr., *The South and the Politics of Slavery, 1828–1856* (Baton Rouge: Louisiana State University Press, 1978), pp. 182–224.

68. J. L. Worley, "The Diplomatic Relations of England and the Republic of Texas," *Southwestern Historical Quarterly* (July 1905), pp. 1–40.

69. Secretary of State John C. Calhoun raised this concern in a letter to British Minister Richard Pakenham on April 27, 1844. Clyde N. Wilson, ed., *The Papers of John C. Calhoun*, vol. 18 (Columbia: University of South Carolina Press, 1988), pp. 348–51. On the Southern reaction to slavery abolition in Britain, see Edward B. Rugemer, "The Southern Response to British Abolitionism: The Maturation of Proslavery Apologetics," *Journal of Southern History* (May 2004), pp. 221–48.

70. It should be remembered that the territory of Texas might have been admitted to the Union as five separate states, each with two senators. The treaty annexing Texas to the United States stated: "New States, of convenient size, not exceeding four in number, in addition to said State of Texas, and having sufficient population, may hereafter, by the consent of said State, be formed out of the territory thereof, which shall be entitled to admission under the provisions of the federal constitution. And such States as may be formed out of that portion of said territory lying south of thirty-six degrees thirty minutes north latitude, commonly known as the Missouri compromise line, shall be admitted into the Union with or without slavery, as the people of each State asking permission may desire." Joint Resolution of March 1, 1845, res. 8, 5 *Stat.* 798.

71. On the protracted Oregon negotiations, see Joseph Schafer, "The British Attitude Toward the Oregon Question, 1815–1846," *American Historical Review* (January 1911), pp. 273–99; R. L. Schuyler, "Polk and the Oregon Compromise of 1846," *Political Science Quarterly* (September 1911), pp. 443–61. Of course, Canada was still a British colony at the time.

72. Piero Gleijeses, "A Brush With Mexico," *Diplomatic History* (April 2005), pp. 223–54. Among those who thought Polk had trumped up a justification for the Mexican War to cover imperialist ambitions was Abraham Lincoln. He was not a member of Congress at the time, but explained his views in an 1848 speech. *Congressional Globe*, Appendix, 30th Cong., 1st Sess. (1848), pp. 93–95. See also Eric Foner, "Lincoln's Antiwar Record," *The Nation* (March 12, 2007), p. 6.

73. William Dusinberre, "President Polk and the Politics of Slavery," *American Nineteenth Century History* (Spring 2002), pp. 1–16.

74. The amendment read: "Provided, That, as an express and fundamental condition to the acquisition of any territory from the Republic of Mexico by the United States, by virtue of any treaty which may be negotiated between them, and to the use by the Executive of the moneys herein appropriated, neither slavery nor involuntary servitude shall ever exist in any part of said territory, except for crime, whereof the party shall first be duly convicted." *Congressional Globe*, 29th Cong., 1st Sess. (1846), p. 1217. On Wilmot, see James H. Duff, "David Wilmot, the Statesman and Political Leader," *Pennsylvania History* (October 1946), pp. 283–89; Richard R. Stenberg, "The Motivation of the Wilmot Proviso," *Mississippi Valley Historical Review* (March 1932), pp. 535–41.

75. Eric Foner, "The Wilmot Proviso Revisited," *Journal of American History* (September 1969), pp. 262–79. Van Buren's efforts to maintain his political alliance with the South included a promise in his inaugural address to "resist the slightest interference" with slavery in the states where it existed.

76. It's worth noting that the Free Soilers were not necessarily abolitionists opposed to slavery per se. Many of the party's members were motivated by other factors, such as opposition to the increasing Southern domination of the Democratic Party. See Michael F. Holt, *The Political Crisis of the 1850s* (New York: W.W. Norton, 1978), p. 52.

77. *Congressional Globe*, 31st Cong., 1st Sess. (1849), p. 28. Emphasis in original.

78. On passage of the territorial provisions of the compromise, see Robert R. Russel. "What Was the Compromise of 1850?" *Journal of Southern History* (August 1956), pp. 292–309.

79. Act of September 18, 1850, ch. 60, 9 *Stat.* 462.

80. Act of February 12, 1793, ch. 7, 1 *Stat.* 302. On problems with enforcement of the act, see Robert M. Cover, *Justice Accused: Antislavery and the Judicial Process* (New Haven: Yale University Press, 1975), pp. 159–74; Fehrenbacher, *Slaveholding Republic*, pp. 213–30.

81. Jeffrey R. Hummel, *Emancipating Slaves, Enslaving Free Men* (Chicago: Open Court, 1996), pp. 55–56. Intriguingly, Hummel suggests (pp. 353–55) that simply allowing the South to secede in 1861 might have destroyed slavery peacefully. The Union could have repealed the Fugitive Slave Law and not only permitted slaves to obtain their freedom by escaping to the North, but actively encouraged them to do so. The slave states would have been boxed in, suffering the steady loss of their slaves with no way to reclaim them or obtain replacements, and facing rising costs of preventing escape across a border difficult to police. Within a few years, the institution might well have died out without a shot being fired. Indeed, many supporters of slavery opposed secession for this very reason. Hummel also says that this is essentially how slavery in Brazil came to an end. Support for this argument can be found in Seymour Drescher, "Brazilian Abolition in Comparative Perspective," *Hispanic American Historical Review* (August 1988), pp. 451–52.

82. Senate Democrats voted 19 to 0 in favor of it and the final vote was 27 to 12. In the House, Democrats supported the measure by a margin of 82 to 17. The final vote was 108 to 76. Castel & Gibson, *Yeas and Nays*, p. 66.

83. See F. H. Hodder, "The Authorship of the Compromise of 1850," *Mississippi Valley Historical Review* (March 1936), pp. 525–36; Holman Hamilton, "Democratic Senate Leadership and the Compromise of 1850," *Mississippi Valley Historical Review* (December 1954), pp. 403–18.

84. Douglas explained his "popular sovereignty" argument most thoroughly in an 1859 article. See Stephen A. Douglas, "The Dividing Line Between Federal and Local Authority," *Harper's Magazine* (September 1859), pp. 519–37. For background, see Robert W. Johannsen, "Stephen A. Douglas, 'Harper's Magazine,' and Popular Sovereignty," *Mississippi Valley Historical Review* (March 1959), pp. 606–31.

85. "Senator Douglas on the Nebraska Bill," *New York Times* (February 2, 1854).

86. In the Senate, Democrats supported the measure by a vote of 32 to 4. The final vote total was 37 to 14. In the House, 99 of the 113 votes for final passage came from Democrats. Castel & Gibson, *Yeas and Nays*, pp. 68–69. On the importance of Democratic Party unity in passing the legislation, see Robert R. Russel, "The Issues in the Congressional Struggle over the Kansas-Nebraska Bill, 1854," *Journal of Southern History* (May 1963), pp. 187–210.

87. Holt, *Political Crisis*, pp. 148–49.

88. See his speeches at Springfield, Illinois on October 4, 1854, and Peoria, Illinois, on October 16, 1854, in Roy P. Basler, *The Collected Works of Abraham Lincoln* (New Brunswick: Rutgers University Press, 1953), vol. 2, pp. 241–83.

89. On the origin of the Republican Party, see Lewis L. Gould, *Grand Old Party: A History of the Republicans* (New York: Random House, 2003), pp. 3–24.

90. Schlesinger, *Age of Jackson*, p. 488.

91. *Congressional Globe*, Appendix, 34th Cong., 1st Sess. (1856), pp. 530–31.

92. Brooks was among the most rabid pro-slavery members of Congress. He once said, "The Constitution of the United States should be torn to fragments and a Southern constitution formed in which every state should be a slave state." Quoted in Robert N. Mathis, "Preston Smith Brooks: The Man and His Image," *South Carolina Historical Magazine* (October 1978), p. 307.

93. William E. Gienapp, "The Crime Against Sumner: The Caning of Charles Sumner and the Rise of the Republican Party," *Civil War History* (September 1979), pp. 218–45; Michael D. Pierson, "'All Southern Society Is Assailed by the Foulest Charges': Charles Sumner's 'The Crime Against Kansas' and the Escalation of Republican Anti-Slavery Rhetoric," *New England Quarterly* (December 1995), pp. 531–57. Interestingly, Sumner seems to have held no malice toward Brooks even though his health suffered as a result of the attack for the rest of his life. See Arnold Johnson, "Recollections of Charles Sumner," *Scribner's Monthly* (August 1874), pp. 482–83.

94. Holt, *Political Crisis*, p. 187. See also Eric Foner, *Free Soil, Free Labor, Free Men* (New York: Oxford University Press, 1970), pp. 263–64.

95. 60 U.S. 393 (1856). It's worth noting that all but one of the votes for the *Dred Scott* decision came from justices appointed by Democrats. Roger Taney, James Wayne, and John Catron were appointed by Andrew Jackson; Peter Daniel was appointed by Martin Van Buren; Robert Grier by James Polk; and John Campbell by Franklin Pierce. Only one Whig appointee, Samuel Nelson, named by John Tyler, voted for the decision. Of the two dissenting votes, one was a Democratic appointee, the other a Whig: John McLean (Jackson) and Benjamin Curtis (Millard Fillmore), respectively.

96. State of the Union message (December 19, 1859).

97. Don E. Fehrenbacher, *The Dred Scott Case* (New York: Oxford University Press, 1978), p. 525.

98. See, for example, his Senate speech of February 6, 1837, in which he argues that slavery is not merely justifiable, but a positive good. Paul Finkelman, *Defending Slavery: Proslavery Thought in the Old South* (New York: Bedford/St. Martin's, 2003), pp. 54–60. See also Bert E. Bradley and Jerry L. Tarver, "John C. Calhoun's Rhetorical Method in Defense of Slavery," in Waldo W. Braden, ed., *Oratory in the Old South, 1828–1860* (Baton Rouge: Louisiana State University Press, 1970), pp. 169–89.

99. Jean Baker, *James Buchanan* (New York: Times Books, 2004), pp. 98–99.

100. Castel & Gibson, *Yeas and Nays*, p. 70. When state legislatures elected senators prior to the Seventeenth Amendment, it was standard practice for them to instruct senators on how to vote on key issues. See Jay S. Bybee, "Ulysses at the Mast: Democracy, Federalism, and the Sirens' Song of the Seventeenth Amendment," *Northwestern University Law Review* (Winter 1997), pp. 517–28.

101. Robert W. Johannsen, "Stephen A. Douglas and the South," *Journal of Southern History* (February 1967), pp. 26–50.

102. Robert W. Johannsen, *Stephen A. Douglas* (New York: Oxford University Press, 1973), p. 571.

103. Allan Nevins, *Ordeal of the Union* (New York: Scribner's, 1947), vol. 2, pp. 107–109.

104. Don E. Fehrenbacher, "The Origins and Purpose of Lincoln's 'House-Divided' Speech," *Mississippi Valley Historical Review* (March 1960), pp. 615–43.

105. Harold Holzer, ed., *The Lincoln-Douglas Debates* (New York: HarperCollins, 1993), p. 111.

106. Holzer, *Debates*, pp. 151–52.

107. Republican candidates actually got more total votes, but the Democrats' gerrymandering gave them more legislative seats, giving Douglas his victory. Richards, *Slave Power*, p. 16.

108. *Congressional Globe*, 35th Cong., 2nd Sess. (1859), pp. 1247, 1257.

109. Breckinridge may have thought he could actually win, but many Southerners supported him in order split the Democratic vote, ensure Lincoln's victory, and thereby bring about secession. See Frank H. Heck, "John C. Breckinridge in the Crisis of 1860–1861," *Journal of Southern History* (August 1955), pp. 316–46; Jeffrey A. Jenkins and Irwin L. Morris, "Running to Lose? John C. Breckinridge and the Presidential Election of 1860," *Electoral Studies* (June 2006), pp. 306–28.

110. More Americans died in combat in World War II, but there were many more deaths from disease and other causes during the Civil War and deaths were much higher as a share of the population. For data: http://www.cwc.lsu.edu/cwc/other/stats/warcost.htm.

CHAPTER 2

1. Kenneth Stampp, *The Era of Reconstruction, 1865–1877* (New York: Vintage Books, 1965), pp. 50–51. It's worth remembering that after Johnson left the White House, he was reelected to the U.S. Senate as a Democrat from the state of Tennessee, where he served from March 4, 1875, until his death on July 31, 1875.

2. Frederick Douglass, "Reconstruction," *Atlantic Monthly* (December 1866), pp. 761–65.

3. A famous historian from the turn of the century, William Dunning of Columbia University, was a strong proponent of this view. His books and those of his students dominated the historical interpretation of Reconstruction until the 1950s. W. E. B. DuBois was really the first scholar to attack their work in his neglected book, *Black Reconstruction in America, 1860–1880* (New York: Harcourt, Brace, 1935), pp. 711–29. For more recent criticism of the Dunning School, see John Hope Franklin, "Mirror for Americans: A Century of Reconstruction History," *American Historical Review* (February 1980), pp. 1–14. For a popular version of the Southerner-as-victim view of Reconstruction, see Claude G. Bowers, *The Tragic Era: The Revolution After Lincoln* (Boston: Houghton Mifflin, 1929).

4. Teddy Roosevelt also held this view. In a 1904 letter, he said, "Jefferson Davis was an unhung traitor." Elting E. Morison, ed., *The Letters of Theodore Roosevelt*, vol. 4 (Cambridge: Harvard University Press, 1951), p. 947.

5. For the latest version of the Lincoln-as-Devil thesis, see Thomas J. DiLorenzo, *Lincoln Unmasked* (New York: Crown Forum, 2006).

6. Hans L. Trefousse, *Andrew Johnson: A Biography* (New York: W.W. Norton, 1989), pp. 17–36.

7. *Congressional Globe*, Appendix, 28th Cong., 1st Sess. (1844), pp. 96–97.

8. *Congressional Globe*, 30th Cong., 1st Sess. (1848), p. 637.

9. As a matter of politics and of reality at that time, Lincoln had no choice except to concede that blacks were not equal to whites, by which he simply meant that they had not yet achieved the advancement of learning or civilization that European whites had then achieved. But he never said that blacks were inherently inferior to whites by nature. One must separate his comments about where blacks were at that moment in time to what he thought their potential was under a completely different set of circumstances. See Don E. Fehrenbacher, "Only His Stepchildren: Lincoln and the Negro," *Civil War History* (December 1974), pp. 293–310; George M. Frederickson, "A Man but Not a Brother: Abraham Lincoln and Racial Equality," *Journal of Southern History* (February 1975), pp. 39–58; Arthur Zilversmit, "Lincoln and the Problem of Race: A Decade of Interpretation," *Journal of the Abraham Lincoln Association* (No. 1, 1980), pp. 22–45.

10. Trefousse, *Andrew Johnson*, pp. 75–79, 111–12.

11. Trefousse, *Andrew Johnson*, pp. 101–2.

12. Quoted in Trefousse, *Andrew Johnson*, p. 98.

13. Trefousse, *Andrew Johnson*, p. 106.

14. *Congressional Globe*, 35th Cong., 1st Sess. (1858), pp. 810–12.

15. *Congressional Globe*, 36th Cong., 1st Sess. (1860), pp. 1367–68. On the slave revolt to which Johnson alludes, see Harvey Wish, "The Slave Insurrection Panic of 1856," *Journal of Southern History* (May 1939), pp. 206–22.

16. In 1860, only one in four Southerners owned any slaves or belonged to a family that did. Just 3,000 Southerners could be considered major slaveholders—owning at least 100 slaves. David Brion Davis, *Inhuman Bondage: The Rise and Fall of Slavery in the New World* (New York: Oxford University Press, 2006), p. 197.

17. Campbell Gibson and Kay Jung, "Historical Census Statistics on Population Totals by Race, 1790 to 1990, and by Hispanic Origin, 1970 to 1990, for the United States, Regions, Divisions, and States," Population Division Working Paper No. 56, U.S. Census Bureau (September 2002), table A-19.

18. In 1860, slaves accounted for just 10 percent of the population of major Southern cities and slaves living in cities accounted for just two percent of the total slave population. C. Vann Woodward, *The Strange Career of Jim Crow*, 3rd ed. (New York: Oxford University Press, 1974), p. 17.

19. For recent reviews of the patrol system in the South, which arrested wandering blacks, pursued runaways, broke up unauthorized meetings of slaves, and often imposed brutal, summary punishment, including flogging and lynching, for infractions of local law and customs, see Adalberto Aguirre Jr. and David V. Baker, "Slave Executions in the United States: A Descriptive Analysis of Social and Historical Factors," *Social Science Journal*

(No. 1, 1999), pp. 1–31; John A. Scott, "Segregation: A Fundamental Aspect of Southern Race Relations, 1800–1860," *Journal of the Early Republic* (Winter 1984), pp. 421–41; Sally E. Hadden, *Slave Patrols: Law and Violence in Virginia and the Carolinas* (Cambridge: Harvard University Press, 2001). Sadly, the evidence shows that the more brutally slaves were treated, the less likely they were to revolt; insurrections mainly occurred where slaves were treated more leniently. See Marion Kilson, "Towards Freedom: An Analysis of Slave Revolts in the United States," *Phylon* (2nd quarter 1964), pp. 175–87. It should be noted that the fear of slave revolts in the South was pervasive among slaveholders and nonslaveholders alike. After the Nat Turner rebellion in 1831, there was a noticeable hardening of attitudes toward slaves throughout the South. See Clement Eaton, *The Growth of Southern Civilization, 1790–1860* (New York: Harper & Row, 1961), pp. 302–3; Harvey Wish, "American Slave Insurrections Before 1861," *Journal of Negro History* (July 1937), pp. 313–14.

20. George Frederickson, *White Supremacy: A Comparative Study in American and South African History* (New York: Oxford University Press, 1981).

21. For a recent statement of this argument by an economist, see Thomas J. DiLorenzo, *The Real Lincoln* (New York: Crown Forum, 2002), pp. 125–29. The only review of this book I could find by a historian called it "a travesty of historical method and documentation." See the review by Richard M. Gamble in the *Independent Review* (Spring 2003), pp. 611–14. Interestingly, there are many on the neo-Confederate, crackpot fringe who still maintain that the Civil War was not about slavery, among whom DiLorenzo's books, which ruthlessly excoriate Abraham Lincoln for every crime known to man, are very popular. See Andrew Ferguson, "When Lincoln Returned to Richmond," *Weekly Standard* (December 29, 2003). In their world, Lincoln's suspension of *habeas corpus* at a time when national survival was at stake is condemned most harshly. (They almost never note that Article I, Section 9 of the Constitution permits suspension of *habeas corpus* "when in cases of rebellion or invasion the public safety may require it.") Meanwhile, the enslavement of millions of Africans brought to America by force to be brutalized and work for nothing in perpetual bondage, lacking even the rights that today we confer on dogs and cats, elicits little concern. For a competent analysis of the economic causes of the war, placing tariffs in their proper, subordinate context, with slavery at the forefront, see Gerald Gunderson, "The Origin of the American Civil War," *Journal of Economic History* (December 1974), pp. 915–50.

22. David W. Bowen, *Andrew Johnson and the Negro* (Knoxville: University of Tennessee Press, 1989), p. 62.

23. Charles H. Coleman, "The Use of the Term 'Copperhead' During the Civil War," *Mississippi Valley Historical Review* (September 1938), pp. 263–64.

24. Richard O. Curry, "The Union As It Was: A Critique of Recent Interpretations of the 'Copperheads,'" *Civil War History* (March 1967), pp. 25–39. The best known history emphasizing the conspiracy angle is Wood Gray, *The Hidden Civil War: The Story of the Copperheads* (New York: Viking Press, 1942).

25. Ray H. Abrams, "Copperhead Newspapers and the Negro," *Journal of Negro History* (April 1935), pp. 131–52; Jennifer L. Weber, *Copperheads: The Rise and Fall of Lincoln's Opponents in the North* (New York: Oxford University Press, 2006).

26. Richard O. Curry, "Copperheadism and Continuity: The Anatomy of a Stereotype," *Journal of Negro History* (January 1972), p. 32. Emphasis in original.

27. *Congressional Globe*, Appendix, 37th Cong., 3rd Sess. (1863), p. 56. Vallandigham's argument that chattel slaves were better off than Northern "wage slaves" was a common racist argument that dovetailed with the growing Marxist critique of industrial capitalism. See Wilfred Carsel, "The Slaveholders' Indictment of Northern Wage Slavery," *Journal of Southern History* (November 1940), pp. 504–20. Later, Vallandigham was arrested for sedition by Union General Ambrose Burnside after urging some of his supporters to "hurl King Lincoln from his throne." Vallandigham was eventually deported to the Confederacy. For details, see Frank L. Klement, *The Limits of Dissent: Clement L. Vallandigham and the*

Civil War (Lexington: University Press of Kentucky, 1970); Geoffrey R. Stone, *Perilous Times: Free Speech in Wartime* (New York: W. W. Norton, 2004), pp. 98–107. Interestingly, the Confederates didn't want Vallandigham, either, viewing his desire for a return to the *status quo ante bellum* as heresy against the cause of independence, so they sent him to Canada. Vallandigham's case is said to have inspired Edward Everett Hale to write his famous short story, "The Man Without a Country," which first appeared in the *Atlantic Monthly* (December 1863), pp. 665–79.

28. *Congressional Globe*, 37th Cong., 1st Sess. (1861), p. 243.
29. Act of July 17, 1862, ch. 190, 12 *Stat.* 589. It's worth noting that the Confederate Congress had previously passed legislation confiscating the property of Union citizens. See Edward McPherson, *The Political History of the United States of America During the Great Rebellion* (Washington: Philp & Solomons, 1864), p. 203.
30. Roy P. Basler, *The Collected Works of Abraham Lincoln* (New Brunswick: Rutgers University Press, 1953), vol. 5, pp. 433–36.
31. The Emancipation Proclamation did not apply in the states of the Union, only to those of the Confederacy. Over the years, many commentators have criticized Lincoln because he freed the slaves only in areas he did not control and not in those that he did, meaning that no slaves actually went free as a consequence. See, for example, Herbert Mitgang, "Was Lincoln Just a Honkie?" *New York Times Magazine* (February 11, 1968), pp. 35, 100–6. However, such criticism overlooks the fact that he did not believe he had the authority to free slaves outside the states that had seceded. In the rebellious states, Lincoln believed he could use his wartime military powers, but not elsewhere. Moreover, he did not wish to give slaveholders outside the Confederacy, especially in Missouri and Kentucky, any reason to join the rebellion. Lincoln's limited action, therefore, was dictated by law and military strategy. See Eugene H. Berwanger, "Lincoln's Constitutional Dilemma: Emancipation and Black Suffrage," *Journal of the Abraham Lincoln Association* (No. 1, 1983), pp. 25–38.
32. Christopher Ewan, "The Emancipation Proclamation and British Public Opinion," *The Historian* (March 2005), pp. 1–19.
33. Frank L. Klement, "Midwestern Opposition to Lincoln's Emancipation Proclamation," *Journal of Negro History* (July 1964), pp. 177–78.
34. James McPherson, *Battle Cry of Freedom: The Civil War Era* (New York: Oxford University Press, 1988), pp. 506–7.
35. Weber, *Copperheads*, p. 79. Senator John Crittenden of Kentucky was a member of the aptly-named Know-Nothing Party. His compromise was a last-ditch effort to keep the South from seceding by basically giving it everything it wanted on slavery. For details, see *Congressional Globe*, 36th Cong., 2nd Sess. (1860), pp. 112–14. It was defeated in the Senate on January 16, 1861, when a Republican substitute was adopted in its place on a 25 to 23 vote. Tellingly, seven Southern Democrats who were present in the chamber, who just voted on another measure a few minutes earlier and could have provided the margin of victory for the Crittenden proposal, did not vote. This strongly suggests that there was no compromise possible that would have prevented secession. See *Congressional Globe*, 36th Cong., 2nd Sess. (1861), p. 409. Further evidence for this view is that prior to the attack on Fort Sumter, both the House and Senate approved a constitutional amendment preserving slavery in places where state law permitted it. The amendment read: "No amendment shall be made to the Constitution which will authorize or give to Congress the power to abolish or interfere, within any State, with the domestic institutions thereof, including that of persons held to labor or service by the laws of said State." It passed the House on February 28, 1861, and the Senate on March 2, 1861. *Congressional Globe*, 36th Cong., 2nd Sess. (1861), pp. 1285, 1403. Of course, it was never ratified by the states.
36. John Cimprich, "Military Governor Johnson and Tennessee Blacks, 1862–65," *Tennessee Historical Quarterly* (Winter 1980), pp. 459–70.
37. Said Butler to Lincoln's emissary, "Ask him what he thinks I have done to deserve the punishment . . . of being made to sit as presiding officer over the Senate, to listen for four

years to debates more or less stupid, in which I can take no part or say a word, nor even be allowed to vote . . . and because of the dignity of the position I had held, not to be permitted to go on with my profession, and therefore with nothing left for me to do save to ornament my lot in the cemetery tastefully, and to get into it gracefully and respectably, as a Vice President should." Benjamin F. Butler, "Vice-Presidential Politics in '64," *North American Review* (October 1885), p. 333. See also Louis T. Merrill, "General Benjamin F. Butler in the Presidential Campaign of 1864," *Mississippi Valley Historical Review* (March 1947), pp. 537–70. Butler later served five terms as a congressman from Massachusetts, during which he helped manage the impeachment trial of Andrew Johnson, the president he could have been.

38. Don E. Fehrenbacher, "The Making of a Myth: Lincoln and the Vice-Presidential Nomination in 1864," *Civil War History* (December 1995), pp. 273–90.

39. McPherson, *Battle Cry*, p. 364.

40. Quoted in Weber, *Copperheads*, p. 185.

41. *Congressional Globe*, 38th Cong., 1st Sess. (1864), p. 712. See also Sidney Kaplan, "The Miscegenation Issue in the Election of 1864," *Journal of Negro History* (July 1949), pp. 274–343.

42. "What Are We Coming To, and When Shall We Reach It?" *New York Times* (March 26, 1864).

43. *House Journal*, 38th Cong., 1st Sess. (1864), p. 812.

44. *Congressional Globe*, 38th Cong., 2nd Sess. (1865), p. 194.

45. Unlike today, newly elected members of Congress in those days didn't take office in January, and a new Congress usually didn't convene until December of the year following an election.

46. *House Journal*, 38th Cong., 2nd Sess. (1865), pp. 170–1.

47. Basler, *Collected Works*, vol. 7, pp. 54–56.

48. Stampp, *Era of Reconstruction*, p. 42.

49. Eric Foner, *Reconstruction: America's Unfinished Revolution, 1863–1877* (New York: Harper & Row, 1988), pp. 61–62.

50. Among other things, this legislation would have required that a majority of a state's adult white males take a loyalty oath before it could be readmitted to the Union. See McPherson, *Political History of the Rebellion*, pp. 317–19.

51. Basler, *Collected Works*, vol. 7, p. 434.

52. The proclamation offering blanket pardons can be found in Edward McPherson, *The Political History of the United States of America During the Period of Reconstruction* (Washington: Solomons & Chapman, 1875), pp. 9–10.

53. In the Thirty-Ninth Congress, Republicans had a majority of 39 to 15 in the Senate and 136 to 57 in the House of Representatives—enough to override presidential vetoes if they all stuck together.

54. Ironically, the Thirteenth Amendment increased the South's political power by eliminating the three-fifths clause of the Constitution. Because blacks now counted the same as whites in terms of apportionment, the South got more representation in Congress than it had previously. For example, in 1860, the 437,000 slaves in Mississippi counted as 262,000 persons for purposes of apportionment on a three-fifths basis. Therefore, the Thirteenth Amendment effectively added 175,000 people to Mississippi's population for allocating House seats. See Stephan Thernstrom and Abigail Thernstrom, *America in Black and White: One Nation, Indivisible* (New York: Simon & Schuster, 1997), p. 31.

55. Summaries of the black codes enacted in every Southern state after the war appear in McPherson, *Political History of Reconstruction*, pp. 29–44. See also Joe M. Richardson, "Florida Black Codes," *Florida Historical Quarterly* (April 1969), pp. 365–79. Interestingly, President Wilson defended the codes when he was in academia. See Woodrow Wilson, "The Reconstruction of the Southern States," *Atlantic Monthly* (January 1901), p. 6; Woodrow Wilson, *A History of the American People* (New York: Harper & Brothers, 1901), vol. 5, pp. 19–22.

56. A transcript of the meeting appears in McPherson, *Political History of Reconstruction*, pp. 52–55.

57. Quoted in LaWanda Cox and John H. Cox, *Politics, Principle, and Prejudice, 1865–1866* (New York: Free Press, 1963), p. 163.

58. *Senate Journal*, 39th Cong., 1st Sess. (1865), p. 50.

59. William Cohen, "Negro Involuntary Servitude in the South, 1865–1940: A Preliminary Analysis," *Journal of Southern History* (February 1976), pp. 31–60; Thomas Wagstaff, "Call Your Old Master—'Master': Southern Political Leaders and Negro Labor During Presidential Reconstruction," *Labor History* (Summer 1969), pp. 323–45.

60. See W. E. B. DuBois, "The Freedmen's Bureau," *Atlantic Monthly* (March 1901), pp. 354–65.

61. The history of land policies relating to former slaves is reviewed in LaWanda Cox, "The Promise of Land for the Freedmen," *Mississippi Valley Historical Review* (December 1958), pp. 413–40. The issue continues to have contemporary relevance because much of the justification for reparations to the descendents of slaves is based on the idea that they were made a promise of "forty acres and a mule," which was reneged upon. In fact, no such promise was made. See John David Smith, "The Enduring Myth of 'Forty Acres and a Mule,'" *Chronicle of Higher Education* (February 21, 2003), p. B11. Nevertheless, it's something that should have been done. For a discussion of how land reform might have improved the lives of both blacks and whites in the South, see Roger L. Ransom, "Reconstructing Reconstruction: Options and Limitations to Federal Policies on Land Distribution in 1866–67," *Civil War History* (December 2005), pp. 364–77.

62. *Senate Journal*, 39th Cong., 1st Sess. (1866), pp. 168–73.

63. *Congressional Globe*, 39th Cong., 1st Sess. (1866), p. 477.

64. *Senate Journal*, 39th Cong., 1st Sess. (1866), pp. 279–85.

65. Cox & Cox, *Politics, Principles, and Prejudice*, pp. 212–13.

66. *Senate Journal*, 39th Cong., 1st Sess. (1866), p. 317. The reason for the different outcome on this vote and that on the Freedmen's Bureau is that two Republicans who had supported the earlier veto switched positions to oppose the Civil Rights Act veto.

67. *House Journal*, 39th Cong., 1st. Sess. (1866), p. 526.

68. In part, this appears to have been a deliberate strategy on Johnson's part to unite the Democratic Party behind him. However, in the process he alienated moderate Republicans who had stood with him up until his veto of the Civil Rights Act. They saw Johnson's veto message as so harsh that it was a virtual repudiation of everything the Republican Party stood for, pushing them over to the radicals. See Cox & Cox, *Politics, Principles, and Prejudice*, pp. 195–232.

69. McPherson, *Political History of Reconstruction*, p. 83. Many Southern sympathizers continue to hold this view. See Thomas E. Woods Jr., *The Politically Incorrect Guide to American History* (Washington: Regnery, 2004), pp. 86–90.

70. Republicans increased their majority in the Senate from 39 seats to 57 seats, with Democrats holding only 9 seats in the Fortieth Congress. In the House, Republicans gained 37 seats and held 173 seats to 47 seats for the Democrats. Republicans only needed 45 votes in the Senate and 150 in the House to override a presidential veto.

71. *Senate Journal*, 39th Cong., 2nd Sess. (1867), p. 67.

72. *House Journal*, 39th Cong., 2nd Sess. (1867), p. 569.

73. *House Journal*, 40th Cong., 1st Sess. (1867), p. 100.

74. Michael Les Benedict, "A New Look at the Impeachment of Andrew Johnson," *Political Science Quarterly* (September 1973), pp. 349–67.

75. C. M. Ellis, "The Causes for Which a President Can Be Impeached," *Atlantic Monthly* (January 1867), pp. 88–92. It should be remembered that the House of Representatives is the sole judge of what is an impeachable offense and the Senate is the sole judge of guilt or innocence. It is important to note that articles of impeachment can be approved by the House on a simple majority vote, but a two-thirds vote in the Senate is needed to convict and remove a president from office. This suggests that the Founding Fathers did not intend impeachment to be overly difficult, but wanted to guard against its abuse.

76. There were eleven articles of impeachment, nine of which dealt with Johnson's alleged abuse of his appointment and removal power. However, the law that he was impeached for violating was probably unconstitutional. See *Myers v. United States*, 272 U.S. 52 (1926). The other two articles were just silly, taking Johnson to task for some intemperate remarks he made. The articles can be found in McPherson, *Political History of Reconstruction*, pp. 266–70.

77. McPherson, *Political History of Reconstruction*, pp. 380–82.

78. Foner, *Reconstruction*, p. 340.

79. *Congressional Globe*, 40th Cong., 3rd Sess. (1869), p. 989.

80. Allen Trelease, *White Terror: The Ku Klux Klan Conspiracy and Southern Reconstruction* (Baton Rouge: Louisiana State University Press, 1971), p. xlvii.

81. Foner, *Reconstruction*, p. 425.

82. Albert Castel and Scott L. Gibson, *The Yeas and the Nays: Key Congressional Decisions, 1774–1945* (Kalamazoo, MI: New Issues Press, Western Michigan University, 1975), p. 93.

83. *Congressional Globe*, 42nd Cong., 1st Sess. (1871), pp. 453–56.

84. Trelease, *White Terror*, p. 415.

85. Another reason for the falloff in violence is that the Klan learned to be more subtle in its intimidation. As one historian explained, "If a party of white men, with ropes conspicuous on their saddlebows, rode up to a polling place and announced that hanging would begin in fifteen minutes, though without any more definite reference to anybody, and a group of blacks who had assembled to vote heard the remark and promptly disappeared, votes were lost, but a conviction on a charge of intimidation was difficult." William A. Dunning, "The Undoing of Reconstruction," *Atlantic Monthly* (October 1901), pp. 440–41.

86. Ronald B. Jager, "Charles Sumner, the Constitution, and the Civil Rights Act of 1875," *New England History* (September 1969), pp. 350–72; James M. McPherson, "Abolitionists and the Civil Rights Act of 1875," *Journal of American History* (December 1965), pp. 493–510.

87. The standard work on this episode is C. Vann Woodward, *Reunion and Reaction: The Compromise of 1877 and the End of Reconstruction* (Boston: Little, Brown, 1951).

88. It's worth remembering that the Democrats won control of the House of Representatives in the 1874 elections and kept their majority until 1880. Consequently, any new civil rights measure would have been dead on arrival. And although Republicans retained control of the Senate, their margin over the Democrats fell sharply from 62–12 in 1870 to 40–35 in 1877. This gave the Democrats enough clout to win some legislative victories. In 1878, they were able to ram though the Posse Comitatus Act, which still forbids using the military for domestic law enforcement, as had been done in the campaign to suppress the Ku Klux Klan. See Matt Matthews, *The Posse Comitatus Act and the United States Army: A Historical Perspective* (Fort Leavenworth, KS: Combat Studies Institute Press, 2006), pp. 30–34.

89. Charles W. Calhoun, *Conceiving a New Republic: The Republican Party and the Southern Question, 1869–1900* (Lawrence: University Press of Kansas, 2006), p. 106. When Hayes thought he had lost the election, his main concern was that Democrats would treat the civil rights amendments as "nullities," with the result that "the colored man's fate will be worse than when he was in slavery." Quoted in Woodward, *Reunion and Reaction*, p. 24.

90. On the impossibility of maintaining federal troops in the South much longer, see William Blair, "The Use of Military Force to Protect the Gains of Reconstruction," *Civil War History* (December 2005), pp. 388–402.

91. 83 U.S. 36 (1873).

92. 92 U.S. 542 (1875). For discussion, see Robert J. Cottrol and Raymond T. Diamond, "The Second Amendment: Toward and Afro-Americanist Reconsideration," *Georgetown Law Journal* (December 1991), pp. 347–48; Stefan B. Tahmassebi, "Gun Control and Racism," *George Mason University Civil Rights Law Journal* (Summer 1991), pp. 75–76.

93. 109 U.S. 3 (1883). For criticism of the Court's reasoning in these cases, see Richard A. Primus, "The Riddle of Hiram Revels," *Harvard Law Review* (April 2006), pp. 1680–1734.

94. 163 U.S. 537 (1896). For historical context, see Stephen J. Riegel, "The Persistent Career of Jim Crow: Lower Federal Courts and the 'Separate but Equal' Doctrine, 1865–1896," *American Journal of Legal History* (January 1984), pp. 17–40.

95. Calhoun, *New Republic*, pp. 270–74. When Democrats got control of the Senate in 1893, they elected Confederate General William Ruffin Cox to be Secretary of the Senate. No apolitical military man, Cox had been actively involved in the secessionist movement and continued to defend secession after the war.

96. Bernard Schwartz, *Statutory History of the United States: Civil Rights* (New York: Chelsea House, 1970), pt. I, pp. 803–5.

97. On black disenfranchisement, see J. Morgan Kousser, *The Shaping of Southern Politics: Suffrage Restriction and the Establishment of the One-Party South, 1880–1910* (New Haven: Yale University Press, 1974); Michael Perman, *Struggle for Mastery: Disenfranchisement in the South, 1888–1908* (Chapel Hill: University of North Carolina Press, 2001). On chain gangs as *de facto* slavery, see Tessa M. Gorman, "Back on the Chain Gang: Why the Eighth Amendment and the History of Slavery Proscribe the Resurgence of Chain Gangs," *California Law Review* (March 1997), pp. 447–52; Alex Lichtenstein, "Good Roads and Chain Gangs in the Progressive South: 'The Negro Convict Is a Slave,'" *Journal of Southern History* (February 1993), pp. 85–110; Matthew J. Mancini, *One Dies, Get Another: Convict Leasing in the American South, 1866–1928* (Columbia: University of South Carolina Press, 1996); Blake McKelvey, "Penal Slavery and Southern Reconstruction," *Journal of Negro History* (April 1935), pp. 153–79; Martha A. Myers and James L. Massey, "Race, Labor, and Punishment in Postbellum Georgia," *Social Problems* (May 1991), pp. 267–86; David M. Oshinsky, *"Worse Than Slavery": Parchman Farm and the Ordeal of Jim Crow Justice* (New York: Free Press, 1996). On the use of lynching as a means of social control, see W. Fitzhugh Brundage, *Under Sentence of Death: Lynching in the South* (Chapel Hill: University of North Carolina Press, 1997); Philip Dray, *At the Hands of Persons Unknown: The Lynching of Black America* (New York: Modern Library, 2002); J. William Harris, "Etiquette, Lynching, and Racial Boundaries in Southern History: A Mississippi Example," *American Historical Review* (April 1995), pp. 387–410; Arthur F. Raper, *The Tragedy of Lynching* (Chapel Hill: University of North Carolina Press, 1933); Stewart E. Tolnay and E. M. Beck, *A Festival of Violence: An Analysis of Southern Lynchings, 1882–1930* (Urbana: University of Illinois Press, 1995).

98. As C. Vann Woodward emphasizes in his great book, *The Strange Career of Jim Crow*, racial discrimination in the South became much more severe in the 1890s, after the Supreme Court, a Democratic Congress, and a Democratic administration systematically eliminated all the federal legal protections for black people that had been enacted by Republicans during Reconstruction.

99. DuBois, *Reconstruction*, p. 30.

100. Republican ineptness was also a factor. See Vincent P. De Santis, "The Republican Party and the Southern Negro, 1877–1897," *Journal of Negro History* (April 1960), pp. 71–87.

101. During those years, Republicans in Congress tried to aid blacks by passing a Force Bill in 1890 that would protect their voting rights in the South, and antilynching bills in 1900 and 1922. But these efforts all fell victim to filibusters and united opposition by Southern Democrats in the Senate. On the Force Bill of 1890, see Calhoun, *New Republic*, pp. 226–59; Thomas A. Upchurch, *Legislating Racism* (Lexington: University Press of Kentucky, 2004); Richard E. Welch Jr., "The Federal Elections Bill of 1890: Postscripts and Prelude," *Journal of American History* (December 1965), pp. 511–26. On the antilynching effort in 1900, see "Debated Ballot Law," *Washington Post* (February 1, 1900). President William McKinley had called for an antilynching law in his inaugural address in 1897 and renewed his request in his State of the Union message on December 5, 1899. On the 1922 effort, see "Antilynching Bill Is Passed by House," *Washington Post* (January 27, 1922); "Democrats Block Antilynching Bill," *Washington Post* (November 30, 1922). This attempt was in response to a call by President Warren G. Harding for an antilynching bill in his address to Congress on April 12, 1921. President Calvin Coolidge also called for an antilynching law in his State of the Union message on December 6, 1923. See George W. Rable, "The South and the Politics of Antilynching Legislation,

1920–1940," *Journal of Southern History* (May 1985), pp. 201–20; David O. Walter, "Legislative Notes and Reviews: Proposals for a Federal Anti-Lynching Law," *American Political Science Review* (June 1934), pp. 436–42.

CHAPTER 3

1. Stephen Kantrowitz, *Ben Tillman and the Reconstruction of White Supremacy* (Chapel Hill: University of North Carolina Press, 2000), p. 73.
2. Eric Foner, *Reconstruction: America's Unfinished Revolution, 1863–1877* (New York: Harper & Row, 1988), p. 571.
3. Quoted in Kantrowitz, *Ben Tillman*, p. 67.
4. Kantrowitz, *Ben Tillman*, p. 74.
5. Kantrowitz, *Ben Tillman*, p. 74.
6. Quoted in James B. Morrow, "Benjamin Ryan Tillman, United States Senator Grew Up as Wild as a Jimson Weed," *Washington Post* (November 18, 1906).
7. Robert Smalls, "Election Methods in the South," *North American Review* (November 1890), pp. 593–600; George B. Tindall, "The Campaign for the Disenfranchisement of Negroes in South Carolina," *Journal of Southern History* (May 1949), pp. 213–15. Note: Smalls had been a black Republican member of Congress from South Carolina until 1886.
8. E. Culpepper Clark, "Pitchfork Ben Tillman and the Emergence of Southern Demagoguery," *Quarterly Journal of Speech* (November 1983), pp. 423–33.
9. Quoted in William A. Mabry, "Ben Tillman Disenfranchised the Negro," *South Atlantic Quarterly* (April 1938), p. 175.
10. Quoted in Mabry, "Ben Tillman," p. 175.
11. George B. Tindall, "The Question of Race in the South Carolina Constitutional Convention of 1895," *Journal of Negro History* (July 1952), pp. 277–303. It goes without saying that these requirements applied only to men; no woman of either race was allowed to vote no matter how wealthy she might have been or how well she could read and understand the state constitution. When women's suffrage became an issue, racists like Tillman opposed it mainly on the grounds that it would allow black women to vote. See Lawrence J. Friedman, *The White Savage: Racial Fantasies in the Postbellum South* (Englewood Cliffs, NJ: Prentice-Hall, 1970), p. 167; William F. Holmes, *The White Chief: James Kimble Vardaman* (Baton Rouge: Louisiana State University Press, 1970), p. 290; Morton Sosna, "The South in the Saddle: Racial Politics During the Wilson Years," *Wisconsin Magazine of History* (Autumn 1970), pp. 45–49.
12. Mabry, "Ben Tillman," pp. 179–80.
13. Kantrowitz, *Ben Tillman*, p. 242.
14. "Two Views of Lynching," *Washington Post* (June 9, 1892); "Ethics of Lynching," *Washington Post* (June 2, 1894).
15. "Mr. Tillman's Tirade," *Washington Post* (January 30, 1896).
16. Quoted in "Mr. Tillman's Tirade." On the bond issue that Tillman was so riled up about, see James A. Barnes, "The Gold-Standard Democrats and the Party Conflict," *Mississippi Valley Historical Review* (December 1930), pp. 428–29; Alexander Dana Noyes, *Thirty Years of American Finance* (New York: G. P. Putnam's, 1898), pp. 234–54.
17. "As Regards Tillman," *Washington Post* (January 31, 1896).
18. See Robert L. Beisner, *Twelve Against Empire: The Anti-Imperialists, 1898–1900* (New York: McGraw-Hill, 1968); John W. Burgess, "How May the United States Govern Its Extra-Continental Territory?" *Political Science Quarterly* (March 1899), pp. 1–18; William Graham Sumner, "The Conquest of the United States by Spain," *Yale Law Journal* (January 1899), pp. 168–93.
19. One who agreed with him on this point was William Jennings Bryan. See Michael Kazin, *A Godly Hero: The Life of William Jennings Bryan* (New York: Alfred A. Knopf, 2006), p. 89.

20. *Congressional Record* (June 30, 1898), pp. 6532–33.
21. *Congressional Record* (June 30, 1898), p. 6532.
22. "Shot By Negroes at Polls," *Washington Post* (November 9, 1898); "No Room for Tolberts," *Washington Post* (November 13, 1898); "Tolberts Out of Jail," *Washington Post* (November 15, 1898); H. Leon Prather, "The Origins of the Phoenix Racial Massacre of 1898," in Winfred B. Moore Jr., Joseph F. Tripp, and Lyon G. Tyler Jr., eds., *Developing Dixie: Modernization in a Traditional Society* (New York: Greenwood Press, 1988), pp. 59–72; Tom Wells, "The Phoenix Election Riot," *Phylon* (1st quarter 1970), pp. 58–69.
23. "Tillman Denounces Whitecaps," *Washington Post* (August 17, 1899).
24. Democrats imposed the death penalty on white and black supporters of the Greenback Party as well. Stephen Kantrowitz, "Ben Tillman and Hendrix McLane, Agrarian Rebels: White Manhood, 'The Farmers,' and the Limits of Southern Populism," *Journal of Southern History* (August 2000), pp. 508–509. The killing of white Republicans in the South by Democrats is a largely untold story. One well documented case is that of John Clayton, a Republican congressional candidate in Arkansas who was murdered by Democrats in 1888 to prevent him from investigating how they had stolen the election from him by destroying most of the black Republican votes. See Kenneth C. Barnes, *Who Killed John Clayton? Political Violence and the Emergence of the New South, 1861–1893* (Durham: Duke University Press, 1998).
25. *Congressional Record* (February 26, 1900), pp. 2244–45.
26. *Congressional Record* (March 23, 1900), pp. 3223–24.
27. B. R. Tillman, "Causes of Southern Opposition to Imperialism," *North American Review* (October 1900), p. 445.
28. Howard Dorgan, "'Pitchfork Ben' Tillman and 'The Race Problem from a Southern Point of View,'" in Cal M. Logue and Howard Dorgan, eds., *The Oratory of Southern Demagogues* (Baton Rouge: Louisiana State University Press, 1981), pp. 47–65; Lindsey S. Perkins, "The Oratory of Benjamin Ryan Tillman," *Speech Monographs* (No. 1, 1948), pp. 1–18.
29. Quoted in "Senator Tillman's Unique Campaign To Save His 'Great Moral Institution,'" *Washington Post* (August 19, 1906). Seventy-five cents in 1906 would be equal to about $16.00 today.
30. C. Vann Woodward, *The Strange Career of Jim Crow*, 3rd ed. (New York: Oxford University Press, 1974), pp. 70–74.
31. "The Political Future of the South," *New York Times* (May 10, 1900).
32. *Congressional Record* (May 7, 1902), pp. 5100–3.
33. Tindall, "Campaign for Disenfranchisement," p. 219. See also, Francis B. Simkins, "Race Legislation in South Carolina Since 1865, Part II: 1869 and After," *South Atlantic Quarterly* (April 1921), p. 177.
34. There was something to this. During Republican William McKinley's administration, McLaurin had been given control of federal patronage in South Carolina. Republicans hoped that McLaurin might lead a new party in the state that would bring together white Republicans, hard money Democrats, and other groups disgruntled with the Tillmanites. See Willard B Gatewood Jr., *Theodore Roosevelt and the Art of Controversy* (Baton Rouge: Louisiana State University Press, 1970), pp. 93–94.
35. Anne M. Butler and Wendy Wolff, *United States Senate Election, Expulsion and Censure Cases, 1793–1990* (Washington: U.S. Government Printing Office, 1995), pp. 269–71.
36. Francis B. Simkins, *Pitchfork Ben Tillman: South Carolinian* (Baton Rouge: Louisiana State University Press, 1944), pp. 408–9.
37. "Negro Vote a Menace," *Washington Post* (February 25, 1903).
38. Simkins, *Pitchfork Ben*, pp. 416–18.
39. Quoted in Gatewood, *Art of Controversy*, p. 112.
40. Francis B. Simkins, "Ben Tillman's View of the Negro," *Journal of Southern History* (May 1937), p. 164. To Tillman, it was inconceivable that there ever could be *consensual* relations between a black man and a white woman. All such relationships, therefore, necessarily constituted rape. See Kantrowitz, *Ben Tillman*, pp. 163, 259.

41. "Fears a Race War," *Washington Post* (October 8, 1906).

42. Quoted in "Tillman Is Unbridled," *Washington Post* (November 26, 1906).

43. Quoted in "Tillman in a Rage," *Washington Post* (November 28, 1906).

44. Kantrowitz, *Ben Tillman*, p. 219.

45. Kantrowitz, *Ben Tillman*, p. 300.

46. Kantrowitz, *Ben Tillman*, p. 307.

47. Simkins, *Pitchfork Ben*, p. 486.

48. Bryant Simon, "The Appeal of Cole Blease of South Carolina: Race, Class, and Sex in the New South," *Journal of Southern History* (February 1996), p. 62.

49. Simkins, *Pitchfork Ben*, p. 485.

50. Simkins, *Pitchfork Ben*, p. 490.

51. Simkins, *Pitchfork Ben*, p. 494.

52. Kantrowitz, *Ben Tillman*, pp. 297–8.

53. Clarence N. Stone, "Bleaseism and the 1912 Election in South Carolina," *North Carolina Historical Review* (January 1963), p. 60.

54. Simon, "Appeal of Cole Blease," pp. 57–60.

55. Simkins, *Pitchfork Ben*, p. 502.

56. Simon, "Appeal of Cole Blease," pp. 81–82.

57. Simon, "Appeal of Cole Blease," pp. 83–84.

58. M. L. McCauley, "Cole Blease and the Senatorial Campaign of 1918," in Logue and Dorgan, *Oratory of Southern Demagogues*, pp. 111–29.

59. *Congressional Record* (May 21, 1928), p. 9300.

60. The defeat of Blease in 1930 had more to do with economics than any change in white mill workers' views on race. See Bryant Simon, *A Fabric of Defeat: The Politics of South Carolina Millhands, 1910–1948* (Chapel Hill: University of North Carolina Press, 1998), pp. 36–58.

61. Joseph Alsop and Robert Kintner, "Sly and Able," *Saturday Evening Post* (July 20, 1940), p. 44; David Robertson, *Sly and Able: A Political Biography of James F. Byrnes* (New York: W.W. Norton, 1994), pp. 34–74.

62. Winfred B. Moore Jr., "James F. Byrnes: The Road to Politics, 1882–1910," *South Carolina Historical Magazine* (April 1983), p. 78.

63. Winfred B. Moore Jr., "The 'Unrewarding Stone,': James F. Byrnes and the Burden of Race, 1908–1944," in Bruce Clayton and John A. Salmond, eds., *The South Is Another Land* (New York: Greenwood Press, 1987), p. 7.

64. *Congressional Record* (April 25, 1917), p. 1101.

65. *Congressional Record* (August 25, 1919), p. 4305.

66. *Congressional Record* (August 25, 1919), p. 4305.

67. *Congressional Record* (August 25, 1919), p. 4303. See also "Race Rioting Blamed on Negro Demagogues and I.W.W. 'Reds,' by Byrnes in a House Address," *Washington Post* (August 26, 1919).

68. "Soviet Influence Behind Race Riots," *Washington Post* (August 27, 1919).

69. *Congressional Record* (August 25, 1919), p. 4304.

70. Robertson, *Sly and Able*, p. 86.

71. "President's Address to Congress on Domestic and Foreign Policies," *New York Times* (April 13, 1921).

72. The opposition was almost entirely Democratic. When the antilynching bill passed the House in January 1922, only eight Democrats supported it, with 102 voting against it. Although seventeen Republicans also voted against the measure, an overwhelming majority of 221 Republicans supported it. See "Antilynching Bill Is Passed By House," *Washington Post* (January 27, 1922). The bill later died in the Senate, victim of a Democratic filibuster. See "Democrats Block Antilynching Bill," *Washington Post* (November 30, 1922).

73. *Congressional Record* (December 19, 1921), pp. 543–44.

74. U.S. Bureau of the Census, *Historical Statistics of the United States: Colonial Times to 1970* (Washington: U.S. Government Printing Office, 1975), p. 422.

75. *Congressional Record* (January 29, 1924), pp. 1659–61.
76. Winfred B. Moore Jr., "New South Statesman: The Political Career of James Francis Byrnes, 1911–1941," Ph.D. dissertation, Duke University (September 1975), p. 55.
77. Moore, "Unrewarding Stone," p. 7.
78. Quoted in Moore, "Unrewarding Stone," p. 10.
79. To his credit, Byrnes refused an offer to secretly join the Ku Klux Klan even though its support might have helped a great deal that year. See Robertson, *Sly and Able*, pp. 91–92.
80. Moore, "New South Statesman," pp. 56, 94–95.
81. Moore, "New South Statesman," pp. 97–160.
82. Moore, "New South Statesman," p. 172.
83. Robert L. Zangrando, *The NAACP Crusade Against Lynching, 1909–1950* (Philadelphia: Temple University Press, 1980), p. 133.
84. Moore, "New South Statesman," pp. 241–2.
85. Moore, "New South Statesman," pp. 248–9.
86. *Congressional Record* (January 11, 1938), p. 310. See also "Declares Party Forsakes South," *New York Times* (January 12, 1939); "Lynching Bill Will Foment Race Hatred, Byrnes Says," *Washington Post* (January 12, 1938); "Senate to Try Gag Rule Vote Today to End Filibustering," *Washington Post* (January 27, 1938); Moore, "New South Statesman," pp. 253–54; Zangrando, *NAACP Crusade*, p. 150.
87. Moore, "New South Statesman," pp. 322–30.
88. Robertson, *Sly and Able*, p. 299. The author suggests that Roosevelt's action may have been designed to mollify racist Southerners opposed to his executive order integrating defense contractors and establishing a Fair Employment Practices Committee, which was signed on June 25, 1941, just a few days after Byrnes' appointment.
89. Robertson, *Sly and Able*, pp. 304–31; Benjamin Stolberg, "James F. Byrnes," *American Mercury* (March 1946), pp. 263–72.
90. Ralph McGill, "What Is Jimmy Byrnes Up to Now?" *Saturday Evening Post* (October 14, 1950), pp. 186–87; Moore, "Unrewarding Stone," p. 21.
91. On Byrnes' Supreme Court record, see Walter F. Murphy, "James F. Byrnes," in Leon Friedman and Fred L. Israel, eds., *The Justices of the United States Supreme Court, 1789–1969* (New York: Chelsea House, 1969), vol. IV, pp. 2517–34; William Pettit, "Justice Byrnes and the United States Supreme Court," *South Carolina Law Quarterly* (June 1954), pp. 423–28; Robertson, *Sly and Able*, pp. 301–4.
92. Quoted in Henry Lesesne, "Red Carpet Out for Gov. Byrnes," *Washington Post* (January 14, 1951).
93. "Byrnes Asks Legislative School Reins," *Washington Post* (January 9, 1952).
94. Edwin A. Lahey, "Byrnes on Integration," *Washington Post* (May 22, 1954).
95. "Former Justice Byrnes: 'Race Relations Are Worsening,'" *U.S. News & World Report* (February 22, 1957), pp. 110–14; "Integration Law Creates Suspicion, Says Byrnes," *Washington Post* (September 23, 1956); "Shaking the Foundations," *Washington Post* (May 20, 1956); "Slippery Logic," *Washington Post* (February 25, 1957); James F. Byrnes, "The South Respects the Written Constitution," *Vital Speeches* (March 15, 1957), pp. 331–35; Thomas S. Morgan, "James F. Byrnes and the Politics of Segregation," *The Historian* (Summer 1994), pp. 645–54.

CHAPTER 4

1. Georgia had what was called a unit vote system similar to the Electoral College in its whites-only Democratic primaries. The eight most populous counties got six unit votes each, the next thirty most populous counties got four votes, and the 121 remaining counties got two votes apiece. In 1940, the eight most populous counties had 34.1 percent of the adult white population, but only 11.7 percent of the unit votes. By contrast, the least populous 121 counties had 39.9 percent of the voters, but controlled 59 percent of the unit

votes. Nominations were based on winning unit votes, not popular votes, thereby giving rural farmers effective control of all statewide elections. See V. O. Key Jr., *Southern Politics* (New York: Alfred A. Knopf, 1949), pp. 117–24.

2. James A. Barnes, "The Gold Standard Democrats and the Party Conflict," *Mississippi Valley Historical Review* (December 1930), pp. 422–50.

3. Karl Marx, *Capital* (New York: Vintage Books, 1977), vol. 1, p. 225.

4. John J. McCusker, *How Much Is That in Real Money?* 2nd ed. (Worcester, MA: American Antiquarian Society, 2001), pp. 101–3.

5. Price V. Fishback, "Debt Peonage in Postbellum Georgia," *Explorations in Economic History* (April 1989), pp. 219–36; George K. Holmes, "The Peons of the South," *Annals of the American Academy of Political and Social Science* (September 1893), pp. 65–74; Forrest McDonald and Grady McWhiney, "The South from Self-Sufficiency to Peonage: An Interpretation," *American Historical Review* (December 1980), pp. 1111–18; C. Vann Woodward, *Tom Watson: Agrarian Rebel* (New York: Macmillan, 1938), pp. 129–30.

6. Woodward, *Tom Watson*, p. 137–40.

7. Woodward, *Tom Watson*, p. 144.

8. Robert M. Saunders, "Southern Populists and the Negro, 1893–1895," *Journal of Negro History* (July 1969), pp. 240–61.

9. Woodward, *Tom Watson*, pp. 223–43.

10. Populism also collapsed because of the fundamental incompatibility of populists in the South and West on the race issue. See Daniel M. Robison, "From Tillman to Long: Some Striking Leaders of the Rural South," *Journal of Southern History* (August 1937), pp. 306–7. Bryan, however, shared Watson's views on race. See Willard H. Smith, "William Jennings Bryan and Racism," *Journal of Negro History* (April 1969), pp. 127–49.

11. On Watson's switch from racial tolerance to racial demagoguery, see Charles Crowe, "Tom Watson, Populists, and Blacks Reconsidered," *Journal of Negro History* (April 1970), pp. 99–116; Eugene R. Fingerhut, "Tom Watson, Blacks, and Southern Reform," *Georgia Historical Quarterly* (Winter 1976), pp. 324–43; G. Jack Gravlee, "Tom Watson: Disciple of 'Jeffersonian Democracy,'" in Cal M. Logue and Howard Dorgan, eds., *The Oratory of Southern Demagogues* (Baton Rouge: Louisiana State University Press, 1981), pp. 85–108; Robert M. Saunders, "The Transformation of Tom Watson, 1894–1895," *Georgia Historical Quarterly* (Fall 1970), pp. 339–56; C. Vann Woodward, "Tom Watson and the Negro in Agrarian Politics," *Journal of Southern History* (February 1938), pp. 14–33. The latest research suggests that Watson's switch may have had more to do with mental illness than politics. See Bertram Wyatt-Brown, "Tom Watson Revisited," *Journal of Southern History* (February 2002), pp 3–30.

12. Woodward, *Tom Watson*, p. 434.

13. Woodward, *Tom Watson*, p. 380

14. Woodward, *Tom Watson*, pp. 402, 432–33.

15. Woodward, *Tom Watson*, pp. 420–1.

16. Woodward, *Tom Watson*, p. 445.

17. "Says Tom Watson Is Frank's Slayer," *New York Times* (August 18, 1915). See also "Frank Lynching Due to Suspicion and Prejudice," *New York Times* (August 20, 1915); "Attacks Watson in Frank Case," *New York Times* (September 13, 1915).

18. Quoted in "Holds Watson Most Guilty," *New York Times* (August 19, 1915). On the Frank case, see Leonard Dinnerstein, *The Leo Frank Case* (New York: Columbia University Press, 1968); Albert S. Lindemann, *The Jew Accused* (New York: Cambridge University Press, 1991), pp. 235–72; Nancy MacLean, "The Leo Frank Case Reconsidered: Gender and Sexual Politics in the Making of Reactionary Populism," *Journal of American History* (December 1991), pp. 917–48; Steve Oney, *And the Dead Shall Rise: The Murder of Mary Phagan and the Lynching of Leo Frank* (New York: Pantheon, 2003). To this day, Watson's family defends the lynching of Leo Frank. In 2000, his grandson, Tom Watson Brown, was quoted as saying that the lynching was justified because the Jews had paid off Governor Slaton to commute Frank's sentence. There is no evidence whatsoever to support this

contention, which certainly wouldn't justify lynching in any case. See Jane Gross, "Georgia Town Is Still Divided Over the 1915 Lynching of a Jew," *New York Times* (August 26, 2000); Bill Hendrick, "'Lynching' Reopens Old Scars for Some Mariettans," *Atlanta Constitution* (August 21, 2000).

19. Woodward, *Tom Watson*, pp. 421, 449.
20. Oney, *Dead Shall Rise*, pp. 605–6; Woodward, *Tom Watson*, pp. 450, 473.
21. Charles P. Sweeney, "Bigotry in the South," *The Nation* (November 24, 1920), p. 585.
22. "'Tom' Watson," *New York Times* (September 27, 1922).
23. Ralph McGill, "Tom Watson: The People's Man," *New Republic* (August 23, 1948), p. 20.
24. Dewey W. Grantham Jr., *Hoke Smith and the Politics of the New South* (Baton Rouge: Louisiana State University Press, 1958), pp. 18–19.
25. Grantham, *Hoke Smith*, p. 33.
26. Woodrow Wilson, "Mr. Cleveland's Cabinet," *Review of Reviews* (April 1893), pp. 286–97, reprinted in Arthur S. Link, ed., *The Papers of Woodrow Wilson*, vol. 8 (Princeton: Princeton University Press, 1970), pp. 160–78.
27. Grantham, *Hoke Smith*, pp. 139–40.
28. Grantham, *Hoke Smith*, p. 145.
29. Grantham, *Hoke Smith*, p. 147.
30. Grantham, *Hoke Smith*, pp. 70, 148–49.
31. Woodward, *Tom Watson*, p. 375.
32. Charles Crowe, "Racial Massacre in Atlanta, September 22, 1906," *Journal of Negro History* (April 1969), p. 152. See also "Blames Tillman and Smith," *Washington Post* (September 24, 1906); Charles Crowe, "Racial Violence and Social Reform—Origins of the Atlanta Riot of 1906," *Journal of Negro History* (July 1968), pp. 234–56.
33. For details on the riot, see Mark Bauerlein, *Negrophobia: A Race Riot in Atlanta, 1906* (San Francisco: Encounter Books, 2001); David F. Godshalk, *Veiled Visions: The 1906 Atlanta Race Riot and the Reshaping of American Race Relations* (Chapel Hill: University of North Carolina Press, 2005).
34. "Atlanta's Night of Terror Ended by Men in Khaki," *Washington Post* (September 24, 1906).
35. "Freedom Hurts Race: Colored Man Not Improving, Declares Hoke Smith," *Washington Post* (June 30, 1907).
36. Ray Stannard Baker, *Following the Color Line: American Negro Citizenship in the Progressive Era* (New York: Doubleday, Page, 1908), p. 245.
37. Grantham, *Hoke Smith*, pp. 159–61.
38. "Unsuited for School: Gov. Smith Tells Educators Few Negroes Can Learn," *Washington Post* (April 15, 1909).
39. "Oppose Negro Police: Senator Hoke Smith Would Have None in Capital," *Washington Post* (July 9, 1912).
40. Grantham, *Hoke Smith*, pp. 272–73.
41. "Says Negro-Baiters Balk Race's Uplift," *New York Times* (May 6, 1914).
42. Grantham, *Hoke Smith*, p. 338.
43. Grantham, *Hoke Smith*, p. 354.
44. William Anderson, *The Wild Man from Sugar Creek: The Political Career of Eugene Talmadge* (Baton Rouge: Louisiana State University Press, 1975), pp. 42–43.
45. As late as 1946, Ralph McGill, editor of the *Atlanta Constitution* and widely viewed in the North as a leading liberal on race, said in a column, "I have always opposed social equality or mixing of races." Quoted in Anderson, *Wild Man*, p. 232.
46. Sarah McCulloh Lemmon, "The Ideology of Eugene Talmadge," *Georgia Historical Quarterly* (September 1954), pp. 226–48.
47. John E. Allen, "Eugene Talmadge and the Great Textile Strike in Georgia, September 1934," in Gary M. Fink and Merl E. Reed, eds., *Essays in Southern Labor History* (Westport, CT: Greenwood Press, 1977), pp. 224–43.
48. "Fascism in the Piney Woods," *Washington Post* (June 6, 1935).
49. Anderson, *Wild Man*, p. 120.

50. Sarah McCulloh Lemmon, "Governor Eugene Talmadge and the New Deal," in J. Carlyle Sitterson, ed., *Studies in Southern History*, James Sprunt Studies in History and Political Science, vol. 39 (Chapel Hill: University of North Carolina Press, 1957), pp. 152–68.

51. Hal Steed, "Talmadge Takes His Issue to the Nation," *New York Times* (May 12, 1935).

52. "Talmadge Assails Roosevelt as Red," *New York Times* (October 10, 1935).

53. Anderson, *Wild Man*, pp. 111, 132.

54. Hamilton Basso, "'Our Gene,'" *New Republic* (February 19, 1936), pp. 35–37; Benjamin Stolberg, "Buzz Windrip—Governor of Georgia," *The Nation* (March 11, 1936), pp. 316–18.

55. Edwin Camp, "Talmadge Raises Race Bogy," *New York Times* (July 12, 1936).

56. Quoted in Calvin M. Logue, *Eugene Talmadge: Rhetoric and Response* (New York: Greenwood Press, 1989), p. 270.

57. Quoted in Anderson, *Wild Man*, p. 161.

58. Howard N. Mead, "Russell vs. Talmadge: Southern Politics and the New Deal," *Georgia Historical Quarterly* (Spring 1981), pp. 28–45.

59. James C. Cobb, "Not Gone, But Forgotten: Eugene Talmadge and the 1938 Purge Campaign," *Georgia Historical Quarterly* (Summer 1975), pp. 197–209.

60. James F Cook, "The Eugene Talmadge-Walter Cocking Controversy," *Phylon* (2nd quarter 1974), pp. 181–92.

61. Quoted in Anderson, *Wild Man*, p. 200.

62. Logue, *Eugene Talmadge*, p. 193. See also Jonathan Daniels, "Witch-Hunt in Georgia," *The Nation* (August 2, 1941), pp. 93–94.

63. "New Regents Oust Georgia Educators," *New York Times* (July 15, 1941); "Talmadge's Regents Oust Two Educators," *Washington Post* (July 15, 1941); "Dictator's Way," *Washington Post* (July 20, 1941); "Aggressive Ignorance," *Washington Post* (July 31, 1941); "College Body Bars 10 in Georgia Group," *New York Times* (December 5, 1941); "Ten Georgia Colleges Lose Merit Rating," *Washington Post* (December 5, 1941); "Educators Rebuke Talmadge Actions," *New York Times* (December 29, 1941).

64. Quoted in William Bradford Huie, "Talmadge: White Man's Governor," *American Mercury* (February 1942), p. 184.

65. "Talmadge Enters Fight to Keep Segregation," *Washington Post* (July 24, 1942).

66. Quoted in Anderson, *Wild Man*, p. 210.

67. "Exit Gene Talmadge," *Time Magazine* (September 21, 1942).

68. Drew Pearson, "Washington Merry-Go-Round," *Washington Post* (June 17, 1946).

69. Anderson, *Wild Man*, p. 225.

70. Anderson, *Wild Man*, pp. 229–30.

71. Talmadge was also aided by a considerable amount of black voter disenfranchisement, despite the court order. See Joseph L. Bernd, "White Supremacy and the Disenfranchisement of Blacks in Georgia, 1946," *Georgia Historical Quarterly* (Winter 1982), pp. 492–513.

72. Drew Pearson, "Washington Merry-Go-Round," *Washington Post* (July 24, 1946).

73. Drew Pearson, "Washington Merry-Go-Round," *Washington Post* (October 9, 1946).

74. For biographical details, see Robert A. Caro, *The Years of Lyndon Johnson: Master of the Senate* (New York: Alfred A. Knopf, 2002), pp. 164–202; Gilbert C. Fite, *Richard B. Russell, Jr.: Senator from Georgia* (Chapel Hill: University of North Carolina Press, 1991); Harold H. Martin, "The Man Behind the Brass," *Saturday Evening Post* (June 21, 1951), pp. 22–23, 42–48.

75. David Daniel Potenziani, "Look to the Past: Richard B. Russell and the Defense of Southern White Supremacy," Ph.D. dissertation, University of Georgia (August 1981), pp. 11–13.

76. Quoted in Potenziani, "Look to the Past," p. 14.

77. Potenziani, "Look to the Past," p. 16.

78. *Congressional Record* (January 25, 1938), pp. 1100, 1102.

79. For a review of how poll taxes were used in this way, see Ralph J. Bunche, *The Political Status of the Negro in the Age of FDR* (Chicago: University of Chicago Press, 1973),

pp. 328–83; Frederic D. Ogden, *The Poll Tax in the South* (Tuscaloosa: University of Alabama Press, 1958).

80. *Congressional Record* (November 17, 1942), p. 8903.
81. *Congressional Record* (August 9, 1944), pp. 6807–9.
82. *Congressional Record* (January 25, 1946), p. 380.
83. *Congressional Record* (January 27, 1949), pp. 569–72.
84. David Potenziani, "Striking Back: Richard B. Russell and Racial Relocation," *Georgia Historical Quarterly* (Fall 1981), pp. 263–77.
85. Campbell Gibson and Kay Jung, "Historical Census Statistics on Population Totals by Race, 1790 to 1990, and by Hispanic Origin, 1970 to 1990, for the United States, Regions, Divisions, and States," Population Division Working Paper No. 56, U.S. Census Bureau (September 2002), pp. 22, 43.
86. *Congressional Record* (August 30, 1957), pp. 16659–62.
87. *Congressional Record* (March 12, 1956), pp. 4459–61.
88. *Congressional Record* (June 16, 1961), p. 10620.
89. Douglas Kiker, "Russell of Georgia: The Old Guard at Its Shrewdest," *Harper's Magazine* (September 1966), pp. 101–106; Don Oberdorfer, "The Filibuster's Best Friend," *Saturday Evening Post* (March 31, 1965), pp. 90–92.
90. The Senate's second office building, which had been known as just the new Senate Office Building, was renamed the Dirksen Senate Office Building at the same time in honor of the late Senator Everett M. Dirksen of Illinois, longtime Republican leader of the Senate. Previously, locals enjoyed referring to the two buildings as the Old SOB and the New SOB.

CHAPTER 5

1. Claira S. Lopez, "James K. Vardaman and the Negro: The Foundation of Mississippi's Racial Policy," *Southern Quarterly* (January 1965), p. 161.
2. Lawrence Grossman, *The Democratic Party and the Negro: Northern and National Politics, 1868–92* (Urbana: University of Illinois Press, 1976), pp. 152–53; J. Morgan Kousser, *The Shaping of Southern Politics: Suffrage Restriction and the Establishment of the One-Party South, 1880–1910* (New Haven: Yale University Press, 1974), pp. 29–30. See also J. M. Stone, "The Suppression of Lawlessness in the South," *North American Review* (April 1894), pp. 500–7. Note: Stone was governor of Mississippi at the time.
3. William F. Holmes, *The White Chief: James Kimble Vardaman* (Baton Rouge: Louisiana State University Press, 1970), p. 38.
4. It's worth remembering that there were more lynchings in Mississippi than any other state between 1882, when records started being kept, and 1968, when lynchings stopped. According to Tuskegee Institute's figures, there were 581 lynchings—539 black and 42 white. The next closest state was Georgia, a much larger state in terms of area and population, with 531 total.
5. Quoted in Holmes, *White Chief*, p. 82.
6. Quoted in Holmes, *White Chief*, p. 85.
7. Quoted in Holmes, *White Chief*, pp. 88–89.
8. Albert D. Kirwan, *Revolt of the Rednecks: Mississippi Politics, 1876–1925* (Lexington: University of Kentucky Press, 1951), pp. 122–35.
9. William M. Strickland, "James Kimble Vardaman: Manipulation through Myths in Mississippi," in Cal M. Logue and Howard Dorgan, eds., *The Oratory of Southern Demagogues* (Baton Rouge: Louisiana State University Press, 1981), pp. 67–82.
10. Holmes, *White Chief*, p. 97.
11. Roosevelt spoke at Tuskegee in 1905. See "Praise for Tuskegee," *Washington Post* (October 25, 1905).
12. "South Is Resentful," *Washington Post* (October 19, 1901); Dewey W. Grantham Jr., "Dinner at the White House: Theodore Roosevelt, Booker T. Washington, and the South," *Tennessee Historical Quarterly* (June 1958), pp. 112–30.

13. Quoted in Holmes, *White Chief*, p. 99.
14. Willard B. Gatewood, *Theodore Roosevelt and the Art of Controversy* (Baton Rouge: Louisiana State University Press, 1970), pp. 33–37.
15. "Bryan on White House Dinner," *Washington Post* (November 1, 1901).
16. "President Deals 'Lily Whites' Another Blow," *New York Times* (November 11, 1902).
17. Quoted in "Negroes in Office," *Washington Post* (November 28, 1902).
18. Theodore Roosevelt later said that the root of the Indianola problem was the arrival of a black doctor who took away much of the black business from "the lowest white doctors of the town," leading to the black doctor being chased out. The mob then decided to get rid of Mrs. Cox for good measure. Theodore Roosevelt to Owen Wister (April 27, 1906), in Elting E. Morison, ed., *The Letters of Theodore Roosevelt* (Cambridge: Harvard University Press, 1952), vol. 5, pp. 227–28.
19. Willard B. Gatewood, "Theodore Roosevelt and the Indianola Affair," *Journal of Negro History* (January 1968), pp. 48–69.
20. Quoted in "Punishes Southern Town," *New York Times* (January 3, 1903).
21. Holmes, *White Chief*, p. 101.
22. Quoted in Holmes, *White Chief*, pp. 110–11. See also Eugene E. White, "Anti-Racial Agitation in Politics: James Kimble Vardaman in the Mississippi Gubernatorial Campaign of 1903," *Journal of Mississippi History* (April 1945), pp. 91–110.
23. Harris Dickson, "The Vardaman Idea," *Saturday Evening Post* (April 27, 1907), pp. 3–5; Garrard Harris, "A Defense of Governor Vardaman," *Harper's Weekly* (February 18, 1905), pp. 236–38.
24. Holmes, *White Chief*, pp. 121–22, 182.
25. Holmes, *White Chief*, pp. 132–45.
26. Holmes, *White Chief*, p. 194; George C. Osborn, "John Sharp Williams Becomes a United States Senator," *Journal of Southern History* (May 1940), pp. 222–36.
27. Heber Ladner, "James Kimble Vardaman, Governor of Mississippi, 1904–1908," *Journal of Mississippi History* (October 1940), pp. 175–205.
28. For details on the "secret caucus," see Kirwan, *Rednecks*, pp. 191–210.
29. Holmes, *White Chief*, p. 286.
30. "War on 'Favorites,'" *Washington Post* (July 26, 1913).
31. "Race Law His Target," *Washington Post* (May 4, 1913).
32. "Calls Lynching Best," *Washington Post* (August 7, 1913).
33. *Congressional Record* (February 6, 1914), pp. 3036–37.
34. Ray Stannard Baker, *Following the Color Line* (New York: Doubleday, Page, 1908), p. 241.
35. The idea that race mixing would somehow destroy the white race has a long history in the South. See James W. Vander Zanden, "The Ideology of White Supremacy," *Journal of the History of Ideas* (June-September 1959), pp. 385–402.
36. "Senator Vardaman," *The Nation* (April 12, 1917), p. 439.
37. Holmes, *White Chief*, pp. 294–327.
38. V. O. Key Jr., *Southern Politics* (New York: Alfred A. Knopf, 1949), p. 243. For background on Bilbo, see Mark Ethridge, "Want-Ridden Southern Workers Elect Bilbo to 'Raise Cain,'" *Washington Post* (September 23, 1934); Mark Ethridge, "New Faces in the Senate—Mr. Bilbo of Mississippi," *Washington Post* (November 10, 1934); Vincent A. Giroux Jr., "The Rise of Theodore G. Bilbo (1908–1932)," *Journal of Mississippi History* (August 1981), pp. 190–209; Jerry A. Hendrix, "Theodore G. Bilbo: Evangelist of Racial Purity," in Logue and Dorgan, *Southern Demagogues*, pp. 151–72; Reinhard H. Luthin, *American Demagogues: The 20th Century* (Boston: Beacon Press, 1954), pp. 44–76; William D. McCain, "Theodore Gilmore Bilbo and the Mississippi Delta," *Journal of Mississippi History* (February 1969), pp. 1–27; Chester M. Morgan, *Redneck Liberal: Theodore G. Bilbo and the New Deal* (Baton Rouge: Louisiana State University Press, 1985); Chester M. Morgan, "Senator Theodore G. Bilbo, the New Deal, and Mississippi Politics (1934–1940)," *Journal of Mississippi History* (August 1985), pp. 147–64; Raymond G. Swing, "Bilbo the Rabble-Rouser," *The Nation* (January 30, 1935), pp. 123–25.

39. *Congressional Record* (January 21, 1938), p. 873.
40. *Congressional Record* (January 21, 1938), p. 882.
41. *Congressional Record* (January 21, 1938), p. 884.
42. *Congressional Record* (January 21, 1938), pp. 883–4.
43. *Congressional Record* (May 24, 1938), pp. 7347–70.
44. *Congressional Record* (April 24, 1939), pp. 4670–1.
45. *Congressional Record* (April 24, 1939), p. 4671.
46. Thurston E. Doler, "Theodore G. Bilbo's Rhetoric of Racial Relations," Ph.D. dissertation, University of Oregon (December 1968), pp. 107–8.
47. Michael W. Fitzgerald, "'We Have Found a Moses': Theodore Bilbo, Black Nationalism, and the Greater Liberia Bill of 1939," *Journal of Southern History* (May 1997), pp. 293–320. On white supremacist support for the back to Africa movement, see Paul A. Lombardo, "'The American Breed': Nazi Eugenics and the Origins of The Pioneer Fund," *Albany Law Review* (Spring 2002), pp. 780–86.
48. A. Wigfall Green, *The Man Bilbo* (Baton Rouge: Louisiana State University Press, 1963), p. 100.
49. Quoted in Hodding Carter, "'The Man' From Mississippi—Bilbo," *New York Times Magazine* (June 30, 1946), p. 12. Carter was editor of the *Delta Democrat-Times* in Greenville, Mississippi. Bilbo was often referred to as "The Man."
50. Quoted in *Time Magazine* (August 27, 1965).
51. Doler, "Bilbo's Rhetoric," pp. 109–12.
52. *Congressional Record* (May 12, 1944), p. 4425.
53. *Congressional Record* (April 17, 1944), p. A1799.
54. *Congressional Record* (April 17, 1944), p. A1801.
55. "Bilbo Runs Amok," *Washington Post* (March 23, 1944).
56. Robert J. Bailey, "Theodore G. Bilbo and the Fair Employment Practices Controversy: A Southern Senator's Reaction to a Changing World," *Journal of Mississippi History* (February 1980), pp. 27–42.
57. Doler, "Bilbo's Rhetoric," pp. 116–7; Green, *Man Bilbo*, pp. 102–3.
58. "'Bilboism' on Trial," *New York Times* (November 18, 1946).
59. Milton Lehman, "Will Bilbo Fool'em Again?" *Saturday Evening Post* (June 29, 1946), p. 19.
60. Quoted in Carter, "Man From Mississippi," p. 12. Linking those supporting rights for blacks to Communists became an increasingly popular technique for Southern racists as the Cold War heated up. See George Lewis, *The White South and the Red Menace* (Gainesville: University Press of Florida, 2004).
61. The statement was made on "Meet the Press." A transcript of the interview was published in the *American Mercury* (November 1946), pp. 525–34.
62. Drew Pearson, "Washington Merry-Go-Round," *Washington Post* (July 2, 1946).
63. "Report on Bilbo," *New Republic* (January 6, 1947), pp. 6–7; Tris Coffin, "Bilbo on the Griddle," *The Nation* (December 21, 1946), pp. 718–19; Tris Coffin, "An Old Southern Custom," *The Nation* (December 28, 1946), pp. 747–8; Richard C. Ethridge, "The Fall of the Man: The United States Senate's Probe of Theodore G. Bilbo in December, 1946, and Its Aftermath," *Journal of Mississippi History* (August 1976), pp. 241–62.
64. Quoted in F. Ross Peterson, "Glen H. Taylor and the Bilbo Case," *Phylon* (4th quarter 1970), p. 346.
65. Anne M. Butler and Wendy Wolff, *United States Senate Election, Expulsion and Censure Cases, 1793–1990* (Washington: U.S. Government Printing Office, 1995), pp. 376–79.
66. It was self-published by Bilbo. The publication information lists Dream House Publishing Company in Poplarville, Mississippi. Poplarville was his home town, where he lived in the "Dream House."
67. John Sharp Williams, *Thomas Jefferson: His Permanent Influence on American Institutions* (New York: Columbia University Press, 1913), pp. 77–78.
68. "Echo of Indianola: John Sharp Williams Says Incident Is Not Dead," *Washington Post* (September 20, 1903).
69. *Congressional Record* (October 1, 1918), p. 10982.

70. George C. Osborn, "The Friendship of John Sharp Williams and Woodrow Wilson," *Journal of Mississippi History* (January 1939), pp. 3–13.

71. *Congressional Record* (January 19, 1922), p. 1427.

72. Quoted in *Time Magazine* (February 14, 1944). Note: Franklin D. Roosevelt did indeed vote for his cousin Teddy in 1904. FDR's Secretary of War, Henry Stimson, had held the same position under Republican William Howard Taft. (He was also Secretary of State under Herbert Hoover.) And FDR's Secretary of the Navy, Frank Knox, was the Republican nominee for Vice President in 1936. Needless to say, most historians view Roosevelt's appointment of prominent Republicans to such key positions as wise and politically astute, helping bring Americans together at a time of crisis and demonstrating that support for the war was bipartisan.

73. Quoted in Joseph Alsop and Stewart Alsop, "Will the Negroes Vote?" *Washington Post* (April 10, 1946).

74. Drew Pearson, "Washington Merry-Go-Round," *Washington Post* (June 11, 1946).

75. *Time Magazine* (November 3, 1947).

76. "Exit Mr. Rankin," *Washington Post* (August 28, 1952).

77. There were no Republican governors in Mississippi between Adelbert Ames, who left office in 1876, and Kirk Fordice, who became governor in 1992. One of the state's senate seats was held by Democrats continuously from James Alcorn, who left office in 1877, and the election of Thad Cochran in 1978. The other seat was held by Democrats continuously between Blanche Bruce, who left office in 1881, and the election of Trent Lott in 1988. Republican Senator Bruce, by the way, was a black man who had been born into slavery. He was the first African American to serve a full six-year term in the Senate.

CHAPTER 6

References to the sixty-nine volumes of Wilson's papers, edited by Arthur S. Link et al. and published by Princeton University Press between 1966 and 1994, are abbreviated as Wilson Papers *and identified by volume and page number in the notes.*

1. For a recent review, see Kendrick A. Clements, *The Presidency of Woodrow Wilson* (Lawrence: University Press of Kansas, 1992).

2. Arthur M. Schlesinger, "Our Presidents: A Rating By 75 Historians," *New York Times Magazine* (July 29, 1962).

3. Arthur M. Schlesinger Jr., "Rating the Presidents: Washington to Clinton," *Political Science Quarterly* (Summer 1997), pp. 179–90. The decline in Wilson's rating may have had something to do with John F. Kennedy, who told Schlesinger Jr. that he didn't think Wilson was a very good president. He had botched the Mexican intervention, messed up the League of Nations fight, and failed in a number of his objectives, Kennedy said. See Arthur Schlesinger Jr., *A Thousand Days: John F. Kennedy in the White House* (Boston: Houghton Mifflin, 1965), p. 675.

4. See Stanley Coben, *A. Mitchell Palmer: Politician* (New York: Columbia University Press, 1963); Roberta S. Feuerlicht, *America's Reign of Terror: World War I, the Red Scare, and the Palmer Raids* (New York: Random House, 1971); Robert K. Murray, *Red Scare: A Study in National Hysteria, 1919–1920* (Minneapolis: University of Minnesota Press, 1955); H. C. Peterson and Gilbert C. Fite, *Opponents of War: 1917–1918* (Madison: University of Wisconsin Press, 1957); Harry Scheiber, *The Wilson Administration and Civil Liberties, 1917–1921* (Ithaca: Cornell University Press, 1960); Geoffrey Stone, *Perilous Times: Free Speech in Wartime* (New York: W.W. Norton, 2004), pp. 220–26; Robert D. Warth, "The Palmer Raids," *South Atlantic Quarterly* (January 1949), pp. 1–23.

5. Arthur S. Link, "Woodrow Wilson: The American as Southerner," *Journal of Southern History* (February 1970), p. 5; John M. Mulder, *Woodrow Wilson: The Years of Preparation* (Princeton: Princeton University Press, 1978), p. 20.

6. Anthony Gaughan, "Woodrow Wilson and the Legacy of the Civil War," *Civil War History* (September 1997), pp. 225–42.

7. Woodrow Wilson to Ellen Louis Axson (November 13, 1884), *Wilson Papers*, 3: 430.

8. Woodrow Wilson, *Division and Reunion: 1829–1889* (New York: Collier Books, 1961), pp. 115–16.

9. Woodrow Wilson, *A History of the American People* (New York: Harper & Brothers, 1901), vol. 5, pp. 59–62.

10. Woodrow Wilson, "The Reconstruction of the Southern States," *Atlantic Monthly* (January 1901), pp. 1–15. For a review of Wilson's views on Reconstruction, see Michael Dennis, "Race and the Southern Imagination: Woodrow Wilson Reconsidered," *Canadian Review of American Studies* (No. 3, 1999), pp. 109–31.

11. Woodrow Wilson to Caleb Thomas Winchester (May 29, 1893), *Wilson Papers*, 8: 220.

12. Woodrow Wilson to Richard Watson Gilder (January 28, 1901), *Wilson Papers*, 12: 84.

13. Arthur S. Link, *Wilson: The Road to the White House* (Princeton: Princeton University Press, 1947), p. 95.

14. According to Princeton's web site, the first black wasn't admitted to the university until 1935—and then by mistake. When the student showed up to register for classes and his race was discovered, he was sent home. It wasn't until World War II that the color barrier at Princeton was finally broken.

15. "Wilson and the Negro," *New York Age* (July 11, 1912).

16. Arthur S. Link, "The Negro as a Factor in the Campaign of 1912," *Journal of Negro History* (January 1947), pp. 83–84; C. Vann Woodward, *Tom Watson: Agrarian Rebel* (New York: Macmillan, 1938), pp. 426–27.

17. Woodrow Wilson to James Calvin Hemphill (January 26, 1906), *Wilson Papers*, 16: 288. See also Mulder, *Years of Preparation*, p. 233.

18. Joseph L. Morrison, *Josephus Daniels: The Small-d Democrat* (Chapel Hill: University of North Carolina Press, 1966), pp. 45–46. Page met Wilson in 1882 while Wilson was briefly practicing law in Atlanta, Georgia. The two quickly hit it off and Page became Wilson's mentor. Woodward, *Tom Watson*, p. 113.

19. The speech can be found in *Wilson Papers*, 18: 631–45.

20. Actually, she was already postmaster when Roosevelt became president. He closed the post office because she was threatened by local racists and forced to resign. On that incident and the appointment of William Crum as customs collector in Charleston, see Willard B. Gatewood Jr., *Theodore Roosevelt and the Art of Controversy* (Baton Rouge: Louisiana State University Press, 1970), pp. 62–134.

21. For details on the Roosevelt dinner with Washington, see Gatewood, *Theodore Roosevelt*, pp. 32–61; and Dewey W. Grantham Jr., "Dinner at the White House: Theodore Roosevelt, Booker T. Washington, and the South," *Tennessee Historical Quarterly* (June 1958), pp. 112–30.

22. "Theodore Roosevelt and the South," *Raleigh News & Observer* (October 1, 1912).

23. Mike Baker, "1898 Race Clash Ruled a Coup," *Washington Post* (June 1, 2006).

24. Helen G. Edmonds, *The Negro and Fusion Politics in North Carolina, 1894–1901* (Chapel Hill: University of North Carolina Press, 1951), pp. 141–42.

25. 1898 Wilmington Race Riot Commission, *Report* (Raleigh: Office of Archives and History, North Carolina Department of Cultural Resources, May 2006), pp. 41, 52–54, 59–94. See also David S. Cecelski and Timothy B. Tyson, *Democracy Betrayed: The Wilmington Race Riot of 1898 and Its Legacy* (Chapel Hill: University of North Carolina Press, 1998); H. Leon Prather, *We Have Taken a City: The Wilmington Racial Massacre and the Coup of 1898* (Southport, NC: Dram Tree Books, 2006).

26. Josephus Daniels, *Editor in Politics* (Chapel Hill: University of North Carolina Press, 1941), pp. 283–312.

27. Daniels, *Editor in Politics*, p. 295.

28. A key difference between the KKK and the Red Shirts is that the latter did nothing to hide their identities. As one historian explained, "The Red Shirts wanted Republicans,

Populists, blacks and the entire white population to know who they were and what they stood for—rule by the Democratic Party and white supremacy." H. Leon Prather, "The Red Shirt Movement in North Carolina, 1898–1900," *Journal of Negro History* (April 1977), p. 175. The Klan had also been active in North Carolina during Reconstruction, acting as the military arm of the Democratic Party and targeting Republicans. See Paul D. Escott, "White Republicanism and Ku Klux Klan Terror: The North Carolina Piedmont During Reconstruction," in Jeffrey J. Crow, Paul D. Escott, and Charles L. Flynn Jr., eds., *Race, Class, and Politics in Southern History* (Baton Rouge: Louisiana State University Press, 1989), pp. 3–34.

29. Wilmington Race Riot Commission Report, p. 67.

30. Daniels, *Editor in Politics*, p. 293.

31. Daniels, *Editor in Politics*, p. 325; J. Morgan Kousser, *The Shaping of Southern Politics: Suffrage Restriction and the Establishment of the One-Party South, 1880–1910* (New Haven: Yale University Press, 1974), pp. 189–95; Morrison, *Josephus Daniels*, pp. 34–35.

32. Quoted in "Eliminate the Negro," *Washington Post* (December 27, 1899).

33. Quoted in "State Surely Democratic," *Washington Post* (September 8, 1900).

34. His exact words were: "A man whose mind runs away into baseless optimism is apt to point to Booker T. Washington as a product of the Negro race. Now Washington is a great and good man, a Christian statesman, and take him all in all the greatest man, save General Lee, born in the South in a hundred years; but he is not a typical Negro." "Stirring Up the Fires of Race Antipathy," *South Atlantic Quarterly* (October 1903), p. 299. See also, Wendell H. Stephenson, "The Negro in the Thinking and Writing of John Spencer Bassett," *North Carolina Historical Review* (October 1948), pp. 427–41.

35. Steve Cohn, "The Bassett Affair and SAQ's Centenary Anniversary," *South Atlantic Quarterly* (Spring 2002), pp. 245–47.

36. Daniels, *Editor in Politics*, pp. 428–36; Morrison, *Josephus Daniels*, p. 39.

37. "An Ugly Chapter," *Raleigh News & Observer* (December 17, 2005); Ted Vaden, "Wilmington, 1898: Revisiting the Riot," *Raleigh News & Observer* (January 15, 2006).

38. Morton Sosna, "The South in the Saddle: Racial Politics During the Wilson Years," *Wisconsin Magazine of History* (Autumn 1970), p. 30.

39. Adrian Anderson, "President Wilson's Politician: Albert Sydney Burleson of Texas," *Southwestern Historical Quarterly* (January 1974), pp. 339–54.

40. E. David Cronon, *The Cabinet Diaries of Josephus Daniels, 1913–1921* (Lincoln: University of Nebraska Press, 1963), pp. 32–33.

41. Kathleen L. Wolgemuth, "Woodrow Wilson's Appointment Policy and the Negro," *Journal of Southern History* (November 1958), pp. 457–71. In 1914, Archibald Grimké of the NAACP testified before Congress that he didn't know a single colored person in Washington or in government service who had expressed any desire for segregation. House Committee on Reform in the Civil Service, *Segregation of Clerks and Employees in the Civil Service*, 63rd Congress, 2nd session (Washington: U.S. Government Printing Office, 1914), p. 22.

42. Link, *Road to the White House*, p. 505.

43. Arthur S. Link, *Wilson: The New Freedom* (Princeton: Princeton University Press, 1956), p. 247.

44. Kathleen L. Wolgemuth, "Woodrow Wilson and Federal Segregation," *Journal of Negro History* (April 1959), p. 161.

45. Desmond King, *Separate and Unequal: Black Americans and the Federal Government* (New York: Oxford University Press, 1995), p. 48–49.

46. Link, *New Freedom*, p. 248.

47. Arthur S. Link, *Woodrow Wilson and the Progressive Era, 1910–1917* (New York: Harper & Row, 1954), p. 65.

48. "White Bosses Is Plea: Citizens Object to Negro Rule in U.S. Departments," *Washington Post* (April 24, 1913); "Pushing Their Plans: Segregation Committee Is Busy Sending Out Literature," *Washington Post* (April 25, 1913).

49. "Takes Up Race Issue: Speaker Demands Segregation in Government Offices," *Washington Post* (April 30, 1913).

50. "Grills Census Office: Fair Play Association Attacks Mingling of Races," *Washington Post* (May 1, 1913); "School U.S. Clerks," *Washington Post* (May 2, 1913).

51. "Race Policy Problem," *Washington Post* (September 30, 1913). According to Arthur Link, "Mrs. Wilson felt much more strongly about the necessity of drawing the color line than did her husband, but both were opposed to social relations between the races." Link, *Road to the White House*, p. 502.

52. "Wants to Part Races: Thompson Introduces Rigid Segregation Bill in House," *Washington Post* (July 16, 1913).

53. "War on 'Favorites,'" *Washington Post* (July 26, 1913).

54. Woodrow Wilson to Oswald Garrison Villard (July 23, 1913), *Wilson Papers*, 28: 65. Villard was owner of the *New York Evening Post* newspaper and *The Nation* magazine, and the grandson of William Lloyd Garrison, the famous abolitionist.

55. Thomas Dixon Jr. to Woodrow Wilson (July 27, 1913); and Woodrow Wilson to Thomas Dixon Jr. (July 29, 1913), *Wilson Papers*, 28: 88–89, 94.

56. Woodrow Wilson to Howard Allen Bridgman (September 8, 1913), *Wilson Papers*, 28: 265.

57. "The President and the Negro," *The Nation* (August 7, 1913), p. 114.

58. "Racial Plot Veiled: Effort to Drive Negro from U.S. Service, Rogers Hears," *Washington Post* (October 17, 1913). Democrats had a majority of 291 to 134 Republicans in the House and a majority of 51 to 44 in the Senate.

59. Nancy J. Weiss, "The Negro and the New Freedom: Fighting Wilsonian Segregation," *Political Science Quarterly* (March 1969), p. 69.

60. "Denied by M'Adoo," *Washington Post* (October 28, 1913).

61. "Segregation His Plea: Aswell of Louisiana Replies to Oswald G. Villard," *Washington Post* (November 13, 1913).

62. House Committee, *Segregation of Clerks*, p. 3.

63. House Committee, *Segregation of Clerks*, p. 12.

64. House Committee, *Segregation of Clerks*, pp. 21–22.

65. Link, *New Freedom*, pp. 343–44; Rayford Logan, *The Betrayal of the Negro: From Rutherford B. Hayes to Woodrow Wilson* (New York: Collier Books, 1965), pp. 362–63.

66. Herbert Aptheker, *A Documentary History of the Negro People in the United States, 1910–1932* (New York: Citadel Press, 1990), pp. 57–58.

67. "The Last Word in Politics," *The Crisis* (November 1912), p. 29, reprinted in Herbert Aptheker, *Writings in Periodicals Edited by W. E. B. DuBois: Selections from The Crisis, 1911–1925* (Millwood, NY: Kraus-Thompson, 1983), p. 45. DuBois even resigned his membership in the Socialist Party in order to support Wilson. See Logan, *Betrayal*, p. 363.

68. "The Election," *The Crisis* (December 1912), reprinted in Aptheker, *Writings*, p. 46.

69. Booker T. Washington to Oswald Garrison Villard (August 10, 1913), in Louis R. Harlan and Raymond W. Smock, eds., *The Booker T. Washington Papers*, vol. 12 (Chicago: University of Illinois Press, 1982), p. 248.

70. Aptheker, *Documentary History*, pp. 63–64.

71. George C. Osborn, "The Problem of the Negro in Government, 1913," *The Historian* (May 1961), pp. 330–47.

72. Henry Blumenthal, "Woodrow Wilson and the Race Question," *Journal of Negro History* (January 1963), p. 8.

73. Wilson later referred to Trotter as "that unspeakable fellow." Woodrow Wilson to Joseph Patrick Tumulty (April 24, 1915), *Wilson Papers*, 33: 68.

74. "President Resents Negro's Criticism," *New York Times* (November 13, 1914). For a report on this meeting by a black newspaper, see "The Trotter Encounter With President Wilson," *Chicago Defender* (November 21, 1914), reprinted in Aptheker, *Documentary History*, pp. 70–73. A transcript of the meeting appears in Christine A. Lunardini, "Standing Firm: William Monroe Trotter's Meetings with Woodrow Wilson, 1913–1914," *Journal of Negro History* (Summer 1979), pp. 255–60.

75. Aptheker, *Documentary History*, pp. 77–78.
76. Link, *New Freedom*, pp. 252–53. See also Raymond A. Cook, "The Man Behind 'The Birth of a Nation,'" *North Carolina Historical Review* (Autumn 1962), pp. 528–35.
77. Quoted in Milton Mackaye, "The Birth of a Nation," *Scribner's Magazine* (November 1937), p. 69.
78. Henry L. Suggs, "The Response of the African American Press to the United States Occupation of Haiti, 1915–1934," *Journal of African American History* (Winter 2002), pp. 70–72.
79. Aptheker, *Documentary History*, p. 139.
80. W. E. B. DuBois, "The Negro Soldier in Service Abroad During the First World War," *Journal of Negro Education* (Summer 1943), pp. 324–34; L. D. Reddick, "The Negro Policy of the United States Army, 1775–1945," *Journal of Negro History* (January 1949), pp. 20–24.
81. Quoted in Jane Lang Scheiber and Harry N. Scheiber, "The Wilson Administration and the Wartime Mobilization of Black Americans, 1917–18," *Labor History* (Summer 1969), p. 441.
82. Quoted in William F. Holmes, *The White Chief: James Kimble Vardaman* (Baton Rouge: Louisiana State University Press, 1970), p. 320.
83. Aptheker, *Documentary History*, pp. 184–85, 203–6, 215–18, 224–26; Edgar A. Schuler, "The Houston Race Riot, 1917," *Journal of Negro History* (July 1944), pp. 300–38.
84. *Wilson Papers*, 53: 340–1.
85. *Wilson Papers*, 55: 471.
86. Margaret Macmillan, *Paris 1919* (New York: Random House, 2001), pp. 306–21.
87. Kenneth O'Reilly, *Nixon's Piano: Presidents and Racial Politics from Washington to Clinton* (New York: Free Press, 1995), p. 94.
88. For example, the Federal Reserve and the income tax, two of Wilson's most progressive accomplishments, had been in the works for years before he took office. Moreover, Wilson gets credit for some reforms, such as women's suffrage, that he really had nothing to do with, while he resisted more radical reforms in many areas than political conditions would have allowed. In short, he was much more conservative and conventional than he is generally portrayed in the history texts. See Richard M. Abrams, "Woodrow Wilson and the Southern Congressmen, 1913–1916," *Journal of Southern History* (November 1956), pp. 417–37; Gabriel Kolko, *The Triumph of Conservatism: A Reinterpretation of American History, 1900–1916* (Chicago: Quadrangle Books, 1967); Martin J. Sklar, "Woodrow Wilson and the Political Economy of Modern United States Liberalism," in Ronald Radosh and Murray N. Rothbard, eds., *A New History of Leviathan: Essays on the Rise of the American Corporate State* (New York: E. P. Dutton, 1972), pp. 7–65; James Weinstein, *The Corporate Ideal in the Liberal State, 1900–1918* (Boston: Beacon Press, 1968).

CHAPTER 7

1. Arthur M. Schlesinger Jr., *The Politics of Upheaval* (Boston: Houghton Mifflin, 1960), p. 430. According to Eleanor Roosevelt confidant Joseph P. Lash, Franklin Roosevelt never had any enthusiasm for equal rights. See Joseph P. Lash, *Dealers and Dreamers: A New Look at the New Deal* (New York: Doubleday, 1988), p. 415.
2. One of Roosevelt's closest advisers, Rexford Tugwell, was appalled at how callously Roosevelt treated Daisy Bonner, a black woman who cooked for him for years at the Little White House in Warm Springs, Georgia. "He didn't know she existed," Tugwell observed. Quoted in Nancy Weiss, *Farewell to the Party of Lincoln: Black Politics in the Age of FDR* (Princeton: Princeton University Press, 1983), p. 19.
3. Geoffrey C. Ward, *A First-Class Temperament: The Emergence of Franklin Roosevelt* (New York: Harper & Row, 1989), pp. 173–74. P.V.L. was the abbreviation for a ship, the *Princessin Victoria Luise*. On other occasions, Roosevelt would refer to blacks as "Africans." See Walter Lord, *The Past That Would Not Die* (New York: Harper & Row, 1965), p. 44.

4. Alonzo Fields, *My 21 Years at the White House* (New York: Coward-McCann, 1961), pp. 41–42.
5. Schlesinger, *Politics of Upheaval*, p. 430.
6. Kenneth O'Reilly, *Nixon's Piano: Presidents and Racial Politics from Washington to Clinton* (New York: Free Press, 1995), p. 95.
7. So close was Roosevelt to his adopted state that there was serious talk of running him for governor of Georgia in the 1920s. His Georgia connection effectively made him the South's candidate for the Democratic presidential nomination in 1932, even though Texan John Nance Garner was also running. See William Leuchtenburg, *The White House Looks South* (Baton Rouge: Louisiana State University Press, 2005), pp. 29–46.
8. Naomi Rogers, "Race and the Politics of Polio," *American Journal of Public Health* (May 2007), p. 787.
9. Charles H. Martin, "Negro Leaders, the Republican Party, and the Election of 1932," *Phylon* (1st quarter 1971), pp. 90–91; Schlesinger, *Politics of Upheaval*, p. 431; Weiss, *Farewell*, p. 20. By all accounts, Garner was fairly moderate on the race question by the standards of the time, when members of the Ku Klux Klan were being elected to statewide office in Texas. Nevertheless, blacks viewed his appointment with great suspicion for the same reason that Southerners applauded it—as a signal that their concerns would be looked after, including those on race. Note: It is generally believed that U.S. Senator Earle Mayfield, Democrat of Texas, who served from 1923 to 1929, was a member of the Klan. See L. C. Speers, "Colorado Hurries Downfall of Klan," *Washington Post* (September 26, 1926); June Rayfield Welch, *The Texas Senator* (Dallas: G.L.A. Press, 1978), pp. 52–55.
10. Quoted in Weiss, *Farewell*, p. 21.
11. Donald J. Lisio, *Hoover, Blacks, & Lily-Whites* (Chapel Hill: University of North Carolina Press, 1985), p. 30.
12. Lisio, *Lily-Whites*, pp. 106–14; Martin, "Negro Leaders," pp. 85–93. Parker was ultimately rejected by the Senate. See Richard L. Watson, "The Defeat of Judge Parker: A Study in Pressure Groups and Politics," *Mississippi Valley Historical Review* (September 1963), pp. 213–34.
13. Richard B. Sherman, *The Republican Party and Black America: From McKinley to Hoover, 1896–1933* (Charlottesville: University Press of Virginia, 1973), pp. 225–29; Walter White, "The Negro and the Flood," *The Nation* (June 22, 1927), pp. 688–89.
14. Leslie H. Fishel Jr., "The Negro in the New Deal Era," *Wisconsin Magazine of History* (Winter 1964–1965), pp. 111–26.
15. O'Reilly, *Nixon's Piano*, p. 115.
16. Roosevelt was right about deflation being the fundamental economic problem. But he and his advisers did not realize that the cause was Federal Reserve policy, which allowed the money supply to shrink by a third between 1929 and 1933. Therefore, the NIRA's price fixing was not only futile, because it did not get at deflation's root cause, but counterproductive, because it prevented the price level from adjusting to the shrunken money supply. It was really the worst policy imaginable under the circumstances and strongly contributed to the length and depth of the Depression. On the counterproductive economic impact of the price-fixing policy, see Harold L. Cole and Lee E. Ohanian, "New Deal Policies and the Persistence of the Great Depression: A General Equilibrium Analysis," *Journal of Political Economy* (August 2004), pp. 779–816. The standard work on Federal Reserve policy during this period is Milton Friedman and Anna Schwartz, *A Monetary History of the United States, 1867–1960* (Princeton: Princeton University Press, 1963), pp. 299–419. There were those at the time who identified monetary policy as the central problem, but unfortunately they were not listened to. See, for example, Lauchlin Currie, "The Failure of Monetary Policy to Prevent the Depression of 1929–32," *Journal of Political Economy* (April 1934), pp. 145–77.
17. Said the Urban League's director of industrial relations, "It is a fact that as wages were raised by virtue of the NRA, employers dismissed their Negro workers in order to pay the higher wages to whites." T. Arnold Hill, *The Negro and Economic Reconstruction* (1937),

in Herbert Aptheker, *A Documentary History of the Negro People in the United States, 1933–1945* (New York: Citadel Press, 1990), p. 275. See also Michael S. Holman, "The Blue Eagle as 'Jim Crow Bird': The NRA and Georgia's Black Workers," *Journal of Negro History* (July 1972), pp. 276–83. It was noted at the time that NRA-mandated wages tended to make some positions historically held by blacks more attractive to whites, thus increasing labor competition to the disadvantage of blacks. See Charles S. Johnson, "Incidence Upon the Negroes," *American Journal of Sociology* (May 1935), p. 738.

18. Philip S. Foner, *Organized Labor and the Black Worker, 1619–1981* (New York: International Publishers, 1981), p. 200.

19. "In Defense of the Humble," *New York Times* (August 19, 1933).

20. The NRA did not employ a single black person with a rank equal to clerk. Bernard Bellush, *The Failure of the NRA* (New York: W. W. Norton, 1975), p. 80.

21. John P. Davis, "Blue Eagles and Black Workers," *New Republic* (November 14, 1934), p. 9.

22. Robert C. Weaver, "A Wage Differential Based on Race," *The Crisis* (August 1934), in Aptheker, *Documentary History*, pp. 109–12.

23. Charles Roos, *NRA Economic Planning* (Bloomington, IN: Principia Press, 1937), pp. 172–73.

24. "Bias Against Negro Laid to New Deal: Tenants Deprived of AAA Aid, Association Report Holds," *New York Times* (January 8, 1935); John P. Davis, "A Black Inventory of the New Deal," *The Crisis* (May 1935), in Aptheker, *Documentary History*, pp. 167–74; Weiss, *Farewell*, p. 55; Raymond Wolters, *Negroes and the Great Depression* (Westport, CT: Greenwood Press, 1970), pp. 3–20.

25. Paul Moreno, "An Ambivalent Legacy: Black Americans and the Political Economy of the New Deal," *Independent Review* (Spring 2002), p. 516.

26. William E. Leuchtenburg, *Franklin D. Roosevelt and the New Deal, 1932–1940* (New York: Harper & Row, 1963), p. 185; Melissa Walker, "African Americans and TVA Reservoir Property Removal: Race in a New Deal Program," *Agricultural History* (Spring 1998), p. 418.

27. Among the many works on labor union racism in the early twentieth century, see Eric Arnesen, "'Like Banquo's Ghost, It Will Not Down': The Race Question and the American Railroad Brotherhoods, 1880–1920," *American Historical Review* (December 1994), pp. 1601–33; John S. Durham, "The Labor Unions and the Negro," *Atlantic Monthly* (February 1898), pp. 221–31; William M. Tuttle Jr., "Labor Conflict and Racial Violence: The Black Worker in Chicago, 1894–1919," *Labor History* (Summer 1969), pp. 408–32.

28. Sterling D. Spero and Abram L. Harris, *The Black Worker: The Negro and the Labor Movement* (New York: Columbia University Press, 1931), pp. 128–46; Warren C. Whatley, "African-American Strikebreaking from the Civil War to the New Deal," *Social Science History* (Winter 1993), pp. 525–58.

29. Raymond Wolters, "Section 7a and the Black Worker," *Labor History* (Summer 1969), pp. 459–74.

30. Marc W. Kruman, "Quotas for Blacks: The Public Works Administration and the Black Construction Worker," *Labor History* (Winter 1975), pp. 37–51; Robert C. Weaver, "Negro Labor Since 1929," *Journal of Negro History* (January 1950), pp. 24–25.

31. Christopher G. Wye, "The New Deal and the Negro Community: Toward a Broader Conceptualization," *Journal of American History* (December 1972), pp. 634–39.

32. David Bernstein, "The Davis-Bacon Act: Vestige of Jim Crow," *National Black Law Journal* (Fall 1994), pp. 276–97.

33. Before the advent of federal housing programs in the 1930s, mortgages were uncommon; people mostly paid cash for homes. When they were financed, down payments of 30 percent to 50 percent were typical, and loans were from three to seven years at most with no amortization.

34. Adam Gordon, "The Creation of Homeownership: How New Deal Changes in Banking Regulation Simultaneously Made Homeownership Accessible to Whites and Out of Reach for Blacks," *Yale Law Journal* (October 2005), pp. 186–223; Kenneth T. Jackson, *Crabgrass Frontier: The Suburbanization of the United States* (New York: Oxford University Press,

1985), pp. 190–218; Dennis R. Judd, "Segregation Forever?" *The Nation* (December 9, 1991), pp. 740–44. Needless to say, the problems of redlining and suburban sprawl are still with us today, and both owe their origins to the New Deal.

35. 295 U.S. 495 (1935).

36. 300 U.S. 379 (1937).

37. See William E. Leuchtenburg, "The Origins of Franklin D. Roosevelt's 'Court-Packing' Plan," *Supreme Court Review* (1966), pp. 347–400; William E. Leuchtenburg, "FDR's Court-Packing Plan: A Second Life, a Second Death," *Duke Law Journal* (June-September 1985), pp. 673–89; Michael Nelson, "The President and the Court: Reinterpreting the Court-Packing Episode of 1937," *Political Science Quarterly* (Summer 1988), pp. 267–93.

38. John Chambers, "The Big Switch: Justice Roberts and the Minimum-Wage Cases," *Labor History* (Winter 1969), pp. 44–73. On the Court's fundamental shift in philosophy in 1937, see Laura Kalman, "The Constitution, the Supreme Court, and the New Deal," *American Historical Review* (June 2005), pp. 1052–79.

39. George E. Paulsen, "Ghost of the NRA: Drafting National Wage and Hour Legislation in 1937," *Social Science Quarterly* (June 1986), pp. 241–54.

40. Jonathan Grossman, "Fair Labor Standards Act of 1938: Maximum Struggle for a Minimum Wage," *Monthly Labor Review* (June 1978), pp. 22–30.

41. Thomas C. Leonard, "Eugenics and Economics in the Progressive Era," *Journal of Economic Perspectives* (Fall 2005), pp. 212–13.

42. F. W. Taussig, *Principles of Economics*, 3rd ed. (New York: Macmillan, 1921), vol. 2, p. 332.

43. John R. Commons, *Races and Immigrants in America* (New York: Macmillan, 1920); Paul H. Douglas, "The Economic Theory of Wage Regulation," *University of Chicago Law Review* (February 1938), pp. 184–218; A. N. Holcombe, "The Legal Minimum Wage in the United States," *American Economic Review* (March 1912), pp. 21–37; Paul U. Kellogg, "Immigration and the Minimum Wage," *Annals of the American Academy of Political and Social Science* (July 1913), pp. 66–77; Francis A. Walker, "Restriction of Immigration," *Atlantic Monthly* (June 1896), pp. 822–29; Sidney Webb, "The Economic Theory of a Legal Minimum Wage," *Journal of Political Economy* (December 1912), pp. 973–98. For a recent analysis supporting some of these arguments, see Daron Acemoglu, "Good Jobs versus Bad Jobs," *Journal of Labor Economics* (January 2001), pp. 1–21.

44. Thomas Leonard, "The Progressive Case for Regulating Women's Work," *American Journal of Economics and Sociology* (July 2005), pp. 757–91; F. W. Taussig, "Minimum Wages for Women," *Quarterly Journal of Economics* (May 1916), pp. 411–42; Clifford F. Thies, "Minimum Wages for Women Only," Independent Institute Working Paper No. 30 (April 2001).

45. *Congressional Record* (April 24, 1939), p. 4657. See also Ralph J. Bunche, *The Political Status of the Negro in the Age of FDR* (Chicago: University of Chicago Press, 1973), pp. 206–7.

46. Quoted in G. V. Doxey, *The Industrial Colour Bar in South Africa* (Cape Town, South Africa: Oxford University Press, 1961), p. 156. See also W. H. Hutt, *The Economics of the Colour Bar* (London: Andre Deutsch, 1964), pp. 79–80; Walter E. Williams, *South Africa's War Against Capitalism* (New York: Praeger, 1989), pp. 62–63.

47. "Wages, 'North' and 'South,'" *New York Times* (February 15, 1938).

48. "Differentials in Wages," *New York Times* (May 21, 1938); "The Wage Bill Compromise," *New York Times* (June 2, 1938); "'No. 1 Economic Problem,'" *New York Times* (July 7, 1938).

49. Robert K. Fleck, "Democratic Opposition to the Fair Labor Standards Act of 1938," *Journal of Economic History* (March 2002), pp. 25–54.

50. John R. Moore, "The Conservative Coalition in the United States Senate, 1942–1945," *Journal of Southern History* (August 1967), pp. 368–76; James T. Patterson, *Congressional Conservatism and the New Deal* (Lexington: University of Kentucky Press, 1967), pp. 149–54.

51. William A. Sundstrom, "Last Hired, First Fired? Unemployment and Urban Black Workers During the Great Depression," *Journal of Economic History* (June 1992), pp. 417, 419.

52. Weiss, *Farewell*, p. 206. See also Ernest M. Collins, "Cincinnati Negroes and Presidential Politics," *Journal of Negro History* (April 1956), pp. 131–33; Elmer W. Henderson, "Political Changes Among Negroes in Chicago During the Depression," *Social Forces* (May 1941), p. 538–46; Edward H. Litchfield, "A Case Study of Negro Political Behavior in Detroit," *Public Opinion Quarterly* (June 1941), pp. 267–74; Samuel Lubell, "The Negro & the Democratic Coalition," *Commentary* (August 1964), pp. 19–27. The Washington bureau chief of the *New York Times* believed that the Roosevelt landslide of 1936 resulted almost entirely from his getting twice as many black votes as in 1932: "If the Negroes had maintained any goodly part of their normal Republican allegiance the election would have been reasonably close, might even have been doubtful." Arthur Krock, "One Deplorable Effect of the Southern 'Purge,'" *New York Times* (August 24, 1938). On the political implications for Democrats of the large exodus of black voters from the Republican Party, see Howard L. Reiter, "The Building of a Bifactional Structure: The Democrats in the 1940s," *Political Science Quarterly* (Spring 2001), pp. 107–29.
53. Leuchtenburg, *Franklin D. Roosevelt*, pp. 186–87.
54. Davis, "Black Inventory," in Aptheker, *Documentary History*, p. 168.
55. Henderson, "Political Changes," p. 542. On the importance of relief to Democrats' gaining the black vote in 1936, see also Henry Lee Moon, "How the Negroes Voted," *The Nation* (November 25, 1944), p. 640.
56. Ira Katznelson, *When Affirmative Action Was White* (New York: W. W. Norton, 2005), p. 41.
57. Theodore H. White, *The Making of the President, 1960* (New York: Atheneum, 1961), p. 232.
58. Robert C. Lieberman, "Race, Institutions, and the Administration of Social Policy," *Social Science History* (Winter 1995), pp. 514–15. See also Linda Gordon, *Pitied But Not Entitled* (Cambridge: Harvard University Press, 1994), p. 5; Katznelson, *When Affirmative Action Was White*, pp. 42–48; Robert C. Lieberman, "Race and the Organization of Welfare Policy," in Paul E. Peterson, ed., *Classifying By Race* (Princeton: Princeton University Press, 1995), pp. 156–87; Jill Quadagno, *The Transformation of Old Age Security* (Chicago: University of Chicago Press, 1988), pp. 115–16.
59. Gareth Davies and Martha Derthick, "Race and Social Welfare Policy: The Social Security Act of 1935," *Political Science Quarterly* (Summer 1997), pp. 219–21.
60. Senate Finance Committee, *Economic Security Act*, 64th Congress, 1st session (Washington: U.S. Government Printing Office, 1935), pp. 640–41.
61. Sidney Olson, "Foe of New Deal Laws Content to Become Maryland Farmer," *Washington Post* (May 19, 1937).
62. On his short list there were seven names: Federal Circuit Court judges Sam Bratton, Joseph Hutcheson, and Samuel Sibley; Walter Stacy, chief justice of North Carolina's Supreme Court; Solicitor General Stanley Reed; and Senators Sherman Minton of Indiana and Hugo Black. See "Nominee No. 93," *Time Magazine* (August 23, 1937).
63. As *Time Magazine* later put it, "No one who had not been in the Klan's good graces could have been elected to the Senate from Alabama in 1926." "Black in White," *Time Magazine* (September 20, 1937). See also William R. Snell, "Fiery Crosses in the Roaring Twenties: Activities of the Revised Klan in Alabama, 1915–1930," *Alabama Review* (October 1970), pp. 256–76; "William R. Snell, "Masked Men in the Magic City: Activities of the Revised Klan in Birmingham, 1916–1940," *Alabama Historical Quarterly* (Fall/Winter 1972), pp. 206–27. These articles note that one of the Klan's prime activities during the time Black was a member was flogging those that earned its ire.
64. Charles N. Feidelson, "Alabama's Super Government," *The Nation* (September 28, 1927), p. 311.
65. Roger K. Newman, *Hugo Black: A Biography* (New York: Pantheon Books, 1994), pp. 92–94.
66. J. Mills Thornton, "Hugo Black and the Golden Age," *Alabama Law Review* (Spring 1985), p. 901.
67. Howard Ball, *Hugo L. Black: Cold Steel Warrior* (New York: Oxford University Press, 1996), p. 56.

68. He said this in a 1967 interview with the *New York Times* that was not published until his death in 1971. It is quoted in his obituary: "Justice Black, Champion of Civil Liberties for 34 Years on Court, Dies at 85," *New York Times* (September 26, 1971).

69. Stephenson was a member of the Klan. See Charles P. Sweeney, "Bigotry Turns to Murder," *The Nation* (August 31, 1921), p. 232.

70. Ray Sprigle, "Black Given Start as Defense Counsel for Priest's Slayer," *Pittsburgh Post-Gazette* (August 20, 1937); Ray Sprigle, "Murder Makes a Senator," *Pittsburgh Post-Gazette* (August 7, 1949).

71. Quoted in Newman, *Hugo Black*, p. 98.

72. "Klan Supports Two in Alabama Primary," *New York Times* (August 9, 1926); L. C. Speers, "Colorado Hurries Downfall of Klan," *New York Times* (September 26, 1926); Richard Oulahan, "Greets Vanguard of New Senators," *New York Times* (December 12, 1926); Richard Oulahan, "Many Big Problems Face New Congress Amid Partisanship," *New York Times* (November 28, 1927).

73. Alabama's other Democratic senator, J. Thomas Heflin, an outspoken bigot, was so disgusted by the Democratic Party's nomination of Smith in 1928 that he supported Republican Herbert Hoover for president, getting him into deep trouble with his fellow Democrats, who expelled him for disloyalty, causing him to lose his Senate seat. See Glenn T. Harper, "'Cotton Tom' Heflin and the Election of 1930: The Price of Party Disloyalty," *The Historian* (May 1968), pp. 389–411; J. Mills Thornton, "Alabama Politics, J. Thomas Heflin, and the Expulsion Movement of 1929," *Alabama Review* (April 1968), pp. 83–112. The Klan strongly supported Heflin in his fight to avoid ejection from the Democratic Party. See "Klan in Alabama Rallies to Heflin," *New York Times* (December 28, 1929).

74. David Rankin Barbee, "Radicalism Near End All Over Dixie Land," *Washington Post* (August 17, 1930).

75. Franklyn Waltman, "Politics and People," *Washington Post* (August 14, 1937).

76. Quoted in "Nominee No. 93."

77. Senator Theodore Bilbo, the Mississippi racist, later said that one reason he voted to confirm Black was precisely because Black had "enjoyed close and intimate" association with the "Ku Kluxers." Chester M. Morgan, *Redneck Liberal: Theodore G. Bilbo and the New Deal* (Baton Rouge: Louisiana State University Press, 1985), p. 170.

78. "Discovery of Black Scoop Is Explained by Sprigle," *Pittsburgh Post-Gazette* (September 23, 1937).

79. Esdale turned on his former friend because Black had ignored his plea for aid when Esdale got into some minor legal trouble that got him disbarred. He believed that a word from one of Alabama's U.S. senators would have made the problem go away. Ray Sprigle, "My Pal—Hugo," *Pittsburgh Post-Gazette* (July 31, 1949).

80. It ran in the *Pittsburgh Post-Gazette* from September 13 through September 18, 1937, and included Photostats of many key documents relating to Black's Klan membership. Sprigle won a Pulitzer Prize for his work on the Black/KKK story.

81. The Klan kept stenographic records of its meetings. A Photostat of this particular one was reproduced in the *Pittsburgh Post-Gazette* on September 15, 1937, leaving no doubt about Black's exact words that night.

82. "Black Ouster Now Is Held Impossible," *New York Times* (September 14, 1937).

83. William V. Nessly, "No Comment By Roosevelt While Black Is In Europe," *Washington Post* (September 15, 1937).

84. Quoted in Ball, *Hugo L. Black*, pp. 98–99.

85. According to Senator Bilbo, an admitted Klan member, "No man can leave the Klan. . . . Once a Ku Klux, always a Ku Klux." See "Senator Bilbo Meets the Press," *American Mercury* (November 1946), p. 529.

86. The text of Black's radio address appeared in the *Pittsburgh Post-Gazette* on October 2, 1937.

87. "Weight of Press Against Black in Radio Plea," *Washington Post* (October 2, 1937); "Nation's Press Almost United in Denouncing Black Speech," *New York Times* (October 3, 1937).

88. Max Lerner, "Hugo Black—a Personal History," *The Nation* (October 9, 1937), p. 367.

89. *Columbia Law Review* (May 1949), p. 718. In the former case, the Supreme Court threw out confessions by four black men because they had been obtained by police compulsion. In the latter, the conviction of a black man on rape charges was set aside because blacks had been systematically excluded from grand jury service.

90. It has been argued that Black's Klan membership may have influenced his position in one case: *Everson v. Board of Education of the Township of Ewing*, 330 U.S. 1 (1947). See Philip Hamburger, *Separation of Church and State* (Cambridge: Harvard University Press, 2002), pp. 454–63.

91. Most people assume that Hitler was just honoring the terms of Germany's treaty with Japan. But that only obliged him to intervene in the event of an American attack on Japan. Since Japan attacked first, the treaty technically did not apply. Therefore, Hitler's action is basically a mystery. See James V. Compton, *The Swastika and the Eagle* (Boston: Houghton Mifflin, 1967), p. 236. One theory recently put forward is that Hitler's declaration of war was no such thing; just a rehash of previous anti-American statements that Roosevelt seized upon and asserted to be a declaration of war. See Richard F. Hill, *Hitler Attacks Pearl Harbor* (Boulder, CO: Lynne Rienner, 2003), pp. 30–34.

92. Hoover had great confidence that the FBI could handle any genuine security threats. He was probably right; there wasn't a single proven act of enemy sabotage in the United States throughout the entire war. See Richard Gid Powers, *Broken: The Troubled Past and Uncertain Future of the FBI* (New York: Free Press, 2004), p. 187.

93. I do not use the term "concentration camp" lightly. That's what they were. See Michi Nishiura Weglyn, *Years of Infamy: The Untold Story of America's Concentration Camps*, 2nd ed. (Seattle: University of Washington Press, 1996).

94. The evacuation order applied only to the West Coast. Oddly, those of Japanese descent living in Hawaii were exempted.

95. Greg Robinson, *By Order of the President: FDR and the Internment of Japanese Americans* (Cambridge: Harvard University Press, 2001), pp. 3, 5.

96. Earl Warren, *The Memoirs of Earl Warren* (New York: Doubleday, 1977), p. 149.

97. William L. Neumann, *America Encounters Japan: From Perry to MacArthur* (Baltimore: Johns Hopkins Press, 1963), pp. 199–202.

98. Franklin D. Roosevelt, "The Average American and the Average Japanese Have Very Cloudy and Often Erroneous Points of View About Relations Between the Two Countries," *Macon Daily Telegraph* (April 30, 1925), reprinted in Donald S. Carmichael, *F.D.R. Columnist* (Chicago: Pellegrini & Cudahy, 1947), pp. 58–60.

99. David S. Wyman, *The Abandonment of the Jews: America and the Holocaust, 1941–1945* (New York: Pantheon Books, 1984), pp. xiv–xv.

100. Katharine Q. Seelye, "Newspaper Group Acknowledges a Holocaust Mistake," *New York Times* (March 13, 2006). See also Laurel Leff, *Buried By the Times: The Holocaust and America's Most Important Newspaper* (New York: Cambridge University Press, 2005).

101. William J. Collins, "Race, Roosevelt, and Wartime Production: Fair Employment in World War II Labor Markets," *American Economic Review* (March 2001), pp. 272–86; Robert A. Margo, "Explaining Black-White Wage Convergence, 1940–1950," *Industrial & Labor Relations Review* (April 1995), pp. 470–81; Robert C. Weaver, "The Employment of Negroes in United States War Industries," *International Labour Review* (August 1944), pp. 141–59. It should be noted that Roosevelt's order integrating the defense industry was issued only because black labor leader A. Philip Randolph threatened to organize a march on Washington if he didn't. In other words, it was a coerced action, not one freely offered. See Herbert Garfinkel, *When Negroes March* (Glencoe, IL: Free Press, 1959); Louis C. Kesselman, *The Social Politics of FEPC: A Study in Reform Pressure Movements* (Chapel Hill: University of North Carolina Press, 1948).

102. Allan Morrison, "The Secret Papers of FDR," *Negro Digest* (January 1951), pp. 3–13, reprinted in Bernard Sternsher, ed., *The Negro in Depression and War: Prelude to Revolution, 1930–1945* (Chicago: Quadrangle Books, 1969), pp. 66–77.

103. Kenneth B. Clark, "The Dilemma of Power," in Talcott Parsons and Kenneth B. Clark, eds., *The Negro American* (Boston: Beacon Press, 1967), p. xiii.

104. Charles Crowe, "Tom Watson, Populists and Blacks Reconsidered," *Journal of Negro History* (April 1970), p. 105.

105. Roy Wilkins, *Standing Fast* (New York: Viking Press, 1982), p. 127.

106. Steve Valocchi, "The Racial Basis of Capitalism and the State, and the Impact of the New Deal on African Americans," *Social Problems* (August 1994), p. 355.

107. Oswald Garrison Villard, "The President's Worst Failure," *The Nation* (June 5, 1935), p. 647.

108. Schlesinger, *Politics of Upheaval*, p. 437. See also Robert L. Zangrando, "The NAACP and a Federal Antilynching Bill, 1934–1940," *Journal of Negro History* (April 1965), pp. 106–17. Claude Pepper was among the leaders of the Southern Democratic filibuster against an antilynching law in 1938. See *Congressional Record* (January 24, 1938), pp. 973–99; Robert C. Albright, "First Night Work Fails to Break Filibuster," *Washington Post* (January 25, 1938). Pepper was defeated for reelection in the 1950 Democratic primary by Congressman George Smathers, who attacked him for being out of step with the state despite his racist pandering on the antilynching bill. Famously, Smathers said of him, "Are you aware that Claude Pepper is known all over Washington as a shameless extrovert [outgoing person]? Not only that, but this man is reliably reported to practice nepotism [favoritism toward a relative in employment] with his sister-in-law, and he has a sister who was once a thespian [actress] in wicked New York. Worst of all, it is an established fact that Mr. Pepper before his marriage practiced celibacy." This incident has gone down in history as the classic case of manipulating ignorant yahoos during a political campaign. The original version appeared in *Time Magazine* (April 17, 1950).

109. Quoted in Walter White, *A Man Called White* (New York: Viking Press, 1948), pp. 169–70.

110. It's worth remembering that in 1936 Roosevelt carried the eleven states of the old Confederacy by an average of 83 percent, ranging from a low of 69 percent in Tennessee to a high of 99 percent in South Carolina.

111. Quoted in Schlesinger, *Politics of Upheaval*, p. 437.

112. It's true that in 1933, Roosevelt declared that lynching was murder. However, he was protesting the lynching of two whites in California, not the routine lynching of blacks in the South. See Leuchtenburg, *White House Looks South*, pp. 64, 438.

113. Quoted in Leuchtenburg, *White House Looks South*, p. 65. It should be noted as well that when Roosevelt finally allowed Japanese Americans to join the Army in 1943, they were kept in a segregated unit, the famous 442nd Regimental Combat Team, immortalized in the 1951 Hollywood movie, "Go For Broke." It is generally considered to have been the most decorated unit in U.S military history.

114. Richard M. Dalfiume, "The 'Forgotten Years' of the Negro Revolution," *Journal of American History* (June 1968), pp. 90–106.

115. For a recent defense of Roosevelt's record on race, see Kevin J. McMahon, *Reconsidering Roosevelt on Race: How the Presidency Paved the Road to Brown* (Chicago: University of Chicago Press, 2004).

CHAPTER 8

1. Michael Gardner, *Harry Truman and Civil Rights* (Carbondale: Southern Illinois University Press, 2002), pp. 4–6.

2. David M. Chalmers, *Hooded Americanism: The History of the Ku Klux Klan*, 3rd ed. (Durham: Duke University Press, 1987), pp. 135–37.

3. It's worth remembering that the Klan was probably at the peak of its political power within the Democratic Party in 1924. Indeed, its presidential nominating convention that year was so heavily dominated by it that historians often refer to it as the "Klanbake" convention. See Chalmers, *Hooded Americanism*, pp. 202–12.

4. Available online at http://www.trumanlibrary.org/oralhist/hindeeg.htm. See also Alonzo L. Hamby, *Man of the People: The Life of Harry S. Truman* (New York: Oxford University Press, 1995), p. 114; David McCullough, *Truman* (New York: Simon & Schuster, 1992), p. 164. The issue of Truman's Klan membership came up during the 1944 campaign, but never got any traction. See William E. Leuchtenburg, *The White House Looks South* (Baton Rouge: Louisiana State University Press, 2005), pp. 160–61.

5. Lawrence H. Larsen and Nancy J. Hulston, *Pendergast!* (Columbia: University of Missouri Press, 1997), p. 104.

6. For background, see Lyle W. Dorsett, *The Pendergast Machine* (New York: Oxford University Press, 1968); Maurice M. Milligan, *Missouri Waltz: The Inside Story of the Pendergast Machine by the Man Who Smashed It* (New York: Scribner's, 1948); Alfred Steinberg, *The Bosses* (New York: Macmillan, 1972), pp. 307–66.

7. Historians note that Truman ran a good campaign in 1934 and that his victory in the Democratic primary resulted more from his strength in Missouri's rural areas than his margin in Kansas City. This may be true, but without Pendergast's support in the first place, Truman never would have considered running or been taken seriously as a candidate for such a high office, since his accomplishments up to that point were extremely modest compared to those of his opponents, both of whom were long-serving congressmen. There is simply no question that Pendergast's support was key to Truman's victory, and both of them knew it. See Gene Schmidtlein, "Truman's First Senatorial Election," *Missouri Historical Review* (January 1963), pp. 128–55.

8. Elliott Thurston, "Missouri Boss Delivers State to New Dealer," *Washington Post* (August 12, 1934).

9. Larsen & Hulston, *Pendergast!*, p. 89.

10. Lyle W. Dorsett, *Franklin D. Roosevelt and the City Bosses* (Port Washington, NY: Kennikat Press, 1977), p. 71.

11. Elliott Thurston, "Pendergast Machine Dominates Missouri," *Washington Post* (August 14, 1934).

12. "President Ousts Roper Assistant to Stop Quarrel," *Washington Post* (June 16, 1935); J. Christopher Schnell, "New Deal Scandals: E.Y. Mitchell and F.D.R.'s Commerce Department," *Missouri Historical Review* (July 1975), pp. 357–75.

13. Larsen & Hultson, *Pendergast!*, p. 101.

14. Elmer Irey, *The Tax Dodgers* (New York: Greenberg Publishers, 1948), p. 227. Irey was the Treasury's top criminal investigator in the 1930s.

15. Robert H. Ferrell, *Truman and Pendergast* (Columbia: University of Missouri Press, 1999), p. 42.

16. Ferrell, *Truman and Pendergast*, p. 43.

17. Irey, *Tax Dodgers*, p. 242.

18. *Congressional Record* (February 15, 1938), pp. 1962–64.

19. "Billion-Dollar Watchdog," *Time Magazine* (March 8, 1943).

20. Ferrell, *Truman and Pendergast*, p. 44.

21. Larsen & Hultson, *Pendergast!*, p. 187.

22. "Pendergast's Foe Replaced by Truman," *Washington Post* (May 4, 1945).

23. Drew Pearson, "Washington Merry-Go-Round," *Washington Post* (May 28, 1945). Truman also pardoned one of those convicted in the 1936 Kansas City vote fraud case. See "Pendergast Worker's Pardon 'Routine,' White House Says," *Washington Post* (July 9, 1946).

24. Arthur M. Schlesinger Jr., "Who Was Henry A. Wallace?" *Los Angeles Times Book Review* (March 12, 2000). See also John C. Culver and John Hyde, *American Dreamer: A Life of Henry A. Wallace* (New York: W.W. Norton, 2000), pp. 130–46.

25. "Text of Wallace Speech Defending Roosevelt Domestic Policy," *Washington Post* (July 26, 1943).

26. "Wallace Tells Negroes They Are Fighting Bigotry," *Washington Post* (March 16, 1944).

27. "Keep Vice President Wallace!" *New Republic* (July 17, 1944), pp. 62–63.

28. David Robertson, *Sly and Able: A Political Biography of James F. Byrnes* (New York: W. W. Norton, 1994), pp. 339–53.

29. Robert C. Albright, "Opposition by Hillman Group Puts Dent in Boom," *Washington Post* (July 19, 1944).

30. Quoted in Leuchtenburg, *White House Looks South*, p. 160.

31. Leuchtenburg, *White House Looks South*, p. 163.

32. Herbert Aptheker, *A Documentary History of the Negro People in the United States, 1933–1945* (New York: Citadel Press, 1974), p. 568.

33. Larry Grothaus, "Kansas City Blacks, Harry Truman and the Pendergast Machine," *Missouri Historical Review* (October 1974), pp. 65–82.

34. Garry M. Fink and James W. Hilty, "Prologue: The Senate Voting Record of Harry S. Truman," *Journal of Interdisciplinary History* (Autumn 1973), pp. 220–22; Gardner, *Harry Truman*, pp. 88–89; Donald R. McCoy and Richard T. Ruetten, *Quest and Response: Minority Rights and the Truman Administration* (Lawrence: University Press of Kansas, 1973), p. 15.

35. "Move to Create Permanent FEPC Reported Blocked," *Washington Post* (May 22, 1945).

36. McCoy & Ruetten, *Quest and Response*, p. 24.

37. "Russell Brands FEPC Wedge for Socialism," *Washington Post* (January 23, 1946); Robert C. Albright, "Foes of FEPC Use Rare Type of Filibuster," *Washington Post* (January 19, 1946); Jack Bell, "Introduction of FEPC Bill Throws Senate into Full-Scale Filibuster," *Washington Post* (January 18, 1946). On the extremely complicated legislative history of the FEPC and the parliamentary tactics used by its congressional opponents to kill it, see Robert A. Garson, *The Democratic Party and the Politics of Sectionalism, 1941–1948* (Baton Rouge: Louisiana State University Press, 1974), pp. 135–44; Will Maslow, "FEPC—A Case History in Parliamentary Maneuver," *University of Chicago Law Review* (June 1946), pp. 407–44.

38. *Congressional Record* (February 7, 1946), pp. 1050–59.

39. Randall B. Ripley, *Power in the Senate* (New York: St. Martin's Press, 1969), pp. 55–67.

40. "Change vs. Rigidity," *Time Magazine* (November 18, 1946).

41. "Police Chief Freed in Negro Beating," *New York Times* (November 6, 1946); "U.S. Accuses Police Chief of Torture," *Washington Post* (September 27, 1946); Gardner, *Harry Truman*, pp. 16–18. The famous folk singer Woodie Guthrie even wrote a song about Woodward, whom he misnamed Woodard. It appeared on his 1946 album, "The Great Dust Storm."

42. "Federal Jury Ready to Sift Ga. Lynching," *Washington Post* (December 3, 1946); Henry Lesesne, "Lynching of Four Goes in Limbo of 'Unsolved,'" *Washington Post* (March 30, 1947); Dillard Stokes, "Truman Sends FBI to Seek Ga. Lynchers," *Washington Post* (July 31, 1946).

43. William E. Juhnke, "President Truman's Committee on Civil Rights: The Interaction of Politics, Protest, and Presidential Advisory Commission," *Presidential Studies Quarterly* (Summer 1989), pp. 593–610.

44. Gerald G. Gross, "Truman Holds Civil Rights a Key to Peace," *Washington Post* (June 30, 1947).

45. Steve F. Lawson, ed., *To Secure These Rights: The Report of President Harry S. Truman's Committee on Civil Rights* (New York: Bedford/St. Martin's, 2004), pp. 160–64.

46. Lawson, *Secure These Rights*, pp. 164–67.

47. On the foreign policy implications of American racial policy at this time, see Mary L. Dudziak, "Desegregation as a Cold War Imperative," *Stanford Law Review* (November 1988), pp. 61–120.

48. Oral history interview with the Truman Library (October 17, 1972), available at http://www.trumanlibrary.org/oralhist/clarktc.htm#oh1.

49. William C. Berman, *The Politics of Civil Rights in the Truman Administration* (Columbus: Ohio State University Press, 1970), pp. 86–87; Monroe Billington, "Civil Rights, President Truman and the South," *Journal of Negro History* (April 1973), pp. 127–39; Garson, *Democratic Party*, p. 233.

50. "Senate Unit Backs Job Rights Bill," *Washington Post* (February 6, 1948).
51. From a speech in Austin, Texas, on May 22, 1948, quoted in Gardner, *Harry Truman*, p. 82. See also Robert A. Caro, *The Years of Lyndon Johnson: Means of Ascent* (New York: Alfred A. Knopf, 1990), p. 125.
52. McCoy & Ruetten, *Quest and Response*, p. 98. On Dewey's support for civil rights legislation in New York, see Anthony S. Chen, "'The Hitlerian Rule of Quotas': Racial Conservatism and the Politics of Fair Employment Legislation in New York State, 1941–1945," *Journal of American History* (March 2006), pp. 1238–64; Gardner, *Harry Truman*, pp. 93–94.
53. Clark M. Clifford to President Truman (November 19, 1947), available online at http://www.trumanlibrary.org/whistlestop/study_collections/1948campaign/large/docs/index.php. Southerners were also aware of the potential political impact of black migration to the North. See John Temple Graves, "The Solid South Is Cracking," *American Mercury* (April 1943), pp. 401–6.
54. Hamby, *Man of the People*, p. 435.
55. Quoted in Mary Spargo, "Southerners Threaten Bolt on Race Issues," *Washington Post* (February 4, 1948).
56. Robert C. Albright, "South Urged to Run Own Candidate," *Washington Post* (February 10, 1948).
57. Robert C. Albright, "Anti-Lynching Bill Approved by House Unit," *Washington Post* (February 26, 1948).
58. Paul T. Murray, "Blacks and the Draft: A History of Institutional Racism," *Journal of Black Studies* (September 1971), pp. 57–76.
59. L. D. Reddick, "The Negro Policy of the United States Army, 1775–1945," *Journal of Negro History* (January 1949), pp. 9–29.
60. Berman, *Politics of Civil Rights*, pp. 108–12.
61. See Richard Hofstadter, "From Calhoun to the Dixiecrats," *Social Research* (June 1949), pp. 135–50; Sarah M. Lemmon, "The Ideology of the 'Dixiecrat' Movement," *Social Forces* (December 1951), pp. 162–71.
62. "Dixie Rebels Nominate Thurmond and Wright," *Washington Post* (July 18, 1948).
63. Harry S. Truman, *Memoirs* (Garden City, NY: Doubleday, 1956), vol. 2, p. 184.
64. Monroe Billington, "Freedom to Serve: The President's Committee on Equality of Treatment and Opportunity in the Armed Forces, 1949–1950," *Journal of Negro History* (October 1966), pp. 262–74.
65. Mary S. Spargo, "Truman Orders Equal Rights in U.S. Jobs, Armed Services," *Washington Post* (July 27, 1948).
66. Gardner, *Harry Truman*, p. 111.
67. Berman, *Politics of Civil Rights*, pp. 121–22. For analysis of the various unsuccessful efforts to abolish poll taxes in Congress, see Frederic D. Ogden, *The Poll Tax in the South* (Tuscaloosa: University of Alabama Press, 1958), pp. 243–49.
68. McCoy & Ruetten, *Quest and Response*, p. 136–38.
69. Garson, *Democratic Party*, pp. 309–10.
70. "The Negro Prefers Truman," *New Republic* (November 22, 1948), p. 8; Berman, *Politics of Civil Rights*, pp. 129–30; Henry Lee Moon, *Balance of Power: The Negro Vote* (Garden City, NY: Doubleday, 1949), pp. 197–214.
71. In these states, the Dixiecrats managed to displace the regular Democratic Party and were listed on the ballots as Democrats along with Truman. In Alabama, Truman wasn't even on the ballot. In states where the Dixiecrats had to run as a genuine third party, they did very poorly. Kari Frederickson, *The Dixiecrat Revolt and the End of the Solid South, 1932–1968* (Chapel Hill: University of North Carolina Press, 2001), p. 184.
72. Clark Clifford, *Counsel to the President* (New York: Random House, 1991), p. 204.
73. In a survey of political experts published less than a month before the election, it was unanimously predicted that Dewey would win easily. See "Election Forecast: 50 Political Experts Predict a GOP Sweep," *Newsweek* (October 11, 1948), p. 20.

74. J. R. Wiggins, "South's Rebellion Dwindles Against Truman, Civil Rights," *Washington Post* (July 14, 1948).

75. Quoted in Gardner, *Harry Truman*, p. 131.

76. On the effectiveness of the "Southern veto" during this period, see Ira Katznelson, Kim Geiger, and Daniel Kryder, "Limiting Liberalism: The Southern Veto in Congress, 1933–1950," *Political Science Quarterly* (Summer 1993), pp. 283–306.

77. Sarah A. Binder and Steven S. Smith, *Politics or Principle? Filibustering in the United States Senate* (Washington: Brookings Institution, 1997), pp. 173–75.

78. "CAA Bans Racial Segregation at National Airport Facilities," *Washington Post* (December 28, 1948); "Restaurant at Airport Wins Suit," *Washington Post* (December 13, 1949).

79. John D. Morris, "2 Agencies Bar Aid to Housing With Bias Pacts Filed After Feb. 15," *New York Times* (December 16, 1949).

80. Gardner, *Harry Truman*, pp. 163–97. See also Philip Elman, "The Solicitor General's Office, Justice Frankfurter, and Civil Rights Litigation, 1946–1960," *Harvard Law Review* (February 1987), pp. 817–52.

81. Kenneth O'Reilly, *Nixon's Piano: Presidents and Racial Politics from Washington to Clinton* (New York: Free Press, 1995), pp. 145–65; Joseph Pierro, "'Everything in My Power': Harry S. Truman and the Fight Against Racial Discrimination," Master's Thesis, Virginia Polytechnic Institute (May 2004), p. 122.

82. Barton J. Bernstein, "The Ambiguous Legacy: The Truman Administration and Civil Rights," in Barton J. Bernstein, ed., *Politics and Policies of the Truman Administration* (Chicago: Quadrangle Books, 1970), p. 299.

83. Berman, *Politics of Civil Rights*, p. 238.

84. Harvard Sitkoff, "Harry Truman and the Election of 1948: The Coming of Age of Civil Rights in American Politics," *Journal of Southern History* (November 1971), pp. 597–616.

85. Peter J. Kellogg, "Civil Rights Consciousness in the 1940s," *The Historian* (November 1979), pp. 18–41.

86. Philip H. Vaughan, "The Truman Administration's Fair Deal for Black America," *Missouri Historical Review* (April 1976), p. 305.

87. Michael J. Klarman, "*Brown*, Racial Change, and the Civil Rights Movement," *Virginia Law Review* (February 1994), pp. 7–150.

CHAPTER 9

1. Richard Cohen, "Was There *That* Much to Like About Ike?" *Washington Post* (November 6, 1990). For a highly critical review of civil rights policy during the Eisenhower years, see Robert F. Burk, *The Eisenhower Administration and Black Civil Rights* (Knoxville: University of Tennessee Press, 1984). For more positive views, see Kasey S. Pipes, *Ike's Final Battle: The Road to Little Rock and the Challenge of Equality* (Los Angeles: World Ahead Media, 2007); David A. Nichols, *A Matter of Justice: Eisenhower and the Beginning of the Civil Rights Revolution* (New York: Simon & Schuster, 2007).

2. State of the Union address (February 2, 1953).

3. "Great Mistake, Talmadge Says," *New York Times* (March 26, 1953).

4. Mark Stern, "Presidential Strategies and Civil Rights: Eisenhower, the Early Years, 1952–54," *Presidential Studies Quarterly* (Fall 1989), pp. 780–81.

5. Kenneth O'Reilly, *Nixon's Piano: Presidents and Racial Politics from Washington to Clinton* (New York: Free Press, 1995), pp. 167–68. During World War II, the FBI became convinced that virtually every black organization in the country had been infiltrated by Communists. See Robert A. Hill, *The FBI's RACON: Racial Conditions in the United States during World War II* (Boston: Northeastern University Press, 1995). Membership in any of these groups blocked many blacks from government appointments. Perhaps in a time less stressful than the immediate postwar era, when Communist subversion was a real threat, the FBI's red flags could have been overcome. But in the wake of the conviction of Julius

and Ethel Rosenberg for spying and of other verified Communist security threats, that just wasn't possible.

6. The White House put out the word that Warren would be appointed to the Court even before there was a vacancy. See Clayton Knowles, "Court Job Open to Warren," *New York Times* (September 4, 1953).

7. The commentary about Warren's selection often noted his liberal views on civil rights. See James Bassett, "'Unpartisan' Chief Justice of the U.S.," *New York Times* (October 11, 1953); Arthur Krock, "Warren Stand Awaited on Key Rights Issues," *New York Times* (October 4, 1953).

8. Michael A. Kahn, "Shattering the Myth About President Eisenhower's Supreme Court Appointments," *Presidential Studies Quarterly* (Winter 1992), p. 49.

9. After leaving office, Eisenhower was critical of Warren and Brennan. However, this was after the Court had adopted a much more liberal stance than Eisenhower would have liked on issues such as criminal rights. But there is no evidence during the time he was president that he didn't fully support the Court's rulings in the area of civil rights, and he often expressed pride in his appointment of Warren, both publicly and privately.

10. Warren was not confirmed by the Senate until March 1, 1954.

11. 275 U.S. 78 (1927).

12. Luther A. Huston, "Administration Urges High Court To Outlaw Segregation in Schools," *New York Times* (December 9, 1953).

13. Beverly Smith, "Earl Warren's Greatest Moment," *Saturday Evening Post* (July 24, 1954), pp. 17–19, 48, 53.

14. Lee Nichols, "Eisenhower Praised On Civil Right Gains," *Washington Post* (December 30, 1954).

15. Ernest B. Vaccaro, "Southern Democrats Assail Ike's Plan to Probe Civil Rights Abuse Charges," *Washington Post* (January 7, 1956).

16. *Congressional Record* (March 12, 1956), pp. 4459–61. This was part of a concerted public relations effort in early 1956 in support of a policy of "massive resistance" against public school desegregation throughout the South. See Numan V. Bartley, *The Rise of Massive Resistance: Race and Politics in the South During the 1950's* (Baton Rouge: Louisiana State University Press, 1969); Sam J. Ervin Jr., "The Case for Segregation," *Look Magazine* (April 3, 1956), pp. 32–33; Thomas R. Waring, "The Southern Case Against Desegregation," *Harper's Magazine* (January 1956), pp. 39–45. Interestingly, when Northern liberals proposed a counter-manifesto, Senator John F. Kennedy was among those who threw cold water on the idea. See Allen Drury, "Democrats Move to Prevent Split," *New York Times* (March 14, 1956).

17. Leo Egan, "Nixon Says G.O.P. Aids Civil Rights," *New York Times* (November 1, 1956).

18. "Powell Sees G.O.P. Winning Negroes," *New York Times* (October 19, 1956).

19. Drew Pearson, "Civil Rights Ike's No. 1 'Must,'" *Washington Post* (February 3, 1957).

20. The House Rules Committee under Smith's chairmanship was notorious as a burial ground for civil rights bills. See Bruce J. Dierenfield, "The Speaker and the Rules Keeper: Sam Rayburn, Howard Smith, and the Liberal Democratic Temper," in Winfred B. Moore Jr., Joseph F. Tripp, and Lyon G. Tyler Jr., eds., *Developing Dixie: Modernization in a Traditional Society* (New York: Greenwood Press, 1988), pp. 199–213.

21. James A. Robinson, "The Role of the Rules Committee in Regulating Debate in the U.S. House of Representatives," *Midwest Journal of Political Science* (February 1961), pp. 59–69.

22. "House Closes Rights Hearing," *Washington Post* (May 18, 1957).

23. "Civil Fight on Civil Rights," *Time Magazine* (June 17, 1957).

24. Richard Lyons, "House Passes Civil Rights Measure," *Washington Post* (June 19, 1957).

25. Monroe Billington, "Lyndon B. Johnson and Blacks: The Early Years," *Journal of Negro History* (January 1977), pp. 26–42; Robert A. Caro, *The Years of Lyndon Johnson: Means of Ascent* (New York: Alfred A. Knopf, 1990), p. 125; Rowland Evans and Robert Novak, *Lyndon B. Johnson: The Exercise of Power* (New York: New American Library, 1966),

p. 121; Mark Stern, *Calculating Visions: Kennedy, Johnson, and Civil Rights* (New Brunswick: Rutgers University Press, 1992), pp. 120–24.

26. Quoted in Robert A. Caro, *The Years of Lyndon Johnson: Master of the Senate* (New York: Alfred A. Knopf, 2002), p. 887.

27. Robert Dallek, *Lone Star Rising: Lyndon Johnson and His Times, 1908–1960* (New York: Oxford University Press, 1991), pp. 517–18.

28. Senator Strom Thurmond, Democrat of South Carolina, apparently didn't get the message and launched a one-man filibuster on August 29, 1957. He holds the record for the longest individual filibuster in Senate history: 24 hours, 18 minutes.

29. *Congressional Record* (August 30, 1957), pp. 16659–62. See also "The Rearguard Commander," *Time Magazine* (August 12, 1957). When Russell lost the vote that put the civil rights bill directly on the Senate calendar, rather than having it sent to the Southern Democrat-dominated Judiciary Committee, where it would never would have been seen again, he knew that killing the bill was not an option and that weakening it was the only strategy remaining. See Howard E. Shuman, "Senate Rules and the Civil Rights Bill," *American Political Science Review* (December 1957), pp. 961–70.

30. Quoted in Doris Kearns Goodwin, *Lyndon Johnson and the American Dream* (New York: St. Martin's Press, 1991), p. 148.

31. Bernard Schwartz, *Statutory History of the United States: Civil Rights* (New York: Chelsea House, 1970), pt. II, p. 838.

32. Quoted in O'Reilly, *Nixon's Piano*, p. 179.

33. C. Vann Woodward, "The Great Civil Rights Debate," *Commentary* (October 1957), pp. 283–91. Recent analyses are more sympathetic to Eisenhower's accomplishments, given the political circumstances. See Donald W. Jackson and James W. Riddlesperger Jr., "The Eisenhower Administration and the 1957 Civil Rights Act," in Shirley Anne Warshaw, ed., *Reexamining the Eisenhower Presidency* (Westport, CT: Greenwood Press, 1993), pp. 85–101; James D. King and James W. Riddlesperger Jr., "Presidential Leadership of Congressional Civil Rights Voting: The Cases of Eisenhower and Johnson," *Policy Studies Journal* (Autumn 1993), pp. 544–55.

34. Quoted in Caro, *Master of the Senate*, p. 893.

35. Creation of a Civil Rights Division within the Justice Department was extremely important to the enforcement of the civil rights laws. For a review of its early activities, see Allan Lichtman, "The Federal Assault Against Voting Discrimination in the Deep South, 1957–1967," *Journal of Negro History* (October 1969), pp. 346–67.

36. "The Eighty-Fifth To Date," *New York Times* (September 1, 1957). Emphasis added.

37. Bartley, *Massive Resistance*, pp. 251–69; Burk, *Eisenhower Administration*, pp. 174–203.

38. "Eisenhower, Faubus and the Court," *New Republic* (September 30, 1957), p. 5.

39. It's also worth noting that the Posse Comitatus Act severely limits use of the federal military for domestic law enforcement purposes. See Matthew Hammond, "The Posse Comitatus Act: A Principle in Need of Renewal," *Washington University Law Quarterly* (Summer 1997), pp. 953–84.

40. Gilbert C. Fite, *Richard B. Russell, Jr.: Senator from Georgia* (Chapel Hill: University of North Carolina Press, 1991), p. 344.

41. Mark Stern, "Eisenhower and Kennedy: A Comparison of Confrontations at Little Rock and Ole Miss," *Policy Studies Journal* (September 1993), pp. 575–88.

42. "The Mouse Comes Forth," *New Republic* (April 25, 1960), pp. 3–4; George McMillan, "Congress' Labor a Mouse to the Negro," *Washington Post* (April 24, 1960).

43. Caro, *Master of the Senate*, pp. 1033–34.

44. This view is consistent with recent scholarship on the Eisenhower presidency, which finds that he was a stronger, more influential president than earlier scholars were able to recognize, owing to his penchant for working behind the scenes in ways that have only become known lately through archival research. See Fred I. Greenstein, "Eisenhower as an Activist President: A Look at New Evidence," *Political Science Quarterly* (Winter 1979–1980), pp. 575–99; Fred I. Greenstein, *The Hidden-Hand Presidency: Eisenhower as Leader* (New

York: Basic Books, 1982); Robert Griffith, "Dwight D. Eisenhower and the Corporate Commonwealth," *American Historical Review* (February 1982), pp. 87–122; Mary S. McAuliffe, "Eisenhower, the President," *Journal of American History* (December 1981), pp. 625–32; Gary W. Reichard, "Eisenhower as President: The Changing View," *South Atlantic Quarterly* (Summer 1978), pp. 265–81; Steven Wagner, *Eisenhower Republicanism: Pursuing the Middle Way* (Dekalb: Northern Illinois University Press, 2006).

45. The public schools were indeed closed in some localities rather than permit integration. Bartley, *Massive Resistance*, p. 275.

46. Michael S. Mayer, "With Much Deliberation and Some Speed: Eisenhower and the *Brown* Decision," *Journal of Southern History* (February 1986), pp. 43–76.

47. Nick Bryant, *The Bystander: John F. Kennedy and the Struggle for Black Equality* (New York: Basic Books, 2006), pp. 54–79; James Reston, "Odd Coalition Won Amendment to Bill," *New York Times* (August 3, 1957).

48. Guy Paul Land, "John F. Kennedy's Southern Strategy, 1956–1960," *North Carolina Historical Review* (January 1979), pp. 41–63; John N. Popham, "Democrats Look to Unity in the South," *New York Times* (August 19, 1956).

49. John F. Kennedy, *Profiles in Courage* (New York: HarperCollins, 2003), p. 140. Even extreme Southern partisans now recognize that this view of Reconstruction is a gross exaggeration. See Ludwell H. Johnson, *Division and Reunion: America, 1848–1877* (New York: John Wiley, 1978), pp. 246–48.

50. Bryant, *Bystander*, pp. 103–5.

51. "Washington Wire," *New Republic* (July 15, 1957).

52. Anti-Catholic bias in the South, which doomed Al Smith in 1928, was also a factor.

53. Bryant, *Bystander*, p. 128.

54. Taylor Branch, *Parting the Waters: America in the King Years, 1954–63* (New York: Simon & Schuster, 1988), pp. 306–7.

55. W. H. Lawrence, "Kennedy Appeals to South to Support His Nomination," *New York Times* (June 28, 1960); O'Reilly, *Nixon's Piano*, p. 198.

56. Bryant, *Bystander*, p. 137.

57. Mark Stern, "John F. Kennedy and Civil Rights: From Congress to the Presidency," *Presidential Studies Quarterly* (Fall 1989), p. 816.

58. Nixon himself insisted upon a stronger civil rights plank in the Republican platform even though he knew it would probably cost him more votes than it would win him. Journalist Theodore White believes it was a matter of conscience with him. Theodore H. White, *The Making of the President, 1960* (New York: Atheneum, 1961), pp. 203–4. See also, Richard M. Nixon, *Six Crises* (Garden City, NY: Doubleday, 1962), p. 325.

59. "The Civil Rights Planks," *New York Times* (July 28, 1960).

60. Full transcripts of the Kennedy-Nixon debates are available at www.debates.org.

61. Branch, *Parting the Waters*, p. 219.

62. Nixon, *Six Crises*, pp. 362–63. See also William Safire, "View From the Grandstand," *New York Times* (April 13, 1987).

63. Branch, *Parting the Waters*, pp. 375–76.

64. Kennedy's people cleverly spread the news of his efforts on behalf of Dr. King only through black newspapers and avoided the major media, thus keeping the news away from racist Southerners who would not have approved.

65. Richard M. Scammon, "How the Negroes Voted," *New Republic* (November 21, 1960), pp. 8–9. Another misstep was Nixon's repudiation of his running mate's promise to appoint a black to the cabinet. Edward C. Burks, "Negro in Cabinet Pledged by Lodge," *New York Times* (October 13, 1960).

66. Burk, *Eisenhower Administration*, p. 260.

67. Senate Commerce Committee, *The Speeches, Remarks, Press Conferences, and Statements of Senator John F. Kennedy, August 1 through November 7, 1960*, Senate Report 994, pt. 1, 87th Cong., 1st Sess. (Washington: U.S. Government Printing Office, 1961), pp. 70, 432, 1011.

68. Senate Commerce Committee, *Kennedy Statements*, p. 576.

69. Kennedy did issue an executive order on March 6, 1961, establishing the President's Commission on Equal Employment Opportunity, reluctantly chaired by Vice President Johnson, to monitor federal contracts. But this was just an extension of the same organization established by Eisenhower and chaired by Nixon that Kennedy had attacked during the campaign for being ineffective. Kennedy's version proved to be equally ineffective. See Bryant, *Bystander*, pp. 228–31; Robert Dallek, *Lyndon B. Johnson: Portrait of a President* (New York: Oxford University Press, 2004), p. 134.

70. Wofford would have preferred to be assistant attorney general for civil rights, but Bobby Kennedy considered him to be a "slight madman." Wofford left the White House after just a year, frustrated at its inaction on civil rights. The vacancy was not filled. See Edwin O. Guthman and Jeffrey Shulman, *Robert Kennedy in His Own Words* (New York: Bantam Books, 1988), pp. 57, 78; Arthur M. Schlesinger Jr., *Robert Kennedy and His Times* (Boston: Houghton Mifflin, 1978), p. 288; Harris Wofford, *Of Kennedys and Kings* (New York: Farrar, Straus & Giroux, 1980), pp. 132–67.

71. "Commitment in New Orleans," *New York Times* (February 9, 1961).

72. O'Reilly, *Nixon's Piano*, p. 190.

73. "Darkened Victory," *Time Magazine* (February 10, 1961).

74. Tom Wicker, *One of Us: Richard Nixon and the American Dream* (New York: Random House, 1991), pp. 185–87.

75. Bryant, *Bystander*, pp. 203–5.

76. "White House Doubts Need of New Rights Laws Now," *New York Times* (May 10, 1961); Arthur M. Schlesinger Jr., *A Thousand Days: John F. Kennedy in the White House* (Boston: Houghton Mifflin, 1965), pp. 930–1.

77. Quoted in O'Reilly, *Nixon's Piano*, p. 200.

78. O'Reilly, *Nixon's Piano*, pp. 207–8.

79. James N. Giglio, *The Presidency of John F. Kennedy* (Lawrence: University Press of Kansas, 1991), p. 43; Schlesinger, *Robert Kennedy*, pp. 307–9; Gerald M. Stern, "Judge William Harold Cox and the Right to Vote in Clarke County, Mississippi," in Leon Friedman, ed., *Southern Justice* (New York: Pantheon Books, 1965), pp. 165–86.

80. Richard E. Mooney, "Officials Hopeful on Housing Order; South Is Critical," *New York Times* (November 22, 1962).

81. Howard Zinn, "Kennedy: The Reluctant Emancipator," *The Nation* (December 1, 1962), p. 373.

82. Schlesinger, *Robert Kennedy*, pp. 313–14.

83. Dean Kotlowski, "With All Deliberate Delay: Kennedy, Johnson, and School Desegregation," *Journal of Policy History* (April 2005), p. 160.

84. O'Reilly, *Nixon's Piano*, pp. 208–9.

85. Martin Luther King Jr., "Bold Design for a New South," *The Nation* (March 30, 1963), pp. 259–62.

86. In his famous "Letter from Birmingham Jail" (April 16, 1963), Dr. King explained the value of "direct action" and "creative tension"—euphemisms for baiting people like Connor into overreacting in order to create sympathy for the civil rights movement. On Connor's election as National Democratic Committeeman for Alabama, see William A. Nunnelley, *Bull Connor* (Tuscaloosa: University of Alabama Press, 1991), p. 170.

87. Anthony Lewis, "Since the Supreme Court Spoke," *New York Times Magazine* (May 10, 1964), p. 91.

88. He was also motivated by a belief that his unpopularity in the South was so great that he had little chance of winning there and needed to increase his percentage of the black vote in the North to win in 1964. See Edward T. Folliard, "Kennedy Can't Count on Any State in the South Now, Talmadge Says," *Washington Post* (June 16, 1963); Rowland Evans and Robert Novak, "Never, Never a Kennedy," *Washington Post* (July 31, 1963); Joseph A. Loftus, "Kennedy and the South," *New York Times* (August 25, 1963).

89. Data available at www.presidency.ucsb.edu/data/popularity.php.

90. James E. Clayton, "Rights Law Is Caught in Crossfire," *Washington Post* (July 23, 1963). Of course, the Justice Department took the course that it did because the Civil Rights Act of 1875, which the Civil Rights Act of 1963 essentially replicated, had been based on the Fourteenth Amendment and was struck down by the Supreme Court in 1883. However, in light of the *Brown* decision, it seems unlikely that the Court would have responded the same way a second time.

91. Alexander M. Bickel, "Civil Rights Act of 1963," *New Republic* (July 6, 1963), pp. 9–12.

92. Branch, *Parting the Waters*, p. 874.

93. David J. Garrow, *Bearing the Cross: Martin Luther King, Jr., and the Southern Christian Leadership Conference* (New York: William Morrow, 1986), p. 283.

94. Kenneth O'Reilly, *"Racial Matters": The FBI's Secret File on Black America, 1960–72* (New York: Free Press, 1989), p. 67.

95. O'Reilly, *Racial Matters*, p. 136.

96. O'Reilly, *Nixon's Piano*, p. 232; Schlesinger, *Robert Kennedy*, p. 360. The Kennedys used the FBI to gather political intelligence on other occasions as well. See Athan Theoharis, *The FBI & American Democracy* (Lawrence: University Press of Kansas, 2004), pp. 124–25. They were also known to use the Internal Revenue Service for political purposes. See John A. Andrew III, *Power to Destroy: The Political Uses of the IRS from Kennedy to Nixon* (Chicago: Ivan R. Dee, 2002), pp. 11–24; David Burnham, *A Law Unto Itself: Power, Politics and the IRS* (New York: Random House, 1989), pp. 77, 244–45, 270–73.

97. Thomas Borstelmann, "'Hedging Our Bets and Buying Time': John Kennedy and Racial Revolutions in the American South and Southern Africa," *Diplomatic History* (Summer 2000), p. 444.

98. "Not Enough," *New Republic* (October 12, 1963), pp. 3–4.

99. Garry Wills, *The Kennedy Imprisonment* (Boston: Little, Brown, 1981), p. 209.

100. Bryant, *Bystander*, p. 467; Bruce Miroff, *Pragmatic Illusions: The Presidential Politics of John F. Kennedy* (New York: David McKay, 1976), p. 225.

101. Clifford M. Lytle, "The History of the Civil Rights Act of 1964," *Journal of Negro History* (October 1966), pp. 275–96.

102. Congressman John Lewis of Georgia, who was active in the civil rights movement, recently commented on the positive impact of violent attacks on civil rights demonstrators by Dallas County, Alabama, Sheriff James Clark in 1965. Said Lewis, "I think we have to give a lot of credit to Clark and other people who beat us because Americans were able to see the contrast. They saw unbelievable, brave, courageous people believing in a dream and participating in nonviolence being brutalized. And it was the contrast that I think did change America and hasten the day of the Voting Rights Act in 1965." "'A Gun on One Hip, A Nightstick on the Other,'" *Newsweek* (June 19, 2007), p. 48.

103. Byrd's filibuster took place on June 9–10, 1964, and lasted fourteen hours, thirteen minutes. As is well known, Byrd was such a racist that he even joined the Ku Klux Klan in his youth. In his memoirs, he expresses remorse about this, but understates his involvement. See Robert C. Byrd, *Child of the Appalachian Coalfields* (Morgantown: West Virginia University Press, 2005), pp. 51–55; Eric Pianin, "A Senator's Shame," *Washington Post* (June 19, 2005); Robert Sherrill, "The Embodiment of Poor White Power," *New York Times Magazine* (February 28, 1971), pp. 50–51.

104. "Now the Talking Begins," *Time Magazine* (February 21, 1964).

105. Murray Kempton, "Dirksen Delivers the Souls," *New Republic* (May 2, 1964), pp. 9–11; E. W. Kenworthy, "Dirksen Shaped Victory for Civil Rights Forces in Fight to Bring Measure to Vote," *New York Times* (June 20, 1964).

106. "The Dirksen Anticlimax," *New York Times* (July 2, 1964).

107. Quoted in Taylor Branch, *Pillar of Fire: America in the King Years, 1963–64* (New York: Simon & Schuster, 1998), p. 94.

108. Johnson lost Louisiana, Mississippi, Alabama, Georgia, and South Carolina. Goldwater voted against the Civil Rights Act of 1964 because he believed it was unconstitutional. He had been told so by William Rehnquist, then a prominent Phoenix attorney and later Chief Justice of the Supreme Court, and Professor Robert Bork of Yale University Law School. See Rick Perlstein, *Before the Storm: Barry Goldwater and the Unmaking of the American Consensus* (New York: Hill and Wang, 2001), pp. 363–64. See also Robert Bork, "Civil Rights—A Challenge," *New Republic* (August 31, 1963), pp. 21–24.
109. Pearl T. Robinson, "Whither the Future of Blacks in the Republican Party?" *Political Science Quarterly* (Summer 1982), p. 212.
110. Paul Burstein, "Public Opinion, Demonstrations, and the Passage of Antidiscrimination Legislation," *Public Opinion Quarterly* (Summer 1979), pp. 157–72; Gerald Pomper, "From Confusion to Clarity: Issues and American Voters, 1956–1968," *American Political Science Review* (June 1972), pp. 415–28.

CHAPTER 10

1. Theodore H. White, *The Making of the President, 1968* (New York: Atheneum, 1969), p. 237.
2. On the advocacy of violence to achieve civil rights goals in the 1960s, see Lance Hill, *The Deacons for Defense: Armed Resistance and the Civil Rights Movement* (Chapel Hill: University of North Carolina Press, 2004); Robert F. Williams, *Negroes With Guns* (New York: Marzani & Munsell, 1962). Of course, this was not a new thing in the black community. More than one hundred years ago, black journalist Thomas Fortune made this colorful comment: "We have cringed and crawled long enough. I don't want any more 'good niggers.' I want 'bad niggers.' It's the 'bad nigger' with a Winchester [rifle] who can defend his home and children and wife." Quoted in the *Washington Post* (August 7, 1901). Indeed, many gun control laws were enacted mainly to restrict blacks' access to firearms. See Clayton E. Cramer, "The Racist Roots of Gun Control," *Kansas Journal of Law & Public Policy* (Winter 1995), pp. 17–25; William R. Tonso, "Gun Control: White Man's Law," *Reason* (December 1985), pp. 22–25.
3. Dan T. Carter, *The Politics of Rage: George Wallace, the Origins of the New Conservatism, and the Transformation of American Politics,* 2nd ed. (Baton Rouge: Louisiana State University Press, 2000), pp. 344–47.
4. An even more overt racist than Wallace, Maddox was elected governor of Georgia in 1966 after making a name for himself as a restaurant owner who refused to serve blacks. When the Civil Rights Act of 1964 forced him to integrate his establishment, he sold it rather than comply with the law. See Marshall Frady, "'You Reckon They Thought I Was a Nut?'" *Saturday Evening Post* (April 22, 1967), pp. 27–29, 80–88; Justin Nystrom, "Segregation's Last Stand: Lester Maddox and the Transformation of Atlanta," *Atlanta History* (Summer 2001), pp. 35–51; Bradley Rice, "Lester Maddox and the Politics of Populism," in Harold P. Henderson and Gary L. Roberts, eds., *Georgia Governors in an Age of Change* (Athens: University of Georgia Press, 1988), pp. 193–210; Bob Short, *Everything Is Pickrick: The Life of Lester Maddox* (Macon, GA: Mercer University Press, 1999).
5. Steven J. Rosenstone, Roy L. Behr, and Edward H. Lazarus, *Third Parties in America*, 2nd ed. (Princeton: Princeton University Press, 1996), pp. 110–11. Maddox was the 1976 nominee of the party Wallace founded, which was known as the American Independent Party.
6. Richard Nixon, *RN: The Memoirs of Richard Nixon* (New York: Grosset & Dunlap, 1978), p. 316.
7. White, *Making of the President*, p. 424. Wallace carried Alabama, Arkansas, Georgia, Louisiana, and Mississippi.
8. Quoted in "Nixon Sped Integration—Wallace," *Washington Post* (September 15, 1968). See also Roy Reed, "Politics—Wallace Accuses Nixon of Courting South While Supporting Civil Rights," *New York Times* (September 12, 1968).

9. Michael K. Fauntroy, *Republicans and the Black Vote* (Boulder, CO: Lynne Rienner, 2007), pp. 127–61; Richard Kluger, *Simple Justice* (New York: Alfred A. Knopf, 1975), p. 761; Reg Murphy and Hal Gulliver, *The Southern Strategy* (New York: Scribner's, 1971); Kenneth O'Reilly, *Nixon's Piano: Presidents and Racial Politics from Washington to Clinton* (New York: Free Press, 1995), pp. 280–86; Jill Quadagno, *The Color of Welfare: How Racism Undermined the War on Poverty* (New York: Oxford University Press, 1994), p. 127; Thomas F. Schaller, *Whistling Past Dixie* (New York: Simon & Schuster, 2006), pp. 40–1.

10. Kevin P. Phillips, *The Emerging Republican Majority* (New Rochelle, NY: Arlington House, 1969), p. 34.

11. Glen Moore, "Richard Nixon: The Southern Strategy and the 1968 Presidential Election," in Leon Friedman and William F. Levantrosser, eds., *Richard M. Nixon: Politician, President, Administrator* (New York: Greenwood Press, 1991), p. 289.

12. David Broder, "GOP Pushes Drive for Minority Votes," *Washington Post* (February 25, 1968); Hugh Davis Graham, *The Civil Rights Era* (New York: Oxford University Press, 1990), pp. 303–4; Dean J. Kotlowski, "Nixon's Southern Strategy Revisited," *Journal of Policy History* (No. 2, 1998), pp. 208–9.

13. Graham, *Civil Rights Era*, pp. 302–3; Nixon, *Memoirs*, p. 268.

14. Quoted in Tom Wicker, *One of Us: Richard Nixon and the American Dream* (New York: Random House, 1991), p. 281. Columnist Pat Buchanan, who worked for Nixon in the 1960s, ghosted this article. He discusses it and Nixon's opposition to Wallace's racism in Patrick J. Buchanan, "Neocons Distort Nixon's '68 Southern Strategy," *Human Events* (January 13, 2003). See also Patrick J. Buchanan, *Conservative Votes, Liberal Victories* (New York: Quadrangle, 1975), pp. 49–71.

15. Robert B. Semple Jr., "Nixon Gives Views on Aid to Negroes and the Poor," *New York Times* (December 20, 1967).

16. See Alan Dessoff, "Transit Pact, Limited Fair Housing Urged by Spiro Agnew in Suburbs," *Washington Post* (July 12, 1966); Alan Dessoff, "Party Backs Mahoney on Occupancy," *Washington Post* (October 14, 1966).

17. "The Candidate from Maryland," *New York Times* (August 9, 1968).

18. Wicker, *One of Us*, p. 282.

19. The classic discussion of the importance of race in Southern politics is V. O. Key Jr., *Southern Politics* (New York: Alfred A. Knopf, 1949). It was Key's view, which strongly influenced a generation of political scientists, that the race issue dominated all others in Southern politics. Studies in the same vein include Earl Black and Merle Black, *The Rise of Southern Republicans* (Cambridge: Harvard University Press, 2002); Jonathan Knuckey, "Racial Resentment and the Changing Partisanship of Southern Whites," *Party Politics* (January 2005), pp. 5–28; Richard K. Scher, *Politics in the New South: Republicanism, Race and Leadership in the Twentieth Century*, 2nd ed. (Armonk, NY: M. E. Sharpe, 1997). Key's view may have been true when he wrote his book, but subsequently the character of the historically insular South changed dramatically as Northerners migrated in when air conditioning became available, blacks migrated out seeking better opportunities, and mass communications integrated the South into the national culture, ending its isolation and undermining its particularism.

20. Gerard Alexander, "The Myth of the Racist Republicans," *Claremont Review of Books* (Spring 2004), p. 11.

21. On the South's anti-union policy and its impact on industrial location, see Timothy J. Bartik, "Business Location Decisions in the United States: Estimates of the Effects of Unionization, Taxes, and Other Characteristics of States," *Journal of Business & Economic Statistics* (January 1985), pp. 14–22; Jeffrey H. Burton, "Membership in Labor Organizations, 1953–1974: A Regional Perspective," in Senate Appropriations Committee, *Selected Essays on Patterns of Regional Change*, Committee Print, 95th Cong., 1st Sess. (Washington: U.S. Government Printing Office, 1977), pp. 178–91; F. Ray Marshall, *Labor in the South* (Cambridge: Harvard University Press, 1967). On the role of federal fiscal

policy in narrowing regional income differences, see *Flows of Federal Funds, 1952–76* (Washington: Advisory Commission on Intergovernmental Relations, 1980); Bernard L. Weinstein and Robert E. Firestine, *Regional Growth and Decline in the United States* (New York: Praeger, 1978), pp. 30–42.

22. See data in Appendix III.
23. Clay Risen, "How the South Was Won," *Boston Globe* (March 5, 2006); W. J. Rorabaugh, "Critical Perspectives: Did Prosperity Contribute to the South's Abandonment of the Democratic Party?" *Journal of Policy History* (No. 4, 2005), pp. 425–32; Byron E. Shafer and Richard Johnston, *The End of Southern Exceptionalism: Class, Race, and Partisan Change in the Postwar South* (Cambridge: Harvard University Press, 2006).
24. Quoted in Joan Hoff, *Nixon Reconsidered* (New York: Basic Books, 1994), p. 79. Emphasis in original.
25. David Lublin, *The Republican South: Democratization and Partisan Change* (Princeton: Princeton University Press, 2004), p. 25.
26. Richard Seltzer and Robert C. Smith, "Race and Ideology: A Research Note Measuring Liberalism and Conservatism in Black America," *Phylon* (No. 2, 1985), pp. 98–105.
27. Nichol C. Rae, "The Democrats' 'Southern Problem' in Presidential Politics," *Presidential Studies Quarterly* (Winter 1992), pp. 135–51.
28. Among the actions taken by liberal Democrats after the 1974 election to diminish Southern influence was the removal of four Southerners from committee chairmanships that they held by virtue of seniority: W. R. Poage of Texas, House Agriculture Committee; F. Edward Hébert of Louisiana, House Armed Services Committee; Wright Patman of Texas, House Banking Committee; and Wilbur Mills of Arkansas, House Ways and Means Committee. On these and other measures that increased the power of Northern liberals and reduced that of Southern Democrats in Congress, see "Democrats Oust Hébert, Poage; Adopt Reforms," *Congressional Quarterly* (January 18, 1975), pp. 111–19; "New Congress Organizes; No Role for Mills," *Congressional Quarterly* (December 7, 1974), pp. 3247–53; Rowland Evans and Robert Novak, "Power Shift in the House," *Washington Post* (December 7, 1974); Nelson W. Polsby, *How Congress Evolves* (New York: Oxford University Press, 2004), pp. 65–73; Spencer Rich, "Liberal Bloc Seeks More Senate Power," *Washington Post* (December 7, 1974); Mary Russell, "Democrats End Hill Era," *Washington Post* (December 8, 1974); Julian E. Zelizer, *On Capitol Hill: The Struggle to Reform Congress and Its Consequences, 1948–2000* (New York: Cambridge University Press, 2004), pp. 156–76.
29. Rowland Evans and Robert Novak, "New Cabinet Choices Seen Revealing How Far Nixon Moves Toward Left," *Washington Post* (November 8, 1968). This was no surprise to those who knew Nixon personally. See William Safire, *Before the Fall: An Inside View of the Pre-Watergate White House* (Garden City, NY: Doubleday, 1975), p. 548; Richard J. Whalen, *Catch the Falling Flag: A Republican's Challenge to His Party* (Boston: Houghton Mifflin, 1972), pp. 37–44; John C. Whitaker, "Nixon's Domestic Policy: Both Liberal and Bold in Retrospect," *Presidential Studies Quarterly* (Winter 1996), pp. 131–53. In recent years, historians have come to accept that on domestic policy, Nixon was operationally liberal. See Michael Barone, *Our Country: The Shaping of America From Roosevelt to Reagan* (New York: Free Press, 1990), pp. 487–89; David Greenberg, *Nixon's Shadow: The History of an Image* (New York: W.W. Norton, 2003), pp. 304–37; Hoff, *Nixon Reconsidered*, pp. 17–49; Herbert S. Parmet, *Richard Nixon and His America* (Boston: Little, Brown, 1990), pp. 530–1; Melvin Small, *The Presidency of Richard Nixon* (Lawrence: University Press of Kansas, 1999), pp. 213–14; Irwin Unger, *The Best of Intentions* (New York: Doubleday, 1996), pp. 300–47.
30. Carroll Kilpatrick, "Moynihan Named Urban Affairs Chief," *Washington Post* (December 11, 1968). On Moynihan's role in the Nixon White House, see Tevi Troy, *Intellectuals and the American Presidency* (New York: Rowman & Littlefield, 2002), pp. 75–112.
31. Norman Kempster, "Finch Promises Racial 'Candor,'" *Washington Post* (December 25, 1968).

32. "Finch Appoints Chief of Civil Rights Office," *Washington Post* (March 30, 1969). When Panetta left the Nixon Administration in 1970, he blasted it for dragging its feet on civil rights. However, Indiana University historian Joan Hoff suggests that Panetta was a bit of a grandstander who went out of his way to promote himself as the lone defender of civil rights in the Nixon Administration in order to advance his personal political fortunes. See Hoff, *Nixon Reconsidered*, pp. 85–88. After leaving HEW, Panetta switched parties and went on to become a Democratic member of Congress from California, serving from 1977 until 1993, when he resigned to became director of the Office of Management and Budget and later White House chief of staff under President Bill Clinton.

33. Quoted in Richard Lyons, "Nixon's Peace Theme Is Well Received," *Washington Post* (January 21, 1969).

34. Peter Milius, "Finch Halts 5 Areas' School Aid But Reopens Desegregation Talks," *Washington Post* (January 30, 1969).

35. Eve Edstrom, "More Schools Face Cutoff of Funds," *Washington Post* (February 13, 1969).

36. Rowland Evans and Robert Novak, "South's GOP Doubts Nixon Could Carry a State," *Washington Post* (February 20, 1969).

37. "U.S. Files 3 Louisiana School Suits," *Washington Post* (February 11, 1969).

38. Peter Milius, "Schools in South Lose Aid," *Washington Post* (July 8, 1969).

39. David S. Broder, "U.S. Files Suit to Desegregate Georgia Schools," *Washington Post* (August 2, 1969).

40. 396 U.S. 1218 (1969).

41. J. D. Alexander, "Mitchell to Press Integration," *Washington Post* (November 11, 1969).

42. Quoted in Dean J. Kotlowski, *Nixon's Civil Rights* (Cambridge: Harvard University Press, 2001), p. 32.

43. Alexander M. Bickel, "'Realistic, Sensible,'" *New Republic* (April 4 & 11, 1970), pp. 14–15.

44. Lawrence J. McAndrews, "The Politics of Principle: Richard Nixon and School Desegregation," *Journal of Negro History* (Summer 1998), pp. 187–200. It's worth remembering that for all of his legislative activity on civil rights, Lyndon Johnson did very little to integrate the schools. By the end of his administration, they were almost as segregated in many Southern states as they had been at the time of *Brown v. Board of Education* in 1954. See Harrell R. Rodgers Jr. and Charles S. Bullock Jr., "School Desegregation: A Policy Analysis," *Journal of Black Studies* (June 1972), pp. 409–21.

45. George P. Shultz, "How a Republican Desegregated the South's Schools," *New York Times* (January 8, 2003).

46. On July 10, 1970, the Internal Revenue Service announced that it was withdrawing the tax-exemption for all-white private schools, which had grown rapidly in the South as desegregation advanced, thereby frustrating efforts to integrate the public schools by reducing the supply of white students. See Peter Milius, "U.S. to Tax Segregated Academies," *Washington Post* (July 11, 1970). On July 16, 1970, Attorney General Mitchell announced that a task force of lawyers was being sent to the South to ensure compliance with desegregation. See Ken W. Clawson, "U.S. Will Send 100 to South To Enforce Desegregation," *Washington Post* (July 17, 1970). Southerners protested both actions vigorously and White House officials tried to assuage them. But at the end of the day, the IRS ruling stood and Justice went ahead with its task force. See Rowland Evans and Robert D. Novak, *Nixon in the White House* (New York: Random House, 1971), p. 174. The point is that historians will often cite internal White House comments or memoranda showing the efforts of Nixon and his staff to calm the ruffled feathers of Southerners on issues such as these and pronounce it proof of the wicked Southern strategy. But then they will ignore the actual policies, which seldom accommodated Southern concerns. In short, the historians implicitly assume that the rhetoric equals the substance. By design, however, the rhetoric was conservative, but the substance was liberal in the Nixon White House. As Attorney General Mitchell told a group of black protesters early in the Nixon Administration: "You'd be better informed if instead of listening to what we say, you watch what we do." Quoted in "'Watch What We Do,'" *Washington Post* (July 7, 1969).

See also Leonard Garment, *Crazy Rhythm: My Journey from Brooklyn, Jazz, and Wall Street to Nixon's White House, Watergate, and Beyond* (New York: Times Books, 1997), p. 220; Kotlowski, *Nixon's Civil Rights*, pp. 20–1.

47. Robert B. Semple Jr., "Schools in South Integrating Fast," *New York Times* (June 6, 1971).

48. Wicker, *One of Us*, pp. 486–87.

49. Frederick Douglass, "The Folly, Tyranny, and Wickedness of Labor Unions," *New National Era* (May 7, 1874), reprinted in Philip S. Foner and Ronald L. Lewis, eds., *The Black Worker: A Documentary History from Colonial Times to the Present*, vol. II (Philadelphia: Temple University Press, 1978), pp. 178–79.

50. W. E. B. DuBois, *The Negro Artisan: A Social Study* (Atlanta: Atlanta University Press, 1902), pp. 153–81; Abram L. Harris, "The Negro Worker: A Problem of Progressive Labor Action," *The Crisis* (March 1930), reprinted in William Darity Jr., ed., *Race, Radicalism, and Reform: Selected Papers of Abram L. Harris* (New Brunswick, NJ: Transaction Publishers, 1989), pp. 193–99; Rayford Logan, *The Negro in American Life and Thought* (New York: Dial Press, 1954), pp. 140–56; Booker T. Washington, "The Negro and the Labor Unions," *Atlantic Monthly* (June 1913), reprinted in Louis R. Harlan and Raymond W. Smock, eds., *The Booker T. Washington Papers*, vol. 12 (Urbana: University of Illinois Press, 1982), pp. 206–23.

51. *American Federationist* (September 1905), reprinted in Philip S. Foner and Ronald L. Lewis, eds., *The Black Worker: A Documentary History from Colonial Times to the Present*, vol. V (Philadelphia: Temple University Press, 1980), p. 124. On the racism of the craft unions, see Herman D. Bloch, "Craft Unions and the Negro in Historical Perspective," *Journal of Negro History* (January 1958), pp. 1–33; Herbert R. Northrup, *Organized Labor and the Negro* (New York: Harper & Brothers, 1944).

52. Herbert R. Northrup, "Organized Labor and Negro Workers," *Journal of Political Economy* (June 1943), pp. 206–21; James S. Olson, "Organized Black Leadership and Industrial Unionism: The Racial Response, 1936–1945," *Labor History* (Summer 1969), pp. 475–86; Robert C. Weaver, "Negro Labor Since 1929," *Journal of Negro History* (January 1950), pp. 23–24; Robert C. Weaver, "Recent Events in Negro Union Relationships," *Journal of Political Economy* (September 1944), pp. 238–41. This is not to say that the CIO was free of racism, only that it was much better than the AFL. See Sumner M. Rosen, "The CIO Era, 1935–55," in Julius Jacobson, ed., *The Negro and the American Labor Movement* (New York: Anchor Books, 1968), pp. 188–208.

53. Orley Ashenfelter, "Race Discrimination and Trade Unionism," *Journal of Political Economy* (May-June 1972), pp. 435–64; Herbert Hill, "Labor Unions and the Negro," *Commentary* (December 1959), pp. 479–88; Herbert Hill, "Racism Within Organized Labor: A Report of Five Years of the AFL-CIO, 1955–1960," *Journal of Negro Education* (Spring 1961), pp. 109–18; Paul D. Moreno, *Black Americans and Organized Labor* (Baton Rouge: Louisiana State University Press, 2006), pp. 236–45. Note: The AFL and CIO merged in 1955.

54. Nixon, *Memoirs*, p. 437.

55. As AFL-CIO President George Meany once remarked, "When I was a plumber, it never occurred to me to have niggers in the union." Quoted in Dean J. Kotlowski, "Richard Nixon and the Origins of Affirmative Action," *The Historian* (Spring 1998), p. 524.

56. John P. Gould and George Bittlingmayer, *The Economics of the Davis-Bacon Act* (Washington: American Enterprise Institute, 1980); Daniel P. Kessler and Lawrence F. Katz, "Prevailing Wage Laws and Construction Labor Markets," *Industrial and Labor Relations Review* (January 2001), pp. 259–74.

57. J. Larry Hood, "The Nixon Administration and the Revised Philadelphia Plan for Affirmative Action: A Study in Expanding Presidential Power and Divided Government," *Presidential Studies Quarterly* (Winter 1993), pp. 145–67.

58. Graham, *Civil Rights Era*, p. 325.

59. Between 1969 and 1972, the staff of the EEOC increased from 359 to 1,640, and its budget more than doubled from $13.2 million to $29.5 million. Hoff, *Nixon Reconsidered*, p. 93.

60. Dean Kotlowski, "Black Power—Nixon Style: The Nixon Administration and Minority Business Enterprise," *Business History Review* (Autumn 1998), pp. 409–45; Parmet, *Richard Nixon*, pp. 597–99.

61. Steven A. Shull, *American Civil Right Policy from Truman to Clinton* (Armonk, NY: M. E. Sharpe, 1999), p. 106. See also *Budget of the United States Government, Fiscal Year 1975: Special Analyses* (Washington: U.S. Government Printing Office, 1974), pp. 171–88.

62. Greenberg, *Nixon's Shadow*, p. 306.

63. Small, *Presidency of Richard Nixon*, p. 176.

64. Hoff, *Nixon Reconsidered*, p. 113.

65. Panetta told me this in conversation at a dinner we both attended on March 13, 2007.

66. William Safire, "Black Republicans," *New York Times* (February 21, 1977). On the improving economic condition of African Americans, see Richard Freeman, "Changes in the Labor Market for Black Americans," *Brookings Papers on Economic Activity* (No. 1, 1973), pp. 67–120.

67. Morton Kondracke, "The G.O.P. Gets Its Act Together," *New York Times Magazine* (July 13, 1980), pp. 18–24, 42–47; James M. Perry, "The GOP and Black Voters," *Wall Street Journal* (December 7, 1977); Pearl T. Robinson, "Whither the Future of Blacks in the Republican Party?" *Political Science Quarterly* (Summer 1982), pp. 207–31.

68. "Energy, Jobs and Black America," *Wall Street Journal* (January 12, 1978); "The NAACP Turns a Corner," *Wall Street Journal* (January 12, 1978); John E. Cooney, "The NAACP: In Welcome Turmoil," *Wall Street Journal* (April 10, 1978); Richard Corrigan, "Energy and the NAACP," *National Journal* (March 18, 1978), p. 438; Paul Delaney, "N.A.A.C.P. in Major Dispute on Energy View," *New York Times* (January 30, 1978); Austin Scott, "NAACP Hits Carter Energy Plan," *Washington Post* (January 12, 1978); Jude Wanniski, "The NAACP—Free at Last," *Wall Street Journal* (February 7, 1978); Roger Wilkins, "Blacks Worry About Position of N.A.A.C.P.," *New York Times* (February 10, 1978); Lena Williams, "N.A.A.C.P. Energy Statement, Seen as Pro-Industry, Causes Dispute," *New York Times* (January 14, 1978).

69. Peter Elkind, "League Study Questions '60s Programs," *Washington Post* (August 9, 1980).

70. Thomas Goldwasser, "Liberal's Liberal Mitchell Is Fiscal Conservative," *Washington Post* (September 15, 1980).

71. On conservatism in black history, see Gayle T. Tate and Lewis A. Randolph, eds., *Dimensions of Black Conservatism in the United States* (New York: Palgrave, 2002).

72. James Alexander, "Economist Williams: New Gospel for Blacks," *Washington Post* (July 27, 1981); Colin Campbell, "Conservative Economist Rides With Reagan Tide," *New York Times* (September 18, 1981); Gordon Crovitz, "A Challenge to Liberalism," *Wall Street Journal* (September 16, 1980); Robert Denton, "Black's Bootstrap Philosophy Attracts Reaganites, Repels Liberals," *Washington Post* (December 6, 1980); John Merwin, "The Right Attitude," *Forbes Magazine* (September 14, 1981), p. 98; William Raspberry, "Leave Laissez Faire Alone," *Washington Post* (November 3, 1980); Sheila Rule, "Black Conservatives Seeking New Approach to Solving Inequities," *New York Times* (November 3, 1980); Thomas Sowell, "Affirmative Action Harms the Disadvantaged," *Wall Street Journal* (July 28, 1981); Thomas Sowell, "A Black 'Conservative' Dissents," *New York Times Magazine* (August 8, 1976), pp. 14–15, 43–46; Thomas Sowell, "Leaders—or, 'Leaders'?" *New York Times* (April 12, 1979); Thomas Sowell, "Ethnic Groups, Prejudice and Economic Progress," *Wall Street Journal* (December 4, 1980); Walter Williams, "Political 'Saviors' Don't Deliver What Blacks Need," *Wall Street Journal* (May 31, 1979); Walter Williams, *Youth and Minority Unemployment* (Washington: U.S. Government Printing Office, 1977).

73. Carl T. Rowan, "Quisling?" *Washington Post* (September 29, 1981). See also "The Backlash Against Sowell," *Business Week* (November 30, 1981), p. 119; Henry Allen, "The Hot Controversy and the Cool Sowell," *Washington Post* (October 1, 1981).

74. Carl T. Rowan, "The Administration's Racist Footprints," *Washington Post* (January 19, 1982).

75. "He Is Not a Bigot," *Washington Post* (July 2, 1982).

76. Lou Cannon, *President Reagan: The Role of a Lifetime* (New York: Simon & Schuster, 1991), pp. 519–25; John P. Diggins, *Ronald Reagan: Fate, Freedom, and the Making of History* (New York: W. W. Norton, 2007), pp. 311–14.

77. This was the view of the Chicago School of economics, which Reagan was very familiar with. It saw free markets, not government regulation, as the best means of helping racial minorities. See Gary S. Becker, *The Economics of Discrimination* (Chicago: University of Chicago Press, 1957); Harold Demsetz, "Minorities in the Market Place," *North Carolina Law Review* (February 1965), pp. 271–97; Milton Friedman, *Capitalism and Freedom* (Chicago: University of Chicago Press, 1962), pp. 108–18; Robert Higgs, *Competition and Coercion: Blacks in the American Economy, 1865–1914* (Chicago: University of Chicago Press, 1977); Alvin Rabushka, *A Theory of Racial Harmony* (Columbia: University of South Carolina Press, 1974); Thomas Sowell, *Race and Economics* (New York: David McKay, 1975).

78. "Reagan Is 'At the Bottom' of Justice Marshall's List," *Washington Post* (September 9, 1987); Ronald Reagan, *Ronald Reagan: An American Life* (New York: Simon & Schuster, 1990), pp. 401–2; Ronald Reagan, *The Reagan Diaries*, ed. Douglas Brinkley (New York: HarperCollins, 2007), pp. 528–29, 548.

79. Dan T. Carter, *From George Wallace to Newt Gingrich* (Baton Rouge: Louisiana State University Press, 1996), pp. 59–68.

80. O'Reilly, *Nixon's Piano*, pp. 360–61.

81. Nicholas Laham, *The Reagan Presidency and the Politics of Race: In Pursuit of Colorblind Justice and Limited Government* (Westport, CT: Praeger, 1998), p. 216.

82. Phil Gailey, "Approval Rating of Reagan by Blacks Has Risen Significantly, Polls Show," *New York Times* (October 15, 1985). On black economic gains the 1980s, see "The Black Middle Class," *Business Week* (March 14, 1988), pp. 62–70; Gary S. Becker, "The American Dream May Be Coming Closer for Blacks," *Business Week* (April 21, 1986), p. 11; Joel Garreau, "Black Elites Transcending Race Barriers: A New Middle Class Is Beginning to Live the American Dream," *Washington Post* (November 29, 1987); James P. Smith and Finis R. Welch, *Closing the Gap: Forty Years of Economic Progress for Blacks* (Santa Monica, CA: Rand, 1986); Lena Williams, "Data Show Blacks Slicing Income Gap," *New York Times* (February 25, 1986).

83. Bush's poor showing among black voters is often blamed on the so-called Willie Horton television ad that he supposedly ran during the 1988 campaign, which criticized Dukakis for setting free on furlough a black convict who used the opportunity to rape a Maryland woman. In fact, the Bush campaign never ran the ad or approved it; it was run by an independent advocacy group. Furthermore, the whole issue of Willie Horton was first raised by Al Gore, who was running against Dukakis for the Democratic presidential nomination in 1988. See Alexander Cockburn and Jeffrey St. Clair, *Al Gore: A User's Manual* (New York: Verso, 2000), pp. 131–34.

84. Louis Bolce, Gerald De Maio, and Douglas Muzzio, "Blacks and the Republican Party: The 20 Percent Solution," *Political Science Quarterly* (Spring 1992), pp. 63–79.

85. Tony Brown, "Becoming a Republican," *Wall Street Journal* (August 5, 1991).

86. Kwame Okampa-Ahoofe, " 'Contract With America' Is Genocide Against America's Poor Minorities," *Amsterdam News* (December 21, 1996), p. 22.

87. "Talk of the Town," *New Yorker* (October 5, 1998), p. 32.

88. Bob Herbert, "Impossible, Ridiculous, Repugnant," *New York Times* (October 6, 2005). Such hyperbole is not uncommon in Herbert's column. A few months earlier, he wrote: "The G.O.P.'s Southern strategy, racist at its core, still lives." Bob Herbert, "An Empty Apology," *New York Times* (July 18, 2005).

89. Cynthia Tucker, "GOP in No Rush to Shed 'Bigot' Label," *Atlanta Journal and Constitution* (April 16, 2003).

90. Cynthia Tucker, "Miller Knows Race-Baiting Lifted GOP," *Atlanta Journal and Constitution* (September 22, 2004).

91. Quoted in John Williams, "Democrats Fight Redistricting Plan with Race Rhetoric," *Houston Chronicle* (June 28, 2003).

92. Comment posted on February 6, 2006.

93. Gregory Kane, "Black Liberals Need to Respond to Insult of Rice by Baraka," *Baltimore Sun* (March 19, 2003).

94. Sam Fulwood III, "Blackwell Not a Friend to Blacks," *Cleveland Plain Dealer* (May 11, 2006).

95. Stephen Evans, "Belafonte's Fires Undimmed at 80," *BBC News* (March 9, 2007). In a 2002 radio interview, Belafonte said, "Colin Powell's committed to come into the house of the master. When Colin Powell dares to suggest something other than what the master wants to hear, he will be turned back out to pasture." Quoted in Todd Purdum, "Powell Finesses a Sour Note from Harry Belafonte, 'a Friend,'" *New York Times* (October 10, 2002).

96. Erin Aubry Kaplan, "Claude Allen's Life Sentence," *Los Angeles Times* (March 15, 2006).

97. Sadly, accusations of "acting white" are often hurled at black students who strive for excellence in school, severely discouraging them from educational achievement, with tragic results. See David Austen-Smith and Roland G. Fryer Jr., "An Economic Analysis of 'Acting White,'" *Quarterly Journal of Economics* (May 2005), pp. 551–83. See also Bob Herbert, "Breaking Away," *New York Times* (July 10, 2003); Jack White, "Are Blacks Biased Against Braininess?" *Time Magazine* (August 7, 2000), p. 81.

98. "Mr. Steele and Race," *Washington Post* (December 4, 2005).

99. Darryl Fears, "Civil Rights Leaders Widen Attack on GOP after Lott Exit; Groups Charge Senator's Actions Reflect Party's Agenda," *Washington Post* (December 23, 2002); Bob Herbert, "The Other Trent Lotts," *New York Times* (December 23, 2002).

100. Michael A. Fletcher and Brian Faler, "Bennett Defends Radio Remarks; Republicans Join Criticism of Talk on Race, Abortion and Crime," *Washington Post* (October 1, 2005).

101. Herbert, "Impossible, Ridiculous, Repugnant."

102. Byrd's Klan activities may not have been widely known when he was elected Whip in January 1971, but they were common knowledge by 1977, when he was elected Senate Majority Leader. That is because Richard Nixon floated Byrd's name as a possible Supreme Court justice—revenge against liberals who had pressured Senate Democrats into defeating his first two Court nominees, Clement Haynsworth Jr. and G. Harrold Carswell. Liberals were forced to publicize Byrd's racist past to keep him off the Court as well, creating ill will between them and Senate Democrats, exactly as Nixon planned. See John Herbers, "Robert Byrd Considered for Supreme Court Seat," *New York Times* (October 10, 1971); William V. Shannon, "Mr. Nixon's Revenge," *New York Times* (October 12, 1971).

103. "Fox News Sunday" (March 4, 2001).

104. Sam J. Ervin Jr., "The Case for Segregation," *Look Magazine* (April 3, 1956), p. 32. See also "Ervin: Compulsory Integration Is 'Fundamentally Wrong,'" *U.S. News & World Report* (November 18, 1955), pp. 90–100; Karl E. Campbell, "Claghorn's Hammurabi: Senator Sam Ervin and Civil Rights," *North Carolina Historical Review* (October 2001), pp. 431–56.

105. Ralph McGill, "How It Happened Down in Georgia," *New Republic* (January 27, 1947), pp. 12–15.

106. Drew Pearson, "Washington Merry-Go-Round," *Washington Post* (November 26, 1946).

107. Herman E. Talmadge, *You and Segregation* (Birmingham, AL: Vulcan Press, 1955), p. 44.

108. Herman E. Talmadge, *Talmadge: A Political Legacy, A Politician's Life* (Atlanta: Peachtree Publishers, 1987), pp. 177–98.

109. "Stennis: 'South Will Oppose Integration to Utmost,'" *U.S. News & World Report* (November 18, 1955), pp. 86–90.

110. "Warning By Hollings," *New York Times* (March 17, 1960).

111. Steven V. Roberts, "Senate Restricts Suits on Prayers in the Schools," *New York Times* (November 17, 1981).

112. Bill Peterson and Dan Balz, "Hollings Issues Apology for Iowa Remark," *Washington Post* (October 13, 1983).

113. Maralee Schwartz, "Hollings Quoted as Referring to Black Workers as 'Darkies,'" *Washington Post* (July 18, 1986).

114. Helen Dewar, "NAACP Chief Calls Hollings an Embarrassment for Remark," *Washington Post* (December 16, 1993).

115. *Congressional Record* (April 1, 2004), p. S3541.

116. Randal C. Archibold, "Dodd Says He Regrets 'Poor Choice of Words,'" *New York Times* (April 16, 2004).

117. Ryan Lizza, "Pin Prick: George Allen's Race Problem," *New Republic* (May 8, 2006), pp. 17–21; Ryan Lizza, "Are, Too: George Allen's Flag Fetish," *New Republic* (May 15, 2006), 10–12; Noam Scheiber, "Religious Conversion," *New Republic Online* (September 8, 2006).

118. As of July 2007, the speech was still posted on Webb's personal web site at: www.jameswebb.com/speeches/confedmemorial.htm.

CONCLUSION

1. Milton Coleman, "Making Black Votes Count," *Washington Post* (July 7, 1985); Paul Frymer, *Uneasy Alliances: Race and Party Competition in America* (Princeton: Princeton University Press, 1999); Derrick Z. Jackson, "Black Voters Get Too Little from Democratic Party," *Boston Globe* (February 23, 2001); William Safire, "The Black Bloc," *New York Times* (December 18, 2000).

2. William Raspberry, "Integration Target: The GOP," *Washington Post* (November 9, 1984).

3. Cash Michaels, "Democrats Have Serious Trouble," *Wilmington Journal* (August 13, 2003).

4. Quoted in David Firestone, "The Republicans Try to Redefine Civil Rights," *New York Times* (December 29, 2002).

5. Lynette Clemetson, "Younger Blacks Tell Democrats to Take Notice," *New York Times* (August 8, 2003); Alexandra Starr, "We Shall Overcome, Too," *Business Week* (July 15, 2002), pp. 86, 89; Juan Williams, "Bush Shouldn't Write Off the Black Vote," *New York Times* (June 16, 2004).

6. Glenn Kessler, "Black Group Seeks Repeal of Estate Tax," *Washington Post* (April 2, 2001); Irvin Molotsky, "Black Business Leaders Campaign Against Estate Tax," *New York Times* (April 5, 2001).

7. Matthew Mosk, "Angling for Hip-Hop Appeal," *Washington Post* (August 25, 2006); Matthew Mosk, "Tyson Ready to Enter the Ring for Steele," *Washington Post* (October 18, 2006); Avis Thomas-Lester, "Leaders Say They Endorsed Republican to Wake Democrats," *Washington Post* (November 6, 2006).

8. Kenneth Couch and Mary C. Daly, "Black-White Wage Inequality in the 1990s: A Decade of Progress," *Economic Inquiry* (January 2002), pp. 31–41.

9. Dalton Conley, "Getting into the Black: Race, Wealth, and Public Policy," *Political Science Quarterly* (Winter 1999–2000), pp. 595–612.

10. Sharmila Choudhury, "Racial and Ethnic Differences in Wealth and Asset Choices," *Social Security Bulletin* (No. 4, 2001–2002), pp. 1–15; Tristan Mabry, "Black Investors Shy Away from Stocks," *Wall Street Journal* (May 14, 1999); Cheryl Winokur Munk, "Trust in Market Shows Racial Divide," *Wall Street Journal* (June 26, 2003).

11. Claudia Deane and Dan Balz, "GOP Puts Stock in 'Investor Class,'" *Washington Post* (October 27, 2003).

12. Zogby News (October 23, 2000), downloaded at www.zogby.com.

13. Accessed at www.pollingreport.com.

14. Jennifer Steinhauer, "After Immigration Bill's Senate Crash, Republicans May Pay Dearly in Latino Votes," *New York Times* (July 1, 2007). According to CNN, 69 percent of Hispanics voted Democratic in the 2006 congressional elections. Data are at www.cnn.com/ELECTION/2006/pages/results/states/US/H/00/epolls.0.html. According to a June, 2007, *USA Today*/Gallup poll, only 11 percent of Hispanics identified themselves as Republicans, down from 19 percent in 2005, while those identifying

as Democrats rose to 42 percent from 33 percent in 2005. Susan Page, "Hispanics Turning Back to Democrats for 2008," *USA Today* (June 27, 2007).

15. Raymond Hernandez, "Hispanic Voters Gain New Clout With Democrats," *New York Times* (June 10, 2007). According to Census Bureau data released on May 17, 2007, between July 1, 2005 and July 1, 2006, the Hispanic population grew 3.4 percent to 44.3 million. Over the same period, the black population grew only 1.3 percent to 40.2 million.

16. Rachel L. Swarns, "Growing Unease for Some Blacks on Immigration," *New York Times* (May 4, 2006); Marjorie Valbrun, "Black Coalition Frets Over Influx of Skilled Foreigners," *Wall Street Journal* (July 7, 2000). One area of recent concern for native-born African Americans has been an influx of foreign-born blacks at many major universities, taking up diversity slots that might otherwise go to native-born black students. See Aditi Balakrishna, "Many Blacks at Ivies Not from U.S.," *Harvard Crimson* (March 9, 2007); Daryl Fears, "In Diversity Push, Top Universities Enrolling More Black Immigrants," *Washington Post* (March 6, 2007); Douglas S. Massey *et al.*, "Black Immigrants and Black Natives Attending Selective Colleges and Universities in the United States," *American Journal of Education* (February 2007), pp. 243–71; Clarence Page, "Black Immigrants Collect Most Degrees," *Chicago Tribune* (March 18, 2007); Sam Roberts, "More Africans Enter U.S. Than in Days of Slavery," *New York Times* (February 21, 2005).

17. Neil Munro, "Immigration Economics," *National Journal* (May 16, 2006). The Pew poll cited is titled, "America's Immigration Quandary" and released on March 30, 2006. It is available at www.people-press.org.

18. Frederick Douglass, *Life and Times of Frederick Douglass* (Hartford, CT: Park Publishing Co., 1881), p. 303.

19. Louis R. Harlan, ed., *The Booker T. Washington Papers* (Chicago: University of Illinois Press, 1974), vol. 3, pp. 584–85.

20. Toni Morrison, "On the Backs of Blacks," *Time Magazine* (December 2, 1993).

21. Choose Black America press release (June 19, 2007); Deborah Schoch and Jonathan Abrams, "Confrontation Kept Under Control," *Los Angeles Times* (June 24, 2007).

22. National Urban League press release (June 5, 2007).

23. Lisa Caruso, "Splits on the Left," *National Journal* (June 30, 2007), pp. 52–53; Jonathan Weisman, "Immigration Divides Allies," *Washington Post* (March 31, 2006).

24. A copy of the ad can be found at www.americanworker.org.

25. George J. Borjas, Jeffrey Grogger, and Gordon H. Hanson, "Immigration and African-American Employment Opportunities: The Response of Wages, Employment, and Incarceration to Labor Supply Shocks," National Bureau of Economic Research Working Paper No. 12518 (September 2006).

26. Quoted in Munro, "Immigration Economics."

27. Randall Robinson, *The Debt: What America Owes to Blacks* (New York: Dutton, 2000); Raymond A. Winbush, ed., *Should America Pay? Slavery and the Raging Debate on Reparations* (New York: Amistad/HarperCollins, 2003).

28. The principal conservative opponent of reparations has been former new left activist David Horowitz. See David Horowitz, *Uncivil Wars: The Controversy Over Reparations for Slavery* (San Francisco: Encounter Books, 2002). See also John McWhorter, "Against Reparations," *New Republic* (July 23, 2001), pp. 32–38; John McWhorter, "Blood Money: Why I Don't Want Reparations for Slavery," *The American Enterprise* (July-August 2001), pp. 19–22.

29. It is quite common for the theft of precious art works to be returned to their rightful owners many decades after the theft occurred. One still hears about paintings that were stolen by the Nazis that have just been identified and returned to the heirs of the original owners.

30. This argument has been made by a prominent libertarian economist. See Walter Block, "On Reparations to Blacks for Slavery," *Human Rights Review* (July 2002), pp. 53–73. For a libertarian critique of reparations, see Richard A. Epstein, "The Case *Against* Black Reparations," *Boston University Law Review* (December 2004), 1177–92. It should be

noted that Epstein's argument is essentially legalistic and is mainly directed against using the courts to obtain reparations, on which he is exactly correct. However, he doesn't really address the moral dimension of the political case for reparations. For other legal analyses of the reparations question, see Boris I. Bittker, *The Case for Black Reparations*, revised ed. (Boston: Beacon Press, 2003); Kim Forde-Mazrui, "Taking Conservatives Seriously: A Moral Justification for Affirmative Action and Reparations," *California Law Review* (May 2004), pp. 685–753; Kevin Hopkins, "Forgive U.S. Our Debts? Righting the Wrongs of Slavery," *Georgetown Law Journal* (August 2001), pp. 2531–56; Eric A. Posner and Adrian Vermeule, "Reparations for Slavery and Other Historical Injustices," *Columbia Law Review* (April 2003), pp. 689–747.

31. Charles Krauthammer, "Reparations for Black Americans," *Time Magazine* (December 31, 1990). See also Charles Krauthammer, "A Grand Compromise," *Washington Post* (April 6, 2001).

32. See Robert S. Browne, "The Economic Case for Reparations to Black America," *American Economic Review* (May 1972), pp. 39–46; William Darity Jr. and Dania Frank, "The Economics of Reparations," *American Economic Review* (May 2003), pp. 326–29; Philip J. Mazzocco *et al.*, "The Cost of Being Black," *DuBois Review* (September 2006), pp. 261–97; Bruce Sacerdote, "Slavery and the Intergenerational Transmission of Human Capital," *Review of Economics and Statistics* (May 2005), pp. 217–34.

33. Cedric Muhammad, "Republicans for Reparations," posted at www.blackelectorate.com (December 18, 2002). Emphasis in original. Alan Keyes, the Republican nominee for the U.S. Senate from Illinois in 2004, proposed during the campaign that all blacks be exempted from paying federal taxes for a generation or two in order to build up capital in compensation for slavery. See Allison Benedikt and David Mendell, "Keyes Has Plan for Reparations," *Chicago Tribune* (August 17, 2004). This shows how a bread-and-butter Republican issue like tax cuts might be tied to reparations.

INDEX